The Nile in Legal and Political Perspective

International Water Law Series

Stephen C. McCaffrey (*The University of the Pacific, McGeorge School of Law*)

VOLUME 11

The titles published in this series are listed at *brill.com/iwl*

The Nile in Legal and Political Perspective

Between Change and Continuity

By

Mahemud E. Tekuya

BRILL | NIJHOFF

LEIDEN | BOSTON

Library of Congress Cataloging-in-Publication Data

Names: Tekuya, Mahemud E., author.
Title: The Nile in legal and political perspective : between change and continuity / by Mahemud E. Tekuya.
Description: Leiden ; Boston : Brill Nijhoff, [2024] | Series: International water law series, 2351-9606 ; volume 11 | Includes bibliographical references and index. | Summary: "Competition over the Nile watercourse is becoming a global crisis. As population growth, economic development, and urbanization increase the demand for water in the Nile Basin while climate change threatens its supply, the region faces a looming water crisis. An effective resolution of this multifaceted issue, which impacts 11 African countries, requires detailed multidisciplinary research"– Provided by publisher.
Identifiers: LCCN 2023019778 (print) | LCCN 2023019779 (ebook) | ISBN 9789004549852 (hardback) | ISBN 9789004549869 (ebook)
Subjects: LCSH: Water–Law and legislation–Nile River Watershed. | Water-supply–Political aspects–Nile River Watershed. | Water resources development–Law and legislation–Nile River Watershed. | Nile River–Water rights.
Classification: LCC KQC660.N55 T45 2024 (print) | LCC KQC660.N55 (ebook) | DDC 341.4/420962–dc23/eng/20230719
LC record available at https://lccn.loc.gov/2023019778
LC ebook record available at https://lccn.loc.gov/2023019779

Typeface for the Latin, Greek, and Cyrillic scripts: "Brill". See and download: brill.com/brill-typeface.

ISSN 2351-9606
ISBN 978-90-04-54985-2 (hardback)
ISBN 978-90-04-54986-9 (e-book)
DOI 10.1163/9789004549869

To all civilians who died due to the armed conflict in Ethiopia,
and
To my brother, Mohammed Eshetu Tikuye, who died because of the war

Contents

Foreword

It is often said today that the world is running out of water. This is not true literally, of course. The quantity of water on Earth has remained the same for billions of years. Yet as human populations grow and water is put to new uses shortages will inevitably occur in many countries.

The present work by Dr. Mahemud Tekuya, a son of Ethiopia, studies this reality in the fraught context of the Blue Nile and other watercourses flowing from Ethiopia to Egypt. Most schoolchildren know something of Egypt, given its fascinating history and culture. This cannot be said of Ethiopia to the same extent, however, despite that country's own highly developed society and, like Egypt, a history free of colonialism.

Egypt has been called the "gift of the Nile." But while most lay people think of "the Nile" referred to in this aphorism as the so-called "White Nile," which originates in the Lake Victoria basin and flows north to Egypt, more water by far, some 85 per cent, comes to Egypt from Ethiopia, via the Blue Nile, and also other rivers, notably the Atbara and the Sobat. It is thus understandable that Egypt would be alarmed by Ethiopia's announcement in 2011 that it would begin constructing what came to be called the Grand Ethiopian Renaissance Dam (the GERD). This action precipitated a tectonic shift in relations among Nile Basin States, and in particular among Egypt, Ethiopia and Sudan.

Given its importance to Nile riparian states, it is perhaps not surprising that a number of agreements have been concluded among those states. Ethiopia's bold move to construct the GERD puts some of those agreements to the test. They will also be stress-tested by climate change, which will no doubt alter the flows of the Blue and White Niles more powerfully than any dam or other human instrumentality could.

For all of these reasons, and others that will emerge with the reading of the present volume, Tekuya's work is of particular importance today. It should form part of the library of anyone interested in how states share fresh water, and indeed how relations between those states can be transformed by natural and artificial events.

Stephen C. McCaffrey
Sacramento, California
March 2023

Preface

Growing up in Wollo, Northeastern part of Ethiopia, I always wondered why my country could be so underdeveloped, despite its resources like the Nile River, while others were blossoming. Being from Wollo, a province adversely impacted by the 1983–1985 famine and where hundreds of thousands of Ethiopians perished as a result, I know firsthand the catastrophic impacts of drought and heavy reliance on rain-fed agriculture.

Although I was born after the 1983–1985 famine and did not lose immediate family members due to the famine, I remember mothers on the playground sobbing, "if it had not been for those evil days, my child would be here playing with you all." In school, I often heard students respond with, "one of my brothers or sisters died during the famine," when asked how many siblings they had. The school I went to was named "Bati Red Cross 77" to honor the organization that saved the lives of many Wolloyes through food and medical aid.

As a child, I remember asking why we (Ethiopians) experienced hunger and my father responded with an Amharic proverb, "*Yabayin lij wuha temaw,*" which literally means "Nile's child got thirsty." What my father was saying is that citizens of a country with a valuable resource like the Nile River were dying from hunger. An epiphany I had as I grew older was that the only way to prevent famines in the future was to use the Nile River for irrigation.

In 2011, while in law school, I heard about the beginning of the construction of the Grand Ethiopian Renaissance Dam (GERD), the first-ever large-scale Ethiopian dam to be built on the Blue Nile in Ethiopia. Like many students, I gave up some of my breakfast funds to raise money to support the project. The construction of the GERD caused me to reflect on how I could do more to help my country. I realized how few Ethiopian experts specialized in international watercourses law and decided to specialize in this field. Upon graduation in 2013, I started working at Dire Dawa University as a lecturer and taught various courses relevant to the subject matter. In 2015, I completed a research paper on the agreement on the declaration of principles between Ethiopia, Sudan, and Egypt; I presented it at a national conference organized by Dire Dawa University.

My teaching and research introduced me to a renowned scholar of international watercourses law, Prof. Stephen C. McCaffrey, who teaches at McGeorge School of Law; I decided to pursue my Ph.D./JSD study under his supervision. In 2017, I began a multidisciplinary study on the legal and hydro-political trajectories of the Nile Basin. From the beginning, I found that the academic discourse regarding the Nile watercourse is primarily dominated by monodisciplinary research. This current research aimed for a broader approach and attempted to provide a retrospective and prospective look at the Nile watercourse through multidisciplinary lenses—commingling history, hydro-politics, climate change, and law.

Indeed, since the Nile Basin presents multifaceted problems, solutions and alternative proposals must deal with myriad issues influencing the legal and hydro-political interest of the Nile Basin States. Throughout this book, I have addressed several intertwined issues that cannot be dealt with in isolation while ensuring that the book does not lack focus.

Given my background as an Ethiopian, it was difficult to be dispassionate on many of the issues discussed in this book. However, I aimed to be as objective, thorough, and non-partisan as possible and tried to avoid subjective and speculative biases, and provided supporting authorities, facts, and figures for all my claims.

Acknowledgments

This book is based on my dissertation written in fulfillment of the requirements for the Ph.D./JSD (Doctor of Juridical Science) in International Water Resources Law at McGeorge School of Law, University of the Pacific, in Sacramento, California. I am extremely grateful to my supervisor, Professor Stephen C. McCaffrey, for allowing me to study under his supervision and tirelessly guiding my academic endeavors. Professor McCaffrey, one of the foremost authorities in the world on international watercourses law, was extremely supportive: This book could not have been completed without his critical review and precious comments. I sincerely appreciate his keen interest in the topic and his unwavering support throughout the development of this book.

I express my deepest gratitude to my distinguished JSD Dissertation Committee—External Examiner, Professor Daniel Magraw, President Emeritus of Center for International Environmental Law (CIEL) and Senior Fellow at Foreign Policy Institute, Johns Hopkins University; Committee Chair, Professor Omar Dajani, Director of Global Center for Business & Development at McGeorge School of Law; and Professor Rachael Salcido, Director of the Environmental Law Program and Sustainable Development Institute at McGeorge School of Law.

My sincere appreciation is also extended to McGeorge School of Law for awarding me the McGeorge Merit-Based Institutional Scholarship and Professor Stephen McCaffrey Scholarship for Water and Environmental Law. I am also grateful to the Open Society Foundations for the Civil Society Scholars Award they awarded me during the 2017/18 academic year. I would not have joined the JSD program at McGeorge School of Law and completed this book without these financial supports. Thank you so much all.

Finally, I would like to thank the two anonymous reviewers of the book for their insightful comments and Zoe Rosenblum, Ph.D. Candidate at Oregon State University, for proofreading the final draft of the book.

•••

Earlier versions of portions of this book have appeared in the following publications: *Governing the Nile Under Climatic Uncertainty: The Need for a Climate-Proof Basin-Wide Treaty,* 59 Nat. Res. J. (2019), and *Sink or Swim: Alternatives for Unlocking the Grand Ethiopian Renaissance Dam Dispute,* 59 Colum. J. Transnat'l L. (2020).

Table

Abbreviations

AHD	Aswan High Dam
AU	African Union
BCM	Billion Cubic Meters
CFA	Cooperative Framework Agreement
CIDA	Canadian International Development Agency
COM	Council of Ministers
CPA	Comprehensive Peace Agreement Development and Environmental Protection of the Nile
DoP	Declaration of Principles
DRC	Democratic Republic of Congo
EIA	Environmental Impact Assessment
ENTRO	Eastern Nile Technical Regional Office
EPLF	Eritrean people's Liberation Front
EU	European Union
GDP	Gross Domestic Product
GERD	Grand Ethiopian Renaissance Dam
GNI	Gross National Income
HDI	Human Development Index
Hydromet	Hydrometeorological Project
IBRD	International Bank for Reconstruction and Development
ICJ	International Court of Justice
ILA	International Law Association
ILC	International Law Commission
IPCC	Intergovernmental Panel on Climate Change
IPoE	International Panel of Experts
JNC	Joint Negotiation Committee
MASL	Meters Above Sea Level
MW	Megawatt
NASA	U.S. National Aeronautics and Space Administration
NBI	Nile Basin Initiative
NBRAP	Nile River Basin Action Plan
NELSAP	Nile Equatorial Lake Subsidiary Action Program
NELSAPCU	Nile Equatorial Lake Subsidiary Action Program Coordination Unit
Nile COM	Nile Basin Council of Ministers
Nile-SEC	NBI Secretariat
Nile-TAC	Nile Technical Advisory Committee
NISRG	National Independent Scientific Research Group

NRBC	Nile River Basin Commission
OAU	Organization of African Unity
PJTC	Permanent Joint Technical Committee
POE	Panel of Experts
RBOs	River Basin Organizations
SAP	Subsidiary Action Programs
SVP	Shared Vision Program
TAC	Technical Advisory Committee
TC	Technical Committee (TC)
TECCONILE	Technical Cooperation Committee for the Promotion of the Development and Environmental Protection of the Nile
TNC	Technical National Committee
TPLF	Tigray People's Liberation Front
UNDP	United Nations Development Program
UNGA	United Nations General Assembly
UNSC	United Nations Security Council
US	United States
USA	United States of America
USAID	United States Agency for International Development
USBR	U.S. Bureau of Reclamation
VCLT	Vienna Convention on the Law of Treaties
VCSSRT	Vienna Convention on State Succession in Respect of Treaties
WMO	World Meteorological Organization

CHAPTER 1

Introduction

1.1 The Global Water Crisis: Finite Supply, Growing Demand

Water, the most precious commodity on Planet Earth, is an essential part of life and human development.[1] "Without water, there simply can be no life. Water flows in the veins and roots of all living organisms, as precious to them as the air they breathe and the food they eat. It is the lifeblood of their collective body."[2] Water is an indispensable and finite resource essential for the very survival of humanity.[3] "Humans can live more than a month without food, but only about a week without water. We use it for everything, from drinking, cooking, bathing, washing and waste disposal to irrigation, industry, power production, transportation, and recreation."[4] However, as Benjamin Franklin observed, we do not seem to appreciate the value of water until we run out of it: "When the well is dry, we know the worth of water."[5]

When the current international institutions were set up eight decades ago, few expected that water scarcity would emerge as a serious global problem.[6] Many at that time thought freshwater resources were so abundant that they

1 *See generally* PETER GLEICK & GILBERT WHITE, WATER IN CRISIS: A GUIDE TO THE WORLD'S FRESH WATER RESOURCES 3 (Peter Gleick & Gilbert White, eds. 1993) [Hereinafter WATER IN CRISIS].

2 DONAL WORSTER, RIVERS OF EMPIRE: WATER, ARIDITY AND THE GROWTH OF THE AMERICAN WEST 19 (1985).

3 The U.S. National Aeronautics and Space Administration (NASA) is searching for water as evidence of the existence of life on the planet Mars. NASA, *The Mars Exploration Program*, https://mars.nasa.gov/programmissions/overview/ ("Among our discoveries about Mars, one stands out above all others: the possible presence of liquid water on Mars, either in its ancient past or preserved in the subsurface today. Water is key because almost everywhere we find water on Earth, we find life.")

4 STEPHEN C. MCCAFFREY, THE LAW OF INTERNATIONAL WATERCOURSES 3 (2019).

5 *Id.* (internal citation omitted).

6 BRAHMA CHELLANEY, WATER, PEACE, AND WAR: CONFRONTING THE GLOBAL WATER CRISIS XI (2013). It should, however, be noted that the United Nations General Assembly (UNGA) recognized the importance of freshwater resources when it adopted Resolution 1401 (XIV) on November 21, 1959, entitled "Preliminary Studies on the Legal Problems Relating to the Utilization and Use of International Rivers." G.A. Res. 1401 (XIV), Preliminary Studies on the Legal Problems Relating to the Utilization and the Use of International Rivers, at 55 (Nov. 21, 1959), https://perma.cc/UZ4W-RGA2.

 | DOI:10.1163/9789004549869_002

would always sustain global demand.[7] "Yet the golden age of safe, cheap, and easily available water has come to an end in most parts of the world, replaced by a new era of increasing supply and quality constraints."[8] Today, the world is facing a looming water crisis,[9] and water scarcity is one of the major concerns of the international community.[10] "More than two billion people are living in countries under water stress and 3.6 billion people face inadequate access to water at least one month per year."[11]

Nevertheless, there is enough water on Earth for all conceivable human needs.[12] Water constitutes 71 percent of the Earth's surface, and the total amount of water in the world is estimated to be 1.4 billion cubic kilometers.[13] However, 97% of this water is saltwater: It is not suitable for domestic consumption, agriculture, and even industrial uses (except cooling) "unless passed through expensive and energy-intensive desalination facilities."[14] This means that only 3 percent of all the water on Earth is freshwater.[15] Although

---

7 CHELLANEY, *supra* note 6, XI.

8 *Id.*

9 *Id.; see generally* GLEICK & WHITE, *supra* note 1; *see also* World Meteorological Organization (WMO), *Wake Up to The Looming Water Crisis, Report Warns* (Oct. 5, 2021), https://public.wmo.int/en/media/press-release/wake-looming-water-crisis-report-warns.

10 *See generally*, U.S. NATIONAL INTELLIGENCE, GLOBAL WATER SECURITY, INTELLIGENCE COMMUNITY ASSESSMENT (2012); WORLD WATER ASSESSMENT PROGRAM (WWAP), THE UNITED NATIONS WORLD WATER DEVELOPMENT REPORT 2019: LEAVING NO ONE BEHIND 1 (2019) [hereinafter WWAP 2019]; *see also generally* WORLD ECONOMIC FORUM, 2016 GLOBAL RISK REPORT (2016), https://www3.weforum.org/docs/GRR/WEF_GRR16.pdf; Joseph Dellapenna & Joyeeta Gupta, *The Evolution of Global Water Law*, in THE EVOLUTION OF THE LAW AND POLITICS OF WATER 1, 3–4 (Joseph Dellapenna & Joyeeta Gupta eds. 2009); MCCAFFREY, *supra* note 4, at 59–60.

11 UNCCD, *Word of the Week: Water Stress* (Oct. 2021), https://knowledge.unccd.int/knowledge-products-and-pillars/unccd-e-library/fact-month-word-week.

12 TESFAYE TAFESSE, THE NILE QUESTION: HYDROPOLITICS, LEGAL WRANGLING, MODUS VIVENDI AND PERSPECTIVES, 1 (2001).

13 Piotr Klimaszyk & Ryszard Gołdyn, *Water Quality of Freshwater Ecosystems in a Temperate Climate*, 12(9) WATER 1–2 (2020); United States Bureau of Reclamation (USBR), *Water Facts: Worldwide Water Supply* (Nov. 4, 2020) https://www.usbr.gov/mp/arwec/water-facts-ww-water-sup.html. It should be noted that "the total supply [of water] neither grows nor diminishes. It is believed to be almost precisely the same now as it was 3 billion years ago. Endlessly recycled, water is used, disposed of, purified and used again. Last night's potatoes may have boiled in what was, ages ago, the bathwater of Archimedes." LUNA LEOPOLD & KENNETH DAVIS, WATER 33 (1966), cited in MCCAFFREY, *supra* note 4, at 5.

14 Stephen McCaffrey, *Water, Water Everywhere, But Too Few Drops to Drink: The Coming Fresh Water Crisis and International Environmental Law*, 28 DENV. J. INT'L L. & POL'Y 329 (2000). *See also* USBR, *supra* note 13. ("97% of the earth's water is found in the oceans (too salty for drinking, growing crops, and most industrial uses except cooling."))

15 *Id.;* McCaffrey, *supra* note 14, 329.

this amount could satisfy global needs, it is not evenly distributed in space and time.[16] More than 68.7 percent of the global freshwater is inaccessible to human consumption as it is trapped in polar ice caps and mountain glaciers.[17] About 30 percent takes the form of groundwater.[18] Only 0.3 percent of the overall freshwater, found in lakes and rivers, is easily accessible for human consumption,[19] and it is not coping with the global demand.

Global water per capita is decreasing at an alarmingly rapid rate mainly due to an increase in the use of water and to population growth.[20] In the words of Herbert Smith, "[o]ne of the most noteworthy features of the last hundred years has been the immense increase in the use of water."[21] Over the past 100 years, worldwide water use has increased by 600 percent[22] and continues to grow at a rate of 1 percent per year.[23] Although such an increase in water use stems from several factors, including economic development and changing consumption patterns,[24] the major threat to water security in most developing countries comes from population growth.[25] "Between 1950 and 1985, [the]

16 *See* Peter Gleick, *An Introduction to Global Fresh Water Issues*, in WATER IN CRISIS, *supra* note 1, at 3; MCCAFFREY, *supra* note 4, at 13. ("Water is often found where people are scarce, and people often live where water is scarce.")

17 *Water Everywhere, But Not Clean Enough to Drink*, REUTERS (March 2008), https://www.reuters.com/article/us-water-factbox-idINL1448398920080319 (accessed on October 31, 2021) (Mentioning that "68.7 percent is frozen in ice caps and glaciers"). *See also* Gleick, *supra* note 16, at 3.

18 *Id;* McCaffrey, *supra* note 14, at 329 (Stating "[g]roundwater constitutes about thirty percent of global freshwater reserves").

19 Gleick, *supra* note 16, at 3.

20 WWAP 2019, *supra* note 10, at 13–15; MCCAFFREY, *supra* note 4, at 5.

21 HERBERT SMITH, THE ECONOMIC USES OF INTERNATIONAL RIVERS 1 (1931).

22 UNITED NATIONS WORLD WATER ASSESSMENT PROGRAM (WWAP), THE UNITED NATIONS WORLD WATER DEVELOPMENT REPORT 2018: NATURE-BASED SOLUTIONS FOR WATER, 10 (2018) [hereinafter WWAP 2018].

23 *Id.; see also* MCCAFFREY, *supra* note 4, at 5 ("Worldwide demand for fresh water grew from 579 cubic kilometers per year in 1900 to 4,130 cubic kilometers in 1990, according to United Nations statistics, and the rate of growth in consumption is itself increasing. This is in part due to economic development: as countries develop, they consume more water on a per capita basis, at least up to a point.")

24 *Id.; see also* WWAP 2018, *supra* note 22, at 10.

25 MCCAFFREY, *supra* note 4, at 5; J. A.A. Jones, *Threats to Global Water Security: Population Growth, Terrorism, Climate Change, or Commercialization*, in THREATS TO GLOBAL WATER SECURITY 3 (Jones et al., eds., 2009). Robert Engelman, When It Comes to Water Scarcity, Population Growth Tops Climate Change, WILSON CENTER, (August 1, 2016), https://www.newsecuritybeat.org/2016/08/water-scarcity-population-growth-trumps-climate-change/ ("[T]he ongoing growth of human population has a greater impact on water availability than [other factors including,] climate change does.")

world population grew at an annual rate of 1.9 percent. … Population growth is now concentrated in the developing regions of Asia, Africa, and Latin America, which accounted for 85 percent of the increase of global population since 1950."[26] To date, the world population is estimated at more than 7.8 billion,[27] a number that is expected to reach beyond 9.8 billion in 2050[28] and stabilize at around 12 billion in 2100.[29]

Mushrooming population growth poses problems of water scarcity. "By 1990, water availability per capita in 18 countries had fallen below 1,000 cubic meters per year—an amount experts consider to be somewhat below that which is required to sustain an adequate standard of living in countries at a level of development of those in North Africa and the Middle East."[30] In the next three years, "over 30 countries will be unable to provide 1,000 cubic meters per person per year, simply because of population growth."[31] The situation is worse in some countries: "in 1990 there were twelve countries in which water availability was less than 500 cubic meters per person per year; this number is projected to increase to nineteen by 2025."[32] In other words, in three years "one out of every three people—almost three and a quarter billion people—will live in as many as 52 countries plagued by water stress or chronic water scarcity."[33] Even today, "2.1 billion people lack safe drinking water at home, more than twice as many lack safe sanitation."[34] Unfortunately, these numbers are likely to increase due to extreme events such as drought and floods associated with global climate change or climate disruption.[35]

---

26 WORLD COMMISSION ON ENVIRONMENT AND DEVELOPMENT, REPORT OF THE WORLD COMMISSION ON ENVIRONMENT AND DEVELOPMENT: OUR COMMON FUTURE, ¶16 (1987) (hereinafter OUR COMMON FUTURE).

27 POPULATION REFERENCE BUREAU, 2020 WORLD POPULATION DATA SHEET (2020), https://www.prb.org/wp-content/uploads/2020/07/letter-booklet-2020-world-population.pdf.

28 UNITED NATIONS, DEPARTMENT OF ECONOMIC AND SOCIAL AFFAIRS, POPULATION DIVISION, WORLD POPULATION PROSPECTS: THE 2017 REVISION, 2 (2017).

29 *Id.*

30 MCCAFFREY, *supra* note 4, at 6.

31 *Id.*

32 *Id.*

33 *Id.*

34 *2.1. Billion People Lack Safe Drinking Water at Home, More Than Twice as Many Lack Safe Sanitation*, WHO/UNICEF (July 2017), https://www.who.int/news/item/12-07-2017-2-1-billion-people-lack-safe-drinking-water-at-home-more-than-twice-as-many-lack-safe-sanitation.

35 Global climate disruption, first coined by President Obama's Science Advisor, John Holdern, is considered to be the most accurate description of the impacts of dumping large amount of carbon dioxide and other greenhouse gases into Earth's atmosphere. *See*

According to the Fifth Assessment Report of the Intergovernmental Panel on Climate Change (IPCC), climate change will cause a significant "reduction of renewable freshwater resources... in most dry subtropical regions...", whereas in regions with snowfall, climate change is already "alter[ing] observed streamflow seasonality."[36] Moreover, in presently dry regions, climate change is predicted to exacerbate "the frequency of meteorological droughts (less rainfall) and agricultural droughts (less soil moisture) by the end of the 21st century."[37] Climate change is also adversely affecting "freshwater ecosystems by changing streamflow and water quality."[38]

In the face of such increasing water scarcity and the uncertainties associated with climate disruption, the management and sustainable utilization of transboundary freshwater resources have become "the single greatest environmental challenge facing the international community."[39] This is especially true for transboundary watercourses that constitute 60 percent of the global freshwater resources and serve as a source of freshwater for 40 percent of the global population.[40]

John Holdern, *Global Climate Disruption: What Do We Know About It and What Should We Do?* (November 6, 2007), https://www.belfercenter.org/sites/default/files/legacy/files/uploads/2007_11-6_Forum_(NXPowerLite).pdf. ("'global climatic disruption' is a more accurate description"). *See also* David Malakoff, *Let's Call It "Climate Disruption," White House Science Adviser Suggests (Again)*, SCIENCEINSIDER (May 2, 2014), https://www.science.org/content/article/lets-call-it-climate-disruption-white-house-science-adviser-suggests-again.This book uses the two terms interchangeably.

36 Nigel W. Arnell et al., *Freshwater Resources*, *in* CLIMATE CHANGE 2014: IMPACTS, ADAPTATION, AND VULNERABILITY. PART A: GLOBAL SECTORAL ASPECTS. CONTRIBUTION OF WORKING GROUP II TO THE FIFTH ASSESSMENT REPORT OF THE INTERGOVERNMENTAL PANEL ON CLIMATE CHANGE 229, 232–233 (C.B. Field et al. eds., Cambridge University Press 2014).

37 *Id.*

38 *Id.*

39 PHILIPPE SANDS, PRINCIPLES OF INTERNATIONAL ENVIRONMENTAL LAW 365 (1995).

40 UNITED NATIONS ENVIRONMENT PROGRAMME, GLOBAL ENVIRONMENT OUTLOOK 5 (GEO-5): ENVIRONMENT FOR THE FUTURE WE WANT, 125 (2012); Nurit Kliot et al, *Institutions for Management of Transboundary Water Resources: Their Nature, Characteristics and Shortcomings*, 3 WATER POL'Y, 229–255, 230 (2001) (Underscoring that management is "even more difficult when water resources are shared by a number of political entities.") *See also* MCCAFFREY, *supra* note 4, at 24–25. "The world's 276 international drainage basins make up more than 45 percent of its land area and hold some 40 percent of the global population These basins cover about 60 percent of both Africa and Latin America, and 65 percent of Asia. Europe has the largest number of international river basins, with sixty-nine, followed by Africa (59), Asia (57), North America (40), and South America (38). Over 95 percent of the territory of thirty-three countries, a number of them quite large, lies within one or more international basins. And these figures leave aside entirely an increasingly important source of fresh water, shared aquifers. Thus,

The fact that the great majority of global freshwater resources lie in transboundary basins means that "states sharing such freshwater resources are both interconnected and interdependent."[41] This interdependence, albeit its potential for interstate cooperation,[42] adds another "dimension to the world's freshwater problems that is of growing significance: the risk of frictions with countries sharing the same sources of water."[43] As early as 1995, a World Bank official remarked: "Many of the wars in this century were about oil, but wars of the next [the twenty-first] century will be over water."[44] Other high international officials, including former UN secretary-general Kofi Annan, also warned that "[f]ierce competition for fresh water may well become a source of conflict and wars in the future."[45] And the current United States vice president, Kamala Harris, stated in 2021: "For years there were wars fought over oil; in a short time there will be wars fought over water."[46]

shared freshwater resources cannot be protected and conserved solely by countries acting alone." *Id.*

41 Tamar Meshel, *Swimming against the Current: Revisiting the Principles of International Water Law in the Resolution of Fresh Water Disputes*, 61 HARV. INT'L L.J. 135, 136 (2020).

42 *Id. See* also Joseph W. Dellapenna, *The Work of International Legal Expert Bodies*, in RESEARCH HANDBOOK ON INTERNATIONAL WATER LAW 26, 33–34 (Stephen C. McCaffrey et al. eds., 2019) (hereinafter RESEARCH HANDBOOK) (stating "unilateral actions by states sharing a water basin only coincidentally optimized utilization of the resource.") THE WORLD BANK DEV. RES. GROUP POL'Y RES. WORKING PAPER NO. 4294 (2007) (arguing that "it is the 'critical need' for a given transboundary resource, and the dispute that may ensue, that provides the impetus for interstate cooperation codified in international water agreements.").

43 MCCAFFREY, *supra* note 4, at 23.

44 Barbara Crossette, *Severe Water Crisis Ahead for Poorest Nations in Next 2 Decades*, N.Y. TIMES (Aug. 10, 1995). Available at https://www.nytimes.com/1995/08/10/world/severe-water-crisis-ahead-for-poorest-nations-in-next-2-decades.html (accessed on November 2, 2021).

45 Press Release, United Nations Secretary-General, *World's Water Problems Can Be Catalyst for Cooperation*, (Feb. 26, 2002). https://www.un.org/press/en/2002/sgsm8139.doc.htm. Former UN secretary-general, Boutros Boutros-Ghali also stated in 1985 that "the next war in the Middle East will be fought over water, not politics." *Talking Point: Ask Boutros Boutros Ghali*, BBC NEWS (June 10, 2002), http://news.bbc.co.uk/1/hi/talking_point/2951028.stm. Secretary Ban Ki moon also remarked in 2007: "The consequences for humanity are grave. Water scarcity threatens economic and social gains and is a potent fuel for wars and conflict." Press Release, United Nations Secretary-General, *Secretary-General, in Message to Inaugural Asia-Pacific Water Summit, Warns That Scarcity Threatens Socio-Economic Gains, Could Fuel Conflicts* (Dec. 3, 2007), https://www.un.org/press/en/2007/sgsm11311.doc.htm.

46 *Vice President Kamala Harris Warns of Looming "Wars Fought Over Water,"* CALIFORNIA NEWS TIMES (April 5, 2021), available in https://californianewstimes.com/vice-president-kamala-harris-warns-of-looming-wars-fought-over-water-cbs-san-francisco/255936/ (Accessed on Nov. 2, 2021).

Indeed, due to political mistrust, power asymmetry, and fragmented water resource governance, states sharing transboundary watercourses often advanced their narrow national interests and exhibited confrontation than cooperation.[47] "As a result, interstate fresh water disputes have arisen in every part of the world, and are likely to continue arising in the future."[48] International law[49] could play an important role not only in resolving such

47 Meshel, *supra* note 41, 136–137 (2020); *see* also *generally* CHRISTINA LEB, COOPERATION IN THE LAW OF TRANSBOUNDARY WATER RESOURCES 35 (2013).

48 Meshel, *supra* note 41, 136–37. Meshel identified several water disputes including, *inter alia*, the Nile River, the Jordan River, the Euphrates and Tigris Rivers, and Lake Malawi in the Middle East and North Africa regions; the Indus River, the Ganges River, the Helmand River, the Mekong River, the Syr Darya basin, and the Aral Sea in Asia; and the Uruguay River, the Silala River, and the Lauca River in South America. *See* Meshel, *supra* note 41, footnote 7 (citing Salman M.A. Salman, *Good Offices and Mediation and International Water Disputes*, in RESOLUTION OF INTERNATIONAL WATER DISPUTES 155, 158 (International Bureau of the Permanent Court of Arbitration ed., 2002); and UNEP, GLOBAL INTERNATIONAL WATERS ASSESSMENT: PATAGONIAN SHELF, GIWA REGIONAL ASSESSMENT 38, at 35–36, 38–39, 80 (2004)). It should be noted, however, that international water resources are more likely to lead to cooperation than conflict. *See generally*, JEROME DELLI PRISCOLI & AARON T. WOLF, MANAGING AND TRANSFORMING WATER CONFLICT (2009). Consider, for instance, the experience of India and Pakistan. Since 1948, the two states have engaged in several wars and skirmishes, largely unrelated to their shared water resources, but they "negotiated and implemented a complex treaty on sharing the waters of the Indus River basin; they carried through with their cooperative water management arrangements even during actual periods of full-scale hostilities." Joseph W. Dellapenna, *International Law's Lessons for the Law of the Lakes*, 40 U. MICH. J.L. REFORM 747, 764 (2007).

49 Restatement of the Law (Third) The Foreign Relations Law of the United States—Restatement of International law—defines international law as: "the rules and principles of general application dealing with the conduct of states and international organizations and with their relations inter se, as well as with some of their relations with persons, whether natural or juridical." RESTATEMENT OF THE LAW (THIRD) THE FOREIGN RELATIONS LAW OF THE UNITED STATES § 101 (1987). International law primarily formulated by states, through their practice and agreements. STEPHEN MCCAFFREY, UNDERSTANDING INTERNATIONAL LAW 4 (2015). While consistent state practice undertaken out of a sense of legal obligation (*opinio juris*) constitutes customary international law, agreements, or treaties, bind states that are parties to them. *See* North Sea Continental Shelf Cases (Ger. v. Den.; Ger. v. Neth.), Advisory Opinions, 1969 I.C.J. 44, ¶ 77 (Feb. 20). For some, international law is not really law because of its lack of central executive, legislative, or judicial institutions. *See*, e.g., John Austin, The Province of Jurisprudence Determined, Lecture I, V and VI (Hart ed. 1954). The decentralized nature of international legal system does not, however, make international law any less real. MCCAFFREY, *supra* note 49, at 4. "The absence of those institutions no more indicates an absence of law in the international system than the absence of those institutions indicated the lack of law

disputes but also in preventing them, "establishing conditions that are conducive to cooperation among states sharing freshwater resources."[50] However, the majority of international watercourses do not have any type of legal and institutional framework for fostering cooperation among water-sharing states.[51] The Nile River, located in northeastern Africa, is one of the watercourses that do not have an all-inclusive framework agreement.

1.2 The Looming Water Crisis in the Nile Basin

The Nile Basin is one of the regions facing a looming water crisis. The Nile extends 6,695 kilometers from the Ruvyironza River in Burundi to the Mediterranean Sea.[52] But this encompasses only the White Nile, one of the river's two major tributaries. The other, the Blue Nile, meets the White in Khartoum, Sudan.[53] The Blue Nile originates in Lake Tana, Ethiopia,[54] and "makes [a] 1,000- kilometer loop through Ethiopian territory, carving a 600-meter-deep gorge through the highlands."[55] It carries considerably more

---

in pre-industrial societies the world over. The international system's less formal processes similarly are law and must be examined carefully to learn both its capabilities and limitations." Joseph Dellapenna, *The Customary International Law of Transboundary Fresh Waters*, 1 INT'L J. GLOB. ENV'T ISSUES 264, 266 (2001).

50 MCCAFFREY, *supra* note 4, at 27.

51 WWAP, THE UNITED NATIONS WORLD WATER DEVELOPMENT REPORT 2015: WATER FOR A SUSTAINABLE WORLD 11– (2015). ("158 of the world's 263 transboundary water basins lack any type of cooperative management framework.")

52 *See* NILE BASIN INITIATIVE, THE WATER RESOURCES OF THE NILE BASIN, *in* STATE OF THE RIVER NILE BASIN 27–28 (2012), http://nileis.nilebasin.org/system/files/Nile%20SoB%20Report%20Chpater%202%20-%20Water%20resources.pdf. The Nile flows from the south to the north. The ancient Egyptian used to consider this as the normal course of any river. *See* WILLIAM KELLY SIMPSON AND WILLIAM W. HALLO, THE ANCIENT NEAR EAST: A HISTORY 261 (1971). "Many words concerned with the movements were determined by the idea of sailing: to travel south is to get upstream, and to travel north is to get downstream, even when referring to traveling outside Egypt." *See also* Yaacov Shavit, *Up the River or Down the River? An Afrocentrist Dilemma, in* THE NILE: HISTORIES, CULTURES, MYTHS 79, 99 (Haggai Erlich & Israel Gershoni eds., 2000) (hereinafter THE NILE: HISTORIES, CULTURES, MYTHS).

53 *See* STEPHEN MCCAFFREY ET AL., PUBLIC INTERNATIONAL LAW: CASES, PROBLEMS AND TEXTS 1046 (2010).

54 *See* MCCAFFREY, *supra* note 4, at 258; *see also* NILE BASIN INITIATIVE, *supra* note 52, at 28; *see also* HAGGAI ERLICH, THE CROSS AND THE RIVER: ETHIOPIA, EGYPT, AND THE NILE 1 (2002).

55 *Id.*

water than the White Nile, but its flow is more volatile, fluctuating with the seasons.[56]

The Nile Basin covers 3.18 million square kilometers, 10 percent of Africa's landmass.[57] Its catchment area spreads over eleven sovereign states: Burundi, the Democratic Republic of Congo (DRC), Egypt, Eritrea, Ethiopia, Kenya, Rwanda, South Sudan, Sudan, Tanzania, and Uganda.[58] The Nile Basin is very diverse in terms of both climate and topographical futures. "[E]xtending over 35° of latitude, from the equatorial zone to the northern subtropics, and over elevations that range from more than 4000 m to sea level …"[59] the Nile River travels through five distinct climate regions.

> Downstream, Egypt and parts of Sudan have a dry, desert like climate with precipitation of less than 200 millimeters (mm) per year. Sudan and small parts of Ethiopia have a steppe climate with rainfall ranging between 200 and 400 mm a year. The precipitation from these two climatic regions does not contribute any water to the Nile. Upstream, the Nile Basin contains the tropical rainforest climate, the tropical savannah climate, and the highland (tropical) climate. These climates serve as the source of the Nile, receiving 1,400 to 1,800 mm of rainfall per year.[60]

As the river flows from its sources, both in Lake Victoria and Lake Tana Basins, to its mouth where it empties into the Mediterranean Sea, it passes through geographical areas where there is a decrease in the amount of precipitation and an increase in potential evapotranspiration.[61] The rainfall parameters of

56 *See* NILE BASIN INITIATIVE, *supra* note 52, at 36. "The Blue Nile (Abay) (60%), Atbara (Tekezze), and Sobat (Baro), contribute between 85 and 90 percent of the annual Nile flows, but the Blue Nile (Abay) can be seen to respond directly to the seasonal rain patterns, exhibiting clear dry and wet spells." The White Nile, on the other hand, "contributes between 10 and 15 percent to the annual Nile discharge, but is fairly stable throughout the year." *Id.*

57 *Id.* at 27–28.

58 THE NILE BASIN INITIATIVE, THE NILE BASIN RESOURCES ATLAS 17 (2016) (hereinafter NBI 2016), http://atlas.nilebasin.org/treatise/location-of-the-nile-basin-in-africa/.

59 *See* Jessica Barnes, *The Future of the Nile: Climate Change, Land Use, Infrastructure Management, and Treaty Negotiations in a Transboundary River Basin*, 8 WIRES CLIM. CHANGE 2 (2017).

60 Alice Shih & Trevor Stutz, *Sink or Swim: Abrogating the Nile Treaties While Upholding the Rule of Law*, 43 ENVT'L L. REP. 10786, 10788 (2013).

61 *See* Meron Teferi Taye et al., T869 *Climate Change: From Science to Lived Experience. The Lived Experience of Climate Change: Water Case Study on the Nile and Rhine River Basins*, UK. OPEN UNIV., at 12 & 14 (2012).

the Basin exhibit a high level of both inter-annual and inter-decadal variability.[62] This means that the Nile River experiences both intra- and inter-seasonal fluctuations in climatic parameters.[63]

For a long time, the Nile Basin States have been affected by such climate variability,[64] and recent climate disruption is exacerbating the vulnerability of the Basin states.[65] Climate change and its ramifications on the Nile watercourse are threatening the lives and livelihoods of the people living in the basin.[66] According to scientific studies, climate-induced problems that lie ahead for the Nile Basin States include: increase and/or decrease in flow of the Nile waters; increase in the frequency of extreme events including floods and droughts; sea-level rise; increase in temperature and evaporation; changes in rainfall, runoff, and sediment yield patterns as well as in ecosystems, vegetation cover, and crop yields; and increase in reservoir and swamp evaporation rates.[67]

Although there is a widespread understanding that climate change will increase the average annual temperature in the Nile Basin and lead to greater loss of water due to evaporation,[68] climate change projections are less certain about future rainfall, river flow, and water availability in the Nile Basin. There

---

62 *Id*; *See also* ANTON EARLE ET AL., TRANSBOUNDARY WATER MANAGEMENT AND THE CLIMATE CHANGE DEBATE at 117 (2015) (Climate variability as an old issue in the Nile basin).

63 *Id.* at 129.

64 THE NILE BASIN INITIATIVE, CHANGE AND ITS IMPLICATIONS FOR THE NILE REGION, in STATE OF THE RIVER NILE BASIN 205, at 210 (2012), http://sob.nilebasin.org/pdf/Chapter%208%20climate%20Change.pdf. COLLINS succinctly explained the impact of climate variability in the Nile Basin, and made the following observation: "In good years enough water could come down from Ethiopian highlands to overflow the river's banks and make the surrounding basin land fertile for crops. The nutrients deposited as alluvial sediment were as important for the cropland as the water itself. In bad years the mountains sent too much water crashing down, destroying everything in its path. People resign themselves to their fate when a great Nile flood swept away their homes, monuments, and temples. But the worst years were when there was not enough, and then the land became caked and barren, hard as cement, and people silently succumbed when the waters did not flow, and famine stalked the land." ROBERT O. COLLINS, THE NILE 1 (2002).

65 NILE BASIN INITIATIVE, *supra* note 64, at 210.

66 UNEP, CLIMATE CHANGE ADAPTATION CAPACITIES IN THE NILE RIVER BASIN 13 (2015), http://wedocs.unep.org/bitstream/handle/20.500.11822/14068/Nile%20Climate%20change%20fa.pdf?sequence=1&isAllowed=y.

67 *See* EARLE ET AL, *supra* note 62, at 130.

68 *Id.;* Declan Conway, *From Headwater Tributaries to International River: Observing and Adapting to Climate Variability and Change in the Nile Basin,* 15 GLOBAL ENVTL. CHANGE, at 106 (2005); *see* UNEP, *supra* note 66, at 13; Heather Cooley et al., *Understanding and Reducing the Risks of Climate Change for Transboundary Waters,* PAC. INST. (2009); *See generally,* Ungtae Kim & Jagath J. Kaluarachchi, *Climate Change Impacts on Water*

is a high probability, however, that climate change will decrease water availability,[69] hindering access to water for drinking and sanitation, irrigation, and energy production.

To make matters worse, climate change is threatening the Nile Basin at a time when the sustainability of the Nile watercourse has been severely strained by other non-climatic factors, such as population growth, economic development, and urbanization, all of which are decreasing water quantity per capita.[70] The Nile Basin is already experiencing a serious problem due to limited water availability and alarming population growth. Despite the river's length, the quantity of fresh water it carries (84 billion cubic meters (BCM)) is only a fraction of that carried by other major rivers like the Mississippi or the Amazon.[71] This relatively small amount of water has to be shared by eleven Nile Basin States in the "most water-deficient parts of the world."[72] Moreover, these states are facing extreme poverty,[73] and rapid population growth is exacerbating the water scarcity in the Nile Basin area.[74]

The Nile Basin States are home to more than 550 million people, though that number is projected to exceed one billion by the end of 2050.[75] 257 million—over 20 percent of Africa's population—live within the basin's boundaries.[76]

Resources in the Upper Blue Nile River Basin, Ethiopia. J. AM. WATER RSRC. ASS. (2009); Barnes, *supra* note 59, 2–6.

69 Manuel Schiffler, *Conflicts over the Nile or Conflicts on the Nile?*, *in* WATER IN THE MIDDLE EAST: POTENTIAL FOR CONFLICTS AND PROSPECT FOR COOPERATION 137, 146 (Waltina Scheumann & Manuel Schiffler eds., 1998) (predicting the Nile's flow will decrease by up to 78%). It should be noted that other studies predicted increasing water quantities by 30%. *Id.*

70 NBI 2016, *supra* note 58, at 15; Arnell et al., *supra* note 36, at 234.

71 *See* COLLINS, *supra* note 64, at 11 (The Nile River constitutes "a mere cup (2 percent) of the Amazon, perhaps a glass (15 percent) of the Mississippi, or at best a pitcher (20 percent) of the Mekong.")

72 Fasil Amdetsion, *Scrutinizing the Scorpion Problematique: Arguments in Favor of the Continued Relevance of International Law and a Multidisciplinary Approach to Resolving the Nile Dispute*, 44 TEX. INT'L L.J. 1, 3 (2008).

73 Except for Egypt, all Nile Basin countries are facing extreme poverty. NBI 2016, *supra* note 58, at 60 ("Poverty is widespread, and socio-economic conditions are difficult for a large majority of the Nile basin population … more than 40 percent of the population of most Nile basin countries live on less than the international poverty line of 1.25 dollar a day [in purchasing power parity terms] PPP").

74 NBI 2016, *supra* note 58, at 50.

75 Addisu Lashitew & Haim Gebeyehu, *Could the Nile Dispute Be an Opportunity to Boost Freshwater Technology?*, BROOKINGS INST (June 18, 2020), https://www.brookings.edu/opinions/could-the-nile-dispute-be-an-opportunity-to-boost-freshwater-technology/.

76 NBI 2016, *supra* note 58, at 11.

With this demography, that eleven states have to share the relatively small quantity of the Nile water means that there will be water scarcity. Further, "the fact that the region's population is growing at 3 percent a year and is projected to reach 859 million in 2025 (up from 245 million in 1990)"[77] will significantly increase competition for access to the Nile's finite water supplies. Between 1960 and 2010, the Nile Basin population "grew by over four-fold,"[78] and with it, the demand for water, food, and energy has increased at an alarming rate.[79] The quantity of fresh water available, per capita, in the Nile Basin is decreasing at a shockingly rapid rate.[80]

The precarious relationship between population growth and water scarcity is visible when examining the three states that dominate the Blue Nile: Egypt, Sudan, and Ethiopia. As a downstream state located in a desert, Egypt receives roughly 98 percent of its surface water from the Nile watercourse.[81] Despite the existence of several huge aquifers, including the Nubian Sandstone that "contains more than 150,000 cubic kilometers of groundwater—more water than the Nile River discharges in 500 years" in the downstream states,[82] almost all of Egypt's current water needs are satisfied by the Nile watercourse.[83] Given its dependency, Egypt is highly vulnerable to fluctuations in the Nile's flow. And because population growth contributes to comparative water scarcity, "further substantial growth in the population, in particular in rural areas, will be very difficult to cope with."[84] Egypt's population is projected to be almost 225 million by the end of this century, exacerbating the existing pressure on the finite resources of the Nile watercourse.[85]

77 Amdetsion, *supra* note 72, at 3.

78 NBI 2016, *supra* note 58, at 50.

79 *Id.*

80 *Id.*

81 Hosam Elemam, *Egypt and Collective Action Mechanisms in the Nile Basin, in* THE RIVER NILE IN THE POST-COLONIAL AGE: CONFLICT AND COOPERATION AMONG THE NILE BASIN COUNTRIES, 219 (Terje Tvedt ed., 2010) (hereinafter THE RIVER NILE IN THE POST-COLONIAL AGE).

82 Mary Morton, *Ancient Water Underlies Arid Egypt: A Hidden Trove of Groundwater Is Left over From the Last Ice vAge,* EOS (June 18, 2019), https://eos.org/articles/ancient-water-underlies-arid-egypt.

83 Elemam, *supra* note 81, at 219 (Nile "satisfies more than 95 per cent of the country's various water requirements").

84 *Id.* at 220.

85 Nada Zaki, *60 Million More Egyptians by 2050: UN Report,* AHRAMONLINE (July 3, 2019), https://english.ahram.org.eg/NewsContent/1/64/337249/Egypt/Politics-/-million-more-Egyptians-by--UN-report.aspx. *See also* Kayla Ritter, *Egypt's Nile River Pressured by Population Growth, Rising Sea Level,* CIRCLE OF BLUE (March 21, 2018),

After South Sudan gained independence in 2011,[86] Sudan also lost almost all of its internal surface waters.[87] It became highly dependent on the Nile, and now receives about 96 percent of its fresh water from the Nile watercourse.[88] It currently draws about 12.5 BCM of water from the Nile,[89] but to accommodate a growing population, Sudan is now planning new hydropower and irrigation projects in the Nile Valley.[90] The country will need an estimated "32 bcm [of water] by 2025 for food security and other essential uses."[91]

Ethiopia, which contributes 85–90 percent of the Nile waters,[92] has a population of more than 115 million and is expected to grow to over 209 million by 2050.[93] Ethiopia, relying on subsistence rainfed agriculture, does not uses the Nile watercourse, and almost all of its surface water is transboundary—less than 3 percent of it remains in the country.[94] Around "85 percent of the

https://www.circleofblue.org/2018/africa/egypts-nile-river-pressured-by-population-growth-rising-sea-level/.

86 After more than five decades of civil war, South Sudan declared independence from the Republic of the Sudan on July 9, 2011, and became the eleventh Nile riparian state. *See* Mohamed Helal, *Inheriting International Rivers: State Succession to Territorial Obligations; South Sudan, and the 1959 Nile Waters Agreement*, 27 EMORY INT'L L. REV.912–14 (2013). Salman, citing the Northern Sudanese political leaders' failure to address South Sudan's social, political, economic, and cultural differences as the reasons for the latter's independence, remarked: "On January 9, 2011, the Southern Sudanese people exercised their right of self-determination and voted by referendum, almost unanimously, to secede from Sudan. The right of self-determination was granted to them, six years before the referendum, by the Comprehensive Peace Agreement ("CPA") that was concluded between the government of the Sudan and the Sudan People's Liberation Movement/Army ("SPLM/A") on January 9, 2005. After the end of an interim period of six months, the Republic of South Sudan emerged on July 9, 2011, as the 193rd member of the global family of nations, and as the 54th African state." Salman M. A. Salman, *South Sudan Road to Independence: Broken Promises and Lost Opportunities*, 26 PAC. MCGEORGE GLOBAL BUS. & DEV. L.J. 344 (2013).

87 UN. FOOD & AGRIC., AQUASTAT COUNTRY PROFILE—SUDAN 5–8 (2015).

88 *Id.*

89 Salman M.A. Salman, *The GERD and the Revival of the Egyptian-Sudanese Dispute Over the Nile Waters*, in ETHIOPIAN YEARBOOK OF INTERNATIONAL LAW 79, 90 (Zeray Yihdego et al. eds., 2018).

90 Fadwa Taha, *The History of the Nile Waters in the Sudan*, in THE RIVER NILE IN THE POST-COLONIAL AGE, *supra* note 81, at 208.

91 *Id*, 208–9.

92 *See* NILE BASIN INITIATIVE, *supra* note 52, at 36.

93 POPULATION REFERENCE BUREAU, *supra* note 27, at 7.

94 Yacob Arsano, *Institutional Development and Water Management in the Ethiopian Nile Basin*, in THE RIVER NILE IN THE POST-COLONIAL AGE, *supra* note 81, at 161.

population live the rural areas."[95] According to a 2016 Nile Basin Initiative (NBI) report, more than 51 percent of Ethiopia's rural population live without access to safe drinking water,[96] some 72 percent without improved sanitation,[97] and more than 92 percent have no access to electricity.[98] Although Ethiopia has enormous potential for irrigation, most of its agriculture is rainfed, and only 5 percent of irrigation-suitable land has been developed.[99] As a result, the country has often experienced chronic food insecurity.[100] More than 22 million Ethiopians currently face acute food insecurity or crisis.[101] In its 2021 development rankings, the United Nations Development Program (UNDP) ranked Ethiopia 175 out of 191 countries.[102] In the 2022 Global Hunger Index, Ethiopia ranked 104 out of 121 countries and is experiencing "a level of hunger that is serious."[103] Therefore, Ethiopia's position is that it must use the Nile waters "to develop the impoverished country."[104]

Ethiopia would need to use the Nile watercourse, including for irrigation, to lift millions of its people out of poverty and ensure food and energy security. As a former World Bank official, David Grey, remarked: "There is no precedent

---

95 Embassy of Eth., Washington DC, *About Ethiopia*, https://ethiopianembassy.org/overview-about-ethiopia/#:~:text=The%20Ethiopian%20peoples%20comprise%20about,live%20in%20the%20rural%20areas.

96 NBI 2016, *supra* note 58, at 61.

97 *Id.*

98 *Id.* at 63.

99 Abeyou Worqlul, *Assessment of Surface Water Irrigation Potential in the Ethiopian Highlands: The Lake Tana Basin,* 129 CATENA 76 (2015).

100 Yacob Arsano & Imeru Tamrat, *Ethiopia and the Eastern Nile Basin,* 67 AQUAT. SCI. 15, 16 (2005).

101 THE WORLD FOOD PROGRAMME, SAVING LIVES CHANGING LIVES, ETHIOPIA ANNUAL COUNTRY REPORT 2022, COUNTRY STRATEGIC PLAN 2020–2025, (2022).

102 UNDP, HUMAN DEVELOPMENT REPORTS, ETHIOPIA (2022).

103 GLOBAL HUNGER INDEX 2022: ETHIOPIA, (2022), https://www.globalhungerindex.org/ethiopia.html.

104 Arsano, *supra* note 94, at 174. Understanding this reality as early as the 1950s, Emperor Haile Selassie articulated Ethiopia's longstanding position regarding the Nile watercourse: "[I]t is of paramount importance to Ethiopia, a problem of the first order that the waters of the Nile be made to serve the life and the needs of our beloved people now living and those who will follow us in centuries to come. However, generally, Ethiopia may be prepared to share this tremendous God given wealth of hers with friendly nations neighboring upon her, for the life and welfare of their people, it is Ethiopia's sacred duty to develop the great watershed which she possesses in the interests of her own rapidly expanding population and economy. To fulfil this task, we have arranged for the problem to be studied in all its aspects by experts in the field. Ethiopia has time and again set this forth as her position regarding the utilization of the Nile waters." *Id* (internal citation omitted).

for a country developing without harnessing its rivers and utilizing its water resources."[105] However, the Nile watercourse is already appropriated by the downstream states. Egypt is the primary user of the Nile River, the mean natural supply of which is measured 84 BCM at the Aswan High Dam (AHD).[106] In 2000, Egypt's total abstraction from the Nile was 68.3 BCM, but this figure has increased to 78 BCM since 2010.[107] Sudan extracts about 12.5 BCM of water annually.[108] In contrast, Ethiopia uses only 0.65 BCM of the Nile waters largely because of the geopolitical realities demonstrated below.[109]

Ethiopia is planning to use the Nile watercourse for irrigation purposes[110] and has begun constructing a massive hydroelectric project—the Grand Ethiopian Renaissance Dam (GERD)—on the Blue Nile.[111] Yet, "[t]he complex unity of a basin hydrology implies that diversions, abstractions or interferences with the flow of a river regime at any point in a basin eventually affect, albeit in varying scales, the quality and volume of water received by the head channels of river courses crossing international borders."[112] Therefore, with the existing pattern of utilization and downstream overexploitation, Ethiopia's future consumptive use may well cause harm, perhaps significant harm, to current and existing uses by the two downstream states.

In view of the political mistrust and competing national interests prevalent in the Nile Basin, the implementation of irrigation schemes in Ethiopia may cause conflict with downstream states. As recently as 2021, Egypt, publicly opposing the filling of GERD (a non-consumptive hydroelectric project), dared Ethiopia to "take a single drop of water from Egypt," and warned of

105 Roger Thurow, *Ravaged by Famine: Ethiopia Finally Gets Help From the Nile,* WALL ST. J. (Nov. 26, 2003), https://www.wsj.com/articles/SB106979937643978400.

106 The average total natural flow of the Nile River as measured in Aswan High Dam (AHD) is 84 BCM. *See* Agreement for the Full Utilization of the Nile Waters, Egypt-Sudan, Nov. 8, 1959, 453 U.N.T.S. 51, Article II, ¶ 4 (1959) [hereinafter 1959 Agreement].

107 UN FOOD & AGRIC., AQUASTAT COUNTRY PROFILE—EGYPT 7–9 (2016).

108 Salman, *supra* note 89, at 90.

109 TAFESSE, *supra* note 12, at 44. *See also* Arsano & Tamrat, *supra* note 100, at 16. ("Ethiopia has only been able to utilize.... a meager 0.6% of the water resources of the Nile basin.") This figure has not been that much changed yet.

110 Arsano, *supra* note 94, at 169–72.

111 *See* INT'L PANEL OF EXPERTS [IPOE] ON THE GRAND ETHIOPIAN RENAISSANCE DAM PROJECT [GERDP], FINAL REPORT, (2013), 7 [hereinafter IPOE FINAL REPORT].

112 Tadesse Kassa Woldetsadik, *International Law and Moderations of Physical Geography: The Nile Setting, in* A HISTORY OF WATER SERIES II, VOLUME 3. WATER, GEOPOLITICS AND THE NEW WORLD ORDER, 472 (Terje Tvedt, et al., eds., 2010).

"inconceivable instability in the region."[113] To accommodate competing desires and historical power imbalances, a comprehensive and binding legal framework is needed. But so far, the Nile Basin States have been unable to agree on basin-wide cooperative water management. Instead of basin-wide cooperation, the hydro-politics of the Nile Basin States have always been unilateral action and the pursuit of egocentric national interests.

1.3 The Legal and Hydro-political Setting of the Nile Basin

The exploitation of the Nile watercourse has had a "political dimension" since the dawn of history.[114] "Even as the ancient empires of Punt and Axum, which correspond to modern-day Ethiopia and parts of Sudan, enjoyed considerable trade relations with ancient Egypt, the issues related to the Nile were predominant."[115] Although the lack of technological capacity prevented Ethiopia from using the Nile watercourse, successive Ethiopian kings and emperors used the Nile water as a political weapon in its relations with Egypt.[116] Indeed, "the idea that the Blue Nile might be blocked or poisoned at its source in Ethiopia, as a means of destroying Egypt, had been canvassed in every age."[117] However, Ethiopian's historical ability to divert the flow of the Nile was "no more than roars of a paper lion."[118]

During the colonial competition, France considered building a dam in upstream countries to adversely affect the interests of Britain in Egypt,[119] and sent unsuccessful military expedition to control the Nile flow at Fashoda—an area where the White Nile and the Sobat River merge together.[120] A few years later, British officials started developing comprehensive plans, known as the

113 Menna Alaa El-Din, *'No One Can Take a Drop of Water From Egypt,' Sisi says on GERD Dispute*, AHRAMONLINE (Mar. 30, 2021), https://english.ahram.org.eg/NewsContent/1/64/408124/Egypt/Politics-/No-one-can-take-a-drop-of-water-from-Egypt,-Sisi-s.aspx.

114 Amdetsion, *supra* note 72, at 44.

115 *Id.*

116 *See generally* Richard Pankhurst, *Ethiopia's Alleged Control of the Nile,* in THE NILE: HISTORIES, CULTURES, MYTHS, *supra* note 52; *see also generally* Emery Van Donzel, *The Legend of Blue Nile in Europe*, in THE NILE: HISTORIES, CULTURES, MYTHS, *supra* note 52.

117 GEBRE TSADIK DEGEFU, THE NILE: HISTORICAL, LEGAL AND DEVELOPMENTAL PERSPECTIVES 150 (2013) (internal citation omitted).

118 Pankhurst, *supra* note 116, at 31.

119 ROBERT COLLINS, THE WATERS OF THE NILE: HYDROPOLITICS AND THE JONGLEI CANAL, 1900–1988, 49 (1990).

120 *Id.*

"Full Nile Control" or the "Century Storage Project," for developing projects in Sudan and upstream countries.[121] However, unlike French's plan, the Full Nile Control was developed to regulate the flow of the Nile, and increase water availability in Egypt.[122] As a means of safeguarding Britain's imperial interests in Egypt and Sudan, the plan did not consider the interests of Ethiopia and other upstream countries.[123]

Along with its "Full Nile Control" plan, Britain also implemented several colonial treaties to safeguard its imperial interests in Egypt, with profound institutional repercussions for the Nile Basin. It concluded, *inter alia*, the 1902 Anglo-Ethiopian Treaty[124] and the 1929 Anglo-Egyptian Treaty,[125] with colonial powers and independent states concerning the use and the flow of the Nile waters. These colonial treaties, which allowed Great Britain and Egypt to construct large-scale projects at the expense of other Nile riparian states or colonies, are very controversial. All the upper Nile Basin States renounced them. Ethiopia rejected the 1902 Anglo-Ethiopian Treaty as early as 1907; Tanganyika (now Tanzania) declared the Nyerere Doctrine in 1961 and denounced the 1929 Anglo-Egyptian Treaty; and Uganda, Kenya, Burundi, DRC, and Rwanda have all subsequently renounced their obligations stipulated under the colonial Nile Waters Treaties.[126]

During the Cold War, the Nile Basin States were also planning and negotiating over large-scale national projects. Ethiopia commissioned the U.S. Bureau

---

121 NURIT KLIOT, WATER RESOURCES AND CONFLICT IN THE MIDDLE EAST 35–37 (1994); COLLINS, *supra* note 64, at 141–56; JOHN WATERBURY, HYDROPOLITICS OF THE NILE VALLEY, 40–42, 87–96 (1979). The notion of full Nile control or the Century Storage plan is simple: "to remove the unpredictable element from the Nile discharge would require storing several successive annual floods; that is, storing the annual difference between the real needs and total discharge. In this manner a series of reserves could be used to bank water against the low years or to hold excess water if the flood promised to be especially high." *Id.*, at 87.

122 WILLIAM GARSTIN, REPORT UPON THE BASIN OF THE UPPER NILE: WITH PROPOSALS FOR THE IMPROVEMENT OF THAT RIVER, 196 (1904), https://archive.org/details/reportuponbasinoodupugoog/page/n280/mode/1up.

123 The William Garstin considered both the Equatorial Lakes and Lake Tana as "natural reservoirs" that would provide "constant and sufficient supply" of water for Egypt. GARSTIN, *supra* note 122, at 195–96.

124 Treaties Relative to the Frontiers Between the Soudan, Ethiopia, and Eritrea, Eth.-U.K., May 15, 1902, [1902] U.K.T.S. 16 [hereinafter 1902 Anglo-Ethiopian Treaty].

125 Exchange of Notes Regarding the Use of the Waters of the River Nile for Irrigation Purposes, Egypt-U.K., May 7, 1929, [1929] U.K.T.S. 17 [hereinafter 1929 Anglo-Egyptian Treaty].

126 *See* discussion *infra* sections 3.1, 3.2 and 3.3.

of Reclamation (USBR) to survey the Blue Nile.[127] Although the study proposed several irrigation and hydropower projects on the Blue Nile in Ethiopia, the geopolitical complexity and domestic political instability of the time made it impossible to implement those projects, except for "the Finchaa agro-industrial plan that was taken up in the 1980s…"[128] On the other hand, Egypt and Sudan concluded the 1959 Agreement and constructed the Aswan High Dam (AHD) and the Roseires Dam. The Agreement, which allocated the entire flow of the Nile between the two countries, is vehemently rejected by upstream states.[129]

Following the end of the Cold War, the Nile Basin States developed several unilateral projects including, *inter alia*, the Toshka project in Egypt, the Merowe Dam in Sudan, and the Grand Ethiopian Renaissance Dam (GERD) in Ethiopia.[130] At the same time, they also attempted to cease their acrimonious relationships through bilateral,[131] and multilateral cooperation initiatives including, *inter alia*, the Technical Cooperation Committee for the Promotion of the Development and Environmental Protection of the Nile (TECCONILE), the Nile Basin Initiative (NBI), and the Cooperative Framework Agreement (CFA).[132]

The CFA was initiated in 1995 as one of the TECCONILE projects (Project D3) to create a basin-wide legal and institutional framework to regulate the interstate utilization and management of the Nile River.[133] At the time, all riparian Nile states,[134] except for Eritrea, which participated in the project as an observer, negotiated the CFA. During the negotiations, the fate of the colonial and immediate post-colonial Nile Waters Treaties (collectively referred to as existing Nile Waters Agreements) was the subject of controversy. The upstream states believed that the purpose of the CFA Project was to produce an inclusive agreement that would replace and supersede the existing Nile Waters Agreements. The lower riparian states—Egypt and Sudan—insisted that the new agreement must explicitly recognize the earlier agreements, referred to as

127 *See* discussion *infra* section 2.3.

128 Arsano, *supra* note 94, at 167.

129 1959 Agreement, *supra* note 106, art II, ¶ 1-2.

130 *See* discussion *infra* sections 5.3 and part III.

131 *See* discussion *infra* sections 5.1.1. and 5.1.2.

132 Agreement on the Nile River Basin Cooperative Framework art 42, *opened for signature* May 14, 2010, INT'L WATER L. PROJECT, http://internationalwaterlaw.org/documents/regionaldocs/Nile_River_Basin_Cooperative_Framework_2010.pdf [hereinafter CFA].

133 *See* discussion *infra* sections 6.1.

134 The riparian Nile states that participated in the negotiations include Burundi, the Democratic Republic of Congo, Egypt, Ethiopia, Kenya, Rwanda, Sudan, Tanzania, and Uganda. Eritrea participated as an observer.

"existing agreements," which would continue to be binding upon all riparian states.[135]

In an attempt to bridge this gap, the negotiators of the CFA introduced the new, non-legal concept of "water security"[136] to replace the provision governing the relationship between the CFA and the existing agreements, on which no agreement could be reached.[137] The idea was that Egypt, which was concerned about water security, could be protected through a new provision and the relationship between the CFA and the "existing agreements" (whether the former supersedes the latter or vice versa) could be governed by the general rules of international law.[138] However, the Nile Basin States were not able to agree on the draft provision on water security contained in Article 14 of the draft CFA.[139] Specifically, the lower riparian states opposed the part of Article 14 providing that the parties "agree, in a spirit of cooperation not to significantly affect the water security of any other Nile Basin State."[140] The lower riparian states insisted that the language should obligate all Nile Basin States "*not to adversely affect the water security and current uses and rights* of any other Nile Basin State."[141]

The position of the lower riparian states brought the long-standing dispute over the existing Nile Waters Agreements back as a request for unequivocal recognition of their validity against upstream states. The upstream states rejected that proposal and opened the agreement for signature on May 14, 2010. The CFA has been signed by six upstream states and subsequently ratified by four states.[142] By its terms, the CFA requires six ratifications to enter into force, and consequently the CFA neither binds the lower riparian states nor governs the entire Nile Basin.[143]

In December 2010, after signing the CFA, Ethiopia also began constructing the GERD an estimated twenty kilometers upstream from the Sudan-Ethiopia

135 Telephone Interview with Professor Stephen C. McCaffrey, Legal and Institutional Consultant, Nile Coop. Framework Project (Nov. 2017) [hereinafter McCaffrey Interview]; *See generally* Dereje Zeleke Mekonnen, *The Nile Basin Cooperative Framework Agreement Negotiations and the Adoption of a 'Water Security' Paradigm: Flight into Obscurity or a Logical Cul-de-Sac?*, 21 EUR. J. INT'L L. 421 (2010).

136 McCaffrey Interview, *supra* note 135; *see also* Mekonnen, *supra* note 135, at 436–40.

137 McCaffrey Interview, *supra* note 135.

138 *Id.*

139 *Id.*

140 *Id.*; Mekonnen, *supra* note 135, at 428.

141 *Id.* CFA, *supra* note 132, Annex on Article 14(b) (emphasis added).

142 Ethiopia, Kenya, Uganda, Burundi, Rwanda, and Tanzania have signed the Agreement; Ethiopia, Tanzania, Rwanda, and Uganda have ratified it.

143 CFA, *supra* note 132.

border on the Blue Nile. Egypt and Sudan initially opposed the GERD, alleging that it would significantly and adversely affect their interests and violate the rules regulating the Nile watercourse.[144] Ethiopia maintains that the GERD will not have a significant adverse impact on the two downstream states, and even proposed the establishment of the International Panel of Experts (IPoE) to study the transboundary impacts of the dam. Ethiopia also contends that the GERD confers enormous benefits to Egypt and Sudan, including a more regular flow of water, better siltation prevention, a reduction in evaporation, and cheaper electricity.[145] In a historic break with its past practice of moving in lockstep with Egypt, Sudan has since 2012 become more receptive to the GERD because of these benefits.[146] Egypt, on the other hand, maintains its view that any upstream dam on the Nile River poses an existential threat.[147] In June 2013, Egypt's president, Mohammed Morsi, warned Ethiopia that "blood is the alternative," if his country "loses one drop" of the Nile water.[148] When Ethiopia responded that no earthly force would stop the construction of the dam,[149] Egypt requested a reduction in the size of the dam.[150] In 2015, after painstaking negotiations,[151] Egypt, Sudan, and Ethiopia signed the Declaration of Principles ("DoP") on the GERD.[152] The DoP provides a framework for further

144 *See* Salman M.A. Salman, *Grand Ethiopian Renaissance Dam: Challenges and Opportunities*, CIP REPORT 23 (Oct. 2011) (stating that Egypt and Sudan considered the GERD a violation of the 1902 Anglo-Ethiopian Treaty).

145 *See* Rawia Tawfik, *The Grand Ethiopian Renaissance Dam: A Benefit-Sharing Project in the Eastern Nile?*, 41 WATER INT'L 574, 576 (2016).

146 *See* Rawia Tawfik, *Revisiting Hydro-Hegemony from a Benefit-Sharing Perspective: The Case of the Grand Ethiopian Renaissance Dam* 24 (German Dev. Inst. Discussion Paper 5/2015, 2015) (describing Sudan's position as "a turning point" in the hydro-political relations between the two downstream countries, Sudan and Egypt). *See* Salman M.A. Salman, *The Grand Ethiopian Renaissance Dam: The Road to the Declaration of Principles and the Khartoum Document*, 42 WATER INT'L 512, 516–17 (2016).

147 *Id.;* Tawfik, *supra* note 145, at 576; *see also* Tawfik, *supra* note 146, at 24.

148 *Egypt Warns Ethiopia Over Nile Dam*, AL JAZEERA (June 11, 2013), https://www.aljazeera.com/news/2013/6/11/egypt-warns-ethiopia-over-nile-dam.

149 *Egypt and Ethiopia Argue Over Dam Project*, DEUTSCHE WELLE (June 14, 2013), https://www.dw.com/en/egypt-and-ethiopia-argue-over-dam-project/a-16880722.

150 Zeray Yihdego, *International Law Connotations of US 'Mediated' Nile Dam Negotiations and Outcomes: Why and How the Parties Should Regain Control* (Mar. 18, 2020) (unpublished working paper) (https://www.researchgate.net/publication/340341053_International_Law_Connotations_of_USsposored_GERD_'mediation'_WorkingPaper_Zeray_Yihdego_18_March_2020).

151 For a description of the negotiation process, *see* Salman, *supra* note 146.

152 Agreement on Declaration of Principles on the Grand Ethiopian Renaissance Dam Project, Mar. 23, 2015, INT'L WATER L. PROJECT, https://www.internationalwaterlaw.org/documents/regionaldocs/Final_Nile_Agreement_23_March_2015.pdf [hereinafter DoP].

negotiation on the filling and annual operation of the dam and reflects Egypt's recognition of the importance of the Nile River to Ethiopia's development.[153]

Despite this framework, however, the dispute over the filling and operation of the GERD persists. At first, the three states disputed the modalities of the two studies—transboundary impact study and hydrological modeling study—recommended by the International Panel of Experts (IPoE).[154] Egypt insisted that the baseline data to determine the impact should be its current use of the Nile waters.[155] Sudan demanded that the 1959 Agreement water allocation serves as the baseline, while Ethiopia rejected both positions.[156] As the dispute persisted, Egypt submitted proposals on the filling and operation of the dam[157] on August 2919, and later effectively internationalized the GERD negotiations[158] by involving the United States government and the World Bank as observers.[159]

The involvement of the United States and the World Bank only served to further complicate the dispute and escalate diplomatic tensions. The United States, seemingly going beyond its status as an observer in the talks, proposed an agreement that Ethiopia considered adverse to its national interest.[160] Ethiopia rejected the proposal and withdrew from the last meeting

153 *Id.*

154 Salman, *supra* note 89, at 95.

155 *Id.*

156 *Id.*

157 *Ethiopia Rejects Egypt Proposal on the Nile Dam*, AL JAZEERA (Sept. 19, 2019), https://www.aljazeera.com/news/2019/9/19/ethiopia-rejects-egypt-proposal-on-nile-dam-operation [hereinafter *Ethiopia Rejects Egypt Proposal 1*]; *Ethiopia Rejects Egypt's Proposal on the Filling, Operation of Grand Dam*, ADDIS STANDARD (Sept. 18, 2019), https://addisstandard.com/news-ethiopia-outright-rejects-egypts-proposal-on-the-fillingoperation-of-grand-dam/ [hereinafter *Ethiopia Rejects Egypt Proposal 2*].

158 *Egypt Seeks International Support to End GERD Talks Deadlock*, DAILY NEWS EGYPT (Oct. 1, 2019), https://www.dailynewssegypt.com/2019/10/01/egypt-seeks-international-support-to-end-gerd-talks-deadlock/ [hereinafter *Egypt Seeks International Support*] (discussing Egyptian President Abdel Fattah el-Sisi's speech in the UN General Assembly); *Egypt Calls on 'Active' US Role Mediating Nile Dam Impasse with Ethiopia*, FRANCE 24 (Sept. 10, 2019), https://www.france24.com/en/20191007-egypt-ethiopia-nile-river-dam-mediating [hereinafter *Egypt Calls on the U.S.*].

159 Press Release, U.S. Dep't of the Treasury, Joint Statement of Egypt, Ethiopia, Sudan, the United States, and the World Bank, (Nov. 6, 2019), https://home.treasury.gov/ [hereinafter Joint Statement 1].

160 Elias Meseret, *Ethiopia Won't Be Forced by the US on Dam, Foreign Minister Says*, ASSOCIATED PRESS (Mar. 13, 2020), https://apnews.com/39183ccfeed1c0796ad38796d459ff3b (interviewing the foreign minister of Ethiopia).

in Washington, DC.[161] The U.S. Department of the Treasury requested that Ethiopia sign the proposed agreement and cautioned Ethiopia to refrain from testing and filling the GERD without an agreement with Egypt and Sudan.[162] When Ethiopia rejected the warning and started filling the GERD, Egypt formally requested the United Nations Security Council ("UNSC") to intervene in the GERD dispute.[163] The UNSC made an unprecedented move and held an open session on the GERD dispute where most members encouraged the three states to resolve their dispute through the African Union (AU).[164] After a year of intermittent tripartite negotiation under the auspices of the AU, Egypt brought the GERD dispute to the UNSC for the second time.[165] The UNSC, after holding another open session on the GERD dispute, again encouraged the three states to resolve their dispute through the AU.[166]

Although disguised in talks over the GERD's filling and operation, the current tension between Ethiopia, Sudan, and Egypt is principally related to their longstanding disagreement over the validity of the 1902 Anglo-Ethiopian Treaty, the 1929 Anglo-Egyptian Treaty, and the 1959 Agreement between Egypt and Sudan (collectively, the "existing Nile Waters Agreements"). These agreements comprise the principal obstacle both to the GERD negotiations and to the sustainable utilization and management of the Nile watercourse. The other challenge pertains to the asymmetric water use and distribution of the Nile Basin, where the downstream states—entirely dependent on the Nile watercourse that originates outside their territories—exploit almost all the Nile waters, while the upstream states that contribute all the waters and

161 *Id.; Ethiopia: US Being 'Undiplomatic' Over Nile Dam Project*, AL JAZEERA (Mar. 4, 2020), https://www.aljazeera.com/news/2020/03/ethiopia-undiplomatic-nile-dam-project-200304060039736 [hereinafter *US Being 'Undiplomatic'*].

162 Press Release, Steven T. Mnuchin, U.S. Sec'y of the Treasury, Statement on the Grand Ethiopian Renaissance Dam (Feb. 28, 2020), https://home.treasury.gov/news/secretary-statements-remarks/statement-by-the-secretary-of-the-treasury-on-the-grand-ethiopian-renaissance-dam [hereinafter Treasury Statement].

163 *See* Permanent Rep. of Egypt to the U.N., Letter dated 1 May 2020 from the Permanent Rep. of Egypt to the United Nations Addressed to the President of the Security Council, U.N. Doc. S/2020/355 (May 1, 2020) [hereinafter Egypt's 2020 Letter to the UNSC 1].

164 *Egypt Warns of 'Existential Threat' from Ethiopia Dam,* AL JAZEERA, (June 30, 2020), https://www.aljazeera.com/economy/2020/6/30/egypt-warns-of-existential-threat-from-ethiopia-dam [hereinafter *Egypt Warns of 'Existential Threat'*].

165 *Meeting on the Grand Ethiopian Renaissance Dam and Regional Relations,* SECURITY COUNCIL REPORT (July 7, 2021), https://www.securitycouncilreport.org/whatsinblue/2021/07/meeting-on-the-grand-ethiopian-renaissance-dam-and-regional-relations-2.php.

166 *UN Ready to Promote 'Win-win Solution' for Blue Nile Dam Project,* UN NEWS (July 8, 2021), https://news.un.org/en/story/2021/07/1095552.

use almost none of them.[167] The asymmetry is also reflected in the power of the Nile Basin States: whereas downstream "Egypt has a superior position of power due to its political support and its military and economical capacity," the upstream states, especially Ethiopia, have "'the power of geography'[with] the ability to control the flow of the river."[168] What makes the issue more problematic is the acrimonious relationship between the Nile Basin States, characterized by historical baggage of animosity and military confrontations. Moreover, the increasing demand for water due to alarming population growth, and the uncertainty associated with the ramifications of global climate change further exacerbate the situation, posing new challenges to the sustainable utilization and management of the Nile watercourse.

1.4 Significance, Objective, and Organization of the Book

This work studies the legal and hydro-political trajectories of the Nile Basin. The Nile Basin and the GERD are the focus of a voluminous body of academic literature. Political scientists have extensively studied the role of power dynamics and the hydro-hegemonic implications of the GERD in their efforts to determine "who gets how much [of the Nile] water, when, where, and why?"[169]

---

167 John Anthony Allan, *Nile Basin Asymmetries: A Closed Fresh Water Resource, Soil Water Potential, The Political Economy And Nile Transboundary Hydropolitics, in* THE NILE: ORIGIN, ENVIRONMENTS, LIMNOLOGY AND HUMAN USE, 749 (Henri J. Dumont, ed. 2019) (In the Nile Basin, "the water endowments and use are asymmetrical"). *See also* KLIOT, *supra* note 121, at 13. (Describing the asymmetric water distribution and the "great contrast between the riparian state which contributes almost all the water to the Nile but uses almost none (Ethiopia) and that which contributes nothing to the Nile but uses most of its water (Egypt)." *Id.*

168 Mathias Devi Nielsen, *The Waters of The Nile: Ethiopia Challenging Regional Hydro-Hegemony,* UNIV. OF COPENHAGEN, 9 (2015) (unpublished MA Thesis); *see* also Mark Zeitoun & Jeroen Warner, *Hydro-Hegemony: A Framework for Analysis of Transboundary Water Conflicts,* 8 WATER POLICY 450 (2006).

169 *See generally* Tawfik, *supra* note 145; Tawfik, *supra* note 146; Rawia Tawfik & Ines Dombrowsky, *GERD and Hydro-Politics in the Eastern Nile: From Water to Benefit-Sharing?,* in THE GRAND ETHIOPIAN RENAISSANCE DAM AND THE NILE BASIN: IMPLICATIONS FOR TRANSBOUNDARY WATER COOPERATION 113 (Zeray Yihdego et al. eds. 2018) [hereinafter GERD IMPLICATIONS]; John Waterbury, *Is the Status Quo in the Nile Basin Viable?,* 4 BROWN J. OF WORLD AFF. (1997); ANA ELISA Cascao, *Changing Power Relations in the Nile River Basin: Unilateralism vs. Cooperation?,* 2 WATER ALTERNATIVES 245 (2009); YACOB ARSANO, ETHIOPIA AND THE NILE DILEMMAS OF NATIONAL AND REGIONAL HYDROPOLITICS (2007); Daniel Kendie, *Egypt and the Hydro-Politics of the Blue Nile River,* 6 NORTHEAST AFR. STUD. 145–46, (1999); Tadesse Woldetsadik, *The Grand Ethiopian Renaissance Dam and Ethiopia's Succession in Hydro-Legal Prominence: A Script in Legal*

Other scholars have addressed whether access to the Nile watercourse and the GERD will be a source of conflict or a catalyst for cooperation.[170] Engineers and hydrologic experts have studied the GERD's positive and adverse effects and proposed various scenarios for the filling and operation of the dam.[171] Legal scholars have explored *some* of the substantive issues concerning the fragmented legal regimes governing the Nile watercourse, including the DoP.[172]

History of Diplomatic Confront (1957–2013), 9 MIZAN L. REV. 369 (2015); Hala Nasr & Andreas Neef, *Ethiopia's Challenge to Egyptian Hegemony in the Nile River Basin: The Case of the Grand Ethiopian Renaissance Dam*, 21 J. GEOPOLITICS 969 (2016); Mohamed Salman Tayie, *The Grand Ethiopian Renaissance Dam and the Ethiopian Challenge of Hydropolitcal Hegemony on the Nile Basin, in* GRAND ETHIOPIAN RENAISSANCE DAM VERSUS ASWAN HIGH DAM 485, 501 (Abdelazim M. Negm & Sommer Abdel-Fattah eds., 2019).

170 *See, e.g.*, Kristin Wiebe, *The Nile River: Potential for Conflict and Cooperation in the Face of Water Degradation*, 41 NAT. RESOURCES. J. 731 (2001); KLIOT, *supra* note 121; SIMON A. MASON, FROM CONFLICT TO COOPERATION IN THE NILE BASIN, (2003); Int'l Crisis Grp., *Bridging the Gap in the Nile Waters Dispute*, Africa Report No. 271, 24–26 (2019); Dale Whittington, John Waterbury & Marc Jeuland, *The Grand Renaissance Dam and Prospects for Cooperation on the Eastern Nile*, 16 WATER POL'Y (2014); *Nile Dam Talks: Unlocking a Dangerous Stalemate*, INT'L CRISIS GROUP (Mar. 16, 2020); Ana Elisa Cascão & Alan Nicol, *Changing Cooperation Dynamics in the Nile Basin and the Role of the GERD*, in GERD IMPLICATIONS, *supra* note 169; Ana Elisa Cascão & Alan Nicol, *GERD: New Norms of Cooperation in the Nile Basin?*, 41 WATER INT'L 550, (2016); SEIFULAZIZ MILAS, SHARING THE NILE: EGYPT, ETHIOPIA AND THE GEO-POLITICS OF WATER (2013).

171 *See, e.g.*, WOSSENU ABTEW & SHIELIS BEHAILU DESSU, THE GRAND ETHIOPIAN RENAISSANCE DAM ON THE BLUE NILE (2018); Kevin G. Wheeler, *Cooperative Filling Approaches for the Grand Ethiopian Renaissance Dam*, 41 WATER INT'L 611 (2016); Ying Zhang, Solomon Tassew Erkyihum & Paul Block, *Filling the GERD: Evaluating Hydroclimatic Variability and Impoundment Strategies for Blue Nile Riparian Countries*, 41 WATER INT'L 593 (2016); Andrew King & Paul Block, *An Assessment of Reservoir Filling Policies for the Grand Ethiopian Renaissance Dam*, 5 J. WATER & CLIMATE CHANGE 233 (2014); Noha Donia & Abdelazim Negm, *Impacts of Filling Scenarios of GERD on Egypt's Water Resources and Their Impact on Agriculture Secto*r, in CONVENTIONAL WATER RESOURCE AND AGRICULTURE IN EGYPT 391 (Abdelazim Negm ed. 2018); Asegdew Mulat & Semu Moges, *Assessment of the Impact of the Grand Ethiopian Renaissance Dam on the Performance of the High Aswan Dam*, 6 J. WATER RES. & PROT. 583 (2014).

172 *See* DEGEFU, *supra* note 117; Amdetsion, *supra* note 72; Mekonnen, *supra* note 135; Dereje Zeleke Mekonnen, *Declaration of Principles on the Grand Ethiopian Renaissance Dam: Some Issues of Concern*, 11 MIZAN L. REV. 255 (2017) (hereinafter *Declaration of Principles*); Dereje Zeleke Mekonnen, *Between the Scylla of Water Security and Charybdis of Benefit Sharing: The Nile Basin Cooperative Framework Agreement—Failed or Just Teetering on the Brink?* 3 GOETTINGEN J. INT'L L. 349 (2011); Salman, *supra* note 89; Salman, *supra* note 146; Salman M. A. Salman, *The Nile Basin Cooperative Framework Agreement: A Peacefully Unfolding African Spring?*, 38 WATER INT'L 17 (2012); TADESSE KASSA WOLDETSADIK, INTERNATIONAL WATERCOURSES LAW IN THE NILE RIVER BASIN: THREE STATES AT A CROSSROADS (2013); MWANGI KIMENYI & JOHN MBAKU, GOVERNING THE NILE RIVER BASIN: THE SEARCH FOR A NEW LEGAL REGIME (2015); ZERAY YIHDEGO, THE

The academic discourse regarding the Nile watercourse and GERD, however, lacks a detailed multidisciplinary study on the legal and hydro-political trajectories of the Nile Basin, analyzing the implications the NBI, CFA, GERD, and the DoP on the use and allocation of the Nile watercourse; appraising the GERD negations in light of the existing Nile Waters Agreements; investigating the legitimacy of the United States' role in the GERD negotiations; scrutinizing the U.S. Treasury statement vis-à-vis international law; prescribing solutions for resolving the GERD dispute; and offering proposals for addressing the ramifications of climate change and developing a basin-wide, climate-proof treaty.

This book intends to fill these gaps in the scholastic discourse on the Nile and GERD negotiations. Specifically, its purpose is fourfold. The first objective is to reconstruct and reflect upon the legal and hydro-political history of the Nile Basin. The initial step towards this objective starts with explaining how the pre-colonial history of the basin affects the current inter-state relationships, how the colonial legacy established the existing status quo, and how the post-colonial reality made unilateralism the *modus operandi* of the Basin. Then, the most important step will be scrutinizing treaty and custom-based arguments vis-à-vis international law.

The second objective of this book is to analyze the legal and hydro-political implications of the NBI, CFA, the GERD, and the DoP. The path towards this objective starts with scrutinizing why the Nile Basin States failed to establish a basin-wide legal and institutional cooperative framework acceptable to them all, and how the GERD is pragmatically changing the existing status quo. These inquiries lead to another question about whether the two legal instruments, CFA and DoP, can invalidate the existing Nile Waters Agreements and bring about a *de jure change* in the status quo. The final and crucial step towards this objective will then be analyzing the ramifications of the existing Nile Waters Agreements on the GERD negotiations, the legitimacy of the United States' role in the GERD negotiations, the U.S. Treasury statement vis-à-vis international law, and solutions for resolving the GERD dispute.

The third objective of this book is to propose mechanisms for governing the Nile watercourse under climatic uncertainties. The journey towards this objective starts with exploring the treaty practices of other shared watercourses and developing frameworks for studying treaty flexibility in the context of the Nile Basin. The latter, in return, leads to analyses of the intrinsic capacity of the fragmented legal regime governing the Nile watercourse to adapt to climate

---

FAIRNESS 'DILEMMA' IN SHARING THE NILE WATERS: WHAT LESSONS FROM THE GRAND ETHIOPIAN RENAISSANCE DAM FOR INTERNATIONAL LAW? (2017).

change. The journey will end by offering specific proposals to the Nile Basin States for addressing the ramifications of climate change and developing a basin-wide, climate-proof treaty.

The last objective of this book is to undertake a detailed multidisciplinary study of the legal and hydro-political trajectories of the Nile Basin. This is especially important because the academic discourse regarding the Nile watercourse is primarily dominated by monodisciplinary studies.[173] This work aims to avoid such categorization and provide a retrospective and prospective look at the Nile watercourse through multidisciplinary lenses—commingling history, geopolitics, climate science, and law.[174]

The book is organized into four parts and ten chapters to achieve its fourfold objectives. Part 1 reconstructs the legal and hydro-political history of the Nile Basin. After introducing the pre-colonial myth and realities of the Nile Basin, this part *deconstructs* and *reflects* upon the colonial legacies that established inequitable and lopsided water utilization in the basin; and *investigates* the postcolonial realities that made unilateralism the *modus operandi* of the Nile Basin (Chapter 2). It then critically examines the legal status of the existing Nile Waters Agreements in light of international law and scrutinizes custom-based legal arguments dominating the Nile discourse (Chapters 3–4).

Part 2 focuses on the post-colonial attempts of the Nile Basin States to change and maintain the status quo. After investigating the legal and hydro-political ramifications of the 1991 Khartoum Declaration[175] and the 1993 Framework for Cooperation[176] as well as other multilateral cooperative initiatives including, *inter alia*, the TECCONILE, the NBI, and the CFA, this part indicates how unilateralism continued to be the *modus operandi* of the Nile Basin during the post–Cold War era (Chapter 5). Moreover, after scrutinizing the sticking points during the negotiation of the CFA, this part analyzes the basic substantive and procedural principles of the CFA vis-à-vis the general rules of international watercourses law. Finally, reflecting upon the institutional structure envisioned in the agreement and analyzing other miscellaneous provisions, it scrutinizes the hydro-political implication of the agreement (Chapter 6).

173 Amdetsion, *supra* note 72, at 5.

174 For earlier multidisciplinary research, *see Id.*

175 Ethiopia-Sudan Peace and Friendship Declaration, December 23, 1991, Sudan-Eth., [1991] copy on file with the author [hereinafter 1991 Khartoum Declaration].

176 *See generally* Framework for General Co-operation, July 1, 1993, Egypt-Eth., INT'L WATER L. PROJECT, https://www.internationalwaterlaw.org/documents/regionaldocs/1993_Ethiopia-Egypt-Framework_Agreement-Nile_Basin.pdf [hereinafter 1993 Framework Instrument].

Part 3 specifically addresses the GERD and the revival of the dispute over the existing Nile Waters Agreements. After providing a brief overview of the GERD, and downstream states' initial reactions to the project, the study reflects upon the negotiation history of the DoP. It then scrutinizes the legal status of the DoP and its relationship with the existing Nile Waters Agreements. Analyzing the legal and hydro-political implications of the DoP, this part submits that the DoP neither abrogated the past treaties nor brought about a *de jure* change in the Egyptian hydro-hegemonic status quo (Chapter 7). Moreover, this part devotes a chapter to the post-DoP negotiations over the filling and annual operation of the GERD (Chapter 8). After providing hydro-political justifications for the involvement of the United States and the World Bank in the GERD negotiations, this chapter explores the implication of the recent sticking points in the GERD talks. It then examines whether—as the U.S. Treasury has suggested—a preliminary agreement is required to fill and test the GERD and further probes the legitimacy under international law of the United States' involvement in the GERD. Finally, after reflecting upon post-Washington GERD negotiations, including the letters that the three states submitted to UNSC, this part provides the way forward for resolving the GERD dispute.

Part 4 looks into the future of the Nile Basin with special emphasis on governing the Nile watercourse under climatic uncertainty. Reviewing the practice of various water-sharing states, this part encapsulates the principal ways of building a climate-proof treaty. It then analyzes treaty flexibility in the Nile Basin and proposes a flexible basin-wide treaty capable of accommodating the ramifications of global climate change. Finally, it calls upon the Nile Basin States to stop approaching the Nile watercourse as a zero-sum game and to cooperate for their mutual benefit.

PART 1

Reconstructing the Legal and Hydro-political History of the Nile Basin

CHAPTER 2

The Politics of the Nile Basin: Water Imperialism, Hydro-political Cold War, and Hegemonic Dominance

Introduction

> To understand the geopolitical status quo, the legal constraints, and diplomatic posturing that determine the current allocation of the Nile's waters, it is necessary to scrutinize the historical record. After all, it is the real and imagined self-representations of contending parties and their historical narratives that form their respective geostrategic outlooks. Historical imaginations drive the dialectic relationship between jurisprudential argument and political stances. Past grievances and confrontations inform political positions, which are in turn legitimized by legal argument.[177]

The Nile watercourse, both as the site of ancient civilization and as a place of enormous diversity, has captivated human imagination since the dawn of history.[178] "The Greek historian Herodotus and the Roman emperor Nero sought to find the source far in the heart of Africa, and failed. The Greek astronomer and geographer Ptolemy speculated about the river's origins."[179] Cambyses, Alexander the Great, and Julius Caesar reportedly sent unavailing expeditions to find the source of the Nile.[180] The Portuguese Jesuit priests, Pedro Paez and Jerome Lobo visited the source of the Blue Nile in Ethiopia in 1618.[181] Pedro Paez was the first foreigner to visit the source of the Nile watercourse, "although the

177 Amdetsion, *supra* note 72, at 13.

178 Haggai Erlich & Israel Gershoni, *Introduction, in* THE NILE: HISTORIES, CULTURES, MYTHS, *supra* note 52, 1.

179 *See* COLLINS, *supra* note 64, at 8.

180 J.N. Blashford-Snell, *Conquest of the Blue Nile,* 136 GEOGRAPHICAL J. 42, 42 (1970) ("Cambyses, Alexander and Julius Caesar so strongly and so unavailingly desired to know" the Nile's source); F. BALTHAZAR TELLEZ, THE TRAVELS OF THE JESUITS IN ETHIOPIA, BOOK I, 12 (1710) (Alexander "fent discoveries throughout Ethiopia, without being able to find ... [the Nile's] Source.")

181 Amdetsion, *supra* note 72, 14 (quoting RICHARD PANKHURST, TRAVELERS IN ETHIOPIA 47 (1965), that Lobo "was one of the first foreigners to reach the source of the Blue Nile").

 | DOI:10.1163/9789004549869_003

famed Scottish traveler James Bruce claimed to be the first European to find the Nile in colorful accounts that enraptured eighteenth-century European high society."[182]

Beyond these expeditions and speculations, the Nile watercourse had different and more concrete meanings to the people living in the basin. The Nile has always meant a source of life and existence for Egyptians.[183] For Ethiopians, the Blue Nile, the father of all rivers, was primarily the symbol of their nation and an abode of spirits—cleansing the people from maladies and iniquities.[184] It was also a significant historical asset that they used as a bargaining chip in dealing religious issues with Egypt.[185]

Indeed, the rulers of ancient Ethiopia had, on several occasions, threatened to divert the flow of the watercourse. Although Ethiopia did not possess the capacity to alter the flow of the Nile watercourse, the threats were so convincing at the time that Egypt invaded Ethiopia in the nineteenth century. With the opening of the Suez Canal in 1869, the Nile watercourse became an arena of water wars and a subject of a river empire. "From source to mouth the river was for the first time controlled from one center; and from London, and by the British government."[186] The British Nile policy subsequently established an inequitable and lopsided water utilization in the Nile Basin.

The lopsided pattern of water utilization continued during the Cold War. The Cold War geopolitical rivalry, as reflected in the development of large-scale projects including, *inter alia*, the AHD, the Roseires Dam, and the Peace Canal as well as the U.S. Bureau of Reclamation (USBR) study on the Blue Nile, also brought about unilateralism in the Nile Basin.[187] Other Cold War developments such as Suez Crisis, the Arab-Israeli conflict, and the Ethio-Eritrea Civil War all have shaped the geopolitics of the Nile Basin.[188] They also enabled the downstream states, particularly Egypt, to develop more hydrologic infrastructures along the Nile watercourse.

---

182 Amdetsion, *supra* note 72, at 13–14.

183 ERLICH, *supra* note 54, 3.

184 Bairu Tafla, *The Father of Rivers: The Nile in Ethiopian Literature,* in THE NILE: HISTORIES, CULTURES, MYTHS, *supra* note 52, at 154–60.

185 ERLICH, *supra* note 54, at 8.

186 Terje Tvedt, *About the Importance of Studying the Modern History of the Countries of the Nile Basin in a Nile Perspective, in* THE RIVER NILE IN THE POST-COLONIAL AGE, *supra* note 81, at 3.

187 *See* discussion *infra* section 2.3.

188 MINA MICHEL SAMAAN, THE NILE DEVELOPMENT GAME TUG-OF-WAR OR BENEFITS FOR ALL? 86-87 (2019).

This chapter scrutinizes major historical events that shaped the geopolitics of the Nile Basin. It *narrates* the ramifications of the precolonial myths that Ethiopia would block the Nile waters from flowing to Egypt; *deconstructs* and *reflects* upon the colonial legacies that established inequitable and lopsided water utilization in the basin; and finally *investigates* the postcolonial realities that made unilateralism the *modus operandi* of the Nile Basin.

2.1 Pre-colonial Myths and Realities

Ethiopia and Egypt do not have a common border, but the natural bond created by the Nile watercourse has intertwined the two nations since the dawn of history.[189] Although the exact sources of the Nile were properly understood only in the early twentieth century,[190] the rulers of Egypt from time immemorial had realized that the Nile originates somewhere in Ethiopia.[191] They were also concerned that Ethiopia might block or divert the flow of the Nile watercourse.[192] These concerns were warranted since Ethiopia was using the Nile River as a diplomatic weapon in its relations with Egypt. For instance, because of the Nile, the ancient Ethiopian kingdom of Axum, which embraced Christianity in the fourth century,[193] was able to recruit its bishops from the Coptic church of Alexandria.[194] Following the Arab conquest of Egypt in the

189 Abadir M. Ibrahim, Note, *The Nile Basin Cooperative Framework Agreement: The Beginning of the End of Egyptian Hydro-Political Hegemony*, 18 MO. ENV'T. L. & POL'Y REV. 282, 289 (2011).

190 ERLICH, *supra* note 54, at 3.

191 *Id.*

192 *Id; see* Pankhurst, *supra* note 116, at 31; *see also* Van Donzel, *supra* note 116, at 121.

193 Axum was the third political entity that accepted Christianity, next to Armenia (A.D. 301) and the Roman Empire under Emperor Constantine (in 312). ERLICH, *supra* note 54, at 16–17. The introduction of Christianity in Ethiopia is "attributed to two young brothers, Frumentius and Aedesius, who were rescued from a shipwreck while en route from India back to Syria, then taken to the Aksumite court. There they acquainted the royal family with Christianity and helped to administer the kingdom." *Id.* Later, Aedesius returned to Syria, while Frumentius went to Alexandria, which was part of the Roman Empire, and told the story to Patriarch Athanasius who "persuaded [him] to return to Ethiopia as a bishop of the Egyptian (later Coptic) Church." The new bishop was given a special title, *abun* ("our father" in Amharic), and a new name, "Abuna Salama." Since then, the Ethiopian Church has linked itself to the Egyptian Church of Alexandria and received its Abun (Patriarchs) from Egypt until 1959. *Id.* at 8.

194 *Id. See also* Pankhurst, *supra* note 116, at 25 ("Ethiopia depended on the Coptic Church of Egypt, from where the Ethiopian abun (patriarch) was selected. Egypt was thus dependent on Ethiopia for its material existence, and Ethiopia was dependent on Egypt for its spiritual existence.")

seventh century, Ethiopian emperors were also able to protect the interest of the Coptic Christians in Egypt.[195] They did so by, *inter alia*, threatening to divert the course of the Nile whenever the Egyptian authorities persecuted the Christians or demolished their churches.[196] To control the sources of the Nile and thereby thwart the possibility of diverting its flow, Egypt invaded Ethiopia in the last quarter of the nineteenth century and suffered successive humiliating defeats by Ethiopia.[197] The following sections *deconstruct* and *reflect* upon these historical events.

2.1.1 *The Nile as a Bargaining Chip for Ancient Ethiopia*

Egypt, as described by Herodotus, is "an acquired country, the gift of the [Nile] river,"[198] and has—for millennia—been dependent upon the Nile waters that originate in the Ethiopian highlands.[199] Because of the inter-annual and inter-decadal rainfall variability in the Ethiopian highlands,[200] the flow of the Nile has experienced both intra-and inter-seasonal fluctuations since the dawn of history.[201] This fluctuation, reflected in low Nile floods and prolonged droughts in Egypt, used to infuriate the Egyptian authorities.[202] Whenever the flood flowing to Egypt decreased due to such climatic reasons, the Egyptian authorities used to believe that the Nile watercourse had been blocked by Ethiopia. According to an Arab historian, Al-Makin, the Nile flood almost disappeared between 1052 and 1090.[203] Devastating to Egypt, the low floodwaters resulted in unimaginable suffering for Egyptians, including disease, and plague.[204] The Egyptian ruler, the Fatimid sultan al-Mustansir bi'llah, who thought Ethiopia

---

195 *Id;* ERLICH, *supra* note 54, at 18–19; COLLINS, *supra* note 64, at 23; Van Donzel, *supra* note 116, at 21; JOHN TRIMINGHAM, ISLAM IN ETHIOPIA, 70–71 (1952).

196 *Id; generally* Pankhurst, *supra* note 116; COLLINS, *supra* note 64, at 23; Van Donzel, *supra* note 116, at 21; ERLICH, *supra* note 54, at 18–19.

197 *See* discussion *infra* section 2.1.2.

198 ALAN MOOREHEAD, THE BLUE NILE 3 (1962).

199 Dynastic Egypt flourished and prospered during the Old, Middle, and New Kingdoms because of good Nile flows. It also disintegrated and even disappeared due to the low flows of the Nile during the first, second, and third intermediate periods (Dark Ages). COLLINS, *supra* note 64, at 18–19. Similarly, after Alexander the Great's conquest of Egypt in 332 BCE, the success of the Greek, Roman, Arab, and Ottoman Turkish rulers was determined as much by the Nile flood as by their military strength, and administrative ability. *Id.* at 19–23.

200 Taye et al, *supra* note 61, at 12 & 14; EARLE ET AL., *supra* note 62, at 117.

201 *Id.* at 129.

202 COLLINS, *supra* note 64, at 22–23.

203 *Id,* 21.

204 *Id.*

had diverted the flow of the Blue Nile, reportedly sent his emissaries to the Ethiopian king, pleading for the release of the water.[205]

The rise of the Zagwe dynasty in Ethiopia around 1137 coincided with the reign of the great Salah al-Din of the Ayyubid dynasty.[206] Because of the Nile, Salah al-Din, who defeated the crusaders in the Holy Land and captured Jerusalem in 1187, exempted Ethiopian Christians from taxes imposed on pilgrims and even gave them spiritual sites in the Holy Land.[207] This cordial relationship and generosity nevertheless ended immediately: The Egyptian rulers started oppressing the Christian Copts, while the Ethiopians continued defending the Christians in Egypt.[208] The great Lalibela,[209] whose reign coincided with the persecution of the Copts in Egypt, allegedly attempted to divert the flow of the Nile.[210] The last Zagwe ruler, Na'akuto La'ab, reportedly

205 ERLICH, *supra* note 54, at 21–22. The Ethiopian king then "ordered a large-enclosed valley to be opened by the cutting of a dam. As soon as this was done the Nile rose ten feet in a single night and the whole land of Egypt was irrigated." *Id.* at 22.

206 *Id.* at 37. It is worth noting that the biblical story of King Solomon and the Queen of Sheba has an Ethiopian version. The legend states: "(1) that Sheba, also known as Makeda, was an Ethiopian queen; (2) that she gave birth to a son by Solomon, a boy by name Menilek [I]; (3) that Menilek [I], after visiting his father in Jerusalem, took the Ark of Covenant to Ethiopia ... and (4) that it was from Menilike that the country's emperors were descended." RICHARD PANKHURST, THE ETHIOPIANS, A HISTORY, 54 (1998). The Zagwe Dynasty, which succeeded the Axumite kingdom, did not fulfill the requirement of this legend and was believed to have usurped power without belonging to the Solomonic line. *Id*, 46.

207 *Id;* TADDESSE TAMRAT, CHURCH AND STATE IN ETHIOPIA: 1270–1527, 58 (2009) (stating that Salah-al-Din gave many sites to the Ethiopians in the Holy Land). In addition to the Nile, it was Ethiopia's favor to prophet Muhammad (PBUH), and Islam during the First Hijra that made Salah al-Din grant Ethiopians this privilege. When Kurish persecuted Muhammad (PBUH) and his followers, he told some of his companions to go to Abyssinia (now Ethiopia) where they would "find a king under whom none are persecuted." ERLICH, *supra* note 54, at 24 (internal citation omitted). True to the words of the prophet, the Aksumite negus, *al-najashi,* Ashama ibn Abjar, had given protection and shelter to the companions. As a showing of gratitude, the prophet also told his companions *Utruku al-habasha ma tarakukum* (leave the Abyssinians alone as long as they leave you alone). *Id.* at 24–25.

208 *Id.* at 37.

209 *Id.* The Great Lalibela "went down in history as the builder of the wondrous rock-hewn churches at the site named after him." *Id.* The rock-hewn churches of Lalibela are remarkable. Made from one stone, "[e]leven churches, all cut out of red volcanic tuff, are situated within little more than a stone's throw apart." *See* PANKHURST, *supra* note 206, at 49. It is believed that Lalibela constructed the beautiful churches to create a new Jerusalem in Ethiopia. *See* TAMRAT, *supra* note 207, at 58–59.

210 JAMES BRUCE, TRAVELS TO DISCOVER THE SOURCE OF THE NILE, 529–30 (VOL. 1, 1790). According to Bruce, Emperor Lalibela "found, by an exact survey and calculation, that there ran on the summit, or highest part of the country, several rivers which could be

demanded tribute from the Egyptians and diverted the Tekeze River when they refused to fulfill his demands.[211]

The Ethiopian kings continued using "the Nile as a bargaining chip" during the Solomonic dynasty.[212] In the fourteenth century, when the Mamluk sultan, al-Nasir Muhammad ibn Qalawun, persecuted the Copts of Egypt and demolished churches, Emperor Amda Seyon (1314–1344) sent an envoy to Cairo, and asked "the Sultan to restore the churches and refrain from persecuting the Copts," threatening that "he would . . . starve the peoples of Egypt by diverting the course of the Nile."[213] Amda-Seyon's grandson, Emperor Dawit (1380–1412) reportedly "held back the Nile waters."[214] Similarly, when the Copts in Egypt

---

intercepted by mines, and their stream directed into the low country southward, instead of joining the Nile, augmenting it and running northward." *Id.* In so doing, Bruce asserts, Lalibela could make the Nile to "never ... rise to a height proper to fit Egypt for cultivation." Bruce also claims that Lalibela actually "intersected and carr[ied] into the Indian Ocean, two very large rivers, which have ever since flowed that way, and ... carr[ied] a level to the lake Zawaia, where many rivers empty themselves in the beginning of the rains, which would have effectually diverted the course of them all." *Id.* Professor Richard Pankhurst challenged Bruce's claims based on three reasons: (1) there is no "visible sign that any river was ever reversed"; (2) "diversion of even a stream from the Nile area to the Indian Ocean [was] virtually impossible," and (3) there is no written account substantiating the story, nor is there "any attempt to divert the Nile included in Lalibela's Gadl (Acts)." Pankhurst, *supra* note 116, at 27–28.

211 *Id.* It is stated in Ethiopian chronicles that "Egyptians refused to pay their accustomed tribute to Ethiopia, whereupon the monarch prayed that the flow of water to the Nile be stopped for three years and seven months. God reportedly listened: Egypt was struck by famine, and its population declined. The Egyptian ruler then dispatched messages to the king, promising tribute and begging him to resume the river's flow." *Id.* at 28.

212 Amdetsion, *supra* note 72, at 14. It is worth noting that the overthrow of Zagewa dynasty in 1270 marked the restoration of power to the Solomonic line. Since then, up until the downfall of Emperor Haile Selassie in 1974, state power was believed to have belonged to the Solomonic line, as all emperors claimed to be the descendants of King Solomon. PANKHURST, *supra* note 206, 53.

213 TRIMINGHAM, *supra* note 195, at 70–71.

214 Pankhurst, *supra* note 116, at 29. Tadesse Tamrat, citing hagiographies, claimed that Dawit fought with the Egyptians and had indeed held back and diverted the Nile waters. TAMRAT, *supra* note 207, at 256. Erlich, mentioning the Ethiopian version of the chronicles, *Ta'amra Maryam,* also claimed that "Dawit prayed to the Virgin [Mary] before raiding Egypt. In reply she advised the emperor, in the name of God, to divert the Nile. The river is referred to in the legends as the 'Abbay' or the 'Geyon' the biblical river of paradise that flows through the land of Kush (Genesis 2:13). When the Egyptians saw that their waters had receded, they sued for peace and promised never again to be the foes of Christianity." ERLICH, *supra* note 54, at 44. But historian Richard Pankhurst disputed this claim stating that "Dawit's alleged Nile diversion does not figure in most of the chronicles, is not mentioned in any Egyptian source, nor is there any archaeological evidence that it ever took place." Pankhurst, *supra* note 116, at 29.

were persecuted and an important church of Mitmaq (al-Magtas) was demolished, Emperor Zar'a Ya'eqob (1434–1468), according to an Egyptian source, sent a delegation carrying a threatening letter to the Egyptian ruler, Sultan Jaqmaq.[215] The relevant part of the letter reads: "And are you aware, you and your Sultan, that the river Nile is flowing to you from our country and that we are capable of preventing floods that irrigate your country? Nothing keeps us from so doing, only the belief in God and his slaves. We have presented to you what you need to know and you should know what you have to do."[216]

The Ethiopian rulers' threats to divert the Nile and thereby reduce Egyptians to destitution had also reached Europe and Western Christendom. The Europeans who visited the Holy Land spoke of a legendary Ethiopian king, Prester John, and his ability "to remove the Nile waters from the Egyptians."[217] Understanding Ethiopia's strategic importance as the source of the Nile, the crusaders were convinced that Ethiopians could be mobilized to defeat the Muslims.[218] The plan of diverting the Nile waters to regain the Holy Land was seriously considered by prominent figures of the time, including, *inter alia*, Pope Benedict XII, Giovanni da Marignolli (John of Marignola), and Marco Polo.[219]

By the early sixteenth century, the legend has reached the Portuguese and begun to play a part in their foreign policy.[220] After controlling the sea route to India in 1510–1511, Alfonso d' Albuquerque, the organizer of the Portuguese hegemony in the Orient, was determined to control the Red Sea and take the spice trade away from Egypt.[221] He contacted Ethiopia in 1513 and envisioned the destruction of Egypt by diverting the course of the Nile to the Red Sea.[222] "To this end he requested his sovereign, Manoel I, to send him workman from Maderia, skilled in cutting rocks and digging irrigation trenches. Albuquerque was, however, soon recalled and his Nile plans were abandoned."[223]

In the following centuries, Ethiopian kings were too busy with internal conflicts and religious rivalries to think of the Nile as a political weapon in their

215 *Id.* at 30; TAMRAT, *supra* note 207, at 261–63; COLLINS, *supra* note 64, at 23; ERLICH, *supra* note 54, at 46.

216 COLLINS, *supra* note 64, at 23 (internal citation omitted). *See* also ERLICH, *supra* note 54, at 46 (internal citation omitted).

217 Pankhurst, *supra* note 116, at 31.

218 *Id.*

219 *Id.* at 31–32, Van Donzel, *supra* note 116, at 122–27.

220 *Id.* at 125; Pankhurst, *supra* note 116, at 32.

221 Van Donzel, *supra* note 116, at 125.

222 *Id.*

223 Pankhurst, *supra* note 116, at 32.

international relations.[224] Belief in the possibility of diverting the Nile nevertheless continued for centuries. Early in the eighteenth century, Emperor Tekle Haymanot (1706–1708), infuriated that Murad, an Armenian trader, and a French ambassador, had been imprisoned by Turkish authorities in Egypt, wrote a threatening letter to the pasha of Cairo and declared: "We could very soon repay you in kind, if we were inclined to revenge the insult you have offered to the man Murad sent on our part; the Nile would be sufficient to punish you, since God hath put into our power his fountain, his outlet, and his increase, and that we can dispose of the same to do you harm."[225]

Recent historians seriously doubt Ethiopian rulers' ability to divert the Nile.[226] Indeed, it would be very unreasonable to expect that those kings could carry out such a grandiose project at the time. Most of the Ethiopian emperors, in fact, "did no[thing] more than pray," while others simply "refrained from any action, either on account of scruples or expediency."[227] As such, Ethiopia's historical ability to divert the flow of the Nile was "no more than roars of a paper lion."[228] But, the myth was so convincing at the time that "[t]hreats were made, fears expressed, prayers uttered, hopes voiced, and travelers' tales published"

---

224 ERLICH, *supra* note 54, 59. One of these conflicts was the war between the Christian highland kingdom and the Muslim sultanates of Ethiopia. In the sixteenth century, a religious and military leader from the Adal sultanate of Harar, (Ahmed Gragn), was able to unite various Muslim communities in Ethiopia. Ahmed, helped by the Ottomans, who occupied Egypt in 1517, managed to launch a series of successful military operations against the Christian highland kingdom of Ethiopia. He occupied Shoa in 1529, Amhara in 1531, Tigre in 1535, and eventually the entire country, except for the Lake Tana islands. ERLICH, *supra* note 54, at 48; PANKHURST, *supra* note 206, at 84–87; *see also generally* ŠIHAB AD-DIN AHMAD BIN ABD AL-QADER BIN SALEM BIN UTMAN, FUTUH AL-HABAŠA: THE CONQUEST OF ABYSSINIA (Paul Lester Stenhouse & Richard Pankhurst, trans., 2003). Regarding Ottoman help, *see* HIOB LUDOLF, A NEW HISTORY OF ETHIOPIA, 221 (1684). After a decade of occupation, the Portuguese expeditionary force, led by Vasco da Gama's son, Dom Christovao da Gama, came to rescue the Christian highland kingdom of Ethiopia. The Portuguese force, which arrived at Massawa in 1541, was able to "help the shattered Ethiopians reorganize," and kill Imam Ahmad in February 1543. PANKHURST, *supra* note 206, at 92; ERLICH, *supra* note 54, at 49. Following the Portuguese military intervention, Jesuit priests came to Ethiopia and created religious friction between Catholicism and Orthodox Christianity which culminated in the proclamation of Catholicism as a state religion of the country. This resulted in bloodshed and chaos in the country, and seriously compromised the power of the central authority. PANKHURST, *supra* note 206, at 97, 103–108, 119–30; TRIMINGHAM, *supra* note 195, at 98–99.

225 JAMES BRUCE, TRAVELS TO DISCOVER THE SOURCE OF THE NILE, 526–27 (VOL. 2, 1790).

226 Pankhurst, *supra* note 116, at 30.

227 *Id.*

228 *Id*, at 31.

about it.[229] It was also a "feature of Ethio-Egyptian statecraft,"[230] and the cause for the "acrimonious inter-state relationship between the two countries that has shaped and is shaping the hydro-politics of the Nile Basin."[231]

2.1.2 *The Nile Wars*

To control the sources of the Nile and thereby thwart the possibility of diverting its flow, Egypt designed a grandiose strategy called "the unity of the Nile Valley" in the nineteenth century.[232] As part of this strategy, Muhammed Ali, an Ottoman governor of Egypt who started modern irrigation,[233] decided to control all of the Nile Basin and administer it under "the green flag of Egypt."[234] He occupied Sudan as early as the 1820s.[235] Using Sudan as a stepping-stone,[236] he then conquered the borderlands of Ethiopia including Kasala in 1834, the garrison town of Metema in 1838, and Ethiopia's maritime gateway, Massawa in 1846.[237]

During those invasions, Ethiopia was in its dark-age. *Zemene Mesafint,* the era of the princes, in which there was no real central authority and regional lords were fighting among themselves for influence.[238] Thus, except for the

229 *Id.* at 35.

230 *Id.*

231 TAFESSE, *supra* note 12, at 59.

232 *Id.* at 60; TRIMINGHAM, *supra* note 195, at 115 (stating that Muhammed Ali, after controlling Sudan, "had now established the political unity of the Nile valley for the first time in history.")

233 During the reign of Mohamed Ali Pasha, Egypt constructed hydraulic structures on the Nile, the Delta Barrages, to regulate the Nile waters. WATERBURY, *supra* note 121, at 33; KLIOT, *supra* note 121, at 32.

234 Czeslaw Jesman, *Egyptian Invasion of Ethiopia*, 58 AFRICAN AFFAIRS, 77 (1959).

235 DEGEFU, *supra* note 117, 44; Kendie, *supra* note 169, at 145.

236 *Id;* DEGEFU, *supra* note 117, 44.

237 *Id*; Kendie, *supra* note 169, at 145.

238 The era of princes, the period known in Ethiopian history as Zamana Masafent, began in 1769 when the Tegeray ruler, Ras Mikael Sehul, killed the reigning emperor, Iyoas and put his own favorite, Emperor Yohannes II, on the throne. *See* PANKHURST, *supra* note 206, at 30. The situation during this period was so serious that Ethiopia, according to a British Traveler, Henry Salt, was "suffering under all those evils that attend an inefficient government" and its emperor was "in the power of one ambitious subject or another; and receives no revenue … from the nearly independent governors of his different provinces, he is incapable of securing a sufficient force to sustain himself, or to prevent them from wasting the resources of the country in mutual hostility." GEORGE ANNESLEY, VOYAGES AND TRAVELS IN INDIA, CEYLON, THE RED SEA, ABYSSINIA, AND EGYPT, 264 (VOL., 3, 1809). This state of affairs would end with the coronation of Kasa Haylu, Tewodros II after his coronation, as the emperor of Ethiopia. BAHRU ZEWDE, A HISTORY OF MODERN ETHIOPIA: 1885–1991, 30 (2001).

battle of Wad Kaltabu where Dejazmach Kinfu Haylu defeated the invading Egyptian army in May 1837,[239] Muhammed Ali did not face much resistance from Ethiopia. The regional lords, despite their repeated appeals for support from the British and French governments,[240] had no modern weapons and were unable to stop the Egyptian invasions. In 1848, Kasa Hailu, later emperor Tewodros II, had confronted the Egyptian invaders and tried to capture Dabarki.[241] But, with his traditional weapons, Kasa Hailu could not withstand the Egyptian troops, who were equipped with modern armaments, and was therefore routed.[242]

Egyptian military encroachments to Ethiopian territory went on unabated during the reign of Khedive Ismail, Muhammad Ali's grandson. Considering himself among the then "progressive forces,"[243] Ismail decided to expand his rule to what he called the "uncivilized tribes in Africa,"[244] and "make the Nile an Egyptian river, annex[ing] to his country all the geographic area of its basin."[245] To this end, he hired military advisors and commanders from the United States and Europe. Of these advisors, a Swiss adventurer, Werner Munzinger (1832–1875), remarked: "Ethiopia with a disciplined administration and army, and a friend of the European powers, is a danger for Egypt. Egypt must either take over Ethiopia and Islamize it, or retain it in anarchy and misery."[246]

Ismail embarked on enforcing this policy by invading Ethiopia. He occupied Kunama in 1869,[247] the city of Harar in 1875,[248] and then subsequently

239 *Id.* at 28.

240 As early as 1805, the ruler of Tigray province, *Ras* (head) Walda Sellase, wrote to King George III of Britain, asking for the "supply of arms and ammunition." PANKHURST, *supra* note 206, 134 (internal citation omitted). In 1838, both Dajazmach Webe Hayla Maryam and Ras Ali Alula, appealed to Queen Victoria of Britain and King Louis-Philippe of France "for help against the Egyptians, who were then invading the country from the west." *Id.* at 136. Dajazmach Wobe Hayla Maryam also asked for arms and ammunitions from France, and in 1849 he wrote again to Queen Victoria, and pleaded that he was seeking her help "because she was so strong 'that [she] may help us lest a Muslim army [Egyptians] should strike and plunder us and deprive[ed] us of our country.'" *Id.* at 136–38. In the same year, he also wrote to Prince Louis Napoleon of France and urged the prince to make the Egyptians withdraw from the broader lands of Ethiopia. *Id.* at 138–39. In 1840, King Sahla Sellase of Shewa province had also written a letter to the British East India Company in Bombay, asking for "guns, cannon, and other things" that he did not have in his country. *Id.* 139–40.

241 *Id.* at 143; ZEWDE, *supra* note 238, at 28.

242 *Id.*, PANKHURST, *supra* note 206, at 143.

243 Jesman, *supra* note 234, at 75.

244 DEGEFU, *supra* note 117, at 43.

245 *Id.* (internal citation omitted).

246 Kendie, *supra* note 169, at 145. (Internal citation omitted).

247 DEGEFU, *supra* note 117, at 44.

248 *Id*, 44 & 46.

marched towards the central part of Ethiopia. In 1875, the Egyptian force, led by Munzinger, set out from the Red Sea coast to the central part of Ethiopia and was annihilated by the Afar people.[249] A second force, led by Colonel Arrendup Bey, departed from Massawa to capture the northern highlands of Ethiopia. "On 15–16 November 1875, this force met with Yohannes's army in Gundet and was virtually wiped out."[250] More than 2,500 Egyptian soldiers, including their commander, Colonel Arrendrup Bey, were routed in the battle.[251]

To avenge his loss, Ismail made a second attempt and sent an invading army of 15,000 men, including a team of U.S. mercenaries headed by General W. Loring, to Ethiopia.[252] On March 7–9, 1876, the invading army, led by Ratib Pasha, launched successive attacks on Ethiopia but suffered an ignominious defeat by Ethiopia at the battle of Gura.[253] In the following years, Egyptian raids against Ethiopia continued until they were brought to a temporary halt when Britain occupied Egypt in 1882.[254]

2.2 The Nile in the Age of Colonialism: the Europeans Scramble for Nile, and the Tana Dam Concession

The scramble for the Nile Basin started with the opening of the Suez Canal on November 17, 1869.[255] The canal provided the shortest maritime route between Europe and Asia, allowing passage from the North Atlantic to the Indian Ocean without rounding Africa via the Cape of Good Hope.[256] This increased Egypt's strategic importance in the eyes of British and French imperialists. "For the British control of Egypt meant more profitable trade with India, its richest colony. For the French, the canal offered quicker access to Indochina, its most lucrative colony."[257] As a result, both countries sought to gain a foothold in

249 ERLICH, *supra* note 54, at 70.
250 *Id.*
251 TAFESSE, *supra* note 12, 61.
252 ERLICH, *supra* note 54, at 70.
253 *Id.*
254 DEGEFU, *supra* note 117, at 44.
255 *Id*, 20–28.
256 *Id*, 21.
257 Andrew Carlson, *Who Owns the Nile? Egypt, Sudan, and Ethiopia's History-Changing Dam*, 6(6) ORIGINS: CURRENT EVENTS IN HISTORICAL PERSPECTIVE (2013), https://origins.osu.edu/article/who-owns-nile-egypt-sudan-and-ethiopia-s-history-changing-dam.

Egypt and control over this strategic sea route. The financial collapse of Egypt due to the debacle at Gura and Gundet and the debt Khedive Ismail owed to the Europeans gave a pretext in 1876 for the French and British to impose their administration on the fiscal matters of Egypt.[258]

In response, the Egyptian troops, who blamed the American and European soldiers for their defeat at the battles of Gura and Gundet, undertook a nationalist revolution against the establishment and European interests in Egypt.[259] In September 1881, the army, led by Colonel Ahmed Orabi, took over the palace and forced Khedive Tewfik, Ismail's son, to dismiss his European advisors.[260] Other riots also erupted in Alexandria around June 1882, and about fifty Europeans were killed.[261] Such developments made Great Britain very concerned, and since other European powers were unable to be directly involved in the dispute,[262] it unilaterally intervened in Egypt in September 1882.[263] After defeating the rebellious army, Britain became "directly responsible for the defence, the debts and development of the country."[264] Describing this event, the British prime minister Gladstone said: "We have done our Egyptian business, and we are an Egyptian government."[265]

2.2.1 *The British One Nile Country Vision and Basin-Wide Planning*

When the British occupied Egypt in 1882, "the cotton industry in Lancashire was searching for ways to reduce its dependency on American cotton, and imports of cheaper but very good cotton from Egypt [had already] become more and more important."[266] Since cotton production was possible only through irrigation from the Nile, Great Britain was interested in the flow of the Nile from the onset of Egypt's occupation.[267] The population growth of Egypt in the

258 DEGEFU, *supra* note 117, at 21.

259 *Id*, 22; PANKHURST, *supra* note 206, at 170.

260 DEGEFU, *supra* note 117, at 22.

261 *Id.*

262 *Id.* (stating "Gladstone, the British Prime Minister, hoped that Britain and France might intervene jointly as the mandatories of Europe. … However, the French government failed to secure the necessary vote of confidence in the Chambers. … The British even tried to secure a joint intervention with Italy, but were unsuccessful.")

263 *Id.*

264 John Gallagher & Ronald Robinson, *The Imperialism of Free Trade*, 6 ECON. HIST. 1, 15 (1953).

265 DEGEFU, *supra* note 117, at 23 (internal citation omitted).

266 Terje Tvedt, *Hydrology and Empire: The Nile, Water Imperialism and the Partition of Africa*, 39(2) THE J. OF IMPERIAL AND COMMONWEALTH HIS., 177 (2011).

267 *Id.* at 187. Great Britain viewed controlling the source of the Nile as a *sine qua non* to safeguard its interests in Egypt and developed "a strategy and a diplomatic and military tactic for establishing a River Empire on the Nile." *Id.*

1880s[268] and the need for more water for irrigation[269] had also obliged Great Britain to make increased water control a top priority from the very beginning.[270] In this regard, Professor Terje Tvedt remarked:

> [N]arrow[ing] the gap between supply and demand for water was a continuous task and a permanent worry to the British. How to increase the Nile yield in the 'timely season', that is, during the summer season, when cotton was grown and the natural Nile discharge was at its lowest? How to protect the agricultural lands against devastating floods? How to dam the excess water in September, October and November for utilization in the season of scarcity? How to construct dams which could reduce the differences in the yearly discharge fluctuations?[271]

At first, Great Britain attempted to bridge the gap by improving existing irrigation facilities and constructing new barrages and dams within the borders of Egypt. To increase water for summer irrigation, Great Britain built the Assiut Barrage (1902), Zifta Barrage (1903), Nag Hammadi Barrage (1909) and Esna Barrage (1909) in Egypt.[272] It also constructed the Old Aswan Reservoir (1902) in Egypt to store 1 BCM of water annually for dry season irrigation.[273] Acclaimed "as a victory of British political, economic, and technological might," the dam was "the biggest reservoir of its kind in the world [and] one of the soundest projects in the history of water control, but [failed] to store sufficient water demanded in the summer."[274]

The failure of Old Aswan to meet water demands made building infrastructures outside of Egypt a much more pressing issue.[275] British hydrologists and engineers had already suggested upstream expansion and control of the Nile as a more efficient way of using the Nile waters.[276] As more planners

268 *Id.* at 176–77 ("The population doubled during a few decades and reached almost ten million in 1897, and the growing number of poor peasants put pressure on the government for more reliable water supplies").

269 *Id.*

270 *Id.*

271 TERJE TVEDT, THE RIVER NILE IN THE AGE OF THE BRITISH: POLITICAL ECOLOGY AND THE QUEST FOR ECONOMIC POWER 22 (2004).

272 KLIOT, *supra* note 121, at 32; WATERBURY, *supra* note 121, at 33.

273 *Id.* ("The height of the dam was raised twice, in 1912 and 34, until its storage capacity grew from 1 billion m^3 to 5.7 billion m^3").

274 TVEDT, *supra* note 271, 102.

275 Tvedt, *supra* note 266, at 179–80.

276 *Id.* at 179.

recommended upstream storage dams, Great Britain started envisioning the Nile Basin as one country that should be controlled under one political planning authority.[277] In explaining Great Britain's vision for the Nile, Sir Sidney Peel remarked:

> It is no longer possible to think of our occupation of Egypt as merely a stepping-stone on the road to India … Egypt is only a portion of the great country of the Nile … all Nile land is one country. No divided sovereignty is possible; there must be one firm hand over all. It would have needed a preternaturally keen eye to perceive that from the moment we began to patch the old Barrage the occupation of the whole valley of the Nile was inevitable. … It sounds a far cry from the snows of Ruwenzori, the lakes and swamps of Equatorial Africa, or the rainswept hills of Abyssinia, to the cotton mills of Lancashire.[278]

To implement this vision, British hydrologists proposed various plans, which collectively known as the "Full Nile control" plan or the "Century Storage Project."[279] The plan, evolved from several sources,[280] envisaged the regulation of the Nile waters along drought and flood seasons by building several dams and reservoirs both on the Blue and White Nile.[281] The first contributor to the plan, William Garstin, published his reports in 1904 and regarded both the Equatorial Lakes and Lake Tana as "natural reservoirs"[282] that would provide

277 *Id.* at 181.

278 SIDNEY PEEL, THE BINDING OF THE NILE AND THE NEW SUDAN, 134–35 (1904), https://archive.org/details/bindingofnilenewoopeel/page/134/mode/2up.

279 KLIOT, *supra* note 121, at 35–37; WATERBURY, *supra* note 121, at 40–42, 87–96; COLLINS, *supra* note 64, at 141–56.

280 British hydrologists such as Sir William Garstin, Sir William Willcocks, Sir Murdoch McDonald, and H. E. Hurst contributed pioneering works for the plan and the hydraulic engineering of the Nile Basin. WATERBURY, *supra* note 121, at 87; KLIOT, *supra* note 121, at 35. Garstin and Willcocks made the first important contribution at the beginning of the twentieth century. McDonald advanced the works of Garstin, and was eventually succeeded by Hurst who "published the six volumes of *The Nile Basin* in which [he] laid the foundation of a total plan for the efficient hydrological development of the Nile Valley. A seventh volume of this monumental work included the detailed, long-term plan for the Nile development along the lines of Garstin's report and introduced the concept of 'Century Storage.'" *Id.*

281 *Id.* at 35–37; WATERBURY, *supra* note 121, at 40–42, 87–96; COLLINS, *supra* note 64, at 141–56.

282 GARSTIN, *supra* note 122, at 195.

"constant and sufficient supply" of water for Egypt.[283] He recommended the construction of dams at the outlets of Lake Victoria, Lake Edward,[284] and on the Blue Nile and Atbara tributaries.[285] He also proposed digging "an entirely new channel" to void "swamp region…altogether" and prevent waters of the White Nile and Sobat River from "entirely wasted in the marshes."[286] Furthermore, Garstin envisaged a large cotton production scheme in the Gezira region and proposed a dam with "a storage reservoir of limited capacity … at or south of the Rosaires rapids."[287] This proposal was implemented with the construction of the Sennar Dam in 1925,[288] although it immediately created tension between Great Britain and Egypt.[289] Egypt, which had received partial independence in 1922,[290] protested that the development of irrigation in Sudan

283 *Id.* at 196. The full Nile control or Century Storage plan focus on increasing the Nile discharge mainly for Egypt. In this regard, Garstin remarked: "To rescue the upper Nile from the marshes in which it has lost more than half its volume—to control and regulate the great Equatorial Lakes, making them add to the flow of the river at will—to cause the waters of the Blue Nile to rise, and irrigate the fertile tracts through which they pass—to secure to Egypt a constant and sufficient supply for the entire area between the cataracts and the Mediterranean—to free that country from the ever-present danger of a disastrous flood." *Id.*

284 *Id.* at 172–74.

285 *Id.* at 183 (remarking that "the best and most certain method of increasing the Blue Nile supply, during the months prior to the annual rise, would be by the construction of regulating works at the outlet of the river from the Tsana lake, using the latter as a storage reservoir, under effective control"). *See also Id.* at 186–87 (discussing the feasibility of building a dam on the Atbara tributary).

286 *Id.* at 174–80.

287 *Id.* at 190.

288 Four years after the Garstin report, "a formal proposal had been drafted to construct a dam at Sennar that would supply enough water to irrigate 50,000 feddans at what was to become the Gezira Cotton Scheme." WATERBURY, *supra* note 121, at 66.

289 TVEDT, *supra* note 271, at 104 (stating that the Sennar was "a very critical topic of strife during the Egyptian revolution and in Egyptian opposition and mistrust of British rule. It was a 'nefarious scheme' which London would use to destroy Egypt.") The dispute had resulted in the assassination of the British governor-general of Sudan, Sir Lee Stack, and forced Great Britain to issue an ultimatum, declaring, *inter alia*, that "the Sudan Government will increase the area to be irrigated in the Gezira from 300,00 feddans to *an unlimited figure as need may arise.*" THE ANNUAL REGISTER, THE ANNUAL REGISTER: A REVIEW OF PUBLIC EVENTS AT HOME AND ABROAD FOR THE YEAR 1924, 124 (1925) (emphasis added).

290 In 1919, the Egyptian revolution, which demanded autonomy for Egypt and abolition of the British protectorate, began, and in 1922 the British government declared Egypt's independence. The declaration ended the protectorate, reserving four matters to Great Britain's discretion: (1) the security of imperial communication, (2) defense, (3) the protection of foreign interests and of minorities, and (4) Sudan. *See* TVEDT, *supra* note 271, at 87–100. It is worth noting that following Egypt's partial independence, "Britain's main

should not damage irrigation, or cause prejudice to future essential projects, in its territories.[291] As discussed below, the two countries established a bilateral Nile Commission and resolved this problem by recognizing the "historic and natural rights" of Egypt in the 1929 Anglo-Egyptian Treaty.[292]

It is also worth mentioning that another project, the Owen Falls Dam, suggested in the Century Storage plan, was constructed at the outlet of Lake Victoria in Uganda. The dam, which was completed in 1954, allowed control of the level of Lake Victoria within a range of three meters and provided annual storage of about 200 BCM.[293] "Egypt paid $1 million to rise the dam one meter higher than planned in order to increase storage, but the main objective was to regulate the discharge from the lake and to generate 150 megawatts of hydroelectric power annually for Ugandan industry."[294] The other proposed projects, including the Jonglei Canal and the dam in Lake Tana, were not implemented during colonization because of geopolitical challenges.

2.2.2 *The Coming of Europeans in the Blue Nile: The Tana Dam Concession*

As noted above, France, despite its strategic interest in the Suez Canal, could not intervene in Egypt with Great Britain in 1882.[295] Thus, to demand concessions from the British government and regain a foothold in Egypt, it decided to control the source of the Nile, including Ethiopia.[296] This made the British very concerned because, as Professor Mesfin Woldemariam remarked, "[t]he power that controlled Ethiopia controlled the Nile Valley including the Sudan and Egypt; the power that controlled the Nile Valley and Egypt controlled the Suez Canal; and the power that controlled the Suez Canal controlled the world."[297] Accordingly, to prevent Ethiopia and the source of the Blue Nile from falling under the sway of France, Great Britain brought Italy into the Horn of Africa.[298]

strategic interest remained the same: to secure its political and military position at Suez and to increase the export of large-staple cotton to Lancashire." *Id.* at 87–88.

291 *Id.* at 141.

292 *See* the 1929 Anglo-Egyptian Treaty, *supra* note 125 (allocating a volumetric quantity of water to Egypt and Sudan: forty-eight billion cubic meters ("BCM") for Egypt and four BCM for Sudan.) *See infra* Chapter 3 for a detailed analysis of the 1929 Anglo-Egyptian Treaty.

293 MCCAFFREY, *supra* note 4, at 311–12.

294 WATERBURY, *supra* note 121, at 89.

295 DEGEFU, *supra* note 117, at 22.

296 ZEWDE, *supra* note 238, at 75; MESFIN WOLDEMARIAM, AN INTRODUCTION TO GEOGRAPHY OF ETHIOPIA, 4 (1972).

297 *Id.*

298 Following Egypt's occupation, the British wasted no time before invading Mahdist Sudan to gain control of the upper Nile. "When their troops encountered resistance from Mahdist

In 1891, Great Britain signed the Anglo-Italian Protocol with Italy and recognized that Ethiopia fell within Italy's sphere of influence.[299] In exchange, Italy agreed that it would not construct on the Atbara irrigation "work which might sensibly modify its flow into the Nile."[300] Great Britain supported Italy's expansion in the Horn of Africa to prevent Ethiopia from falling under the influence of France, its principal rival in the scramble for the Nile.[301] In 1896, the Italians invaded Ethiopia and suffered a humiliating defeat at the battle of Adwa.[302] "Ethiopia's victory against Italian forces ... gave Ethiopia more influence at the diplomatic table where countries jostled for control over the Horn."[303]

Because of Adwa, France and Great Britain were thwarted from invading Ethiopia. Moreover, France, craving Menelik's support to control Fashoda in Sudan,[304] offered 100,000 rifles to

forces, however, the British turned to the Ethiopian Emperor Yohannes and signed the Adwa (or Hewitt) Treaty, in which Ethiopia committed herself to assisting British troops and Great Britain pledged to allow Ethiopia free passage of goods through the previously Egyptian-controlled Port of Massawa." Amdetsion, *supra* note 72, at 17. Yohannes kept his promise in good faith "by driving out Mahdist forces, thereby salvaging Britain's presence in the Horn, but the British reneged by giving Massawa to Italy instead of Ethiopia." *Id.*

299 F. Earnest Work, *Italo-Ethiopian Relations,* 20 J. NEGRO HIST. 4389 (1935).

300 Protocol for the Demarcation of Their Respective Spheres of Influence in East Africa from Ras Kasar to the Blue Nile, art. III, Gr. Brit.-Italy, Apr. 15, 1891, *quoted in* DEGEFU, *supra* note 117, at 95.

301 PANKHURST, *supra* note 206, at 171. Explaining the Anglo-Italian alliance, Professor Bahru Zewde stated that after the occupation of Egypt, "[p]reventing the mortal enemy, France, from encroaching on the waters of the Nile became the primary objective of British imperialism. While the British were prepared to guard the White Nile themselves, they wanted someone to watch over the Blue Nile and its Ethiopian source and tributaries. This was the genesis of the Anglo-Italian collusion over Ethiopia: the Italians were desperate to control Ethiopia, and the British were ready to support them as long as they acted as a watch dog of British imperial interests." ZEWDE, *supra* note 238, at 75.

302 *Id.* at 76–85; PANKHURST, *supra* note 206, at 188–94; JOHN WATERBURY, NILE BASIN: NATIONAL DETERMINANTS OF COLLECTIVE ACTION 61 (2002).

303 Amdetsion, *supra* note 72, at 18.

304 Explaining the reason why the French chose Fashoda, COLLINS remarked: "[A]nyone at the time, or even today, casually looking at the configuration of the upper Nile basin without any specific knowledge of its hydrology would observe that all of the many tributaries of the White Nile come together to form a single mighty river at Fashoda ... [which] ... would be able to control all the waters rising in the equatorial regions of central and eastern Africa, thereby making the British position in Cairo completely untenable. With a French force at Feshoda, how could the British refuse to negotiate the evacuation of Egypt once they had lost control of the irreplaceable water supply?" COLLINS, *supra* note 119, at 49–50. To this end, the French sent an expeditionary force and gained control of Fashoda in 1898. That same year, a British expeditionary force, led by Sir Horatio Kitchener, arrived at Fashoda. After heated arguments, the leaders of the two forces "agreed to refer the matter to their respective governments." DEGEFU, *supra* note 117, at 34–35. Eventually, the

Ethiopia.[305] Great Britain, in contrast, decided to pursue diplomatic avenues to protect its interests over the Nile, and avoid military confrontations with Ethiopia.[306] As such, in 1902, Great Britain signed an agreement with Emperor Menelik and settled a long-standing boundary dispute between Ethiopia and Sudan.[307] Further, when Garstin suggested building a dam at the outlet of Lake Tana in 1904,[308] Great Britain opted to use diplomatic means to get concessions from Ethiopia. As the dam in Lake Tana would "store three trillion cubic meters of water," and allow "almost limitless expansion of Gezira irrigation,"[309] Great Britain, in 1904, offered Ethiopia the sum of £10,000 sterling annually to build the dam in Lake Tana.[310] The offer was, however, withdrawn in 1907 as Menelik was not ready to accept the terms.[311]

During the negotiations, Ethiopia was bedeviled by the problem of succession.[312] By 1904, the health of Emperor Menelik, who had no recognized son at the time, had seriously deteriorated, and Ethiopia was already vulnerable to European intervention.[313] In 1906, Great Britain, France, and Italy signed a Tripartite Treaty, which, *inter alia*, made the Blue Nile and the regulation of the Nile waters part of Great Britain's sphere of influence.[314] Based on the treaty, the three powers also directly intervened in Ethiopia's affairs and took part in

desire to prevent war, and to balance military power (i.e., French force was outgunned and outnumbered) forced the France government to back down and withdraw from Fashoda. Amdetsion, *supra* note 72, at 18. In March 1899, the two colonial powers entered into an agreement and determined their spheres of influence, which left Sudan under the complete control of Great Britain. DEGEFU, *supra* note 117, at 34–35.

305 DEGEFU, *supra* note 117, at 35.

306 WATERBURY, *supra* note 302, at 61.

307 The 1902 Anglo-Ethiopian Treaty, *supra* note 124. *See infra* Chapter 3 for a detailed analysis of the 1902 Anglo-Ethiopian Treaty.

308 GARSTIN, *supra* note 122, at 195.

309 James McCann, *Ethiopia, Britain, and Negotiations for the Lake Tana Dam*, 14 INT'L J. AFR. HIST. STUD. 667 (1981).

310 TVEDT, *supra* note 271, at 114.

311 *Id.*

312 PANKHURST, *supra* note 206, at 200.

313 *Id.*

314 *See* Agreement between the United Kingdom, France, and Italy, Respecting Abyssinia, Dec. 13, 1906 (hereinafter 1906 Tripartite Treaty). Accessed from Am. J. Int'l L., Apr. 1907, Vol. 1, No. 2, Supplement: Official Documents, 226–230 (1907). The Treaty also recognized the interests of Italy in the hinterland of its colonies in Eritrea and Somaliland and their territorial connection with the west of Addis Ababa, as well as the interests of France in the hinterland of the French Protectorate on the Somali Coast, and in the territories "necessary for the construction and working of the railway from Djibouti to Addis Ababa." *Id.* at 4(b-c).

overthrowing the successor of Emperor Menelik, Lij Iyasu V (1913–1916) for his "failure to cooperate with European legations, on issues such as Tana."[315]

After Iyasu had been deposed, Ethiopia was ruled by the daughter of Emperor Menelik, Empress Zauditu (1916–1930), and the regent and heir to the throne, Ras Tafari Mekonnen (later became Emperor Haile Selassie).[316] Tafari saw the Tana Dam concession both as a risk and an opportunity. As regent, he had strong rivals in regions along the Nile. Since Ras Hailu of Gojjam and Ras Wale of Begemder—both powerful aristocrats—had control over the Lake Tana area,[317] he considered the Lake Tana concession as a "potential Trojan horse," allowing European powers to penetrate into Ethiopia, and thereby "giving ammunition to his strong rivals."[318] He also considered the Lake Tana concession as an opportunity to get Great Britain's "backing for his ascent to the throne."[319] He even presented himself to the British officials as a would-be reformer who could grant Great Britain the Lake Tana concession should he become an emperor.[320]

Accordingly, in 1923 Great Britain offered Tafari a generous cash payment (£50, 000 first payment, £150,000 on the completion of the reservoir, and annual rent of up to £30,000) and promised to help him control territories on the borders of Ethiopia.[321] However, Great Britain simultaneously frustrated Ethiopia by opposing its admission to the League of Nations and demanding for "access road from the Sudan to [lake] Tana."[322] Tafari feared that the dam on Lake Tana would undermine the power of the central government, and so he cut off the negotiations.[323] Great Britain, on its part, continued coordinating with Italy and signed an exchange of notes in 1925.[324]

---

315 McCann, *supra* note 309, at 673. In addition to the Lake Tana concession, Iyasu's "material and moral support to Sayyid Muhammad Abdille Hassen, the Somali patriotic leader who have been challenging the British and Italian colonial rules" in the Horn of Africa had also "alarmed the tripartite powers." ZEWDE, *supra* note 238, at 127.

316 *Id.* at 130–36; PANKHURST, *supra* note 206, at 208–14; WATERBURY, *supra* note 302, at 63.

317 *Id.*

318 *Id.*

319 *Id.*

320 Tafari reportedly promised that "[i]f he were emperor … many questions would by now be settled, but he explained how his hands were tied by the empress and her supporters who were mainly obstructionists to the welfare of Abyssinia." McCann, *supra* note 309, at 679.

321 TVEDT, *supra* note 271, at 119.

322 WATERBURY, *supra* note 302, at 63; McCann, *supra* note 309, at 681–82.

323 WATERBURY, *supra* note 302, at 63.

324 No. 1211—British and Italian Interests in Abyssinia, 50 L.N.T.S. 281 (1925) (hereinafter the 1925 Treaty).

In the notes (hereinafter the 1925 Anglo-Italian Treaty), Italy recognized "the prior hydraulic rights of Egypt and Sudan on the Nile" and committed "not to construct on the head waters of the Blue Nile or the White Nile or their tributaries or affluents any work which might sensibly modify their flow into the river."[325] Great Britain, in return, recognized "the existing water rights of the populations of the neighboring territories which enter into the sphere of exclusive Italian economic influence,"[326] and allowed Italy the construction of a "railway connecting Eritrea and Somaliland."[327] The two countries also pledged to grant Britain the Tana concession, and agreed if one of the governments secured concession before the other, "the Government which had obtained satisfaction would not relax their wholehearted efforts to secure a corresponding satisfaction for the other Government concerned."[328]

Understandably, the 1925 Anglo-Italian Treaty angered Ethiopia: Tafari, infuriated that he was not involved in the discussions, expressed his opposition by sending a letter to each government.[329] He also brought the case to the League of Nations, disputing the validity of the 1925 Anglo-Italian Treaty.[330] The League found the treaty not binding on Ethiopia.[331] Despite this decision, however, political jostling over the Lake Tana concession continued. Great Britain tried to reopen the Lake Tana negotiations with Ethiopia in mid-1927,[332] although Tafari refused because of his suspicion that the British would use the concession as "an excuse to push the Sudan frontier up as far as the Lake [Tana]."[333] In the same year, Tafari reached an agreement with the J. G.

---

325 *Id.* at 285.

326 *Id,* at 293.

327 *Id.*

328 *Id.* at 285.

329 *See* HAILE SELLASSIE I, THE AUTOBIOGRAPHY OF EMPEROR HAILE SELLASSIE: MY LIFE AND ETHIOPIA'S PROGRESS, VOL. 1, at 134–35 (Edward Ullendorff, trans., Ann., 1999). He stated, in the letter to the Italian government: "The fact that both of you have reached agreement and that you have considered it proper jointly to inform Us of this agreement in identical notes, raises some disgusting thoughts in Us. ... [I]t is right [to] place the matter before the League of Nations, as it requires to be carefully examined in the first place." *Id.* He also stated in a similar letter to Great Britain that "[t]he British Government had already entered into negotiations with the [Ethiopian] Government in regard to its proposals, and we had imagined that, whether that proposal was carried into effect or not, the negotiations would have been concluded with us: We should never have suspected that the British Government would come to an agreement with another Government regarding our lake." *Id.*

330 *Id.* at 135–37; KLIOT, *supra* note 121, at 82–84.

331 *Id.;* HAILE SELLASSIE I, *supra* note 329, at 144.

332 TVEDT, *supra* note 271, at 131.

333 *Id.*

White Engineering Corporation of New York to build the Lake Tana dam.[334] This sent a clear message to Great Britain: "We will carry out the project with our own resources, and it will be under the sovereign control of Ethiopia."[335]

Two years later, Tafari, who became Emperor Haile Selassie I, "signed a letter awarding the construction concession to the American" White Engineering company, and approached Great Britain for "an agreement specifying the amount to be paid annually for the water."[336] He undertook several conferences with the United States and Great Britain, but his attempt to implement the Tana project failed immediately.[337] Due to the Great Depression (1929–1930), the demand for cotton decreased internationally, and the Gezira scheme faced an enormous financial crisis.[338] Meanwhile, Great Britain concluded the 1929 Anglo-Egyptian Treaty with Egypt, and Sudan gained enough water (4 BCM) to expand the Gezira scheme, making the Lake Tana dam less relevant.[339] All those factors and "Ethiopia's Achilles heel, a backward economy with no international creditworthiness,"[340] made the implementation of the Lake Tana project impossible.[341]

Having exhausted all alternatives, Haile Selassie uncovered Great Britain's promise to Menelik II to pay £10,000 per year in return for Ethiopia's 1902 agreement not to arrest the flow of the Blue Nile, and he requested that Great Britain "make good on the arrears amounting to £230,000."[342] When Great Britain rejected this request,[343] he invited all parties to a conference held in May 1935

334 *Id.* at 134; McCann, *supra* note 309, 687; WATERBURY, *supra* note 302, at 64.

335 *Id.*

336 McCann, *supra* note 309, at 691.

337 *Id.* at 695.

338 *Id* ("Hit hard by the general decline in demand, Sudanese cotton prices dropped 55 percent in six years from 1929–1935. Although yields improved after 1934, prices did not recover until after the Second World War.")

339 *Id.*

340 WATERBURY, *supra* note 302, at 64.

341 *Id;* McCann, *supra* note 309, at 695.

342 *Id.* at 693; WATERBURY, *supra* note 302, at 63; HAILE SELLASSIE I, *supra* note 329, at 145 (stating that "the Ethiopian government had earlier given an undertaking to the effect that it would not cut off [arrest] the flow of the small rivers entering the Blue Nile ... without the agreement of British-Sudan Government, and therefore the British-Sudan Government was to pay to the Ethiopian Government an annual sum of ten thousands guineas. When We noticed in Our record the non-payment to the Ethiopian Government of this money ... ever since [1902], we wrote to the British Minster at Addis Ababa asking that the money be paid in accordance with the terms of the letter.")

343 Rejecting Ethiopia's claim, Great Britain asked Egypt to finance the implementation of the Lake Tana project, but Egyptian nationalists opposed the project as they considered it as "a wily scheme by which British were inveigling Egypt into paying for the work that

at Addis Ababa.[344] However, the British, who would officially recognize Fascist Italy's invasion of Ethiopia a year later, declined to attended the meeting as it did not want to "aggravate the present unfortunate controversy between Italy and Ethiopia."[345] In October 1935, Fascist Italy transported 500,000 troops through the Suez Canal and invaded Ethiopia.[346] By May 1936, Italy had captured significant parts of Ethiopia, including the capital city, Addis Ababa, and forced Emperor Haile Selassie into exile.[347] However, Ethiopian patriots continued fighting Fascist Italy without any central government until World War II broke out in 1941 and emperor Haile Selassie returned from exile.[348] The same year, Ethiopia defeated fascist Italy with the help of Great Britain and regained its independence.[349]

In the years following the end of World War II, Egypt launched a campaign to instate the unity of the Nile Valley. It did everything possible to incorporate Sudan into its territory.[350] Anticipating that Sudan would make common cause with Egypt, "Egypt [also] argued for the annexation of Eritrea to Sudan."[351] Contrary to the wishes of the Egyptian leaders, however, "the UN decided to federate Eritrea with Ethiopia in 1952. Sudan also unequivocally decided not to unite with her northern neighbor, but declared independence in 1956."[352]

---

would principal[ly] benefit British cotton interest in Sudan." TVEDT, *supra* note 271, at 165.

344 HAILE SELLASSIE I, *supra* note 329, at 144; McCann, *supra* note 309, at 696.

345 *Id* (internal citation omitted).

346 Kendie, *supra* note 169, at 147. *See* also ZEWDE, *supra* note 238, at 226 (stating that the invasion started in October 1935).

347 *Id*, 235–36.

348 *Id*, 243–249. It is worth noting that Ethiopia, as a member of the League of Nations, asked for "a loan of £10,000,000, but Britain and France opposed it. Ethiopia was even refused permission to buy six airplanes from excess government stocks in England, which it needed for legitimate self-defense." Kendie, *supra* note 169, at 147. Great Britain and France were concerned that Mussolini would join the Axis forces during World War II, and pressured the League of Nations not to help Ethiopia. However, "Mussolini was neither grateful nor appeased and joined Hitler as an ally." *Id.* The League of Nation's inaction, which enabled Fascist Italy to overturn Ethiopia, and crush patriotic resistance using poison gas, was "a death blow to the League." A. J. P. TAYLOR, THE ORIGINS OF THE SECOND WORLD WAR 95 (1961).

349 ZEWDE, *supra* note 238, 243–249; Kendie, *supra* note 169, at 147.

350 *Id;* ARSANO, *supra* note 169, at 88.

351 *Id.*

352 *Id.*

2.3 The Nile in the Age of Cold War: Hydro-political Rivalry and the Scramble for Dominance

After World War II, Great Britain lost its colonial presence in the Nile Basin.[353] All of Britain's East African colonies got their independence: Sudan in 1956, Tanganyika (now Tanzania after unifying with Zanzibar) in 1961,[354] Uganda in 1962,[355] and Kenya in 1963.[356] The other Nile Basin countries such as Zaire (now the Democratic Republic of Congo), and Burundi and Rwanda gained their independence from Belgium in the early 1960s.[357] Nevertheless, the geopolitical importance of the Red Sea and the Suez Canal, which half a century earlier led to the Anglo-French competition over the Nile, brough about another great power competition between the United States and the Soviet Union.[358]

Geopolitical rivalry during the Cold War, as reflected in the study and (non) implementation of large-scale national projects, brought about unilateralism in the Nile Basin. Disregarding the Century Storage Scheme suggested by early British studies, the Soviet Union helped Egypt to build the Aswan High Dam (AHD), from early 1960s to 1970.[359] The United States, for its part, conducted the Blue Nile study from 1959 to 1964 and assisted Ethiopia in the construction of Finchaa dam in the early 1970s.[360] However, when Ethiopia joined the Soviet camp following the downfall of Emperor Haile Selassie in 1974,[361] the United States shifted its policy to Egypt and conducted essential maintenance work on AHD to "improve the performance of [its] 12 turbines."[362] Furthermore, the geopolitics of the Cold War facilitated the construction of the Roseires Dam and the suspension of the Jonglei Canal in 1983.[363] Other developments, such

353 TVEDT, *supra* note 271, at 189–96, 200–202; SAMAAN, *supra* note 188, at 87;

354 *Id;* YILMA MAKONNEN, INTERNATIONAL LAW AND THE NEW STATES OF AFRICA 30–41 (1983).

355 *Id.* at 32; SAMAAN, *supra* note 188, at 87-88.

356 *Id.* MAKONNEN, *supra* note 354, at 35.

357 *Id.* at 40–41; SAMAAN, *supra* note 188, at 87-88.

358 SAMAAN, *supra* note 188, at 88.

359 *Id.* 87; WATERBURY, *supra* note 121, at 109; *See* also TRANSBOUNDARY FRESHWATER DISPUTE DATABASE, NEWS EVENT DATA IN THE NILE BASIN (2008), http://gis.nacse.org/tfdd/event.php?BCODE_Input=NILE& (hereinafter TRANSBOUNDARY FRESHWATER DISPUTE DATABASE).

360 *See generally* U.S.B.R, LAND AND WATER RESOURCES OF THE BLUE NILE BASIN, ETHIOPIA (1964A) (hereinafter U.S.B.R BLUE NILE REPORT A); *see also* CHRISTOPHER SNEDDON, CONCRETE REVOLUTION: LARGE DAMS, COLD WAR GEOPOLITICS, AND THE U.S. BUREAU OF RECLAMATION 98–99 (2015); SAMAAN, *supra* note 188, at 87.

361 ERLICH, *supra* note 54, at 164.

362 TRANSBOUNDARY FRESHWATER DISPUTE DATABASE, *supra* note 359.

363 *See* SAMAAN, *supra* note 188, at 87.

as the Suez Crisis, the Arab-Israeli war, the civil war in Ethiopia, and the Ethio-Somali war, also shaped the geopolitics of the Nile Basin.[364] The following sections analyze the ramifications of these historical events on the use and allocation of the Nile watercourse.

2.3.1 *The Hydro-political Cold War and Downstream Hydraulic Works*

In September 1952, two months after Colonel Gamal Abdel Nasser overthrew King Farouk on July 23, 1952, Egypt decided to build a high dam at Aswan.[365] The construction of the AHD, initially described as "not worthy of serious consideration"[366] and "full of mad ideas for the Nile,"[367] was the antithesis of the Century Storage Scheme and the basin-wide approach that dominated water management on the Nile since the beginning of 20th century.[368] Nasser, committed to conserving the Nile for his country, scrapped several upstream projects in favor of the AHD.[369] "The dam did what Nasser wanted: end the Egyptian dependency on the Africans upstream who possessed but did not control the Nile waters."[370]

The dam has regulated the Nile waters over seasons and years, providing adequate summer water for Egypt's irrigation.[371] It also prevents the most devastating floods and generates a massive amount of electricity.[372] However, the dam, which offered these enormous benefits for Egypt, has come at huge socio-economic and environmental costs.[373] These costs, according to Professor Robert Collins, include "forced relocation of tens of thousands of Sudanese Nubians[,] decreased fertility in surrounding agricultural land, serious erosion downstream, inundation of the delta with seawater, increases in soil salinity and waterlogging, increased seismic activity from the weight of the reservoir on fault lines and decreases in fish populations in the Mediterranean Sea."[374] To be sure, the implication of those costs is staggering by itself.[375] But, what is more remarkable is the 10–15 BCM annual water evaporation at Lake Nasser

364 *Id.*
365 *Id.* 88; COLLINS, *supra* note 64, at 117; WATERBURY, *supra* note 302, at 66.
366 TVEDT, *supra* note 271, at 260 (internal citation omitted).
367 *Id* (internal citation omitted).
368 *Id.* at 261.
369 WATERBURY, *supra* note 121, at 96.
370 COLLINS, *supra* note 64, at 25.
371 *Id.* at 4.
372 *Id.*
373 *Id.*
374 *Id.*
375 *Id.*

that makes the AHD "the wrong dam in the wrong place," providing "a local, short-term, and one-sided political solution."[376]

When Sudan gained its independence in 1956, it opposed the construction of the AHD.[377] It protested against the dam not only because it was not informed of the technical details of the project, but also because it favored the early British plan—the Century Storage Scheme—with a number of smaller dams in Uganda and Ethiopia, and the Jonglei Canal in Sudan.[378] In 1954, while the study on the AHD was being conducted, Sudan had decided to construct the Roseires Dam on the Blue Nile.[379] Both Egypt and Sudan tried to get funds for their respective projects from the International Bank for Reconstruction and Development (IBRD), which later became the World Bank.[380] However, since the AHD would have significant socio-economic impacts on Sudan, including the displacement of 50,000 Sudanese Nubians and flooding of large areas of the Sudan, the IBRD required the two countries to reach an agreement to get the funds.[381]

In December 1955, Egypt received a financial offer for funding the AHD with a $56 million grant from the United States, $14 million aid from Great Britain and $200 million loan from the IBRD.[382] A year later, Egypt accepted the offer from the Western block, but the United State and Great Britain withdrew their offers on the pretext that "the Egyptian economy could not bear the strain of building the dam (presumably because of the arms purchases)."[383] Egypt

376 ERLICH, *supra* note 54, at 132.

377 MCCAFFREY, *supra* note 4, at 312–14.

378 *Id.*

379 SAMAAN, *supra* note 188, at 89; COLLINS, *supra* note 64, at 166; COLLINS, *supra* note 119, at 251; TVEDT, *supra* note 271, at 267.

380 *Id.* at 267–270; SAMAAN, *supra* note 188, at 89; WORLD BANK, WORLD BANK GROUP ARCHIVISTS' CHRONOLOGY 1944–2013, 55, 102 (2013); MOHAMED-HATEM EL-ATAWY, NILOPOLITICS: A HYDROLOGICAL REGIME, 1870–1990 (48) (1996); WATERBURY, *supra* note 302, at 67; WATERBURY, *supra* note 121, at 101 (stating that Egypt approached the IBRD for funding the AHD in January 1953).

381 WATERBURY, *supra* note 302, at 67; WATERBURY, *supra* note 121, at 101–105; TVEDT, *supra* note 271, at 270; SAMAAN, *supra* note 188, at 89; R. K. Batstone, The Utilisation of the Nile Waters, 8 INT'L & COMP. L.Q. 525 (1959); EL-ATAWY, *supra* note 380, 48 ("Sudan also needed [a] financial assistan[ce] to build Rosaries Dam and was informed by IBRD that Egyptian consent was a prerequisite.") For the socio-economic cost, *see* Salman, *supra* note 146, at 514 (stating "[t]he AHD flooded large areas of the Sudan and forced the relocation [of] 50,000 Sudanese Nubians whose lands and main town, Wadi Halfa, and 27 of their villages were submerged under the reservoir of the AHD that extended for 150 km inside the Sudan.")

382 WATERBURY, *supra* note 121, at 105; TVEDT, *supra* note 271, at 270.

383 WATERBURY, *supra* note 121, at 107. The real reasons why the United States and Great Britain withdraw their offer includes, *inter alia*, "Egypt's growing ties with Czechoslovakia

swiftly reacted by nationalizing the Suez Canal to get the funds necessary for the construction of the AHD.[384]

Not surprisingly, Egypt's decision provoked Great Britain and France, and with the support of Israel, they conducted a coordinated attack (the Suez Crisis or Tripartite Aggression) against Egypt in late October 1956.[385] However, Egypt's fierce resistance, the possibility of Soviet Union's intervention, and the pressure from the United States and United Nations halted the attack immediately.[386] Subsequently, Great Brain and France contemplated using the Nile waters as a political weapon against Egypt. In particular, Great Britain had "shown much interest in the possibility that, by stopping or reducing the flow of the White Nile at Owen Falls, severe damage may be caused to the Egyptian economy."[387] Great Britain contemplated to harm Egypt by the constructing the Roseires Dam and other irrigation projects in Sudan.[388] Nevertheless, Great Britain did not put this plan into action as it would violate the 1929 Anglo-Egyptian Treaty, and would not have an immediate disastrous impact on Egypt.[389]

The Suez Crisis or Tripartite Aggression brought the superpowers, the United States and the Soviet Union, into Nile politics.[390] In the years following

---

and the Soviet Union," Nasser's condemnation of "the Baghdad Pact (later known as the Central Treaty Organization), and the conclusion of ... expensive $200 million arms agreement with the Soviet Union." COLLINS, *supra* note 64, at 179–80.

384 In the nationalization speech, Nasir remarked: "The income of the Suez Canal Company in 1955 reached £ E. 35 million, or 100 million dollars. Of this sum, we, who have lost 120,000 persons, who have died in digging the Canal, take only £ E. 1 million or 3 million dollars ... [T]he Suez Canal Company ... was dug for the sake of Egypt and its benefit ... We shall not repeat the past. We shall eradicate it by restoring our rights in the Suez Canal. This money is ours ... The Suez Canal Company in Paris is an imposter company. It usurped our concessions. But history will never repeat itself. On the contrary, we shall build the High Dam. We shall restore our usurped rights. We shall build the High Dam as we want it ... Thus, today, citizens, when we build the High Dam, we are actually building the dam to defend our dignity, freedom and pride, and to eradicate humiliation and submission ... Today, citizens, the Suez Canal Company has been nationalized. This order has been published in the Official Journal. It has become a matter of fact." *See* SUEZ CANAL PROBLEM, JULY 26—SEPTEMBER 22, 1956, 27–29 (1956).

385 TVEDT, *supra* note 271, at 310; WATERBURY, *supra* note 121, at 70; SAMAAN, *supra* note 188, at 93.

386 *Id. See also The Suez Crisis, 1956*, OFFICE OF THE HISTORIAN, https://history.state.gov/milestones/1953-1960/suez, *See generally*, Pnina Lahav, *The Suez Crisis of 1956 and Its Aftermath: A Comparative Study of Constitutions, Use of Force, Diplomacy, and International Relations*, 95 B.U. L. Rev. 1297 (2015).

387 TVEDT, *supra* note 271, at 308 (internal citation omitted).

388 *Id.* at 309; SAMAAN, *supra* note 188, at 93.

389 *Id. See also* TVEDT, *supra* note 271, at 310.

390 SAMAAN, *supra* note 188, at 93; WATERBURY, *supra* note 121, at 70–71.

the crisis, Egypt received financial support from the Soviet Union for constructing the AHD.[391] This further damaged the bilateral relationship between Egypt and Sudan: Sudan immediately endorsed the "Eisenhower Doctrine which provided for direct U.S. military support to Middle East states threatened by 'communist aggression.'"[392] Openly rejecting the 1929 Anglo-Egyptian Treaty, Sudan also unilaterally extended the Gezira scheme and raised the height of the Sennar Dam.[393] Furthermore, opposing the AHD, Sudan endorsed the Century Storage Scheme as its own national Nile plan, after including "additional dams for Lake Kyoga, [and] the upper Blue Nile, at Semna."[394]

In November 1958, General Ibrahim Abboud, who deposed the Sudanese Umma government with the help of Egypt, became the president of Sudan and broke the deadlocked negotiations over AHD.[395] On November 8, Sudan and Egypt entered into the 1959 Agreement and allocated the 32 BCM that was unallocated under the 1929 Anglo-Egyptian Treaty.[396] The agreement authorized Egypt to build the AHD "[i]n order to make use of the full natural river supply and stop the flow of any excess to the sea,"[397] although it left 10 BCM for annual evaporation and seepage losses at the Reservoir.[398] It also allowed Sudan to construct the Roseires Reservoir on the Blue Nile, "[i]n order to enable the Republic of Sudan to exploit their share," as well as "any other works deemed necessary by Sudan for the same purpose."[399] Furthermore, the Agreement contemplated the possibility of implementing water conservation projects in Sudan and instructed the two states to share the construction costs and water benefits of such projects equally.[400] In particular, it specified projects for the prevention of water "loss" in the Sudd wetlands of Sudan.[401]

Subsequently, Egypt, after receiving 400 million rubles of assistance from the Soviet Union,[402] started constructing the AHD.[403] Sudan, on the other hand, secured $32.5 million in financial assistance from the IBRD and

391 *Id.* at 71 ("An accord had been the precondition for IBRD funding, but it was apparently not for Soviet funding.")

392 *Id.* at 70.

393 *Id.* at 71.

394 COLLINS, *supra* note 119, at 259.

395 *Id.* at 255; WATERBURY, *supra* note 121, at 70–71.

396 1959 Agreement, *supra* note 106, at art. I, ¶ 1. *See infra* note 730.

397 *Id.* at Article II, ¶ 1.

398 *Id.* at Article II, ¶ 4.

399 *Id.* at Article II, ¶ 2.

400 *Id.* at Article III.

401 *Id.*

402 WATERBURY, *supra* note 121, at 109.

403 *Id.* at 109–11.

$19 million from West Germany and constructed the Roseires Dam on the Blue Nile.[404] The dam was completed in 1966, and its reservoir can impound about 3 BCM of water.[405] In 1964, Sudan also implemented the Managil extension and constructed the Khashm El Girba Dam on the Atbara tributary to relocate the Nubian inhabitants, who had been displaced by the construction of AHD, in the New Halfa irrigation project.[406]

In the following decades, Egypt embarked on ambitious and very controversial out-of-basin desert reclamation projects. One of these projects is a large irrigation scheme in northern Sinai through the construction of the Peace Canal.[407] The canal is expected to provide 4.5 BCM of water[408] for the reclamation of 228.36 thousand acres of land in the west of the Suez Canal (phase I) and 415.2 thousand acres of land in the Sinai (phase II).[409]

Ever since its inception in 1979, Ethiopia fiercely opposed the project and threatened to divert the flow of the Blue Nile.[410] Egypt's leader, Anwar Sadat, on the other hand, responded in strong words: "We do not need permission from Ethiopia or the Soviet Union to divert our Nile water … If Ethiopia takes any action to block the Nile waters, there will be no alternative for us but to *use force*. Tampering with the rights of a nation to water is tampering with its life and a decision to go to war on this score is indisputable in the international community."[411] Despite such belligerent rhetoric, however, the tension between the two countries was short-lived as Sadat was assassinated on

404 COLLINS, *supra* note 119, at 274.

405 Taha, *supra* note 90, at 195–96.

406 *Id.* at 193–194; SAMAAN, *supra* note 188, at 97.

407 Amal Othman et al., *El-Salam Canal Is a Potential Project Reusing the Nile Delta Drainage Water for Sinai Desert Agriculture: Microbial and Chemical Water Quality*, 3(2) J. ADV. RES. 100 (2012).

408 ABTEW & DESSU, *supra* note 171, at 21; SAMAAN, *supra* note 188, at 110.

409 THE EGYPTIAN STATE INFORMATION SERVICE, SINAI DEVELOPMENT PROJECTS (2006), http://www.sis.gov.eg/newVR/sinia/html/esinia10.htm.

410 WATERBURY, *supra* note 302, at 70–71.

411 KIMENYI & MBAKU, *supra* note 172, at 99 (internal citation omitted). Ironically, Sadat, who threatened Ethiopia not to use its equitable share of the Nile waters, traveled to Israel and offered to transfer the Nile waters to the Negev desert in Israel. In his speech at Haifa, Sadat informed the Israelis that "[a]fter the tunnel is completed, I am planning to bring the sweet Nile waters—this is the sweetest of the four big rivers of the whole world—to the Sinai. Well, why not send you some of this sweet water to the Negev Desert as good neighbors." *Id. See* William Claiborne, *Sadat Offers Israel Water from the Nile*, WASH. POST (Sept.7, 1979), https://www.washingtonpost.com/archive/politics/1979/09/07/sadat-offers-israel-water-from-the-nile/c07ab59e-fde0-489c-88aa-24020196444e/.

October 6, 1981.[412] Following the assassination, the construction works of the Peace Canal continued, despite Ethiopia's persistence objection to the legality of the project.[413]

Regarding the water conservation projects envisaged in the 1959 Agreement, Egypt and Sudan decided to construct the Jonglei Canal following the end of the first round of civil war in southern Sudan in 1972.[414] Although the international environmental community opposed the project due to the benefits of wetlands to the environment and local populations,[415] Egypt and Sudan started building the Jonglei Canal in 1978.[416] By 1983, two-thirds of the canal had been completed, but the second round of the South Sudanese civil war erupted, and the project was completely abandoned.[417]

2.3.2 *The Cold War Rivalry and Upstream Hydraulic Plans*

While Nasser's Egypt was supported by the Soviet Union, Ethiopia was a strategic ally of the Western bloc. Haile Selassie allowed the United States to establish a U.S. Army radio station at Kagnew in the province of Eritrea.[418] The station, which hosted thousands of American soldiers, as well as marine research and National Aeronautics and Space Administration (NASA) observation centers, gave the United States a foothold on the Red Sea during the height of the Cold War.[419] The United States, in return, provided significant financial and military support to Ethiopia.[420]

In 1959, the United States started conducting an extensive study on the Blue Nile. The study, conducted by the USBR, is the first extensive survey of the Blue

412 David B. Ottaway, *Sadat Assassinated at Military Show*, WASH. POST (Oct. 7, 1981), https://www.washingtonpost.com/archive/politics/1981/10/07/sadat-assassinated-at-military-show/604a2b32-408f-4e99-972d-ad6379c880c2/. *See also* SAMAAN, *supra* note 188, at 113.

413 *Id. See* the discussion *infra* section 5.1. for the details of Ethiopia's legal arguments.

414 WATERBURY, *supra* note 302, at 140; COLLINS, *supra* note 64, at 199–201.

415 *Id.* at 205–12.

416 WATERBURY, *supra* note 302, at 140.

417 *Id.* at 140, 146; COLLINS, *supra* note 64, at 199–201.

418 ZEWDE, *supra* note 238, at 185–86; PANKHURST, *supra* note 206, at 259; WATERBURY, *supra* note 302, at 67–78.

419 *Id.*; ZEWDE, *supra* note 238, at 185–86; PANKHURST, *supra* note 206, at 259.

420 ZEWDE, *supra* note 238, at 186 (stating "American military influence was most evident in the fields of training and equipment. US military aid in the period between 1946 and 1972 came to over $US 180 million. Over 2.500 Ethiopians underwent diverse form[s] of military training in the United States between 1953 and 1968. The jet aircraft, anti-tank and anti-aircraft weapons, naval craft, infantry weapons and sometimes even uniform were of American origin. In both equipment and training, the air force remained the most prestigious show-piece of American military aid in Ethiopia." *Id.*)

Nile.[421] The USBR issued its final report in 1964 after five years of investigation of the irrigation and hydroelectric power potentials of the entire Blue Nile Basin.[422] In its report, the USBR outlined "plans for projects that would irrigate 433,754 hectares of land … and for power projects capable of producing 8,660,000 kilowatts to add to the present limited supply. The flows … reaching the Ethiopia-Sudan border would be depleted by irrigation uses and evaporation losses from reservoir surfaces by about 5,400 million cubic meters annually (10%)."[423]

Implementing all Blue Nile projects would not adversely affect the interests of Egypt and Sudan. Instead, they would increase the amount of water available for irrigation in the Nile Basin. In this regard, Professor Robert Collins remarked: "Even if Ethiopia were simply to pursue its own objective of managing the reservoir to maximize hydropower production, without considering the interest of Egypt and Sudan, the amount of water to downstream riparian would not substantially be affected."[424] Had Ethiopia been able to implement the Blue Nile Plan, Collins further asserted, "drawing off six km3, Egypt and Sudan would still benefit from the construction of reservoirs in the Blue Nile, if properly managed, a maximum loss of only 2.5 KM3, a trivial amount compared to the total Nile flow and sources of additional water available in the equatorial lakes."[425]

The Blue Nile Plan had a clear message for Egypt: The Ethiopians, who threatened to cut off the flow of the Nile for centuries, were taking the first step to do just that with the help of the United States. Thus, the Plan, "provoked a knee-jerk reaction from Egypt."[426] Egypt started creating havoc in Ethiopia by, *inter alia*, instigating an Arab revolution in Eritrea. Radio Cairo broadcasts started urging "Eritreans to take up arms and to struggle for their independence."[427] Egypt opened an office for the Eritrean Liberation Front in Cairo[428] and provided training, and generous financial and arms support to various guerrilla liberation fronts fighting against Ethiopia.[429] It also supported Somalia in its border dispute with Ethiopia.[430]

---

421 *See generally*, U.S.B.R BLUE NILE REPORT A, *supra* note 360.

422 Robert O. Collins, *History, Hydropolitics and the Nile: Myth or Reality?*, in THE NILE: SHARING A SCARCE RESOURCE, 122 (Paul P. Howell & J. Antonio Allan, eds., 1994).

423 U.S.B.R BLUE NILE REPORT A, *supra* note 360, 40–41.

424 Collins, *supra* note 422, at 123.

425 *Id.* at 123–24.

426 Waterbury, *supra* note 169, at 288.

427 Kendie, *supra* note 169, 154.

428 *Id.* at 155.

429 *Id.*

430 *Ethiopia Accuses Egypt*, N.Y. TIMES (Feb. 17, 1978), https://www.nytimes.com/1978/02/17/archives/ethiopia-accuses-egypt-little-more-than-gesture.html.

Ethiopia, for its part, pushed for the implementation of the projects and asked the United States to quickly begin constructing the dams on the Blue Nile. Complaining about the delay in the implementation of the projects, Haile Selassie asked the United States government to help him in building the Finchaa Dam.[431] In response, the head of the United States Agency for International Development (USAID), who was alarmed by Haile Selassie's complaints, advocated for the Finchaa Dam, affirming that "the project as conceived was technically and financially sound, and that it would make a significant contribution to the economic development of Ethiopia."[432] Further, the director of the Bureau of the Budget confirmed that the United States "has a serious political stake in Ethiopia as a moderately pro-Western state with a good record of political stability and considerable influence in the African world."[433] Therefore, the director concluded, the Finchaa Dam was a worthwhile project "both [in] economic and political terms."[434]

The construction of the dam began in 1968, "the cornerstone laid in November 1970 by Emperor Haile Selassie, and the commissioning took place in 1972. The total value of the project was put at $34 million (in 1968 dollars) of which $23 million was in foreign exchange. The World Bank put up most of the foreign exchange, while the USAID contributed $2.8 million."[435] The dam could generate 90 MW of electricity through three turbines.[436] Initially, the dam had 0.6 BCM of water storage capacity, but it was later upgraded and can now store about 1.2 BCM of water.[437]

The following years saw improvements in the relationship between Ethiopia, Sudan, and Egypt. In February 1972, Haile Selassie and the World Council of Churches mediated the conflict between Sudan and southern Sudanese rebel groups and brokered a deal (the 1972 Addis Ababa Accord) that ended the civil

431 SNEDDON, *supra* note 360, at 98. "We ... asked the Americans to build a dam on the Finchaa River, a tributary to the Blue Nile. It took them five years to make a survey and the dam is not even started. Meanwhile, you have doubtless heard of the big fuss further down the Nile where the Russians dedicated a much bigger dam which they built not in 40 years but in about five years." *Id.* (internal citation omitted).

432 *Id.* at 99.

433 *Id.* (internal citation omitted).

434 *Id.* (internal citation omitted).

435 WATERBURY, *supra* note 302, at 118.

436 *Id.* at 119.

437 *Id.*

war.[438] In March 1973, an Egyptian journalist, Abd al-Tawwab Abd al-Hayy, came to Ethiopia at the invitation of Haile Selassie, and was briefed about Ethiopia's water development plans, and visited the sites of the proposed projects on the Blue Nile and Lake Tana.[439] By May 1973, Haile Selassie had gone to Cairo and requested Sadat's assistance for maintaining the Organization of African Unity's (OAU) headquarters in Addis Ababa and for curbing the Somali aggregation in Ethiopia.[440] Sadat accepted those requests and endorsed Addis Ababa as the headquarter of the OAU.[441] In return, Haile Selassie promised that "Ethiopia would never interfere with the Nile before consulting with the other riparian countries."[442]

This cordial relationship immediately ended, however, with the overthrow of Haile Selassie by Colonel Mengistu Haile Mariam, leader of the Dergue, or military junta, in 1974.[443] Following a "bloody path to power," Mengistu "liquidate[d] all [his] political contenders" and established a communist regime in Ethiopia.[444] This took Ethiopia into the Soviet camp, and Ethiopia "all the while guarding its ambitions to develop the Blue Nile, lost its access to Western sources of funding."[445] The Soviet Union provided weapons for Mengistu, but did not "make Ethiopia a showcase for other African countries by developing Ethiopia's economy, which would have been more impressive than flooding the country with armaments."[446]

While Ethiopia was heading to the Soviet camp, Sadat had already taken Egypt into the Western camp. In 1971, he terminated the alliance with the Soviet Union,[447] and he attacked Israel in 1973.[448] Following the deadly military confrontation, Egypt and Israel accepted the United Nations' request for a ceasefire, started negotiating under the auspices of the United States,

438 *Id.* at 139–40.

439 ERLICH, *supra* note 54, at 200.

440 *Id.*

441 *Id.*

442 *Id.*

443 *Id.* at 164.

444 *Id.*

445 Waterbury, *supra* note 169, at 288–289.

446 GETACHEW METAFERIA, ETHIOPIA AND THE UNITED STATES: HISTORY, DIPLOMACY, AND ANALYSIS 68 (2009).

447 ANOUSHIRA EHTESHAMI & EMMA MURPHY, THE INTERNATIONAL POLITICS OF THE RED SEA 51 (2011). *See also* SAMAAN, *supra* note 188, at 106.

448 *Id. See also The October Arab-Israeli War of 1973: What Happened?*, AL JAZEERA (Oct. 8, 2018), https://www.aljazeera.com/features/2018/10/8/the-october-arab-israeli-war-of-1973-what-happened.

and eventually entered into the 1978 Camp David Treaties and the 1979 Peace Agreement, which give Egypt all its occupied lands.[449] Following the accords, Egypt became a strategic partner to the United States in, *inter alia*, its efforts to mediate the Israeli-Arab conflict. Thus, the United States helped Egypt reopen the Suez Canal, build its economy, and maintain the AHD during the 1970s and the 1980s.[450]

The reversal of alliances brought about significant changes in the region. Sadat, now aligning with Saudi Arabia, Sudan, and the United States, continued supporting Somalia in its aggression against Ethiopia.[451] Mengistu, for his part, aligned himself with the Soviet Union and defended the territorial integrity of Ethiopia.[452] In March 1978, he defeated Siad Barre's (the Somali president) armies, who were supported by Egypt and the United States, and drove them out of Ethiopia's territory.[453] In retaliation, Ethiopia resorted to the Nile, and announced, at the U.N. Water conference in Mar de Plata, that it would abstract 4 BCM from the Nile waters to irrigate 91,000 hectares on the Blue Nile and 28,000 hectares on the Baro areas.[454] It also underscored "the sovereign right of any riparian state, in the absence of an international agreement, to proceed unilaterally with the development of water resources within its territory."[455]

A year later, Mengistu commissioned Soviet experts to survey Lake Tana.[456] This action seriously provoked Egypt, and Sadat, on May 13, 1978, declared: "We depend upon the Nile 100 percent in our life, so if anyone, at any moment thinks to deprive us of our life, we shall never hesitate [to go to war] because [Nile] is a matter of life or death."[457] Ethiopia, for its part, made it abundantly clear that "no one in his right mind could question Ethiopia's inalienable and self-evident right to use its natural resources for the benefit of its people."[458]

449 *Id;* EHTESHAMI & MURPHY, *supra* note 447, at 51; SAMAAN, *supra* note 188, at 106.

450 *Id;* TRANSBOUNDARY FRESHWATER DISPUTE DATABASE, *supra* note 359.

451 EHTESHAMI & MURPHY, *supra* note 447, at 51–52.

452 *Id.* at 54 (stating "Moscow emerged as the key Ethiopian ally (1977) and aided it in a major military campaign against Somalia.")

453 ERLICH, *supra* note 54, at 166–67.

454 Woldetsadik, *supra* note 169, at 391.

455 ARSANO, *supra* note 169, at 90 (Internal citation omitted).

456 SAMAAN, *supra* note 188, at 109; ASHOK SWAIN, MANAGING WATER CONFLICT: ASIA, AFRICA, AND THE MIDDLE EAST 103 (2004).

457 WATERBURY, *supra* note 121, at 78 (Internal citation omitted).

458 DEGEFU, *supra* note 117, at 150 (internal citation omitted).

In addition to the war rhetoric, Egypt used its strategic position in the Middle East as leverage to block international funds that were intended to help Ethiopia develop the Nile.[459] Meanwhile, Ethiopia lacked funds to develop irrigation projects[460] and continued relying on rain-fed agriculture. This heavy reliance on traditional farming left many Ethiopians vulnerable to hunger, and a series of droughts have long kept millions of families "on the ragged edge of starvation."[461] From 1983 to 1985, more than one million Ethiopians died prematurely from illnesses related to malnutrition.[462] The result, according to the *Wall Street Journal*, was "one of Africa's cruelest ironies: the land that feeds the Nile is unable to feed itself."[463]

Following the famine, Ethiopia, securing a significant donation from European countries,[464] started the Tana-Beles project to generate power and irrigate 150,000 hectares of land in the Lake Tana area.[465] "Italian assistance alone was $246 million in 1988, including generous aid to the 'development' project of Tana-Beles."[466] In return, Mengistu contracted with an Italian company, Cellini, to undertake the project.[467] Meanwhile, Egypt, concerned about its potential adverse impacts, "protested vigorously" against the project[468] and blocked funding from the African Development Bank.[469] As a result, the Tana-Beles project could not be implemented during the communist regime in Ethiopia.

By the beginning of the 1990s, the devastating drought and the conflict in the northern Ethiopia significantly eroded the power of Mengistu's government;

459 For instance, Egypt blocked African Development Bank funds meant to aid Ethiopia in exploiting the Nile. *See* Ashok Swain, *The Nile River Basin Initiative: Too Many Cooks, Too Little Broth,* 22 SAIS REV. 293, 298 (2002); *see also* Thurow, *supra* note 105 ("Modern geopolitics have favored Egypt because of its strategic position in the Middle East. Major international lenders and development agencies have been loath to support anything upstream on the Nile that might disrupt the vital flow of water to Egypt.")

460 *Id.*

461 *Id.*

462 Kathryn Reid, *1980s Ethiopia famine: Facts, FAQ s, and How to Help*, WORLD VISION (June 8, 2018), https://www.worldvision.org/disaster-relief-news-stories/1980s-ethiopia-famine-facts.

463 Thurow, *supra* note 105.

464 AFRICA WATCH: A DIVISION OF HUMAN RIGHTS WATCH, EVIL DAYS: 30 YEARS OF WAR AND FAMINE IN ETHIOPIA, 366–67 (1991) (hereinafter EVIL DAYS).

465 WATERBURY, *supra* note 302, at 117.

466 EVIL DAYS, *supra* note 464, 365–66.

467 WATERBURY, *supra* note 302, at 117.

468 DEGEFU, *supra* note 117, at 212.

469 Kendie, *supra* note 169, at 158.

the Tigray People Liberation Front (TPLF) and Eritrean People Liberation Front (EPLF), which had been fighting the government since the 1960s, started controlling significant parts of Ethiopia.[470] The United States also continued pressuring the military regime by, *inter alia,* , supporting the rebel groups and launching hostile propaganda through the Amharic program of the Voice of America.[471] Even worse, the Soviet Union, adopting "Gorbachev Doctrine of superpower cooperation," unequivocally warned Mengistu that it "would not continue assisting Ethiopia as itself was undergoing radical changes in domestic policies,"[472] and that he should " make a rapprochement with the United States and ...seek political solutions to its domestic problems, especially to the Eritrean issue."[473] Then, on May 20, 1991, the EPLF and the TPLF gained control of Addis Ababa, the capital city of Ethiopia on May, and the next day Mengistu "secretly fled to Harare, Zimbabwe."[474]

Conclusion

This chapter has investigated the geopolitics of the Nile Basin during the pre-colonial, colonial, and Cold War periods. Even since the early Axumite period, Ethiopia had been using its "power of geography" against Egypt and was threatening to divert or control the flow of the Nile waters. Although Ethiopia's historical ability to divert the flow of the Nile has always been very unrealistic, the myth was so convincing at the time that it made Egyptians pursue a hydrological strategy towards controlling the source of the Nile, in Ethiopia. In the nineteenth century, Egypt invaded Ethiopia and was forced to swallow successive defeats by Ethiopia.

During the colonial period, Great Britain controlled the White Nile all the way from its source in Lake Victoria to its mouth on the Mediterranean Sea. As the guardian of the Nile, Great Britain sought to secure plenty of water for Egypt both to provide cotton production for its textile industries in Lancashire and safeguard its interests in the Suez Canal. Accordingly, Great Britain developed the Century Storage Plan to increase water availability in Egypt. It also invested in downstream hydraulic works that established inequitable and lopsided water utilization in the basin. Further, it concluded several colonial treaties

470 METAFERIA, *supra* note 446, at 71.
471 *Id*, 69–70.
472 *Id*, at 70.
473 *Id.*
474 ZEWDE, *supra* note 238, at 267–68; METAFERIA, *supra* note 446, at 70.

to safeguard its imperial interests in Egypt and thereby shaped institutional practices in the Nile Basin. Through the 1902 Treaty with Ethiopia, and the 1929 Treaty with Egypt, Britain set the rules of the game, prohibiting upstream states from utilizing the waters of the Nile without the consent of those downstream. After decolonization, Egypt followed in Britain's footsteps, concluding the 1959 Agreement with Sudan, which effectively institutionalized that same status quo.

Following independence, the Nile Basin States challenged the colonial legacy and decided to develop active unilateral projects within their territories. Nevertheless, Cold War geopolitics and bipolar rivalry between the United States and the Soviet Union helped Egypt to effectively control the Nile waters by unilaterally constructing the AHD within its territory. Egypt also attempted to foreclose Ethiopia's future use by establishing facts on the ground through its controversial desert reclamation projects, namely, the North and South Valley Development Projects. In the same epoch, Egypt followed the second of the options offered by Munzinger that "Ethiopia … is a danger for Egypt. Egypt must … retain it in anarchy and misery."[475] In this regard, it supported the Eritrean and the Tigrayan Liberation Fronts to prevent Ethiopia from implementing the projects proposed by the USBR and forcing it to devote its limited resources towards resolving internal turmoil. Egypt also backed Somalia's aggression against Ethiopia and threatened, on so many occasions, to bomb Ethiopia.

In addition to these forms of sabotage, the 1974 revolution, which overthrew Haile Selassie and brought about the communist regime in the country, closed access to Western sources of funding, which Ethiopia needed to implement its ambitious projects on the Blue Nile. Moreover, Egypt, using its strategic position in the Middle East as leverage, blocked international funds intended to help Ethiopia develop the Nile. As a result, international financial institutions refused to fund upstream projects in Ethiopia. Meanwhile, Ethiopia lacked funds to implement its Nile projects and could not use the Nile watercourse throughout the Cold War era.

475 Kendie, *supra* note 169, at 145.

CHAPTER 3

The Status of Colonial Nile Waters Treaties under International Law

Introduction

During colonization, Great Britain used normative agreements to secure the uninterrupted flow of the Nile. It concluded several treaties with colonial powers and independent states concerning the use and the flow of the Nile waters.[476] After independence, all the upper Nile Basin States renounced the colonial Nile Waters Treaties. Ethiopia rejected the English version of the 1902 Anglo-Ethiopian Treaty as early as 1907.[477] The newly independent Tanganyika (now Tanzania) declared the Nyerere Doctrine in 1961, renouncing the 1929 Anglo-Egyptian Treaty signed on its behalf by Great Britain.[478] Following Tanzania's path, Uganda, Kenya, Burundi, DRC, and Rwanda have also renounced their obligations stipulated under the colonial Nile Waters Treaties.[479] Egypt, on the other hand, invokes the law of state succession and claims that the colonial Nile Waters Treaties are binding upon the upstream states.[480]

This chapter critically scrutinizes the claims and counterclaims of the Nile Basin States in light of international law. The next section introduces colonial Nile Waters Treaties and analyzes the content and scope of the most controversial agreements. Section 3.2. investigates the immediate post-colonial dispute over colonial Nile Waters Treaties. Sections 3.3 and 3.4 respectively analyze

476 *See* discussion in Chapter 2.

477 WOLDETSADIK, *supra* note 172, 88; BONAYA ADHI GODANA, AFRICA S SHARED WATER RESOURCES: LEGAL AND INSTITUTIONAL ASPECTS OF THE NILE, NIGER AND SENEGAL RIVER SYSTEMS 197 (1985) ("Ethiopia simply does not acknowledge any existing treaty or other obligations preventing it from freely disposing of the Nile waters on its territory.")

478 GODANA, *supra* note 477, 146–156.

479 *Id.* ARTHUR OKOTH-OWIRO, THE NILE TREATY: STATE SUCCESSION AND INTERNATIONAL TREATY COMMITMENTS: A CASE STUDY OF THE NILE WATER TREATIES, 14 (2004).

480 Shih & Stutz, *supra* note 60, 10796–10805; Samir Ahmed, *Principles and Precedents in International Law Governing the Sharing of Nile Waters, in* THE NILE: SHARING A SCARCE RESOURCE, 351, 355–57 (Paul P. Howell & J. Antonio Allan, eds., 1994); GODANA, *supra* note 477, 143–44.

 | DOI:10.1163/9789004549869_004

the colonial Nile Waters Treaties in light of international law of state succession and the principle of fundamental change in circumstance.

3.1 The Colonial Nile Waters Treaties

As demonstrated in Chapter 2, several bilateral agreements concluded between riparian states and their former colonial powers concerning the flow of the Nile since the end of the 19th century. Of these colonial treaties, the 1902 Anglo-Ethiopian Treaty and the 1929 Anglo-Egyptian Treaty are the most relevant and disputed.[481] This section analyzes the content and scope of these treaties.

3.1.1 *The 1902 Anglo-Ethiopian Treaty*

The 1902 Anglo-Ethiopian Treaty is a bilateral treaty concluded between Great Britain, on behalf of Sudan, and Ethiopia to determine the boundary between Ethiopia and Sudan.[482] Although the Treaty is about boundary delineation, article III is about the waters of the Nile, in which Ethiopia undertook "not to construct, or allow to be constructed, any work across the Blue Nile, Lake Tana, or the Sobat which would *arrest* the flow of their waters into the Nile except in agreement with His Britannic Majesty's Government and the Government of the Soudan."[483]

Noticeably, the physical scope of the article is very limited and governs only the Blue Nile, Lake Tana, and the Sobat River. The Tekeze river, which originates in Ethiopia and contributes about 12–15 BCM to the Nile,[484] is exempted from this Treaty.[485] Further, the "treaty allegedly restricted constructions on or across the Blue Nile, Lake Tana or the Sobat which would arrest the flow of their waters into the main Nile."[486] Both the Blue Nile and Sobat River are joined by various tributaries as they flow from their sources in Ethiopia into the main Nile in Sudan.[487] For instance, from the whole Blue Nile waters flowing to Sudan, only about 3.5 BCM of waters leaves Lake Tana annually, and

481 Amdetsion, *supra* note 72, 22; Mekonnen *supra* note 172, 351–55; *see also* Salman, *supra* note 172, 18.

482 *See* generally 1902 Anglo-Ethiopian Treaty, *supra* note 124.

483 *Id.* art. III (emphasis added).

484 MCCAFFREY, *supra* note 4, 305–306.

485 WOLDETSADIK, *supra* note 172, 59.

486 *Id.*

487 *Id.*

about 46 BCM of the mean annual outflow of the Blue Nile waters is derived from the river's major tributaries in the north and north-western Ethiopia.[488] The question would then be whether the 1902 Anglo-Ethiopian Treaty includes these tributaries.

Approached from a geographical point of view, or the notion of a drainage basin, the Blue Nile, Lake Tana, and the Sobat river referred to in the 1902 Anglo-Ethiopian Treaty would include tributaries, underground waters, and rainfall in Ethiopia.[489] The main streams of the Blue Nile or Sobat watercourses are nothing, but parts of the entire riverine hydrology.[490] Hydrologically, the drainage basin or unity of the river system means that any interference with or withdrawal of water from tributaries of the Blue Nile, Lake Tana, or Sabot Rivers would affect the overall quantity and quality of the flow of waters reaching the downstream states.[491] Therefore, if we follow an approach that adopts the unity of river systems, or drainage basin, it is likely that the tributaries of the Blue Nile or Sobat River would automatically be included in the Treaty.[492]

However, the text of the 1902 Anglo-Ethiopian Treaty does not support such an approach. Article III is very restricted in scope and does not extend its application to tributaries of the Blue Nile and the Sobat River.[493] Although Great Britain had in past advocated for the prohibition of all forms of interference in the Nile River Basin,[494] it had employed the phrase "across the Blue Nile, Tsana, and Sobat" in the Treaty without an explicit or implicit reference to the tributaries of the Blue Nile and Sobat River.[495] This is either because Great Britain could not get a better concession from Ethiopia or satisfied with the Treaty's current design.[496] The possible justifications notwithstanding, one fact is abundantly clear: Great Britain did not excluded the tributaries of the

488 *Id.*

489 Int'l Law Ass'n 52nd Conference, Helsinki, Fin., Aug. 1966, The Helsinki Rules, art. II, (1962) [hereinafter Helsinki Rules] (Defining an international drainage basin as "a geographical area extending over two or more States determined by the watershed limits of the system of waters, including surface and underground waters, flowing into a common terminus.")

490 *Id*; WOLDETSADIK, *supra* note 172, 59.

491 *Id*, 60. *See* also 1994 Y.B. INT'L L. COMM'N, vol. 2, pt. 2, p. 90, ¶ 4 (1997). (Stating "[b]ecause the surface and groundwaters form a system, and constitute by virtue of their physical relationship a unitary whole, human intervention at one point in the system may have effects elsewhere within it.")

492 WOLDETSADIK, *supra* note 172, 59.

493 1902 Anglo-Ethiopian Treaty, *supra* note 124, art III.

494 WOLDETSADIK, *supra* note 172, 72.

495 *Id*, 65.

496 WOLDETSADIK, *supra* note 172, 65.

Blue Nile and Sobat River from the Treaty due to lack of foresight regarding potential consequences of its action.[497]

Quite the contrary, the various treaties concluded by Great Britain during the same period demonstrate that it intentionally excluded the tributaries of the Blue Nile and Sobat River from the 1902 Anglo-Ethiopian Treaty.[498] For instance, the 1906 Tripartite Treaty between Great Britain, France, and Italy included a specific provision that protected the interest of Great British in "the Nile basin, and more specifically as regards the regulation of the waters of that river and its *tributaries*."[499] Further, under the 1925 Anglo-Italian Treaty, Italy recognized "the prior hydraulic rights of Egypt and Sudan," promising that it will "not to construct on the head waters of the Blue Nile or the White Nile or their tributaries or affluents any work which might sensibly modify their flow into the river."[500] Similarly, article VI of the 1909 Anglo-American Treaty signed between the United States of America (USA) and Great Britain (representing Canada) explicitly stipulated that "Saint Mary and Milk Rivers and their *tributaries* are to be treated as one stream for purposes of irrigation and power."[501]

To be sure, all the aforementioned treaties had their own unique political and historical circumstances that necessitated their conclusions. However, notwithstanding the difference in their respective context, there is no plausible reason justifying why the British, who had significant bargaining power and "an imposing position [at the time] could not have framed Article III along the *same model* reiterated above, if indeed such objective had been contemplated."[502] Therefore, it can be concluded that Article III of the 1902 Anglo-Ethiopian Treaty does not include hydraulic works on the tributaries of the Blue Nile and Sobat River.

3.1.2 *The 1929 Anglo-Egyptian Treaty*

The 1929 Anglo-Egyptian Treaty grew out of a 1926 report the Joint Commission established through an exchange of notes between Egypt and the United Kingdom on January 25, 1925.[503] The Commission, which was mainly created

497 *Id.*

498 *Id.*

499 The 1906 Tripartite Treaty, *supra* note 314, art 4 (a). (Emphasis added).

500 The 1925 Treaty, *supra* note 324, at 285.

501 Treaty with Great Britain Relating to Boundary Waters, and Questions Arising Between the United States and Canada, Jan. 11, 1909, art. IV, 36 Stat. 2448, T.S. No. 548.

502 WOLDETSADIK, *supra* note 172, 66.

503 Exchange of notes of January 26, 1925, contained in annex A to the 1929 Anglo-Egyptian Treaty, *supra* note 125 [Hereinafter Exchange of notes of January 26, 1925]. The commission was established "for the purpose of examining and proposing the basis on which

to resolve the dispute between Great Britain and Egypt regarding the expansion of the Gezira cotton scheme, had "decided to approach its task with the object of devising a practical working arrangement which would respect the needs of established irrigation, while permitting such program of extension as might be feasible under present conditions and those of the near future, without at the same time compromising in any way the possibilities of the more distant future."[504]

Notwithstanding its clear mandate to propose irrigation plans in Sudan that would not be "detriment to [Egypt's] natural and historic rights,"[505] the Commission recognized that irrigation projects in Sudan would necessarily affect the historic rights of Egypt, and disregard Egypt's absolute rights over its historical uses.[506] Recognizing the necessity of irrigation development in Sudan, the Commission remarked:

> Any abstraction of water in flood time in Sudan must affect these levels to the detriment of the basin irrigation, and therefore to admit that the lands in question have an absolute right to undiminished natural levels must preclude any abstraction of water by Sudan ... The present Commission is not disposed to enter into an argument on general principles as to how far the maintenance of levels can be regarded as an established right. Approaching the matter as a body of engineers invited to advise on a practical question, the Commission considers that development or conservation works in the upper part of the river should not be indefinitely restricted by considerations of the natural levels lower down, but that Sudan should accept a limited rate of progress, so as to afford Egypt the opportunity to overtake the effect of development in Sudan by [the] construction of the works which formed her part of the original program.[507]

Approaching the problem from a practical point of view,[508] the Commission recommended that "[t]he natural flow of the river should be reserved for the

irrigation can be carried out with full consideration of the interests of Egypt and without detriment to her natural and historic rights." *Id*, ¶ 1.

504 *Id*, ¶ 21.

505 *Id*, ¶ 1.

506 *Id*, ¶ 37.

507 *Id*, ¶37 and ¶56.

508 MCCAFFREY, *supra* note 4, 310. (Stating "while the Commission declined to enter into a debate on whether Egypt had an 'established right' to the maintenance of historic levels, it found that as a practical matter Egypt should not be regarded as having an absolute right to the precise manner of use that had been made there historically; such would be

benefit of Egypt from the 9th January, to the 5th July,"[509] and "foresees that it will be necessary from time to time to review the questions discussed in this Report."[510] In spite of its attempts to "find a practical and workable basis for irrigation, and to foresee, and, as far as possible, to provide for, any difficulties that may arise in the future,"[511] the Commission expected the possibility of disputes relating to the interpretation, or factual issues.[512] Finally, the Commission declared its desire to record its view "that neither the elaborate drafting of an agreement nor the provision of special machinery for adjudication should be allowed to obscure the importance of mutual confidence and cooperation in all matters concerning the river and its waters."[513]

The report of the Joint Commission was annexed to the 1929 Anglo-Egyptian Treaty and considered an integral part thereof.[514] The Treaty allocated forty-eight billion cubic meters ("BCM") for Egypt and four BCM for Sudan, a ratio of 12:1.[515] In the Treaty, Egypt acknowledged the fact that "the development of Sudan requires a quantity of the Nile water greater than that which has been so far utilized by Sudan,"[516] but agreed to future development in Sudan only insofar as it "does not infringe Egypt's natural and historical right in the waters of the Nile and its requirements of agricultural extension."[517] In return, Great Britain, representing Sudan and its other East African colonies (Kenya, Uganda, and Tanganyika), recognized Egypt's veto power over any projects in its colonies. Article 4 (ii) of the Treaty stipulates:

> Save with the previous agreement of the Egyptian Government, no irrigation or power works or measures are to be constructed or taken on the River Nile and its branches, or on the lakes from which it flows, so far as all these are in … Sudan or in countries under British administration, which would, in such a manner as to entail any prejudice to the interests

incompatible with development of irrigation in Sudan. Instead, the latter development could be phased in gradually, so that Egypt would have time to complete the necessary compensating works").

509 Exchange of notes of January 26, 1925, *supra* note 503, ¶ 88 (i).

510 *Id*, ¶ 89. It also noted that it was "all established irrigation should be respected in any future review of the question." *Id*.

511 *Id*, ¶ 91.

512 *Id*, ¶ 92.

513 *Id*, ¶ 91.

514 The 1929 Anglo-Egyptian Treaty, *supra* note 125, art 3.

515 MCCAFFREY, *supra* note 4, 311. *See* also 1959 Agreement, *supra* note 106 at art. I, ¶ 1 (characterizing these quantities as the "established right" of the parties).

516 The 1929 Anglo-Egyptian Treaty, *supra* note 125, art 2.

517 *Id*.

of Egypt, either reduce the quantity of water arriving in Egypt, or modify the date of its arrival, or lower its level.[518]

Alice Shih and Trevor Stutz argued that this clause "applies ... to all riparian countries since it references all irrigation and power works or measures on the lake."[519] While the clause has significant implications for some upstream states, the argument that it "applies to all riparian countries" is a bit of a stretch as Ethiopia, Eritrea, and Congo were not "under British administration" at the time. In addition to the principle of privity of treaty or *pacta tertiis nec nocent nec prosunt,*[520] the clause itself explicitly restricted its scope and applicability on states that were "under British administration."[521] Even the states on whose behalf Great Britain concluded the treaty (Sudan, Kenya, Uganda, and Tanzania) vehemently rejected the clause after they gained their independence in the 1950 and 60s.[522] Egypt, meanwhile, insists that the 1929 Anglo-Egyptian Treaty is still binding, and claims veto power over projects in these former British East African colonies.[523]

3.2 Immediate Post-colonial Dispute over the Colonial Nile Waters Treaties

Having outlined the content and scope of the 1902 and 1929 treaties, this section scrutinizes the immediate post-colonial disputes over the colonial Nile Waters Treaties. In so doing, it scrutinizes the claims and counterclaims of the Nile Basin States vis-à-vis international law.

---

518 *Id*, art. 4 (ii).

519 Shih & Stutz, *supra* note 60, 10793.

520 *See* Vienna Convention on the Law of Treaties art. 34, May 23, 1969, 1155 U.N.T.S. 331. [hereinafter VCLT].

521 The 1929 Anglo-Egyptian Treaty, *supra* note 125, art. 4 (ii).

522 GODANA, *supra* note 477, 146–153.

523 Report of the Commission to the General Assembly, 1974 U.N.Y.B. Int'l L. Comm'n 157, 203 (1974), https://legal.un.org/ilc/publications/yearbooks/english/ilc_1974_v2_p1.pdf (hereinafter 1974 Report). (Nothing Egypt's reply to Tanganyika which "maintained that pending further agreement, the 1929 Nile Waters Agreement, which had so far regulated the use of the Nile waters, remained valid and applicable.") Ahmed, *supra* note 480, 355–57; Shih & Stutz, *supra* note 60, 10796–10805; GODANA, *supra* note 477, 143–144; Christina Carroll, *Past and Future Legal Framework of the Nile River Basin*, 12 GEO. INT'L ENVT'L. L. REV. 269, 270, 279 (1999) (Stating "that Egypt has maintained that the colonial agreements are controlling, but other former colonies have disagreed with this position.")

3.2.1 *Swimming against the Current: Revisiting Ethiopia's Arguments against the 1902 Anglo-Ethiopian Treaty*

The 1902 Anglo-Ethiopian Treaty is the only colonial treaty addressing Nile access applicable to Ethiopia. But, as Shih and Stutz note, the Treaty is often overlooked:[524] Many Ethiopian scholars avoid discussing the treaty,[525] and some others even implicitly deny its existence altogether.[526]

While the agreement's binding effect is up for debate, there is no doubt that Britain (on behalf of Sudan) and Ethiopia concluded the 1902 Anglo-Ethiopian Treaty, imposing boundary issues between the two countries with lasting legacies.[527] The Treaty, which has both English and Amharic versions, requires Ethiopia "not to construct, or allow to be constructed, any work across the Blue Nile, Lake Tana, or the Sobat which would *arrest* the flow of their waters into the Nile except in agreement with His Britannic Majesty's Government and the Government of the Soudan."[528]

Given these seemingly unfavorable terms, Ethiopia has made several arguments disputing the validity of the 1902 Treaty. First, Ethiopia questions the very relevancy of the 1902 Anglo-Ethiopia Treaty, contending that the Treaty never entered into force as neither Britain, nor Ethiopia ratified it,[529] and that Ethiopia persistently objected to the Treaty since the 1950s.[530] Second, Ethiopia

---

524 Shih & Stutz, *supra* note 60, 10789.

525 *See*, e.g., Mekonnen, *supra* note 135, Mekonnen *Declaration of Principles, supra* note 172; Mekonnen *supra* note 172; Dereje Zeleke Mekonnen, *From Tenuous Legal Arguments to Securitization and Benefit Sharing: Hegemonic Obstinacy—The Stumbling Block against Resolution of the Nile Waters Question*, 4 MIZAN L. REV. 232 (2010); KIMENYI & MBAKU, *supra* note 172. It should be noted that few scholars tried to address this treaty, although Professor Woldetsadik book is the most visible exception in this regard. WOLDETSADIK, *supra* note 172. *See* also Shih & Stutz, *supra* note 60; Ahmed, *supra* note 480; YIHDEGO, *supra* note 172.

526 Shih & Stutz, *supra* note 60, 10789 (challenging Amdetsion's assertion that "Ethiopia has not entered into any binding treaties with either Egypt or Sudan concerning the allocation of the Nile's waters.")

527 *See generally*, 1902 Anglo-Ethiopian Treaty, *supra* note 124.

528 *Id*, art. III (emphasis added).

529 Ibrahim, *supra* note 189, 299 (arguing that "the treaty never came into force as Britain did not ratify it"); Tesfaye Tafesse, *Ethiopia's Position on the Nile Water Agreements, in* COOPERATIVE DIPLOMACY, REGIONAL STABILITY AND NATIONAL INTERESTS: THE NILE RIVER AND THE RIPARIAN STATES, 69 (Korwa Adar & Nicasius Check, eds. 2011) (arguing that the treaty is void because it "has never been ratified either by Ethiopia or the British parliament"); DEGEFU, *supra* note 117, 97 (claiming that Ethiopia never ratified the treaty).

530 Ibrahim, *supra* note 189, 299 (mentioning Ethiopia's rejection as a ground for abrogating the treaty); DEGEFU *supra* note 117, 98 (arguing that "Ethiopia's practice ... negates the

invokes the doctrine of unequal treaty, and alleges that it is not bound by the Treaty.[531] Third, Ethiopia invokes the later-in-time, or *lex posterior* principle, and alleges that the 1902 Anglo-Ethiopian Treaty is void because Sudan and Egypt concluded the 1959 Agreement.[532] Forth, Ethiopia considers Britain's recognition of fascist Italy's annexation of Ethiopia in 1936[533] as a material breach the 1902 Anglo-Ethiopian Treaty, and abrogates the validity of the Treaty. Finally, Ethiopia, relying on an alleged discrepancy between the English and Amharic versions of the 1902 Anglo-Ethiopian Treaty, submits that the treaty does not prohibit Ethiopia from equitably using the Nile watercourse.[534]

Though meritorious in some aspects, most of the arguments face significant flaws. To take each in turn: The first argument combines a pair of premises about ratification and later rejection of the Treaty. The first premise is misleading: Article v of the 1902 Anglo-Ethiopian Treaty requires ratification only from Britain, not Ethiopia.[535] Moreover, the Treaty was in fact ratified by Britain.[536] The claim also fails when considering Ethiopia's historical practice: during a war with Eritrea in 1998–2000, Ethiopia cited some articles of the 1902 Anglo-Ethiopian Treaty before the Eritrea-Ethiopia Boundary Commission, arguing for their continuing binding applicability.[537] Thus, regardless of the ratification, it is difficult to accept that the Treaty never entered into force, since Ethiopia has admitted its operationality.[538] As for the second premise: under international law, persistent objection or denunciation is not a valid method of abrogating a treaty.[539]

---

continued binding force of the Treaty as Ethiopia declared that she no longer regard herself bound by the old treaty obligation.")

531 DEGEFU, *supra* note 117, 99.

532 *Id.*

533 Ibrahim, *supra* note 189, 299.

534 *Id.* WOLDETSADIK, *supra* note 172, at 54–56.

535 1902 Anglo-Ethiopian Treaty, *supra* note 124, art. v.

536 Britain's ratification was delivered at Addis Ababa on October 28, 1902. HB Deb. (Dec. 8, 1902) (vol. 116) cols. 204–05. The U.K. Foreign & Commonwealth Office lists the ratification date as August 21, 1902. U.K. FOREIGN & COMMONWEALTH OFFICE, https://treaties.fco.gov.uk/awweb/pdfopener?md=1&did=74175.

537 *See* Decision Regarding Delimitation of the Border Between Eritrea & Ethiopia, XXV R.I.A.A. 83 (Eri.-Eth. Boundary Comm'n 2002). *See* also Shih & Stutz, *supra* note 60, 10798.

538 The maxim "[s]auce for the goose is sauce for the gander" also supports this conclusion as a state that "invokes a true or supposed rule of international law for [its] own advantage today, cannot deny its existence for someone else's benefit tomorrow." *See* C. D' O. Farran, *The Nile Waters Question in International Law*, 41 SUDAN NOTES AND RECORDS 90 (1960).

539 VCLT, *supra* note 520, art. 56.

The second argument relies inappropriately on the theory of unequal treaties, which challenges validity of treaties based on inequality of obligation.[540] Though there have been some exceptions,[541] historically state practice has not supported the invalidation of unequal treaties.[542] And at present, "[t]here is... no rule of international law..., prescribing that there must be a balance of obligations in treaties," and that even substantial inequality of obligation "could, in and of itself justify their nullity or annulment."[543] Britain doubtless wielded significant influence during negotiations.[544] Even so, it remains unlikely that British influence or even coercion constituted the "duress" required to render the Treaty void under international law.[545]

The third argument, which invokes the 1959 Agreement to invalidate the 1902 Treaty, is not grounded in international law. It assumes that Ethiopia may relieve itself from treaty obligations simply because Sudan and Egypt concluded the 1959 Agreement outside the context of the 1902 Anglo-Ethiopian Treaty.[546] The later-in-time, or *lex posterior*, principle under international law does indeed permit states to supersede past treaties by concluding a new treaty governing the same matter.[547] But this principle applies only to states that are parties to both the former and the new treaties.[548] Ethiopia was a third party in the case of the 1959 Agreement.[549]

The fourth argument, on the import of British recognition of Italian occupation, presupposes the existence of material breaches of the treaty. Article 60 of the Vienna Convention on the Law of Treaties ("VCLT") allows states to terminate, in whole or in part, a bilateral treaty if the other party violates "a provision essential to the accomplishment of the object or purpose of the treaty."[550] The main purpose of the 1902 Anglo-Ethiopian Treaty, as articulated in its preamble, was to ensure friendly relations between Ethiopia and Britain by settling a longstanding boundary dispute between Sudan and Ethiopia.

540 VCLT, *supra* note 520, art. 34.

541 Law of Treaties, 1966 U.N.Y.B. Int'l L. Comm'n 1, 17 (1966) (*See* the positions of Byelorussian, Ecuadorian, and Iraqi delegations).

542 Albert H. Putney, *Termination of Unequal Treaties*, 21 AM. SOC'Y INT'L L. PROC. 87, 89 (1927); Lucius Caflisch, *Unequal Treaties*, 35 GERMAN Y.B. INT'L L. 52, 67–69 (1992).

543 *Id.* 69.

544 WOLDETSADIK, *supra* note 172, at 54–56 & 66; Shih & Stutz, *supra* note 60, at 10798.

545 VCLT, *supra* note 520, arts. 51–52; Shih & Stutz, *supra* note 60, at 10798.

546 *Id.*

547 VCLT, *supra* note 520, art. 59.

548 *Id.*

549 *See* the 1959 Agreement, *supra* note 106.

550 VCLT, *supra* note 520, art. 60.

Ethiopia's independence and sovereignty were arguably essential to that goal. In recognizing Italy's invasion of Ethiopia and the inclusion of Ethiopia's territories into the Italian East Africa colony,[551] Britain arguably committed a material breach of the 1902 Anglo-Ethiopian Treaty, opening the door for Ethiopia to terminate Article III of the Treaty, at least.[552]

The fifth argument is based on alleged discrepancies between the English and Amharic versions of the Treaty, and thus requires a proper investigation of the two versions of the Agreement. The English version of Article III of the Treaty reads:

> His Majesty Emperor Menelik, King of Kings of Ethiopia, engages himself towards the Government of his Britannic Majesty not to construct or allow to be constructed any work across the Blue Nile, Lake Tsana, or the Sobat, which would arrest the flow of their waters into the Nile except in agreement with His Britannic Majesty's Agreement and the Government of the Soudan.[553]

Whereas the Amharic version of the Treaty reads:

> **ጃንሆይ ዳግማዊ ምኒልክ ንጉሠ ነግስት ዘ-ኢትዮጲያ ከጥቁር አባይና ከባህረ ጣና ከሶባት ወንዝ ወደ ነጭ አባይ የሚወስደውን ውሃ ከእንግሊዝ መንግስት ጋር አስቀድመው ሳይስማሙ ወንዝ ተዳር እዳር የሚደፍን ስራ የሚደፍን ስራ እንዳይሰሩ ወይም ወንዝ የሚደፍን ስራ ለማሰራት ለማንም ፈቃድ እንዳይሰጡ በዚህ ውል አድርገዋል።** [554]

The Amharic version, as translated by Professor Tadesse Woldetsadik, reads:

> His Majesty Menelik II, King of Kings, Ethiopia, has agreed into this treaty not to construct, nor authorize anyone to construct a work that blocks up/stops up from riverbank to riverbank the water descending from the Black Abbay, from the Tana Sea, and from the Sobat River

551 For a discussion of the French and British responses to the Italian invasion of Ethiopia, *see* generally R.A.C. Parker, *Great Britain, France and the Ethiopian Crisis 1935–1936*, 89 ENG. HIST. REV. 293 (1974).

552 Given the general preference for the stability of treaties, and considering the fact that VCLT makes treaty withdrawal or termination very narrow, one can dispute this argument and contend that Britain recognition of Italy's invasion of Ethiopia cannot constitute a material breach of the 1902 Anglo-Ethiopian Treaty. Gabčíkovo-Nagymaros Project (Hung./Slovk.), Judgment, 1997 I.C.J. 7, ¶ 46 (Sept. 25).

553 1902 Anglo-Ethiopian Treaty, *supra* note 124, art. III.

554 *Id. See* also WOLDETSADIK, *supra* note 172, 57.

> towards the White Abbay without previously agreeing with the English Government.[555]

As the Amharic version demonstrates, the 1902 Anglo-Ethiopian Treaty does not prohibit Ethiopia from equitably using the Nile waters. The Treaty only prohibits Ethiopia from *blocking up* or *stopping up* the entire flow of the Nile waters without the consent of Britain. The Treaty leaves within Ethiopia's discretion irrigational, industrial, or domestic uses of the Nile waters. However, Britain's understanding of the Treaty was different, and Britain advocated for a broader view that prohibits Ethiopia from arresting the flow of the Nile waters in any way without prior authorization.[556]

Pursuant to Article 33 of VCLT, both versions of the Treaty are equally authentic texts, and the terms of the Treaty are presumed to have the same meaning in each text.[557] It is presumed that the term arrest in Article III of the Treaty has the same meaning as its Amharic equivalent. The root verb in the Amharic version, daffana, denotes the English equivalent meaning of "to stop up, to fill, plug or close tightly, or to block a passage."[558] Similarly, the lexical and contextual meaning of the term arrest in the English version of the Treaty conveys "to stop, check, break automatically a motion; to cease … or discontinue or as a device for stopping motion."[559]

Both the Amharic and English versions of the Treaty are clear: neither the term arrest nor its equivalent daffana "appear to insinuate a controversial language."[560] The description of the English version echoes "the corresponding Amharic text which had been constituted as '**ወንዙን ከዳር እስከ ዳር የሚደፍን ስራ እንዳይሰሩ**'; literally, the latter translates to denote the meaning 'not to block up/stop up from riverbank to riverbank.'"[561] Therefore, both the Amharic and English versions of the Treaty do not prohibit Ethiopia from equitably using the Nile waters without Britain's consent. The Treaty requires Great Britain's consent only for works on the Blue Nile, Lake Tana, and Sobat River that would completely stop their water flow.

555 *Id.* The translation of the treaty is Professor Woldetsadik's own. *Id.*

556 *Id*, 72.

557 VCLT, *supra* note 520, art. 33. Article V of the 1902 Anglo-Ethiopian Treaty also explicitly stipulates both versions are authentic. 1902 Anglo-Ethiopian Treaty, *supra* note 124, art. V.

558 WOLDETSADIK, *supra* note 172, at 75.

559 *Id.*

560 *Id.*

561 *Id.*

This conclusion is also in line with the object and purpose of the Treaty.[562] As noted, the preamble of the Treaty, which forms part of the context and can thus be considered in interpretation,[563] stipulates that the main purpose of the Treaty was "to confirm friendly relations" between Ethiopia and Great Britain and to "settle the frontier between Sudan and Ethiopia."[564] While the narrow interpretation of the Treaty ensures a friendly relationship between the two countries, the wider interpretation of the Treaty, which prohibits Ethiopia from arresting the flow of the Nile waters in any way without prior authorization, defeats the very purpose and object of the 1902 Anglo-Ethiopian Treaty.[565] It is also contrary to the principle of good faith in treaty interpretation recognized under customary international law.[566]

The import of Sudanese consent also arises in the discrepancies between the English and Amharic versions of the Treaty. Unlike the English version, the Amharic version mentions only Britain and does not require Sudanese consent for the construction of works that would completely block the water flow of the Blue Nile, Lake Tana, or Sobat.[567] Here the inconsistency is real, and cannot be reconciled through the application of the general rules of interpretation codified under articles 31 and 32 of the VCLT.[568]

In such a situation, article 33 ¶ 4 of the VCLT stipulates that "the meaning which best reconciles the texts, having regard to the object and purpose of the treaty, shall be adopted."[569] This can be achieved by applying the version of

562 VCLT, *supra* note 520, 31, ¶ 1. ("A Treaty shall be interpreted in good faith in accordance with the ordinary meaning to be given to the terms of the treaty in their context and in the light of its object and purpose.") This provision is a codification of customary international law. Territorial Dispute (Libyan Arab Jamahiriya v. Chad), Judgment, 1994 ICJ Reports,¶ 41 (Feb. 3).

563 VCLT, *supra* note 520, 31, ¶ 2.

564 1902 Anglo-Ethiopian Treaty, *supra* note 124, preamble.

565 In addition to object and purpose, VCLT requires to consider "[a]ny relevant rules of international law applicable in the relations between the parties." VCLT, *supra* note 520, 31, ¶ 3 (c). The parties to the 1902 Anglo-Ethiopian Treaty recognized the principles of equitable utilization and no significant harm as governing rubric of the Nile Basin. Supporting the narrow interpretation of Article III of the 1902 Anglo-Ethiopian Treaty, these principles allow each riparian state to use the Nile waters equitably and reasonably without causing significant harm to the interest of other riparians. *See* discussion *infra* sections 4.2, 5.1., 6.2.1., & 7.2.

566 *See*, Territorial Dispute (Libyan Arab Jamahiriya v. Chad), Judgment, 1994 ICJ Reports, ¶ 41 (Feb.3).(recognizing the VCLT, *supra* note 520, 31, ¶ 1 as a codification of customary international law).

567 1902 Anglo-Ethiopian Treaty, *supra* note 124, art III.

568 VCLT, *supra* note 520, arts. 31–32.

569 VCLT, *supra* note 520, art article 33 ¶ 4.

the Treaty that reinforces the object and purpose of the 1902 Anglo-Ethiopian Treaty. Arguably, the Amharic version best reinforces the purpose of ensuring friendly relations between Ethiopia and Britain. As noted, Britain concluded the Treaty on behalf of Sudan.[570] Both versions of the Treaty require Britain's consent which represent Sudan's consent for all practical purposes at that time.[571] Therefore, the Amharic version of Article III of the 1902 Treaty best reconciles the texts' discrepancies regarding the consent of Sudan.

It is therefore reasonable to conclude that Article III of the Treaty requires only Britain's prior authorization[572] of construction or approval of works on and across the Blue Nile, Lake Tana, or Sobat River (not in their tributaries) that would arrest or completely block the flow of their waters to the White Nile.

3.2.2 *The Nyerere Doctrine and the 1929 Anglo-Egyptian Treaty*

The validity of the colonial Nile Waters Treaties vis-à-vis the Equatorial Lake States has been a very controversial issue since the 1950s. Following Sudan's independence in 1956, and during the negotiation of the 1959 Agreement, Britain underscored, in a statement sent to Egypt, that it considered the 1929 Anglo-Egyptian Treaty subject to revision, and that it intended to negotiate new terms on behalf of its East African colonies.[573] On August 27, 1959, Britain also sent official notes to Egypt, Sudan, and Ethiopia, reiterating the fact that "the territories of British East Africa will need for their development more water than they at present use and will wish their claims for more water to be recognized by other states concerned."[574] Forecasting that those upstream states "will find it difficult to press ahead with their own development until they know what new works downstream states will require on the headwaters within British East African Territory," Britain also called upon Egypt, Sudan, and Ethiopia for "an early settlement of the whole Nile waters question."[575]

Following Great Britain's suit, Tanganyika (now Tanzania) rejected the validity of the colonial Nile Waters Treaties as soon as it became independent in

570 *See generally*, 1902 Anglo-Ethiopian Treaty, *supra* note 124.

571 *Id*, art. III.

572 International Law of state succession governs the issue whether Sudan's consent is required for the construction or approval of works on and across the Blue Nile, Lake Tana, or Sobat River that would arrest or block up the flow of their waters to the White Nile. *See* discussion *infra* section 3.3.

573 WATERBURY, *supra* note 121, at 72; DEGEFU, *supra* note 117, 140–41.

574 *Id* (Internal citation omitted).

575 *Id* (Internal citation omitted).

1960.[576] On 9 December 1961, the Prime Minister of Tanganyika, Julius Nyerere, made the following declaration to the Secretary-General of the United Nations:

> As regards bilateral treaties validly concluded by the United Kingdom on behalf of the territory of Tanganyika or validly applied or extended by the former to the territory of the latter, the Government of Tanganyika is wilting to continue to apply within its territory, on a basis of reciprocity, the terms of all such treatments for a period of two years from the date of independence (i.e., until 8 December 1963) unless abrogated or modified earlier by mutual consent. At the expiry of that period. the Government of Tanganyika will regard such of these treaties which could not by the application of the rule of customary international law be regarded as otherwise surviving, as having terminated.[577]

Concerning the 1929 Anglo-Egyptian Treaty, Nyerere further declared "that an agreement that purported to bind Tanganyika for all time to secure the prior consent of the Egyptian Government before it undertook irrigation or power works or other similar measures on Lake Victoria or in its catchment area was incompatible with its status as an independent sovereign State."[578] Therefore, Nyerere concluded, "the provisions of the 1929 Agreement purporting to apply to the countries 'under British Administration' are not binding on Tanganyika."[579]

This position, known as the Nyerere doctrine, was immediately adopted by other newly independent states, including Kenya, Uganda, Burundi, and Rwanda, and heralded as the governing principle of international law regarding treaties concluded by former colonial powers.[580] In effect, the Nyerere doctrine is the modified version of the "tabula rasa" or "clean slate" principle, according to which "successor states do not inherit obligations arising out of the treaties concluded by their predecessors."[581] However, unlike the classic

576 GODANA, *supra* note 477, 147.

577 *See* United Nations Conference on Succession of States in Respect of Treaties, at 18 (1977–1978), https://digitallibrary.un.org/record/36222?ln=en#record-files-collapse-header [hereinafter United Nations Conference].

578 *Id*, 33, §27 (commenting on Article 12, discussing Tanganyika's declaration).

579 Okoth-Owiro, *supra* note 479, 14 (quoting Nyerere's letter to Egypt, Great Britain, and Sudan).

580 MAKONNEN, *supra* note 354, 216–17; C. O. Okidi, *Review of Treaties on Consumptive Utilization of Waters of Lake Victoria and Nile Drainage System*, 22 NAT. RESOURCES J. 175 (1982).

581 Yehenew Walilegne, *The Nile Basin: From Confrontation to Cooperation*, 27 DALHOUSIE L.J. 503, 511 (2004). For a detailed analysis of "tabula rasa" or "clean slate" doctrine and

"tabula rasa" or "clean slate" articulations, which render a new sovereign free from any of its predecessor's obligations,[582] the Nyerere doctrine tempers itself, recognizing that some treaty obligations may be regarded as "surviving" through customary international law.[583]

Although international law of state succession has faced extraordinarily inconsistent state practice, there is a well-established rule of customary international law that state succession does not affect boundary regimes.[584] Some scholars also try to expand this rule to territorial obligations establishing international servitudes, claiming that those obligations should be devolved to newly independent states as an exception to the general rule of non-transmissibility of treaty obligations.[585] The claim has long been controversial,[586] and currently neither scholarship nor state practice provides clear answers about which territorial obligations constitute exceptions to the clean slate doctrine under the general international law.[587]

Even so, some scholars invoke the territorial obligations exception and argue for the continued validity of colonial Nile Waters Treaties.[588] For instance, Bonaya Godana, arguing the 1929 Anglo-Egyptian Treaty includes territorial obligation, asserted that "[t]he survival of this particular treaty is unmistakably attested to by available evidence."[589] But the "available evidence" is difficult to ascertain: Godana, seemingly contradicting himself, remarked that "[i]t seems

its applicability to the Nile Basin States, *see generally* MAKONNEN, *supra* note 354 & GODANA, *supra* note 477.

582 *Id*, 137; MAKONNEN, *supra* note 354, 132–33.

583 *See* United Nations Conference, *supra* note 577, at 18.

584 1974 Report, *supra* note 523, 201. *See also* JAMES R CRAWFOR, BROWNLIE'S PRINCIPLES OF PUBLIC INTERNATIONAL LAW 440 (8th ed. 2012).

585 D.P. O CONNELL, THE LAW OF STATE SUCCESSION 51–52 (1956); LORD MCNAIR, THE LAW OF TREATIES 256 & 656 (1961); D.P. O CONNELL, STATE SUCCESSION IN MUNICIPAL LAW AND INTERNATIONAL LAW 14–15 (1967).

586 MAKONNEN, *supra* note 354, 270–71 (Arguing that any attempt for the transfer of territorial treaties to successor states "based on misconception arising from the Roman Law analogy should be dismissed as being of no international legal significance in determining the effect of state succession on treaties.") *Id*. *See* also CRAWFOR, *supra* note 584, 440. (Stating that "there is insufficient evidence in either principle or practice for the existence of this exception to the general rule. First, much of the practice is equivocal and may rest on acquiescence. Secondly, the category is difficult to define and it is not clear why the treaties apparently included should be treated in a special way.")

587 *See supra* note 586 and accompanying texts.

588 Shih & Stutz, *supra* note 60, 10796–10805; Ahmed, *supra* note 480, 355; GODANA, *supra* note 477, 156.

589 GODANA, *supra* note 477, 156.

doubtful that the 1929 agreement was seriously regarded or even intended as permanent in the sense that it would bind all successor states in perpetuity."[590]

Despite the controversy, Egypt still considers the 1929 Anglo-Egyptian Treaty perpetually binding on the former British East African colonies.[591] Rejecting the Nyerere Doctrine, it maintained that "pending further agreement, the 1929 Nile Waters Agreement, which had so far regulated the use of the Nile waters, remained valid and applicable."[592] It further asserted that the Treaty is valid based on the law of state succession.[593] The next part scrutinizes the rules of state succession and determines their applicability to the colonial Nile Waters Treaties.

3.3 The Colonial Nile Waters Treaties and State Succession

States are the primary subjects of international law,[594] and possess various rights and obligations.[595] States can be created in various ways, including through independence from a colonial power, succession from an already existing state, balkanization of a state into two or more states, or unification of two or more states into one.[596] "In all these cases, the original international personality of the State disappears, and a new international person appears on the scene. In other words, there occurs a succession of one international person (the State) by another."[597] Such an occurrence, often called state succession, "does not entail an automatic transfer of rights and obligations" from the original person (predecessor state) to the new one (the successor state).[598]

The decolonization of African States in the 1950s and 1960s and the dissolution of the Soviet Union in the 1980s forced the international legal community to develop two conventions dealing with the ramifications of state

590 *Id*, 143.
591 *Id*, 143–144.
592 1974 Report, *supra* note 523, 203.
593 GODANA, *supra* note 477, 143–144.
594 MCCAFFREY, *supra* note 49, 135; CRAWFOR, *supra* note 584, 115–16.
595 *Id*; MCCAFFREY, *supra* note 49, 135.
596 Yimer Fisseha, *State Succession and the Legal Status of International Rivers, in* THE LEGAL REGIME OF INTERNATIONAL RIVERS AND LAKES, 177, 177 (Ralph Zacklin & Lucius Caflisch eds., 1981).
597 *Id*, 177–78.
598 Shih & Stutz, *supra* note 60, at 10802; *see* also Okoth-Owiro, *supra* note 479, 10. (Remarking that "state succession in fact does not entail automatic juridical substitution of the factual successor state in the complex sum of rights and obligations of the predecessor state").

succession.[599] Even so, international law of state succession continues to face "great uncertainty and controversy."[600] State practice in the area has always been equivocal,[601] and jurists are virtually unanimous in asserting that the conventions do not necessarily reflect customary international law, which itself remains underdeveloped.[602]

State succession theory has historically split into two camps.[603] Until the late 19th century, the theory of "universal succession," or the doctrine of "universal continuity" of rights and obligations was the prevailing approach.[604] Developed from Roman Civil Law governing inheritance cases, the theory advocates for an automatic transfer of the entirety of rights and obligations of the predecessor state to the successor or newly independent state.[605] Since the end of the 19th century, the "clean slate" or "tabula rasa" theory has gained popularity.[606] As the names suggest, it takes the opposite tack: treaty rights

599 Shih & Stutz, *supra* note 60, at 10802. *See* also Vienna Convention on the Succession of States in Respect of Treaties arts 16, 11 and 12, Aug. 23, 1978, 1946 U.N.T.S. 3. (Hereinafter VCSSRT); Vienna Convention on Succession of States in Respect of State Property, Archives and Debts, Apr. 8, 1983, U.N. Doc. A/CONF.117/14 (1983).

600 IAN BROWNLIE, PRINCIPLES OF PUBLIC INTERNATIONAL LAW 650 (7th ed. 2008).

601 Okoth-Owiro, *supra* note 479, 10. (Remarking "[s]tate succession is an area of great uncertainty and controversy. Not many settled legal rules have emerged as yet ... In other words, it is not clear, from either writings on international law or the practice of states, how and to what extent a legal principle of state succession applies in the sense of the transmissibility of rights and obligations from one state to another.") Jeffrey Azarva, *Conflict on The Nile: International Watercourse Law and the Elusive Effort to Create a Transboundary Water Regime in The Nile Basin*, 25 TEMP. INT'L & COMP. L.J. 473 (2011).

602 *See, e.g.*, Shih & Stutz, *supra* note 60 at 10802 ("The Committee on State Succession set up by the International Law Association (ILA) in 1961 examined the effect of independence on treaties, and after four years of study felt that 'the problem is too novel and the practice insufficiently coherent to permit it to take attitude with respect to the law.'" (quoting PRAKASH MENON, THE SUCCESSION OF STATE IN RESPECT OF TREATIES, STATE PROPERTY, ARCHIVES, AND DEBT 118, viii (1991) (quoting THE EFFECT OF INDEPENDENCE ON TREATIES: A HANDBOOK, THE INTERNATIONAL LAW ASSOCIATION xiii (1965)))). *see* also Helal, *supra* note 86, 907; Matthew C.R. Craven, *The Problem of State Succession and the Identity of States under International Law*, 9 EURO. J. INT'L L. 142, 148 (1998).

603 Shih & Stutz, *supra* note 60 at 10802–10803.

604 *see* HUGO GROTIUS, THE RIGHTS OF WAR AND PEACE 684 (Richard Tuck, ed. 2005) (1625).

605 *Id, See, e.g.*, Shih & Stutz, *supra* note 60 at 10802; *Craven, supra* note 602, 147–48; Fisseha, *supra* note 596 , 178–79; MAKONNEN, *supra* note 354, 129–32; Yilma Makonnen, *State Succession in Africa: Selected Problems*, 200 RECUEIL DES COURS 93, 104 (1987).

606 *Id*, 107; *Craven, supra* note 602, 147–48; Fisseha, *supra* note 596, 178–79; MAKONNEN, *supra* note 354, 132–36.

and obligations of the predecessor do not automatically transfer to the new state.[607]

3.3.1 *The Vienna Convention on State Succession in Respect of Treaties*

The debate surrounding these theories was apparent in the development of the Vienna Convention on State Succession in Respect of Treaties (hereinafter VCSSRT). Max Huber, a renowned international law scholar, advocated for the doctrine of "universal continuity," while scholars such as Berriedale Keith went "to the other extreme and den[ied] that there can be any succession to treaty rights and obligations."[608] The final draft reconciled these two extreme positions, "embracing the 'clean slate' doctrine for the newly independent states that emerged during decolonization while maintaining a limited set of important exceptions to the 'clean slate' that survive state succession."[609] Those exceptions include[610] boundary and territorial regimes: both remained unaffected by state succession, meaning that new states could not suddenly become free from previous boundary and territorial obligations.[611]

In this regard, Article 11 of the VCSSRT, addressing boundary regimes, stipulates that state succession does not affect "a boundary established by a treaty; or … obligations and rights established by a treaty and relating to the regime of a boundary."[612] During the drafting of the VCSSRT, this Article was supported by the overwhelming majority of states.[613] "States had described article 11 as right, reasonable, balanced and realistic, incontestable, well-established and universally recognized, or in full harmony with State practice and the general

607 Makonnen, *supra* note 605, 107; *Craven, supra* note 602, 147–48; Fisseha, *supra* note 596, 178–79; MAKONNEN, *supra* note 354, 132–36.

608 *See also* Shih & Stutz, *supra* note 60, at 10802–03 (describing the distinctions between Huber and Keith's perspectives, and quoting Menon, *supra* note 602, vii).

609 Shih & Stutz, *supra* note 60, 10803.

610 Article 16 of the VCSSRT recognized the clean slate theory, proclaiming that "[a] newly independent State is not bound to maintain in force, or to become a party to, any treaty by reason only of the fact that at the date of the succession of States the treaty was in force in respect of the territory to which the succession of States relates." VCSSRT, *supra* note 599, art 16.

611 *Id*, arts 11 & 12.

612 *Id*, art 11 (a), (b) & (c).

613 1974 Report, *supra* note 523, 199¶ 10 (Cognizant of the fact that "[t]he exception of treaties establishing a boundary from the fundamental change of circumstances rule … was endorsed by a very large majority of the States at the United Nations Conference on the Law of Treaties," the International Law Commission (ILC) concluded that the policy justification that necessities the exception applies "with the same force to a succession of States" and that "the attitude of States towards boundary treaties at the United Nations Conference on the Law of Treaties is extremely pertinent also in the present Convention.")

principles of international law."[614] Determined to avoid the instabilities that would emanate from renegotiating boundaries,[615] almost all states considered the proposal as a codification of customary international law.[616]

Of the colonial Nile Waters Treaties, only the 1902 Anglo-Ethiopian Treaty makes assertions regarding boundary demarcations.[617] But those portions of the treaty are isolated from Article III, which deals exclusively with the use of the Blue Nile, Lake Tana, and Sobat River within Ethiopian territory.[618] This segmentation raises questions about whether the customary international law boundary regime exception, as codified in Article 11 of the VCSSRT, applies to Article III of the Treaty. Article 11 of the VCSSRT applies only to boundaries; it does not apply to the validity or "the continuance in force or otherwise of a treaty between the parties."[619] It explicitly distinguishes boundary regimes from the treaties establishing the boundary[620] and exclusively governs only "the effect of the succession of States on the boundary settlement."[621] It follows that Article III of the 1902 Anglo-Ethiopian Treaty is not about boundary settlement and should therefore be treated separately from the provisions governing the Sudanese-Ethiopian boundary. Therefore, the boundary regime exception should not apply to Article III of the 1902 Anglo-Ethiopian Treaty.

The other exception relevant to the colonial Nile Waters Treaties regards the territorial regimes. Article 12 of the VCSSRT stipulates:

---

614 Int'l L. Comm., United Nations Conference on Succession of States in Respect of Treaties: First Sessions, Official Records, at 119 (1977), https://digitallibrary.un.org/record/57002?ln=en (hereinafter 1977 United Nations Conference).

615 *Id.* Endorsing article 11, the delegate of Ghana underlined that the article "was of overriding importance for the maintenance of international peace and security." *Id.* The delegate of Hungary also remarked that: "article 11 was linked with the need to establish international peace and security." *Id.* Similarly, India affirmed that this provision was "vital to the maintenance of world peace and security ... and that chaos would ensue if newly independent States unilaterally repudiated the boundaries they had inherited." *Id.* at 121.

616 *See id.* 122–23. Almost all delegates supported ILC's conclusion that "[t]he weight of the evidence of State practice and of legal opinion in favor of the view that in principle a boundary settlement is unaffected by the occurrence of a succession of States is strong and powerfully reinforced by the decision of the United Nations Conference on the Law of Treaties to except from the fundamental change of circumstances rule a treaty which establishes a boundary." 1974 Report, *supra* note 523, 201¶ 17.

617 *See generally*, 1902 Anglo-Ethiopian Treaty, *supra* note 124.

618 *Id*, Article III.

619 1974 Report, *supra* note 523, 201¶ 18. (Stating "in the present draft the question is not the continuance in force or otherwise of a treaty between the parties; it is the obligations and rights which devolve upon a successor State").

620 *Id*, 201 ¶ 18; VCSSRT, *supra* note 5995, art 11.

621 1974 Report, *supra* note 523, 201¶ 18.

1. A succession of States does not as such affect:
   (a) obligations relating to the use of any territory, or to restrictions upon its use, established by a treaty for the benefit of any territory of a foreign State and considered as attaching to the territories in question;
   (b) rights established by a treaty for the benefit of any territory and relating to the use, or to restrictions upon the use, of any territory of a foreign State and considered as attaching to the territories in question.
2. A succession of States does not as such affect:
   (a) obligations relating to the use of any territory, or to restrictions upon its use, established by a treaty for the benefit of a group of States or of all States and considered as attaching to that territory;
   (b) rights established by a treaty for the benefit of a group of States or of all States and relating to the use of any territory, or to restrictions upon its use, and considered as attaching to that territory.[622]

The International Law Commission's (ILC) commentary explains how the article should be interpreted. The commentary includes in its definition of territorial regimes, the "rights of transit on international waterways or over another State, [and] the use of international rivers."[623] The ILC also states: "Treaties concerning water rights or navigation on rivers are commonly regarded as candidates for inclusion in the category of territorial treaties."[624] It then mentions the 1929 Anglo-Egyptian Treaty but notes that its parties disputed the Treaty's validity.[625]

Applying the territorial treaty exception provided in the VCSSRT to all colonial Nile Waters Treaties, Samir Ahmed argues that "[i]t is an agreed principle of international law that such territorial status agreements constitute an obligation and a limitation on the contracting parties' territory, unaffected by a

622 VCSSRT, *supra* note 599, art 12.

623 1974 Report, *supra* note 523, 196–197. Commenting on Article 12, ILC remarked: "The question of what will for convenience be called in this commentary "territorial treaties" is at once important, complex and controversial. In order to underline its importance the Commission need only mention that it touches such major matters as international boundaries, rights of transit on international waterways or over another State, *the use of international rivers*, demilitarization or neutralization of particular localities, etc." *Id.*

624 *Id*, 203 ¶ 26.

625 *Id.* ¶ 27.

change of sovereignty … They cannot be amended or abrogated except by the agreement of the signatories or in accordance with the measures stipulated by the Vienna Convention on the Law of Treaties of 1969."[626] Concurring with Ahmed, Shih & Stutz also characterize the colonial Nile Waters Treaties as territorial in nature, and argue that all the Nile Basin States "are bound by treaty not to interfere with the flow to Egypt of the Nile's waters."[627] Any arguments to the contrary, they submit, "simply do not stand up to international law."[628]

Given that both Ahmed and Shih & Stutz relied on the VCSSRT to justify the continued validity of the colonial Nile Waters Treaties, one may expect that the VCSST is the proper authority. But, according to its own Article 7 ¶ 1, the VCSST applies only to the succession of states that occurred after the Convention's entry into force in 1996.[629] The succession of the Nile Basin States occurred long before then.[630] The VCSSRT does not provide controlling authority that justifies the continued validity of the colonial Nile Waters Treaties.

And so the question remains: what law governs the fate of the colonial Nile Waters Treaties? The doctrine of intertemporal law, as articulated in the Island of Palmas arbitration case, provides a valuable contribution to this inquiry. There Judge Huber found, "[a] juridical fact must be appreciated in the light of the law contemporary with it, and not of the law in force at the time when a dispute in regard to it arises or falls to be settled."[631] The doctrine, now recognized in customary international law,[632] necessitates evaluating the ramifications of Nile Basin States' succession using under the rules then in effect. In

626 Ahmed, *supra* note 480, 355.

627 Shih & Stutz, *supra* note 60, 10805.

628 *Id.*

629 VCSSRT, *supra* note 599, art 7 ¶1.

630 MAKONNEN, *supra* note 354, at 30–35 (Underlining that Britain's East African colonies gained their full independence in the early 1960s: Sudan in 1956, Tanganyika in 1961 (now Tanzania after unifying with Zanzibar), Uganda in 1962, and Kenya in 1963).

631 Island of Palmas (U.S. v. Neth.), II R.I.A.A. 829, 845 (Perm. Ct. Arb. 1928).

632 *Id. See* also Taslim O. Elias, *The Doctrine of Intertemporal Law*, 74 AM. J. INT'L L. 285 (1980) (Noting that "[t] he doctrine may also be regarded as having general applicability in various fields of customary international law … Judge Max Huber's famous arbitral award in that case made it clear that the doctrine is of general applicability in customary international law.") Over the years, the principle has been applied in several court decisions. *See*, e.g., Minquiers and Ecrehos, (Fr. V. U.K.) 1953 I.C.J. Rep. (Nov. 17) ; Dispute Regarding Navigational and Related Rights (Costa Rica v. Nicar.), Judgment, 2009 I.C.J. Rep. 213 (July 13); Rights of Nationals of United States of America in Morocco (Fr. v. U.S.), Judgment, 1952 I.C.J. Rep. 193 (Aug. 27); Island of Palmas, II R.I.A.A. at 845; Grisbadarna (Nor. v. Swed.) XI R.I.A.A. 155 (Perm. Ct. Arb. 1909).

other words, the customary international law applicable during the succession of the Nile Basin States governs the fate of colonial treaties.

3.3.2 *The Intertemporal Customary International Law*

Since the applicable intertemporal law varies case by cases bases, this section analyses its application in 1902 and 1929 separately.

3.3.2.1 The Intertemporal Law for the 1929 Anglo-Egyptian Treaty

According to the doctrine of intertemporal law, the fate of the 1929 Anglo-Egyptian Treaty should be determined by customary international law around state succession as it existed when Tanzania, Uganda, and Kenya gained their independence in the early 1960s. Determining the customary international law of that era requires a look at state practice, the norms and governance of international organizations like the United Nations, and the drafting history of the VCSSRT.

State practice relied heavily on the clean slate doctrine, which perfectly suited the purpose of colonial exploitation, as the rule of governing state succession arising from colonization.[633] For instance, when France occupied Madagascar in 1896, it disavowed all obligations of Madagascar.[634] Similarly, when Great Britain occupied Burma in 1866, it rejected all of the former obligations of Burma.[635] But after the Second World War the European colonial powers, particularly Britain, changed tack and began supporting the doctrine of "universal succession" or "universal continuity."[636] The colonial powers, seeing their roles shift to that of predecessor states, sought to maintain their interests in perpetuating "colonial domination and exploitation of African and Asian countries."[637] Newly independent states, advocating for a clean slate doctrine, strongly opposed these efforts by colonial powers to safeguard their colonial wealth through the doctrine of universal succession.[638]

---

633 MAKONNEN, *supra* note 354, 152–53. "None of the obligations of the Afro-Asian States were taken over or recognized by colonial powers." *Id.*

634 *Id.* It should be noted also that following the occupation of Algiers in 1830, France also rejected all former treaties concluded by Algiers with foreign powers. *Id.*

635 *Id.* Great Britain "denied that any obligations of the defunct State had passed *ipso facto* to new sovereign or that silence could be construed as implied assumption." *Id.*

636 *Id*, 157.

637 *Id.*

638 *Id*, 158. (Nothing that the "practice of most of the new States which achieved independence between 1945 and the 1960s also provide overwhelming evidence that the new States exercised their freedom of choice as to what they wished to take over from their respective predecessor States.")

Supporting the newly independent states, the United Nations also started following the clean slate doctrine. In 1947, when Pakistan asked for the continuity of its membership in the United Nations General Assembly based on the earlier membership of India, the UN Secretariate asserted: "The territory which breaks off, Pakistan, will be a new State. It will not have the treaty rights and obligations of the old State and will not of course have membership in the United Nations."[639] The UN was "inspired by the clean-slate doctrine [which] was the 'traditional' and generally accepted" law governing state succession at the time.[640] This was also apparent in its approach to treaty depositories: the Secretary-General always requested notification from newly independent states regarding their consent to be bound by treaties concluded by predecessor states.[641]

Though the clean-slate doctrine was widely applied, laws governing state succession remained controversial during the period of decolonization. In 1961, the International Law Association (ILA) established the Committee on State Succession to study the issue.[642] Examining the effect of independence on treaties and after four years of study, the ILA referred to the 1929 Anglo-Egyptian Treaty as "an agreement of a territorial character" that would continue to be "disputed" by the parties.[643] Emphasizing the disputed nature of the subject matter, the ILA concluded that "the problem is too novel and the practice insufficiently coherent to permit it to take [an] attitude with respect to the law."[644]

Subsequently, the ILC became interested in laws governing state succession and started drafting the VCLSST. Many jurists and scholars considered the Convention "an example of the progressive development of international law, rather than a codification of customary international law."[645] This assertive development in international law was met with mixed reviews. Daniel Patrick O'Connell argued that treaty succession was "a subject altogether unsuited to the processes of codification, let alone of progressive development."[646]

639 1974 Report, *supra* note 523, 211¶ 4.
640 *Id.*
641 MAKONNEN, *supra* note 354, 160.
642 Shih & Stutz, *supra* note 60, 10802.
643 *Id*, 1083 (Internal citation omitted).
644 *Id* (Internal citation omitted).
645 ANTHONY AUST, MODERN TREATY LAW AND PRACTICE 369 (2007).
646 D.P. O Connell, *Reflections on the State Succession Convention*, 39 ZEITSCHRIFT FÜR AUSLÄNDISCHES ÖFFENTLICHES RECHT UND VÖLKERRECHT 725, 726 (1979), http://www.zaoerv.de/39_1979/39_1979_4_a_725_739.pdf.

Meanwhile, Matthew G. Malone submitted that the Convention reflected "an altogether sensible compromise between conflicting interests."[647]

Unlike the ILC proposal on boundary regimes, Article 12 of the VCSSRT was particularly controversial during the drafting of the Convention. As noted by the U.S. representative, "article 12 was perhaps the one which had caused the International Law Commission the greatest difficulties,"[648] and according to the Italian delegate "[t]here was something disturbing, if not vaguely nightmarish" about that Article.[649] Three decades later after the VCSSRT entered into force in 1996, many jurists continued to support the clean-slate doctrine, arguing that Article 12, "imposes no requirement that treaties continue in operation with regard to newly independent states."[650]

Considering the inconsistency of state practice and the absence of *opinio juris* on the part of newly independent states when Article 12 was drafted,[651] the territorial treaty regime that it stipulated can hardly be regarded as customary international law at the time. And so without any territorial regime exception firmly in place, the clean-slate doctrine continued to govern the fate of the 1929 Anglo-Egyptian Treaty. It follows that the agreement's attendant obligations do not pass on to Tanzania, Kenya, and Uganda.

Article 12 has since attained the status of customary international law. For example, while determining the status of the 1977 Treaty Between the Hungarian Peoples Republic and the Czechoslovak Socialist Republic, in Gabčíkovo-Nagymaros case, the International Court of Justice (ICJ) remarked "that Article 12 reflects a rule of customary international law."[652] But, because of the inconsistent state practice and absence of *opinio juris*, the Article was far from reflecting international customary law in the early 1960s. Even if one were to consider the Article as customary international law, it does not bind Tanzania, Uganda, and Kenya: The three states, which have rejected the continuation of the 1929 Anglo-Egyptian Treaty obligations since decolonization,

647 Matthew G. Maloney, *Succession of States in Respect of Treaties: The Vienna Convention of 1978*, 19 VA. J. INT'L L. 885, 913–14 (1979).

648 Helal, *supra* note 86, 971 (Internal citation omitted).

649 *Id* (Internal citation omitted).

650 LUNG-CHU CHEN, AN INTRODUCTION TO CONTEMPORARY INTERNATIONAL LAW: A POLICY-ORIENTED PERSPECTIVE 488 (2015).

651 North Sea Continental Shelf Cases (Ger. v. Den.; Ger. v. Neth.), Advisory Opinions, 1969 I.C.J. 44, ¶ 77 (Feb. 20) (discussing the two elements of customary international law, state practice and *opinio juris*).

652 Gabčíkovo-Nagymaros Project (Hung./Slovk.), Judgment, 1997 I.C.J. 7, ¶ 123 (Sept. 25).

can claim the "persistent objector" exception to the development of territorial regime as customary international law.[653]

To invoke this exception, the three states should "persistently and openly" object to the territorial regime, while the practice was developing into a rule of customary international law.[654] They did so by rejecting the validity of colonial Nile Water Treaties and declaring the Nyerere doctrine as the governing principle of state succession. Moreover, during the drafting of the VCLSST, Tanzania, and Kenya advocated for the nullification of treaties that restricted their ability to exploit natural resources within their territories.[655] Tanzania, calling for the total exclusion of draft Article 12, stated: "The international servitudes which article 12 sought to create in favor of other States in the territory of a successor State constituted an endorsement of former colonial situations and were inconsistent with the independent status of the successor State."[656] Opposing draft Article 12, Kenya suggested revisions to recognize the right of newly independent states to terminate territorial obligations established by predecessor states and renegotiate new treaties that would protect "the vital interests of [the] beneficiary State[s] [without] jeopardizing the successor States' independence."[657] The three states continue to vehemently oppose a territorial regime exception to clean-slate doctrine and reject the validity of the 1929 Anglo-Egyptian Treaty to this day.[658] As "persistent objectors," they are not bound by Article 12 despite its current status as customary international law. It follows from this analysis that Tanzania, Uganda, and Kenya did not inherit the obligations that Britain stipulated in the 1929 Anglo-Egyptian Treaty, and that Egypt lacks veto power over upstream projects in their territories.[659]

653 Fisheries case (United Kingdom v. Norway), Judgment of 18 December 1951, ICJ Reports, 1951, p. 116 ff., p. 131.

654 Int'l L. Ass'n, Comm. on Formation of Customary (Gen.) Int'l L., *Statement of Principles Applicable to the Formation of General Customary International* Law, art 15 (2000).

655 1977 United Nations Conference, *supra* note 614, at 131, ¶ 25 & 135.

656 *Id*, 131, ¶ 25.

657 *Id.* at 135.

658 *See generally* OKOTH-OWIRO, *supra* note 479 (articulating the position of the Nile Basin States on the territorial regime and colonial Nile waters treaties).

659 It should be noted that the restrictions provided in the 1929 Anglo-Egyptian Treaty were included based on the political and economic interests of Great Britain. The Treaty was not concluded to establish perpetual obligations and does not create a territorial regime as contemplated in article 12 of the VCSSRT. In this regard, the report of the 1925 joint commission—annexed in and an integral part of the 1929 Anglo-Egyptian Treaty—states: "The Commission foresees that it will be necessary from time to time to review the questions discussed in this Report." Exchange of notes of January 26, 1925, *supra* note 503, ¶ 89. Therefore, even assuming, *arguendo*, that 12 of the VCSSRT is controlling authority, the 1929 Anglo-Egyptian Treaty cannot be considered a territorial treaty, and as such

3.3.3.2 The Intertemporal Law for 1902 Anglo-Ethiopian Treaty

The fate of the 1902 Anglo-Ethiopian Treaty also depends on the customary international law governing state succession when relevant states succeeded prior ones. Here, that was 1956, when Sudan gained independence.[660] As noted above, the clean-slate doctrine was the governing rule of state succession during the 1950s.[661] But later, the territorial regime exception began to gain purchase in customary international law.[662] Unlike the former British colonies that persistently objected to the development of this exception, Ethiopia supported the ILC draft Article 12 during the drafting of the VCSSRT in 1977.[663] Supporting the draft Article 12 at the United Nations 19th meeting regarding the question of succession of States in respect of treaties, Ethiopia asserted:

> The provisions of article 12 could affect the vital interests of countries, particularly in the sphere of rights relating to water, navigation and transit, which could not be compromised without endangering peace and security. The article was more particularly concerned with economic questions, and to delete it might compromise the economic situation of the States concerned or even "strangle" certain countries. Since the rule stated in article 12 was firmly based on international law, and in view of the facts which had to be faced in regard to international servitudes, there was no alternative but to accept the International Law Commission's text.[664]

Given this history of support for the territorial regime exception as a principle of international law, Ethiopia can hardly invoke the clean-slate doctrine to object to the transfer of rights from the 1902 Anglo-Ethiopian Treaty to Sudan. Ethiopia similarly cannot invoke the "persistent objector" doctrine to argue against the customary status of Article 12 of the VCSSRT. Accordingly, Article 12 determines the fate of the 1902 Anglo-Ethiopian Treaty. The Treaty established

---

Tanganyika, Kenya, and Uganda did not inherit any right or obligation stipulated in the Treaty.

660 Egypt's independence in 1918 is irrelevant because it cannot inherit a right, if there is any, from the Treaty. This is because Great Britain concluded Treaty only for Sudan. The Treaty is about boundary delineation between Ethiopia and Sudan, and Article III of the English version mentions only "His Britannic Majesty's government and the Government of Sudan." *See generally* 1902 Anglo-Ethiopian Treaty, *supra* note 124.

661 1974 Report, *supra* note 523, 211¶ 4.

662 Gabčíkovo-Nagymaros Project (Hung./Slovk.), Judgment, 1997 I.C.J. 7, ¶ 123 (Sept. 25).

663 1977 United Nations Conference, *supra* note 614, at 133 ¶ 41.

664 *Id*, ¶ 42.

a perpetual arrangement, "binding on [the parties] themselves, their heirs and successors."[665] It satisfies the requirements of the territorial regime exception as provided in the VCSSRT. It follows that upon independence, Sudan inherited the rights and obligations set out by the Treaty, including Article III's governance of water resources.

It should be remembered, however, that Article III of the 1902 Anglo-Ethiopian Treaty requires Ethiopia to get prior authorization from Great Britain for construction or approval of works on and across the Blue Nile, Lake Tana, or Sobat River (not in their tributaries) that would arrest or completely block the flow of their waters to the White Nile. Since Sudan inherited Britain's right to consent, Ethiopia may therefore be required to obtain Sudanese consent before initiating these types of undertakings.

3.4 Fundamental Change of Circumstances

"*Rebus sic stantibus*," or the principle of fundamentally changed circumstances, presents another approach to nullifying the colonial Nile Waters Treaties. The principle, codified in Article 62 of the VCLT,[666] and recognized as customary international law,[667] "allow[s] state parties to an agreement to withdraw from or terminate an agreement due to a fundamental change of circumstances that occurred after its conclusion."[668] However, reliance on *rebus sic stantibus* to abrogate some of the colonial Nile Waters Treaties faces challenges: the VCLT carved out exceptions to the doctrine, stipulating that a fundamental change of circumstances may not be invoked to terminate or withdraw from a treaty that establishes a boundary.[669] The 1902 Anglo-Ethiopian Treaty establishes the Sudanese-Ethiopian boundary. So it can be hard to imagine that *rebus sic stantibus* may apply to this Treaty. But the Treaty is not a monolith: while some parts of the 1902 Anglo-Ethiopian Treaty demarcate boundaries, Article III's focus is on the Nile and its sources in Ethiopia.[670] "If only parts of the treaty contain rules on boundaries," the *rebus sic stantibus* principle can "still

665 1902 Anglo-Ethiopian Treaty, *supra* note 124, preamble.
666 VCLT, *supra* note 520, art 62.
667 Gabčíkovo-Nagymaros Project (Hung./Slovk.), Judgment, 1997 I.C.J. 7, ¶ 104 (Sept. 25); Fisheries Jurisdiction (Federal Republic of Germany v. Iceland), Judgment, 1973, I.C.J. ¶ 43 (Feb. 2).
668 *See* VCLT, *supra* note 520, art. 62 (1); *See* also MALCOLM N. SHAW, INTERNATIONAL LAW, 951 (6TH ed. 2008).
669 VCLT, *supra* note 520, art. 62 ¶ 2 (a).
670 *See* 1902 Anglo-Ethiopian Treaty, *supra* note 124, art. III.

be invoked in respect of the remainder of [non-boundary related]...provisions."[671] Therefore, the principle of fundamentally changed circumstances may well apply to the 1902 Treaty.

If so, it can be argue that in addition to decolonization, the ever-increasing demand for water and water resources development in the Nile Basin, prompted by profound changes in the social and economic circumstances facing the upstream countries since the end of the 19th century, present the fundamental change of essential circumstances required.[672] When the 1902 and the 1929 colonial Nile Waters Treaties were signed, allocating the majority of the Nile waters to Egypt could arguably be justified by the British geopolitical interests and Egypt's thorough dependence on the Nile.[673] But due to rapid population growth, "the water availability, economic well-being, and health of the Nile Basin have so drastically changed in the past eight decades to fundamentally change the circumstances such that human rights are violated" in upstream countries.[674]

For centuries, Egypt used the Nile waters exclusively and ensure water and food security.[675] "While Egypt has demonstrated incredible improvement over the years in food security, water sanitation, access to drinking water, and human development, most of the other riparian countries have stayed stagnant or slipped backward. These countries are no longer able to sustain a minimal standard of living for their populations without additional sources of water."[676]

671 MARK E. VILLIGER, COMMENTARY ON THE 1969 VIENNA CONVENTION ON THE LAW OF TREATIES 775 (2009). ("[F]undamental change of circumstances may not be invoked as a ground for terminating or withdrawing from a treaty in *two* cases ... The *first* is if the treaty establishes a boundary (sub para. 2[a]). If only parts of the treaty contain rules on boundaries, the change may still be invoked in respect of the remainder of the provisions.")

672 Shih & Stutz, *supra* note 60, 10807.

673 *See generally* TVEDT, *supra* note 271; Shih & Stutz, *supra* note 60, 10807.

674 *Id.*

675 For a detailed analysis of Egypt's provision of water security, food security, and development, *see* Shih & Stutz, *supra* note 60, at 10809–10.

676 *Id*, 10808. The capacity of Nile Basin States to provide access to safe drinking water, sanitation, and electricity to their populations varies widely. Although substantial improvements have been made in providing safe drinking water to urban populations, most rural people, who constitute more than 75 percent of the entire Nile Basin population, still lack access to safe drinking water. *See* NBI 2016, *supra* note 58, at 61. Except in Egypt, where 99 percent of the population has access to improved drinking water, "the proportion of [the] rural population with access to safe drinking water is [extremely] low by international standards." *Id*, 61. The upstream states also lag behind Egypt in providing functioning sanitation: while 95–97 percent of Egypt's population has access to an improved sanitation facility, most residents of upstream states lack access. *Id.* In Ethiopia, for instance, less than 28 percent of the population has access to improved sanitation. *Id.*

Historically, upstream states have relied on rainfed agriculture. Droughts left their populations vulnerable to hunger and starvation.[677] Millions died prematurely from hunger and malnutrition-related illnesses.[678] "Clearly other sources of water in upper riparian countries are not enough to develop the irrigable land," and ensure food security.[679] If upstream countries continue to rely on rainfed agriculture, many more millions of people will face hunger and starvation.

Upstream states are not alone in facing changed circumstances: Egypt's water needs have also changed fundamentally since colonization. Back then, Egypt's economy was entirely dependent on irrigation and cotton production.[680] Now, the economy is less dependent on agriculture, which composes only 11.7 percent of GDP and supplies 25.8 percent of jobs.[681] Although agricultural crops remain one of Egypt's main exports,[682] this economic interest alone may not justify existing inequitable water allocations. It is arguably unreasonable "to justify allocating water for Egypt's cotton growth when other States do not have enough water for drinking and growing food."[683] Egypt has also

---

The same is true for electricity. Outside of Egypt, where the entire population has access to electricity, the percentage of populations with access to electricity in the Basin remains extremely low by global standards. *Id*, 62. The upstream states provide electricity access to between 4 and 27 percent of their population. *Id*. On a per capita basis, electricity consumption reveals a stark contrast: "Egypt's … consumption is more than double the combined per capita electricity consumption of 6 Nile Basin countries." *Id*. In terms of development, Egypt is more generally developed than the other Nile Basin States. UNITED NATIONS DEVELOPMENT PROGRAM, HUMAN DEVELOPMENT REPORTS (2020), http://hdr.undp.org/en/indicators/137506# (Egypt ranks 116th out of 189 countries for the highest Human Development Index (HDI). *Id*. Burundi ranks 188th, South Sudan ranks at 185th, Eritrea 180th, DRC 175th, Ethiopia 173rd, Sudan 170th, Tanzania 162nd, Rwanda 160th, Uganda 159th, and Kenya 143rd. *Id*. Egypt has the highest Gross Domestic Product (GDP) and Gross National Income (GNI) in the region, followed by Sudan compare to other Nile Basin countries. NBI 2016, *supra* note 58, 59. Almost the entire Egyptian population lives above the income poverty line. *Id*, 60 Meanwhile, poverty is widespread in the Nile Basin countries: "by income alone, more than 40 % of the population of most of the Nile basin countries lives on less than the international poverty line of 1.25 dollars a day (in purchasing powers parity terms)." *Id*.

677 Thurow, *supra* note 105.

678 Reid, *supra* note 462.

679 Shih & Stutz, *supra* note 60, 10809.

680 *See generally*, Tvedt, *supra* note 266 (elaborating how Egypt's economy was dependent on irrigation and cotton production during colonization).

681 *Egypt, The World Factbook*, CENTRAL INTELLIGENCE AGENCY (2021) https://www.cia.gov/the-world factbook/countries/egypt/#economy.

682 *Egypt's agricultural exports hit $1.25 billion in first half of 2021/2022*, EGYPT TODAY, March 31, 2022.

683 Shih & Stutz, *supra* note 60, 10810.

benefitted from the discovery of substantial groundwater resources and the continued development of desalination technology,[684] making it less dependent on the Nile waters that it was during colonization. It can therefore be argued that circumstances across the Nile Basin have changed so fundamentally that the colonial Nile Waters Treaties cannot remain binding.[685] "To abrogate them would be to uphold the rule of law."[686]

But the mere existence of these socioeconomic and geopolitical changes does not alone abrogate the treaties. Per ICJ's decision in the Gabciıkovo–Nagymaros Project case, *rebus sic stantibus* would apply only if these changes were unforeseen during the conclusion of the colonial Nile Waters Treaties.[687] The decolonization of the Nile Basin States; the rapid population growth in the Basin; the ever-increasing demand for Nile waters in upstream countries; the importance of the Nile waters to ensure water security, food security, and human development in upstream countries; the existence of alternative water resources (ground water and desalination technology) in downstream countries all were not foreseen during the conclusion of the 1902 and 1929 treaties.[688] Therefore, the upstream Nile Basin States can invoke *rebus sic stantibus* principle and nullify the colonial Nile Waters Treaties.

Conclusion

The foregoing analysis regarding the status of the colonial Nile Waters Treaties under international law yields several conclusions. First, while the international law of state succession invalidates most of the colonial Nile Waters Treaties, the 1902 Anglo-Ethiopian Treaty may have survived state succession due to Ethiopia's support and willful admission of the territorial exception to the "clean slate" doctrine. However, in recognizing Italy's invasion of Ethiopia, and the inclusion of Ethiopia's territories into the Italian East Africa colony,[689] Britain committed a material breach of the 1902 Anglo-Ethiopia Treaty.

684 *See* Morton, *supra* note 82; David L. Chandle, *Solar-Powered System Offers a Route to Inexpensive Desalination*, MIT, Feb. 14. 2022. https://news.mit.edu/2022/solar-desalination-system-inexpensive-0214.

685 Shih & Stutz, *supra* note 60, 10810.

686 *Id.*

687 Gabciıkovo–Nagymaros (Hung. v. Slovak.), Judgement, 1997 I.C.J Rep. 56, 65, ¶ 104 (Sept. 19970).

688 For a detailed analysis of Egypt's provision of water security, food security, and development, *see* Shih & Stutz, *supra* note 60, at 10809-10.

689 Parker, *supra* note 551, 293.

Therefore, per Article 60 of the VCLT, Ethiopia is allowed to terminate Article III of the Treaty, at least.

Even if Ethiopia is not allowed to invoke Article 60 of the VCLT, the obligation imposed in the 1902 Anglo-Ethiopian Treaty does not prohibit Ethiopia from equitably using the Nile waters without Britain's consent (or now that of Sudan). The treaty requires Great Britain's consent only for works on the Blue Nile, Lake Tana, and Sobat river (not on the tributaries) that would completely stop up or block up their water flow. Finally, this chapter submits that the circumstances under which the colonial Nile Waters Treaties were executed have changed so fundamentally that they are no longer valid under international law. "The degree of water and food scarcity in the upstream countries today is so dire and so fundamentally different than during the colonial era" that under *Rebus sic stantibus* doctrine the treaties can be abrogated.[690]

The logic underlying the colonial Nile Waters Treaties was a desire to prohibit upstream states from utilizing the waters of the Nile without the consent of those downstream. This conception, which violates the very foundation of international watercourses law,[691] is no longer viable. The colonial treaties simply do not have the intrinsic capacity for addressing the many challenges facing the Nile watercourse.[692] Although contracted by independent states, the 1959 Agreement is not better. In stark contrast with modern international watercourses law, it allocates the entire flow of the Nile between Egypt and Sudan. The next chapter focuses on this agreement and other principles of customary international law relevant to the Nile Basin.

---

690 Shih & Stutz, *supra* note 60, 10822.

691 *See* discussion *infra* section 4.2.

692 Carroll, *supra* note 523, 275.

CHAPTER 4

Legal Arguments Based on the 1959 Agreement and Customary International Law

Introduction

As has already been seen, Chapters 2 and 3 investigated the geopolitics of the Nile Basin during the precolonial, colonial, and Cold War periods, and determined the status of colonial Nile Waters Treaties. This chapter examines the legal arguments based on the 1959 Agreement and customary international law. It begins by overviewing the negotiation history and the content of the 1959 Agreement. After briefly introducing the dispute over Sudan's unused "share" of the Nile waters, this chapter then turns to scrutinize the ramifications of the 1959 Agreement vis-à-vis upstream states and the newly independent State of South Sudan. Finally, this chapter encapsulates basic customary international watercourses law principles and determines their relevancy in the Nile Basin.

4.1 The 1959 Agreement

The 1959 Agreement is a source of dispute between the Nile Basin States.[693] Egypt and Sudan allocated the entire flow of the Nile to themselves in this Agreement.[694] They further invoked "historic rights" and "established rights" doctrines and claim that they are legally entitled to the water share allocated in the Agreement.[695] As non-signatory third parties, the upstream states vehemently rejected this claim and considered the 1959 Agreement as an infringement of their rights to an equitable share of the Nile watercourse and demanded the adoption of a new legal framework that would protect their interests.[696]

693 Salman, *supra* note 172, 19.

694 1959 Agreement, *supra* note 106, arts I–II.

695 Salman, *supra* note 172, 19.

696 *Id*; Valerie Knobelsdorf, *The Nile Waters Agreements: Imposition and Impacts of a Transboundary Legal System*, 44 COLUM. J. TRANSNAT'L L 633 (2006) ("In the cases of Ethiopia, Tanzania, and Kenya, national leaders have directly refused to be bound by the 1929 and 1959 Agreements, arguing that these were signed on their nations' behalf and without their consultation.") *See* also Mekonnen, *supra* note 172, 355 (Stating that "the

 | DOI:10.1163/9789004549869_005

Although the Nile Basin States negotiated a basin-wide cooperative framework for 13 years, an all-inclusive legal agreement could not be reached because of their dispute over the exciting Nile Waters Treaties.[697] At the height of the dispute, the people of South Sudan seceded from Sudan and declared their independence in January 2011.[698] The birth of South Sudan has brought about new dimensions to the dispute, involving several adjacent areas of international law including the law of state succession, international law of treaties, and the law of non-navigational uses of international watercourses.[699]

There are three fundamental legal questions worth asking regarding the 1959 Agreement: (1) Does the 1959 Agreement invalidate the 1929 Anglo-Egyptian Treaty? (2) Are the upstream states bound by the water allocation provided for in the 1959 Agreement? (3) Is the 1959 Agreement binding on South Sudan? This section answers those questions, after reflecting on the negotiating history and content of the Agreement.

4.1.1 *The 1959 Agreement: Negotiating History, Content, and Dispute over Water Loan*

As noted in Chapter 2, Sudan was planning to construct the Roseires Dam on the Blue Nile and expand the Gezira irrigation scheme in 1954.[700] However, with the water rights of Sudan already reaching the limits of 4 BCM under the 1929 Anglo-Egyptian Treaty, the implementation of these projects was not possible. Hence, following its independence in 1956, Sudan "formally stated that she did not consider herself bound by a treaty [the 1929 Anglo-Egyptian Treaty] entered into on her behalf by the British."[701] On the other hand, Egypt, committed to providing for its future water security, decided, in 1952, to build a high dam at Aswan, whose reservoir would extend some 250 kilometers into Sudan.[702] Sudan protested the dam not only because it was not informed of

pattern of inter-riparian relationship has long been a tug of war between the two downstream riparians, which strive to endlessly perpetuate the *status quo,* and the upstream riparians, which call for its demise and replacement by an inclusive, fair and equitable regime.")

697 *See* discussion *infra* sections 5.3 & 6.1.

698 Helal, *supra* note 86, 912–14; Salman, *supra* note 86, 344; Salman M.A. Salman, *The New State of South Sudan and the Hhydro-Politics of the Nile Basin,* 36 WATER INT'L 154–166 (2011); *see* also generally, Charles L. Katz, *Another Cup at the Nile's Crowded Spigot: South Sudan and its Nile Water Rights,* 44 GEO. J. INT'L L 250–54 (2013).

699 Helal, *supra* note 86, 910–11.

700 COLLINS, *supra* note 64, at 166; COLLINS, *supra* note 119, at 251; TVEDT, *supra* note 271, at 267.

701 MCCAFFREY, *supra* note 4, at 313–14 (Internal citation omitted).

702 *Id.*

the technical details of the project, but also because it favored the early British plan—the Century Storage Scheme—with a number of smaller dams in Uganda and Ethiopia, and the Jonglei Canal in Sudan.[703]

Following protracted negotiations, Sudan accepted the construction of the AHD but submitted several preconditions for approving the project.[704] First, Sudan demanded that its "ultimate share in the natural flow of the river measured at Aswan should be determined before work was started on the High Dam."[705] Second, Sudan proposed the inclusion of an explicit provision in the future agreement, stipulating that it "would be free to build on the main river, or on any of its tributaries, any dams or control works which, in its opinion, were essential to the full utilization of its share."[706] This condition was intended to exonerate Sudan from the application of Article III of the 1929 Anglo-Egyptian Treaty, which granted the virtual veto power to Egypt over waterworks in Sudan and other former British East African colonies.[707] Third, Sudan insisted that "Egypt should bear the entire cost of transferring the displaced people," from the Sudanese village of Wadi Halfa.[708] "Sudan demanded a compensation of 35 million Egyptian pounds, while Egypt insisted on paying only 10 million pounds."[709] Finally, Sudan demanded that the net water benefit to be gained from the construction of the AHD should be divided "in ratio to the annual flow of the river. This could be done, [Sudan] maintained, on the basis of the relative population of both countries."[710] Egypt outright rejected Sudan's preconditions, contending "that the proposals produced by the Sudan delegation were most unreasonable, and that, had they been applied, Egypt would have had to sacrifice a part of her established right to her present share."[711]

---

703 *Id.*

704 Helal, *supra* note 86, 926. *See* also I.H. Abdalla, *The 1959 Nile Waters Agreement in Sudanese-Egyptian Relations*, 7 MIDDLE E. STUD. 331–32 (1971).

705 Abdalla, *supra* note 704, at 331–32.

706 *Id*, at 332.

707 *Id. see* also Helal, *supra* note 86, 926.

708 Abdalla, *supra* note 704, at 332; Helal, *supra* note 86, 926.

709 Salman, *supra* note 89, 86.

710 Abdalla, *supra* note 704, at 332.

711 *Id.* Explaining the advantage of this proposal for Sudan, Abdalla remarked: "As the Sudanese were not then expected to be less than half as numerous as the Egyptians, the Sudan would, accordingly, get not less than 28 milliards or one-third of the river's annual discharge. The division could also be effected on the basis of the potential irrigable lands in Egypt and the Sudan. This alternative proposal, if it were applied, would have given the Sudan even more water as the potential irrigable lands of the Sudan exceed by far those of Egypt." *Id.*

Although the two States continued a series of difficult negotiations, they could not strike a deal acceptable to them all. The stalemate continued "until political developments in Sudan provided the opportunity for a breakthrough."[712] In November 1958, General Ibrahim Abboud, who deposed the Sudanese Umma government with the help of Egypt, become the president of Sudan and broke the deadlocked negotiations over AHD.[713] On November 8, the Sudan and Egypt entered into the 1959 Nile Agreement.[714]

In terms of content, the 1959 Agreement includes a preamble, eight articles, and two annexes.[715] Contrary to Sudan's statements repudiating the previous treaty,[716] the preamble of the 1959 Agreement confirms it was concluded based on the 1929 Anglo-Egyptian Treaty.[717] Egypt and Sudan further recognized, in Article I of the 1959 Agreement, the allocation provided in the 1929 Anglo-Egyptian Treaty (48 BCM to Egypt and 4 BCM to Sudan) as the established rights of the two countries.[718]

Article II stipulates the "*quid pro quo*" obligations of the two countries.[719] Sudan endorsed the construction of AHD, and Egypt approved the construction of the Roseires Dam in Sudan.[720] Regarding water allocation, article II ¶ 4 of the Agreement estimated the 32 BCM gross gain expected after the construction of the AHD.[721] After deducting 10 BCM for evaporation and seepage,[722] this paragraph divides the remaining 22 BCM in a 2:1 ratio in favor of Sudan, or 14.5 BCM for Sudan and 7.5 BCM for Egypt.[723] Then, by adding the net benefits to

712 Helal, *supra* note 86, 927.

713 *Id*, COLLINS, *supra* note 119, 255; WATERBURY, *supra* note 121, 70–71; *Knobelsdorf, supra* note 696, 629.

714 1959 Agreement, *supra* note 106.

715 *Id.*

716 MCCAFFREY, *supra* note 4, at 313–14.

717 1959 Agreement, *supra* note 106, preamble ¶ 3; *Knobelsdorf, supra* note 696, 629. Helal, *supra* note 86, 927.

718 1959 Agreement, *supra* note 106, art I.

719 Helal, *supra* note 86, 927.

720 *Id. See* also 1959 Agreement, *supra* note 106, *Id*, art II, ¶ 1–2.

721 *Id*, art II, ¶ 4.

722 *Id.*

723 *Id;* As the 1929 Anglo-Egyptian Treaty determined the "established right[s]" of the two states, the 1959 Agreement allocated only the net benefit generated from the construction of the AHD. Of the 32 BCM gross gain expected after the construction of AHD, the Agreement deducts 10 BCM for evaporation and seepage, and divides the remaining 22. BCM in a two-to-one ratio in favor of Sudan or 14.5 BCM for Sudan and 7.5 BCM for Egypt. *Id.* art. II, ¶ 3–4. The net benefit is as follows:
Mean natural river supply at Aswan 84 BCM
Less over-year storage losses -10 BCM
Egypt's established right -48 BCM
Sudan's established right -4 BCM

the established rights of each State, it allocates 55.5 BCM to Egypt and 18.5 BCM to Sudan.[724] In article II ¶ 6, Egypt agreed to pay Sudan 15 million Egyptian Pounds as full compensation for damages incurred by the Sudanese residents of Wadi Halfa.[725]

Article III contemplates the possibility of implementing water conservation projects in Sudan and instructed the two States to share the construction costs and water benefits of such projects equally.[726] In particular, it specified projects for the prevention of water "loss" in the Sudd wetlands of Sudan.[727] Article IV establishes the Permanent Joint Technical Committee (PJTC) and sets forth its function, which is restricted to administrative matters like overseeing construction and storage works, and facilitation of cooperation between the two countries.[728]

Article V governs the relationship between the two parties to the agreement on one hand, and the other Nile Basin States, on the other.[729] If any question concerning the Nile waters needs negotiation with the governments of upstream countries, Egypt and Sudan would agree beforehand on a unified view based on the study to be conducted by PJTC.[730] "This unified view would henceforth form the basis of instructions to be followed by the Committee in the negotiations with the governments concerned."[731] Thus, Egypt and Sudan were able to create a downstream hydro-hegemonic alliance through the Committee.[732] Moreover, should these negotiations "results in the acceptance

Total net benefit 22 BCM

Gretta Goldenman, *Adapting to Climate Change: A Study of International Rivers and Their Legal Arrangements*, 17 ECOLOGY L.Q. 741, 753–54 (1990).

724 1959 Agreement, *supra* note 106, art II, ¶ 3–4.

725 *Id*, art II ¶ 6.

726 *Id*, art. III. While the article encourages the two states to undertake the projects jointly and share the water benefit and the total costs of the projects equally, it also allowed "Egypt a unilateral right to carry out such projects by itself if Sudan does not need such waters at that time." Salman, *supra* note 89, 88. The article gives Egypt the right to "carry out such a project by itself after notification of Sudan to this effect," means that Sudan's approval is not necessary. *Id*. "Thus, the provisions in the 1959 Agreement on the presence of the Egyptian irrigation staff in Sudan and the unilateral right of Egypt to build the canals in South Sudan have sealed the hydro hegemony of Egypt over Sudan and its Nile waters. Those provisions have raised serious concerns in Sudan as impinging on the sovereignty of Sudan." *Id*.

727 1959 Agreement, *supra* note 106, art. III.

728 *Id*, art. IV.

729 *Id*, art V.

730 *Id*, art V, ¶ 1.

731 Salman, *supra* note 89, 87.

732 *See* Salman, *supra* note 89, at 85–89.

of allotting an amount of the Nile water to" other riparian States, that "amount shall be deducted from the shares of the two Republics in equal parts, as calculated at Aswan."[733]

The last three Articles govern miscellaneous matters including, *inter alia*, the transitional period until the construction of AHD and enter into force of the Agreement.[734] Annex I provide for a special provision governing the water loan required by Egypt.[735] Here, Sudan agreed to grant Egypt a water loan of 1.5 BCM from its share of the Nile waters until 1977.[736] Although the notions of water loan assume repayment, there is nothing mentioned in the 1959 Agreement (or the Annex) as to when and how "the water loan would be repaid by Egypt to Sudan."[737] However, this is not surprising "because Sudan has failed since the conclusion of the 1959 Nile Waters Agreement to use more than 12 BCM of its share of 18.5 BCM specified in the Agreement."[738]

Sudan's concessions during the protracted negotiations, "particularly the submergence of Wadi Halfa town and its 27 villages, and the agreement to give Egypt a water loan helped eventually in increasing Sudan's share to 18.5 BCM."[739] Despite all these concessions, however, Sudan has failed to use 18.5 BCM from the inception of the Agreement until now.[740] Salman Mohammed Ahmed Salman, explaining this unfortunate reality, remarked:

> Indeed, from the very early days following the conclusion of the 1959 Agreement, it became clear to both sides that Sudan was only able to use no more than two-thirds, at best, of its Nile waters share of 18.5 BCM. Each side kept quiet about this fact for its own reasons. Sudan was hoping that this embarrassing and unfortunate situation would gradually change and Sudan would be able to put its Nile house in order by using its full

733 1959 Agreement, *supra* note 106, art V, ¶ 2. Commenting on this paragraph, Salman captured the unfortunate reality "that whatever Nile waters that may be allotted to another Nile riparian is the ultimate decision of the two parties (which may choose to allot none) and not a right to such a riparian under international water law. Indeed, under the Agreement, such allotted amount of the Nile waters to another riparian is more of a donation from Egypt and Sudan to such a riparian rather than a right." Salman, *supra* note 89, 87. Therefore, the 1959 Agreement is "not consistent at all with the cardinal principle of international water law of the equality of all the riparians to a shared watercourse." *Id.*

734 1959 Agreement, *supra* note 106, VI, VII & VIII.

735 *Id*, Annex 1.

736 *Id.*

737 Salman, *supra* note 89, 86.

738 *Id.*

739 *Id*, 89.

740 *Id*, 88.

> share of water allotted under the 1959 Agreement. Egypt, on the other hand, did not want to embarrass its allies in the Ministry of Irrigation in Khartoum by divulging this critical fact and was hoping at the same time that this happy and unexpected situation would become permanent.[741]

Although leading Nile water experts and international financial institutions have documented Sudan's failure to use its share of the Nile waters under the 1959 Agreement, Sudan's official answer has long been "unequivocal—Sudan was using its full and entire share of the Nile waters of 18.5 BCM allotted under the 1959 Agreement."[742] However, as recently as August 2011, "the then Sudanese Minister of Irrigation and Water Resources, Engineer Kamal Ali Mohamed, divulged the full story. ... that Sudan had only been using 12 BCM of its annual share of the Nile waters of 18.5 BCM" and that it "plans to use its full share."[743]

As discussed below, Sudan's unused "share" of the Nile waters is one of the most crucial and fundamental issues determining the entire Nile water relations between the two downstream States.[744] Egypt, invoking the notion of "existing use and rights," is claiming "every drop of water" that currently flows into the Lake Nasser reservoir of the AHD, including the waters that Sudan fails to use.[745] Sudan is insisting that its annual "share" of the Nile waters of 18.5 BCM should be respected.[746] Considering its unused water as a loan to Egypt, Sudan declared it "will soon stop its water loan to Egypt."[747] Egypt, in its part, is alleging "that Sudan has been using its full share of the Nile waters."[748]

4.1.2 *The Upstream States and the 1959 Agreement*

The 1959 Agreement between Sudan and Egypt is a subject of bitter controversy, both between downstream and upstream states and within academic discourse. Scholars have expressed "mixed reviews" regarding this Agreement.[749] For Samir Ahmed, the Agreement is "a model International River water-sharing agreement [that] contains some 'advanced' ideas and principles governing cooperation and sharing of efforts and burdens relative to the international

741 *Id*, 89.
742 *Id.*
743 *Id*, 90.
744 *See* the discussion *infra* section 8.1.1.
745 Salman, *supra* note 89, 100.
746 *Id.*
747 *Id*, 101.
748 *Id.*
749 Helal, *supra* note 86, 929.

river," including equity.[750] But to Salman, the Agreement violates "the cardinal principle of international water law," and presents a means of establishing downstream hegemonic control over the Nile.[751] A third view underlines the importance of the 1959 Agreement for the upstream countries and asserts that its conclusion abrogated the 1929 Anglo-Egyptian Treaty.[752] Yet another perspective threats the 1959 Agreement as binding upon all upstream states.[753]

The Agreement entailed several significant ramifications for upstream countries. First, while the establishment of the PJTC in the 1959 Agreement was a novel development at the time, assertions that the Agreement represents "a model International River' water-sharing agreement"[754] are vastly overstated. For starters, the Agreement does not "contain provisions for issues that have gained importance in modern times, such as environmental protection and sustainable river management."[755] Moreover, contrary to Ahmed's view that the Agreement includes "advanced" ideas and principles of equity and cooperation,[756] the regime it set forth fails to allocate the Nile watercourse in an equitable manner.[757] Instead, the Agreement allocates the entire flow of the Nile waters only to Egypt and Sudan, excluding the other Nile Basin States entirely.[758] "Even Ethiopia, the major contributor to Nile flow, does not receive an allocation. Thus, the current arrangement is not equitable and is not a practical system for regulating water quality and allocating water from a resource shared by [eleven] states."[759]

750 Ahmed, *supra* note 480, 357.

751 Salman, *supra* note 89, 85–89.

752 Joseph Dellapenna, *The Nile as a Legal and Political Structure, in* THE SCARCITY OF WATER 128, (Edward H.P. Brans et al. eds., 1997); C. O. Okidi, *History of the Nile Basin and Lake Victoria Basins Through Treaties, in* THE NILE: SHARING A SCARCE RESOURCE, 321, 329 (Paul P. Howell & J. Antonio Allan, eds., 1994); Fisseha, *supra* note 596, at 189; *see* Carroll, *supra* note 523, 279. (Reiterating Ethiopia's argument that "it could denounce the colonial Nile agreements, not only under the clean slate doctrine of state succession, but based on the Egyptian and Sudanese practice of denouncing treaties signed by Britain on their behalf if they no longer reflect their development needs.") *Id.* Mekonnen, *supra* note 135, 434–35. (Stating that the 1929 Anglo-Egyptian Treaty has "long been reduced to a thing of the past for Egypt and Sudan and, *a fortiori,* for the former British colonies of Kenya, Tanzania, and Uganda as well, as it was superseded by the 1959 Agreement"). For a similar assertion *see* Mekonnen *supra* note 172, 361; Mekonnen, *supra* note 525, 241–43.

753 *See* Knobelsdorf, *supra* note 669, 629.

754 Ahmed, *supra* note 480, 357.

755 Carroll, *supra* note 523, 282.

756 Ahmed, *supra* note 480, 357.

757 Carroll, *supra* note 523, 282.

758 1959 Agreement, *supra* note 106, art II, ¶ 3–4; *see* also *supra* note 723, and accompanying text.

759 Carroll, *supra* note 523, 282.

In addition to this inequitable allocation, and violation of the no significant harm rule,[760] the Agreement subordinates any possible water claims of upstream states to the "present acquired rights" of downstream states,[761] empowers Egypt and Sudan to allot (or not to allot) the Nile waters to the upstream states,[762] and tasks the PJTC to supervises the water consumption of upstream states.[763] These provisions support Salman's view that the 1959 Agreement is "not consistent at all with the cardinal principle of international water law of the equality of all the riparians to a shared watercourse."[764] Moreover, the fact that Egypt and Sudan agreed to hold a "unified view" in their engagement with upstream states[765] means that they created a downstream hydro-hegemonic alliance through the 1959 Agreement.[766]

Okidi, a proponent of the third view—the 1959 Agreement abrogated the 1929 Anglo-Egyptian Treaty—claims that "Egypt considered the 1929 Agreement temporary pending determination of the political future of the Sudan."[767] If the 1929 Anglo-Egyptian Treaty applied to the two downstream countries only temporarily, Okidi concludes, "there is no reason why it should have [a] longer life for Kenya, Tanzania, or Uganda."[768] He further asserts that in concluding the 1959 Agreement Egypt and Sudan "were beginning nearly with [a] *tabula rasa* as far as the utilization and control of Nile waters ... concerned."[769]

As demonstrated in Chapter 3, Kenya, Tanzania, and Uganda can very well challenge the 1929 Anglo-Egyptian Treaty based on the international law of state succession and fundamental change of circumstances.[770] However,

760 1959 Agreement, *supra* note 106, art II, ¶ 3–4; *see* also *supra* note 723, and accompanying text. Underlining the fact that "harm may, in effect, flow upstream, in the form of effective foreclosure of future uses in upstream states by virtue of the operation of the "no-harm" rule," McCaffrey remarked that the allocation strategy in 1959 Agreement "would seem on the face of it to leave little margin for upstream consumptive-use development without causing the downstream countries significant harm, and [is therefore] prima facie in violation of the 'no-harm' rule recognized under international watercourses law." MCCAFFREY, *supra* note 4, 317.

761 Azarva, *supra* note 601, 473.

762 1959 Agreement, *supra* note 106, art V, ¶ 2; *see* also *supra* note 733, and accompanying text.

763 1959 Agreement, *supra* note 106, art V, ¶ 2. (Stipulating that PJTC "shall make the necessary arrangements with the states concerned, in order to ensure that their water consumption shall not exceed the amounts agreed upon").

764 Salman, *supra* note 89, 85–89.

765 1959 Agreement, *supra* note 106, art V, ¶ 1.

766 *See* Salman, *supra* note 89, at 85–89.

767 Okidi, *supra* note 752, 329.

768 *Id.*

769 *Id*, 333.

770 *See* the discussion in Chapter 3.

Okidi's argument that the 1959 Agreement abrogated the 1929 Anglo-Egyptian Treaty faces significant objections. Although the *later-in-time*, or *lex posterior*, principle under international law permits states to supersede past treaties by concluding new ones governing the same matters, the principle applies only to states that are parties to both the former and latter treaties.[771] No upstream states—including Kenya, Tanzania, and Uganda, parties to the 1929 Agreement—are parties to the 1959 Agreement. And per the principle of privity of the treaty, the treaty does not create any right to the third parties.[772] The upstream states therefore cannot invoke the 1959 Agreement to invalidate the 1929 Anglo-Egyptian Treaty.

Instead of abrogating the 1929 Anglo-Egyptian Treaty, the 1959 Agreement explicitly recognized the prior legal framework and the rights and obligations it established.[773] Egypt and Sudan noted in the 1959 Agreement's preamble that it was an extension of the 1929 Anglo-Egyptian Treaty.[774] Article I of the 1959 Agreement also adopted the water allocation provided in the previous treaty (48 BCM to Egypt and 4 BCM to Sudan) as the established rights of the two countries.[775] This all suggests that the conclusion of the 1959 Agreement did not abrogate the 1929 Anglo-Egyptian Treaty, but rather intended to facilitate the "full utilization" of the Nile waters and the allocation of the additional water that would be generated from the construction of AHD.[776]

Finally, Valerie Knobelsdorf, articulating the fourth view, asserts that "the 1959 Agreement effectively bound all upstream riparians to the allocations" stipulated under the Agreement.[777] Concurring with Knobelsdorf, other Ethiopian scholas also suggest that Egypt and Sudan sought to bind upstream states as third parties to the 1959 Agreement.[778] It is clear that Egypt and Sudan

771 VCLT, *supra* note 520, art. 59.

772 *Id*, art. 34.

773 Shih & Stutz, *supra* note 60, 10801.

774 *Id. See* 1959 Agreement, *supra* note 106, preamble ¶ 3 (Reiterating that Egypt and Sudan agreed the 1959 Agreement because "the Nile waters Agreement concluded in 1929 provided only for the partial use of the Nile waters and did not extend to include a complete control of the River waters.")

775 *Id*, art I.

776 *Id* art. II, ¶ 3–4. *See also* Shih & Stutz, *supra* note 60, 10822.

777 *See* Knobelsdorf, *supra* note 696, 629.

778 See Shih & Stutz, *supra* note 60, 10802 (challenging Amdetsion's clime that "[b]oth countries continue to argue (and Egypt in particular) that all Nile riparian states must abide by the Agreement's terms, despite the fact that no upper riparian state was a party to the 1959 Agreement.") Mekonnen also attacks the 1959 Agreement based on privity of treaty. *See* Mekonnen, *supra* note 135, 435; Mekonnen *Declaration of Principles, supra* note 172, 260; Mekonnen, *supra* note 525, 243.

cannot bind upstream states, and the 1959 Agreement is devoid of any legal relevance vis-à-vis the non-signatory third parties.[779] But this is not the real legal question: Egypt's argument is that the allocation set out under the 1959 Agreement established a regional custom within the Nile Basin, which effectively bound—and still binds—upstream states.[780]

True, principles established by treaty can ultimately become customary law; but this requires consistent state practice and *opinio juris* over an extended period of time.[781] Here, there has been neither consistent state practice nor *opinio juris* that justifies the water allocation provided in the 1959 Agreement: disregarding the water allocation provided in the Agreement, in the intervening years, upstream states have planned and sometimes executed unilateral projects impacting the Nile River, effectively preventing the formation of consistent and uniform state practices.[782]

Notwithstanding these projects, upstream states have been largely unable to equitably use the Nile watercourse.[783] This lack of equitable use or substantial development results from the geopolitical complexities of the region, not out of respect for the 1959 Agreement.[784] The upstream states did not exercise forbearance in exploiting the Nile watercourse and constructing large-scale dams dam earlier out of any sense of legal obligation (*opinio juris*). Any such forbearance was due to a combination of other factors, including threats from Egypt[785] and a lack of funding from international financial institutions.[786]

---

779 VCLT, *supra* note 520, art. 34. *See also* Shih & Stutz, *supra* note 60, 10802.

780 *See* Salman, *supra* note 172, at 19 (Stating that Egypt and Sudan claim historical and established rights based on the Treaty). *See* also Azarva, *supra* note 601, at 469. ("Egypt continues to rely on the 1929 and 1959 agreements … invoking the notion of 'natural and historical rights.'")

781 *See* North Sea Continental Shelf Cases (Ger. v. Den.; Ger. v. Neth.), Advisory Opinions, 1969 I.C.J. 44, ¶ 77 (Feb. 20) (discussing the two elements of customary international law, state practice and *opinio juris*).

782 *See* the discussion in section 2.3. *See* also the discussion *infra* section 5.1.

783 *See generally*, THE RIVER NILE IN THE POST-COLONIAL AGE, *supra* note 81 (discussing the water resource development plans in each Nile Basin country).

784 *See* the discussion section 2.3.

785 As discussed in Chapter 2, Egyptian officials have previously been willing to threaten war on Ethiopia in their attempt to safeguard Egypt's hegemonic status in the Nile Basin. Early on, Anwar el-Sadat signaled that Egypt was ready to go to war to avert "any action that would endanger the water of [the] Blue Nile." In 1988, Boutros Boutros-Ghali, then Egyptian Minister of State of Foreign Affairs, also stated that "… the next war in our region will be over the waters of the Nile, not politics." Hosni Mubarak, former Egyptian President threatened to "bomb Ethiopia" if it built any dam on the Blue Nile. More recently, Morsi, who took power following President Mubarak, emotionally revealed that Egypt would trade a drop of blood for every drop of its Nile waters. *See* Mahemud Eshtu Tekuya, *The Egyptian Hydro-Hegemony in the Nile Basin: The Quest for Changing the Status Quo*, 26 J. WATER L. 11 (2018).

786 *See* Swain, *supra* note 459 and accompanying text.

The upstream states, especially Ethiopia and Tanzania, have also undermined the establishment of a regional custom around the 1959 Agreement by explicitly objecting to the 1929 and 1959 Agreements over time, as well as to Egyptian and Sudanese unliteral exploitation of the Nile. Ethiopia opposed the 1929 Anglo-Egyptian Treaty almost immediately, contending it protected Egypt's interests without reciprocity.[787] During the negotiations over the 1959 Agreement, Ethiopia sent aides-memories to all diplomatic missions in Cairo, notifying that "[it] has the right and obligation to exploit its water resources for the benefit of present and future generations of its citizens [and] must, therefore, reassert and reserve now and for the future, the right to take all such measures in respect of its water resources."[788] Tanzania similarly opposed the Nile legal regime in its 1962 letter to the Egyptian government which has since become the foundation of the Nyerere doctrine.[789] Thus, the upstream states can be considered persistent objectors that are not bound by any custom that could be established in the 1959 Agreement.

4.1.3 *South Sudan and the 1959 Agreement*

The people of South Sudan seceded from Sudan, establishing their own independent state in January 2011.[790] The secession raises legal question as to whether South Sudan is bound by the 1959 Agreement or whether it inherited the Agreement's rights and obligations. This question is critical, especially to Egyptian and Sudanese interests: the entire swamp region of the Sudd, where most of the tributaries of the White Nile converge, are now located in South Sudanese territory.[791] "[A]bout 90% of southern Sudan falls in the Nile Basin, and about 20% of the Nile Basin falls in southern Sudan. … About 28% of the flow of the Nile River, representing about 23 BCM of the total flow of the Nile of 84 BCM measured at Aswan, crosses southern Sudan into northern Sudan and eventually into Egypt."[792]

787 Amdetsion, *supra* note 72, at 27–28.

788 For the aides-memories, *see* Letter dated 22 June 2020 from the Permanent Rep. of Eth. to the United Nations addressed to the President of the Security Council, U.N. Doc. S/2020/567, annex III (June 22, 2020) [hereinafter Ethiopia's 2020 Letter to the UNSC 1].

789 Okoth-Owiro, *supra* note 479, 14 (quoting Nyerere's letter to Egypt, Great Britain, and Sudan). *See* also United Nations Conference, *supra* note 577, at 18 (highlighting Julius Nyerere's declaration to the Secretary-General of the United Nations).

790 Helal, *supra* note 86, 912–14; Salman, *supra* note 86, 344; Katz, *supra* note 698, at 250–54; Salman, *supra* note 698, 154–166.

791 *Id*, 157.

792 *Id*.

South Sudan and Sudan " neither signed or any agreement, whether pre-or post-independence, concerning its use of the Nile."[793] The 2005 Comprehensive Peace Agreement between the Government of the Republic of Sudan and the Sudan People's Liberation Movement/Sudan People's Liberation Army (CPA)—which provided for the framework for South Sudan's separation—lacked any provision regarding the Nile or the fate of the 1959 Agreement.[794] Instead, it contemplates that the two parties would address those issues in the future.[795] Similarly, the 2009 South Sudan Referendum Act listed water as one of the key post-referendum issues.[796] Then the 2010 Mekelle Memorandum of Understanding on Post-Referendum Issues and Arrangements, signed by the National Congress Party of Sudan and the Sudan People's Liberation Movement, established teams to negotiate several post-referendum substantive issues including, *inter alia*, water resource issue and the fate of the 1959 Agreement.[797] But the negotiators failed to resolve those issues, and since then no agreement has been reached addressing use of the Nile Watercourse.[798] Therefore, South Sudan does not inherit Agreement through a devolution agreement with Sudan.[799]

---

793 Katz; *supra* note 698, 1252.

794 The Comprehensive Peace Agreement Between the Government of the Republic of Sudan and the Sudan People's Liberation Movement/the Sudan People's Liberation Army, Chapeau, Sud.-SPLM/SPLA (Jan. 7, 2005) (hereinafter CPA) https://peacemaker.un.org/sites/peacemaker.un.org/files/SD_060000_The%20Comprehensive%20Peace%20Agreement.pdf. It should be noted that CPA gave the national government exclusive jurisdiction over "Nile Water Commission, the management of the Nile Waters, transboundary waters and disputes arising from the management of interstate waters between northern states and any dispute between northern and southern states." CPA, schedule A, p 40, ¶ 33. *See* also Katz, *supra* note 698 , at 250 (The CPA "did not include an agreement on South Sudan's rights to the Nile after independence").

795 CPA, *supra* note 794, Chap. 3, Sect. 2.1. ("Without prejudice to the position of the parties with respect to ownership of land and subterranean natural resources, including in South Sudan, this Agreement is not intended to address the ownership of those resources. The parties agree to establish a process to resolve this issue.")

796 Southern Sudan Referendum Act, 32, ¶ 67 (3) i, (2009), https://www.parlament.cat/document/intrade/6546.

797 Mekelle Memorandum of Understanding between the NCP and the SPLM on Post-referendum Issues and Arrangements (2010), https://www.peaceagreements.org/viewmasterdocument/752.

798 Katz; *supra* note 698, 1252.

799 It should be noted that South Sudan could be bound by the 1959 Agreement based on the operation of the VCSSRT, if it is a party to it. The VCSSRT is relevant here because South Sudan become independent after its coming into force in 1996. VCSSRT, *supra*

But, as discussed in Chapter 3, South Sudan might have succeeded to the rights and obligations provided in the 1959 Agreement based on customary international law, if the treaty established territorial regimes.[800] As noted, the ICJ, in its decision in the Gabčíkovo-Nagymaros Project, considered Article 12 of the VCSSRT as a reflection of customary international law.[801] In that case, the court found that the 1977 Treaty, governs the construction and joint operation of a large scale, integrated and indivisible complex of structures on specific parts of the two countries,[802] "established the navigational régime for an important sector of an international waterway [that] ... inescapably created a situation in which the interests of other users of the Danube were affected."[803] The Court then concluded that "the content of the 1977 Treaty indicates that it must be regarded as establishing a territorial régime within the meaning of Article 12 of VCSSRT. It created rights and obligations 'attaching to' the parts of the Danube to which it relates" as envisioned under Article 12 of the Convention.[804]

Mohamed Helal applied this decision to the 1959 Agreement and remarked that "like the 1977 Gabčíkovo-Nagymaros Treaty, the 1959 Agreement established a territorial regime for the management of the Nile River in Egypt and Sudan."[805] He reasoned that the 1959 Agreement "bears many resemblances to the 1977 Gabčíkovo-Nagymaros Treaty. Both treaties authorized the construction of major waterworks in two riparian States, created a joint management system for parts of international watercourses, and included provisions

note 599, art 7 ¶1. And, as per article 34 of the VCSSRT, the doctrine of the continuity of treaty applies to non-colonial state succession. VCSSRT, *supra* note 599, art 34. The South Sudan succession is not related to decolonization, and as such it could be governed by the principle of continuity provided in the Convention. However, since neither Sudan nor South Sudan accedes to the VCSSRT, it is not the controlling authority for determining the fate of the 1959 Agreement. Sudan signed the VCSSRT on August 23, 1978, but has not ratified the Convention thus far. https://treaties.un.org/Pages/ViewDetails.aspx?src=IND&mtdsg_no=XXIII-2&chapter=23&clang=_en. Regarding the status of article 34 of VCSSRT, Mohamed Helal remarked: "It seems premature ... to assert that the rule of *ipso jure* treaty continuity has been confirmed, and that an indisputable *opinio juris* has crystallized supporting the rule's status as customary international law." *See* Helal, *supra* note, 963.

800 Gabčíkovo-Nagymaros Project (Hung./Slovk.), Judgment, 1997 I.C.J. 7, ¶ 123 (Sept. 25).

801 *Id.*

802 *Id.*

803 *Id.*

804 *Id.*

805 Helal, *supra* note 86, 981.

affecting the interests of third parties."[806] Therefore, Helal submitted, the 1959 Agreement established a "territorial regime that South Sudan has inherited."[807]

It is true that under contemporary international law, territorial regimes remain unaffected by state succession.[808] However, the argument that the 1959 Agreement established a territorial regime is very questionable. First, unlike the 1977 Treaty, the 1959 Agreement did not establish a "navigational régime" on the Nile watercourse.[809] Indeed, like the 1977 Treaty, the 1959 Agreement authorized the construction of hydraulic works such as AHD and Roseires Reservoir.[810] But unlike the 1977 Treaty where obligations are created on the territory of Slovakia, the obligations as to the construction of the AHD and Roseires Reservoir are restricted to the territory of Egypt and North Sudan and do not include any territory of South Sudan.[811]

The 1959 Agreement envisioned the construction of projects in South Sudan's territory "for the increase of the River yield by preventing losses of waters of the Nile Basin in the swamps of Bahr el Jebel, Bahr el Zeraf, Bahr el Ghazal and its tributaries, the Sobat River and its tributaries and the White Nile Basin."[812] Unlike the 1977 Treaty, this provision neither specifies the content of these projects nor provides clear rights and obligations constituting a territorial regime, as stipulated under Article 12 of the VCSSRT.[813] Indeed, the Jonglei Canal is among the projects envisioned under the 1959 Agreement.[814] But, due to several factors including opposition from the environmental community and the Sudanese civil war,[815] the canal was abandoned permanently in 1978 before creating any right and obligation,[816] let alone establishing a territorial regime. Further, even if the projects were implemented, it is unlikely that they would "inescapably create a situation in which the interests of other users"[817] of the Nile waters would be affected. This suggests that the 1959 Agreement is different from the 1977 Treaty, creating no territorial regime in South Sudan's

806 *Id.*
807 *Id.*
808 Gabčíkovo-Nagymaros Project (Hung./Slovk.), Judgment, 1997 I.C.J. 7, ¶ 123 (Sept. 25).
809 *See generally* 1959 Agreement, *supra* note 106.
810 1959 Agreement, *supra* note 106, art II.
811 *Id.*
812 1959 Agreement, *supra* note 106, art III, ¶ 1.
813 *Id.*
814 COLLINS, *supra* note 64, 199–201; WATERBURY, *supra* note 302, 140.
815 COLLINS, *supra* note 64, 199–212.
816 WATERBURY, *supra* note 302, at 140.
817 Gabčíkovo-Nagymaros Project (Hung./Slovk.), Judgment, 1997 I.C.J. 7, ¶ 123 (Sept. 25).

territory. South Sudan is therefore not bound by the Agreement following its independence in 2011.

4.2 Customary International Watercourses Law

After establishing that the 1959 Agreement does not bind South Sudan and other upstream states, this section now scrutinizes basic customary international watercourses law principles and determines their relevancy in the Nile Basin.[818]

In the absence of all-inclusive binding treaties, customary international law principles govern the utilization of international watercourses.[819] Although some commentators argue that international law does not have a coherent set of customary rules governing the utilization of international watercourses,[820] the status of this area of law has evolved over the years to "widely applicable and accepted standards."[821]

---

818 Four major international legal bodies participated in the development of international watercourses law. In 1911, the International Institute of Law (IIL) adopted the Madrid Declaration, focusing on the absolute prohibition of harm, and later shifted to equitable utilization in its 1961 Salzburg Resolution. The ILA promulgated the 1966 Helsinki Rules, further codifying international watercourses law. In 1971 the U.N. General Assembly asked the ILC to work on "the codification and progressive development" of international watercourses law. After almost three decades of preparatory work, the UN General Assembly adopted the UN Watercourse Convection in 1997. Convention on the Law of the Non-Navigational Uses of International Watercourses, May 21, 1997, 2999 U.N.T.S. 52106 (Hereinafter U.N. Watercourses Convention). Drowning upon the Convention, ILA updates the Helsinki Rules and developed Berlin Rules on Water Resources in 2004. International Law Association, The Berlin Rules on Water Resources, Berlin Conference: Water Resources Law, 4 (2004) (hereinafter Berlin Rules). Following its adoption, international tribunals, including the international court of justice (ICJ) heavily relied on the U.N. Watercourses Convention in resolving disputes between water sharing states. Although the Convention came into force only in 2014, it has long been considered as the most authoritative body of law governing transboundary watercourses, and its principles have been accepted as customary international law. For an overview of the historical development of international watercourses law, *see* Shih & Stutz, *supra* note 60, 10811–10812; MCCAFFREY, *supra* note 4, 410–440.

819 *See* Shih & Stutz, *supra* note 60, 10811. *See also* MCCAFFREY, *supra* note 4, at 445; Dellapenna, *supra* note 49, 269–72.

820 Charles Bourne, *The Primacy of the Principle of Equitable Utilization in the 1997 Watercourses Convention*, 1997 CAN. Y.B. INT'L L. 215, 215–16 (1997). *See also* Fisseha, *supra* note 596, 177. (Describing international watercourses law as "one of the most unsettled areas of international law" that has very "few rules of general application or validity.")

821 Shih & Stutz, *supra* note 60, 10811. *See* Joseph Dellapenna, *International Water Law in a Climate of Disruption,* 17 MICH. ST. J. INT'L L. 43, 60 (2008); Dellapenna, *supra* note

International watercourses law evolved through various stages.[822] The law, developed from the rules of navigation, expanded to regulate non-navigational uses of international watercourses in the early 20th century.[823] It started with the doctrines of sovereign absolutism over natural resources and has over the years shifted towards the doctrine of limited sovereignty in the utilization of transboundary resources.[824] This section examines the relevancy and applicability of these doctrines in the Nile Basin. It first reflects on two diametrically opposed doctrines—absolute territorial sovereignty and absolute territorial integrity. Thereafter, it turns to the two modern doctrines—limited territorial sovereignty and community of interest—which reflect currently prevailing views and forms the foundation for current customary international principles of water law, including notions of equitable and reasonable utilization, and of no significant harm.

4.2.1 *Theoretical Foundation International Watercourses Law*

4.2.1.1 Two Archaic Doctrines: Absolute Territorial Sovereignty and Territorial Integrity

The doctrine of absolute territorial sovereignty or the "Harmon Doctrine", stemming from an opinion delivered in 1895 by American Attorney General Judson Harmon during the dispute between the United States and Mexico over the use of Rio Grande waters,[825] states that an upstream state "could do

49, 261 (Underscoring the existence of a settled and "well developed" body of international watercourses law for "addressing transboundary water problems" and considering the Berlin Rules as codification of "customary international law applicable to the management of waters, and not just to the waters of the waters of an international drainage basin.")

822 Shih & Stutz, *supra* note 60, 10811–10812.

823 *See* MCCAFFREY, *supra* note 4, 69–71.

824 Shih & Stutz, *supra* note 60, 10811.

825 In this dispute, Mexico opposed "the increasing diversions of Rio Grande waters by farmers in the United States reduced the supply of water to Mexican communities in the vicinity of Ciudad Juarez, located across the Rio Grande from El Paso, Texas." In advising the Secretary of State on Mexico's claims, Attorney General Harmon stated: "The fundamental principle of international law is the absolute sovereignty of every nation, as against all others, within its territory... The immediate as well as the possible consequences of the right asserted by Mexico show that its recognition is entirely inconsistent with the sovereignty of the United States over its national domain...The case presented is a novel one. Whether the circumstances make it possible or proper to take any action from considerations of comity is a question which does not pertain to the Department [of Justice]; but that question should be decided as one of policy only, because, in my opinion, the rules, principles, and precedents of international law impose no liability or obligation upon the United States." Stephen McCaffrey, *The Harmon Doctrine One Hundred Years Later: Buried, Not Praised*, 36 NAT. RESOURCES J. 981-982 (1996) (quoting Attorney General Harmon).

virtually as it pleased with the portion of an international watercourse within its territory … irrespective of the harmful consequences in the downstream state."[826] While there are instances in which states use this doctrine as an argument in negotiation,[827] the doctrine of absolute territorial sovereignty has never been considered as reflection of international watercourses law.[828] "It is at best an anachronism that has no place in today's interdependent, water-scarce world."[829]

The second doctrine, the doctrine of absolute territorial integrity, promoting downstream states' rights to an uninterrupted flow of water, posits that downstream states have an absolute right to an uninterrupted and undiminished flow of water, and that "the upstream state[s] may do nothing that might affect the natural flow of the water into the downstream state[s]."[830]

Ironically, the United States, which is associated with the doctrine of absolute territorial *sovereignty,* is among the countries that have invoked this doctrine in the *Trail Smelter* case.[831] In this case, the Legal Adviser of the U.S. Department of State argued: "It is a fundamental principle of the law of nations that a sovereign state is supreme within its own territorial domain and that it and its nationals are entitled to use and enjoy their territory and property without interference from an outside source."[832]

Despite the rhetoric, the doctrine of absolute territorial integrity has not been practically applied like that of absolute territorial sovereignty.[833] Even so in the Nile Basin, upstream and downstream states invoke these conflicting doctrines to justify their diametrically opposed positions regarding rights to the Nile. Although there are arguable instances in which upstream states invoke absolute territorial sovereignty over the Nile watercourse,[834] all

826 *Id.* 967.

827 *Id.*

828 MCCAFFREY, *supra* note 4, 103. (United States itself did not consider the "Harmon Doctrine" as the international law of the time, given that "the dispute was ultimately settled in the 1906 Convention concerning the *Equitable Distribution* of the Waters of the Rio Grande for Irrigation.")

829 *Id,* 100.

830 *Id,* 116.

831 *Id,* 117.

832 *Id* (internal citation omitted).

833 *Id,* 118. (Even the Trail Smelter Tribunal neglected to follow the doctrine as it "allowed the smelter to continue operating, but subjected it to both a very stringent emissions regime designed to avoid unreasonable harm in Washington, and the duty to provide compensation for any damage caused despite compliance with the regime.")

834 For instance, Godana suggested that Ethiopia "still stands by the Harmon Doctrine, as is shown by a series of terse statements issued by her Ministry of Foreign Affairs in 1978 and in which Ethiopia once again asserts and reserves for herself 'all the rights to exploit her

upstream States have long pushed for the principle of equitable use and no significant harm rule,[835] undercutting arguments for absolute territorial integrity.

Egypt, a downstream state which often considers upstream projects as an existential threat, has frequently advocated for the doctrine of absolute territorial integrity, and believed that it has "natural and historical rights," or "acquired rights" in the flow of the Nile waters.[836] In 1981, Egypt explicitly asserted the doctrine of absolute territorial integrity, stating at a regional meeting that it "has the full right to maintain the status quo of the rivers flowing on its territory" and "that no country has the right to undertake any positive or negative measure that could have an impact on the river's flow in other countries."[837] Egypt, addressing upstream states, has also asserted that "a river's upper reaches should not be touched lest this should affect the flow of quantity of its water;" and that "any works at a river's upper reaches that may affect the countries at the lower reaches are banned unless negotiations have taken place."[838]

Despite this rhetoric, Egypt has agreed in practice to some upstream projects such as the Owen Falls Dam in Uganda at the outlet of Lake Victoria[839] and the GERD in Ethiopia,[840] undercutting arguments for absolute territorial integrity.[841] While holding extreme positions may serve short-term political interests, ultimately the irreconcilable "doctrines of absolute territorial sovereignty

---

natural resources.'" GODANA, *supra* note 477, 36. McCaffrey, succinctly explaining the historical background of the statements, arrived in different conclusion. "Even taken at face value, however, it is important to recognize that the Ethiopian statement quoted above does not necessarily constitute a denial of obligations toward downstream states with regard to the use of an international watercourse. That is, it is universally recognized that a state is fully entitled to exploit its natural resources. Ethiopia only said that she reserves for herself "all the rights to exploit her natural resources." Ethiopia clearly has rights to do just that. The statement does not deny that Ethiopia also has obligations nor that Egypt does not have rights. To acknowledge a right to exploit natural resources within a state is in no way to admit that in exploiting such resources the state may cause harm to other states sharing them or ignore their rights to an equitable and reasonable sharing of the resource. Therefore, Ethiopia cannot be placed in the Harmon Doctrine camp on the basis of this or similar statements." *See* MCCAFFREY, *supra* note 4, 111.

835 Mohammed Abdo, *The Nile Question: The Accords on the Water of the Nile and their Implication on Cooperative Schemes in the Basin,* 9 PERCEPTIONS J. INT'L AFF. 51 (2004).

836 *See* MCCAFFREY, *supra* note 4, 118–119.

837 *Id,* (internal citation omitted).

838 *Id,* (Internal citation omitted).

839 *Id.*

840 *See* the discussion *infra* Chapter 7.

841 Amdetsion, *supra* note 72, at 30 (Stating that "no state has ever accepted a diplomatic settlement on this basis, no arbitral decision has ever been awarded by virtue of this principle, and no prominent jurists have advocated this view").

and absolute territorial integrity are dead letters" in the eyes of international law.[842] Yet, the continued rhetoric along these absolute sovereignty doctrines by the Nile Basin significantly undermines cooperation and the formation of a basin-wide treaty.[843]

4.2.1.2 Two Modern Doctrines: Limited Sovereignty and Community of Interest

The doctrine of limited territorial sovereignty, a relative compromise, is the dominant and prevailing theory governing international watercourses today.[844] Rather than conferring states absolute rights over international watercourses, it imposes moderate restrictions on their use of shared resources.[845] The doctrine, as applied to the Nile, suggests that each Basin state can freely use waters of the Nile in its territory, provided that it also respects the rights and interests of the other Basin states.[846] The sovereignty of a state over its territory is therefore limited to the extent that it would otherwise use its territory or resources in a manner that would cause significant harm to the rights of other Basin states.[847]

The doctrine is fundamental to the smooth functioning of any region where states share limited resources.[848] It is widely recognized in domestic legal systems[849] and supported by state practice,[850] international

842 Shih & Stutz, *supra* note 60, 10813.

843 Takele Soboka Bulto, *Between Ambivalence and Necessity: Occlusions on the Path Toward a Basin-Wide Treaty in the Nile Basin,* 20 COLO. J. INT'L ENVTL. L. & POL'Y 291, 302 (2009).

844 *See* MCCAFFREY, *supra* note 4, 125.

845 *Id,* 125–126.

846 *Id.*

847 *Id,* 126. McCaffrey made two remarks regarding the nomenclature, "limited territorial Sovereignty." "First, sovereignty has never been absolute. If it were, international law could not regulate the relations between states. Instead, sovereignty carries with it a set of obligations owed to other states. These obligations may be based on treaties, customary international law, general principles of law recognized by the nations of the world, and certain fundamental principles of morality including norms of *jus cogens*. Therefore, to speak of "limited" territorial sovereignty is in this sense a redundancy. But the word "limited" was presumably thought necessary to distinguish this doctrine from that of "absolute" territorial sovereignty. The second initial point is that the theory of limited territorial sovereignty should not be understood to be confined to the obligation of a state not to use its territory in such a way as to cause significant harm to other states—at least as "harm" is normally understood. It is equally applicable, and increasingly important, with respect to issues of quantitative allocation and may thus be seen as the theoretical precursor of the obligation of equitable and reasonable utilization."

848 *Id.*

849 *Id.*

850 Second Report on the Law of the Non-Navigational Uses of International Watercourses, Doc. A/CN.4/399, ILC Yearbook 1986, Vol. II (Part 1), 87 at 103–13. (Hereinafter Second Report).

tribunals,[851] and the commentaries of international law scholars.[852] The doctrine has been incorporated in the U.N. Watercourses Convention and serves as the foundation for the main substantive and procedural rights and obligations recognized in international watercourses law, including the principles of equitable and reasonable utilization, and the no significant harm rule.[853]

The fourth doctrine, the doctrine of community of interest, often considered "idealistic," recognizes equality of rights of watercourses states over their shared watercourses.[854] The doctrine was recognized by the Permanent Court of International Justice (PCIJ) as early as 1929 in the case concerning navigation on the River Oder.[855] In that case, PCIJ had to decide whether states other than Poland had the right of navigation "under the provisions of the Treaty of Versailles, to the sections of the tributaries of the Oder, the Warthe (Warta), or Netze (Noteć), that are situated in Polish territory."[856] Interpreting Article 331 of the Treaty of Versailles based on the "principles governing international fluvial law,"[857] the PCIJ stated the following:

> [W]hen consideration is given to the manner in which States have regarded the concrete situations arising out of the fact that a single waterway traverses or separates the territory of more than one State, and the possibility of fulfilling the requirements of justice and the considerations

851 Lake Lanoux (Fr. v. Spain), 12 R.I.A.A. 281 (Arb. Trib. 1957); Gabčíkovo-Nagymaros Project (Hung./Slovk.), Judgment, 1997 I.C.J. 7 (Sept. 25); Pulp Mills on the River Uruguay (Arg. v. Uru.), Judgment, 2010 I.C.J. 14 (Apr. 20). Case relating to the Territorial Jurisdiction of the International Commission of the River Oder, Judgment, 1929 PICJ (Sept. 10); The Corfu Channel Case (United Kingdom v. Albania), Judgment. 1949 ICJ (April 9); Trail Smelter Arbitration (United States v. Canada), RIAA III 1949 (April 16). For detail detailed discussion of the decisions, *see* Second Report, *supra* note 850, at 113–122.

852 *See* MCCAFFREY, *supra* note 4, 137–38 (The theory of limited territorial sovereignty is "supported by the writings of commentators dating at least from the nineteenth century, has been endorsed by learned societies since as early as 1911, and ... is the dominant theory today").

853 *Id*, 157–58.

854 *Id*, 99, 139–157.

855 Territorial Jurisdiction of Int'l Comm'n of River Oder (U.K. v. Pol.), Judgment 1929 P.C.I.J. at 16 (Sep. 10).

856 MCCAFFREY, *supra* note 4, 139.

857 Territorial Jurisdiction of Int'l Comm'n of River Oder (U.K. v. Pol.), Judgment 1929 P.C.I.J. at 26 (Sep. 10).

> of utility which this fact places in relief, it is at once seen that a solution of the problem has been sought not in the idea of a right of passage in favour of upstream States, but in that of a community of interest of riparian States. This community of interest in a navigable river becomes the basis of a common legal right, the essential features of which are the perfect equality of all riparian States in the use of the whole course of the river and the exclusion of any preferential privilege of any one riparian State in relation to the others.[858]

Quoting this passage, ICJ in the Gabciıkovo–Nagymaros Project case extended the applicability of this doctrine to "non-navigational uses of international watercourses."[859] The doctrine, as applied to the Nile, suggests that all Nile Basin States share an interest in the Nile River, and that this shared interest forms a type of community.[860] It also affirms the "perfect equality" of rights of all Nile Basin States in the use of the Nile Watercourse, independent on any prior degree of development or use.[861] As equality of rights does not entitle equal shares to all Nile Basin States, the actual apportionment of the Nile watercourse would be governed by the principle of equitable and reasonable utilization as discussed below.

4.2.2 *Basic Principles of International Watercourses Law*

4.2.2.1 Equitable and Reasonable Utilization

The principle of equitable and reasonable utilization, historically developed largely through domestic court judgments over water apportionment disputes in federal states,[862] is the "pillar of interstate interactions over the uses of international waters."[863] Its status as the fundamental norm of international watercourses law is recognized by the decision of ICJ in the Gabčíkovo-Nagymaros

---

858 *Id*, 27–28.

859 Gabciıkovo–Nagymaros (Hung. v. Slovak.), Judgement, 1997 I.C.J Rep. 56, 65, ¶ 85 (Sept. 19970).

860 *Id*. Stephen C. McCaffrey, *Intertwined General Principles*, in RESEARCH HANDBOOK, *supra* note 42, 87 (Commenting on the doctrine generally).

861 *Id* (Commenting on the doctrine generally).

862 For United States Supreme Court decisions, *see* Kansas v. Colorado, 206 U.S. 46, 104 (1907); New Jersey v New York, 283 U.S. 336 (1931); Nebraska v. Wyoming, 325 U.S. 589, 618 (1945); Colorado v. New Mexico (Vermejo I), 459 U.S. 176, 184 (1982), remanded to Spec. Master, (Vermejo II), 467 U.S. 310 (1984); Connecticut v Massachusetts, 282 U.S. 660 (1931); Wyoming v Colorado, 259 U.S. 419 (1922), modified, 260 U.S. 1 (1922), vacated, 353 U.S. 953 (1957). For decisions of other federal courts, *see* MCCAFFREY, *supra* note 4, 288–300.

863 Bulto, *supra* note 843, 308.

Project (Hungary/Slovakia) case.[864] The Berlin Rules, which replaced the Helsinki Rules,[865] and the U.N. Watercourses Convention also treat equitable utilization as the overarching principle of international watercourses law.[866] State practice and academic opinion both consistently assert that the principle of equitable and reasonable utilization wholly reflects customary international law.[867]

The principle asserts that states hold equal rights over shared water resources.[868] Conceptually, two initial points require clarification. First, the terms "equitable" and "reasonable" are not synonymous, and they govern different areas of international watercourses law.[869] Equitable utilization governs the division or apportionment of waters,[870] while "reasonable utilization looks at how water is used to determine if the purpose for which the water is being used and the amount[s] used are reasonable under the circumstances."[871]

864 Gabčíkovo-Nagymaros Project (Hung./Slovk.), Judgment, 1997 I.C.J. 7 ¶ 8, 85, 147 & 150 (Sept. 25); *see* also Pulp Mills on the River Uruguay (Arg. v. Uru.), Judgment, 2010 I.C.J. 14 (Apr. 20).

865 Berlin Rules, *supra* note 818, arts, 12–14.

866 MCCAFFREY, *supra* note 4, 445.

867 *Id.*

868 *Id*, 449.

869 Margaret J. Vick, *The Law of International Waters: Reasonable Utilization*, 12 CHI.-KENT J. INT''L & COMP. L. 145 (2012).

870 MCCAFFREY, *supra* note 4, 445. It should be noted in U.S. Supreme Court cases it is referred as the doctrine of equitable "apportionment". *Id.* Nine decades ago, United States Supreme Court well-articulated the philosophical underpinnings of the doctrine in the case between New Jersey v New York. "A river is more than an amenity, it is a treasure. It offers a necessity of life that must be rationed among those who have power over it. New York has the physical power to cut off all the water within its jurisdiction. But clearly the exercise of such a power to the destruction of the interest of lower States could not be tolerated. And on the other hand equally little could New Jersey be permitted to require New York to give up its power altogether in order that the river might come down to it undiminished. Both States have real and substantial interests in the River that must be reconciled as best they may. The different traditions and practices in different parts of the country may lead to varying results but the effort always is to secure an equitable apportionment without quibbling over formulas." New Jersey v New York, 283 U.S. 342–3(1931). Explaining the concept of equitable utilization, McCaffrey commented on this decision, and indicated how the Court "effectively rejects both the absolute territorial sovereignty and the absolute territorial integrity theories." *See* MCCAFFREY, *supra* note 4, 446.

871 Vick, *supra* note 869, 145; *see* also MCCAFFREY, *supra* note 4, 449 (Admitting the existence very "few examples in international jurisprudence of what constitutes an unreasonable use of shared freshwater resources," McCaffrey imagined "possibilities, including wasteful uses, sale of withdrawn water outside the basin, excessive withdrawals for use by the

Second, the notion of equality of rights does not guarantee a numerically equal quantity of water to all riparian states; rather, it simply entitles every watercourse state to an equal right to an equitable share of the uses of a watercourse and the benefit derived from it.[872] Those equitable shares embody not only actual water quantities but also, for example, the capacity to generate electricity using hydropower.[873] Fundamental to equitable division is the idea that "no state has an inherently superior claim to the use of the watercourse. … [T]he rights of each [state sharing] … the watercourse are equal. … One of them may not destroy the rights of the other by using some or all of the waters of the river, whether that use [is] prior or subsequent to the use of the other state."[874]

The principle of equitable and reasonable utilization provides a general and flexible legal framework for allocating the use of an international watercourse.[875] Given its generality, it is essential to take all objective relevant factors, including priority of use and water contribution, into consideration when determining equitable and reasonable utilization in particular cases.[876] "While priority of use is an important consideration, priority alone is not decisive; even less is the place where the watercourse system originates controlling."[877] Transboundary harm is also a crucial factor to consider when allocating equitable utilization of shared water resources. But factual harm is tolerated under international law, and it is only "deprivation of a state's equitable share, that is prohibited."[878]

The U.N. Watercourses Convention provides a list of key factors for determining equitable and reasonable utilization of international watercourses:

> (*a*) geographic, hydrographic, hydrological, climatic, ecological, and other factors of a natural character; (*b*) the social and economic needs of the watercourse States concerned; (*c*) the population dependent on the watercourse in each watercourse state; (*d*) the effects of the use or uses of the watercourses in one watercourse State on other watercourse States; (*e*) existing and potential uses of the watercourse; (*f*) conservation,

withdrawing state outside the basin, serious pollution of the watercourse, as by toxic or hazardous substances" that constitute unreasonable use).

872 *Id*, 451.

873 *Id.*

874 *Id.*

875 *Id*, 447–48.

876 *Id.*

877 *Id*, 447.

878 *Id*, 449.

> protection, development and economy of use of the water resources of the watercourse and the costs of measures taken to that effect; [and] (*g*) availability of alternatives, of comparable value, to a particular planned or existing use.[879]

In determining equitable and reasonable use, decisions should be made holistically, while weighing each factor "by its importance in comparison with that of other relevant factors."[880] In principle, no use of water should be given priority over another.[881] But in cases of conflict between uses, special regard should be "given to the requirements of vital human needs."[882] Therefore, "while States must weigh all other competing interests based on their relative importance in a given context, satisfying vital human needs will always take precedence."[883]

In the Nile Basin, the principle of equitable utilization is historically intertwined with downstream states' claims for prior use and historical rights.[884] During the negotiations for the 1929 Anglo-Egyptian Treaty, Britain explicitly recognized prior use or historical rights, while also asserting that waters beyond that use should be equitably apportioned.[885] The 1959 Agreement also followed a similarly selective approach, applying equitable utilization only to Egypt and Sudan, while disregarding the interest of all other riparian states.[886] In negotiations preceding the Agreement, Sudan stated: "It is not disputed that Egypt has established a right to the volumes of water which she actually uses for irrigation. Sudan has a similar right."[887] The 1959 Agreement accordingly apportioned net benefits generated from AHD (22 BCM) between Sudan and Egypt in a two-to-one ratio in favor of Sudan.[888] It also provides that should the

879 U.N. Watercourses Convention, *supra* note 818, art. 6 ¶1. The Berlin Rules includes two additional factors: sustainability of proposed or existing uses and minimization of environmental harm. The Berlin Rules, *supra* note 818, art. 13 ¶ 2 h & i.

880 U.N. Watercourses Convention, *supra* note 818, art 6, ¶ 3.

881 *Id*, art 10, ¶1.

882 *Id*, art 10, ¶ 2.

883 Shih & Stutz, *supra* note 60, 10815.

884 *Id. see* also MCCAFFREY, *supra* note 4, 128.

885 During the negotiation, Britain stated that the Nile watercourse "must be considered as a single unit, designed for the use of the peoples inhabiting their banks … [I]t is recognized that Egypt has a *prior right* to the maintenance of her present supplies of water for the areas now under cultivation, and to an equitable proportion of any additional supplies." 1974 Y.B. Int'l L. Comm'n, Vol. 2, 2, 322, 326 (emphasis added). *see* also MCCAFFREY, *supra* note 4, 128.

886 1959 Agreement, *supra* note 106, art II ¶ 3–4.

887 MCCAFFREY, *supra* note 4, 129 (internal citation omitted).

888 1959 Agreement, *supra* note 106, art II ¶ 3–4.

annual yield increase, surplus water would be divided into equal shares among the two states, again excluding all others in the Basin.[889] Hosni argues that this arrangement "confirms the idea that the parties drifted further towards the concept of equitable shares."[890] He further submits that in the 1959 Agreement "the concept of established rights and prior appropriation found little recognition, perhaps no more than an element to be taken into consideration in determining what should be an equitable share."[891]

While the 1959 Agreement does consider the notions of equity when dividing the 22 BCM between Sudan and Egypt, the claims that it gives no or little recognition to the concept of established rights and prior appropriation are debatable. For one, the Preamble and Article I explicitly recognized the "established rights" of the two states over the Nile watercourse.[892] Moreover, "drifting ... towards the concept of equitable share" would at least require the Agreement to recognize the equality of rights of all riparian States over the Nile Watercourse. Yet, the Agreement neither recognizes this right nor allocates a single drop of water to the upstream states, including Ethiopia which contributes between 85 and 90 percent of the Nile waters.[893]

Upstream states have long called for equitable and reasonable utilization of the Nile watercourse. As discussed in a subsequent chapter, the Nile Basin States recognized equitable utilization as a fundamental principle of the CFA.[894] Although Egypt and Sudan have yet to accede to the CFA, they both signed a shared declaration of principles with Ethiopia, regarding the GERD, which recognized the principles of equitable utilization and no significant harm as the governing rubric of the Blue Nile.[895]

4.2.2.2 No Significant Harm

The no significant harm principle, or *sic utere tuo ut alienum non laeda* (so use your own as not to harm that of another), prohibits states from using their territory in such a way that would cause harm to other states.[896] Generally considered a reflection of sovereign equality of states, the principle "appears to

---

889 *Id*, art III.

890 MCCAFFREY, *supra* note 4, 314 (internal citation omitted).

891 *Id* (internal citation omitted).

892 1959 Agreement, *supra* note 106, preamble, ¶ 3 & art I.

893 1959 Agreement, *supra* note 106, art II ¶ 3–4. NILE BASIN INITIATIVE, *supra* note 52, at 36 (Ethiopia "contribute[s] between 85 and 90 percent of the annual Nile flows").

894 *See* discussion *infra* section 6.2.

895 *See* discussion *infra* section 7.2.

896 MCCAFFREY, *supra* note 4, 477. *See* also Shih & Stutz, *supra* note 60, 10816 (discussing the Roman origin of the no harm principle).

have acquired customary force, as is attested by international practice."[897] It is enshrined in several international law instruments[898] and has been reaffirmed by various decisions of international tribunals.[899] Contemporary state practice also supports the principle, affirming that "no one state may claim to use the waters in such a way as to cause material injury to the interests of another, or to oppose their use by another state unless this causes material injury to itself."[900]

Drawing on the doctrine of absolute territorial integrity, some depict the obligation to prevent significant harm as an absolute prohibition against harming the interests of downstream states.[901] This approach has been advanced to maintain existing use, prior appropriation, and historical or established rights arguments.[902] Nevertheless, "the no-harm principle is not, and has never been, conceived as absolutely prohibiting the causing of significant harm in all circumstances."[903]

Rather, the no significant harm principle imposes due diligence obligations on the use of transboundary watercourses.[904] Watercourse states are required to "take all appropriate measures to prevent the causing of significant harm to other watercourses States."[905] The concept of due diligence is a flexible one, accounting for generally accepted standards, the nature and magnitude of a given harm, and the capacity of the states involved.[906]

Although the extent of obligations to prevent significant harm to other riparian states vary by case, certain general circumstances tend to be present. First, to invoke the principle, there must be "actual or threatened" transboundary

---

897 MCCAFFREY, *supra* note 4, 477 (internal citation omitted).

898 *See*, e.g., U.N. Watercourses Convention, *supra* note 818, art. 7; Berlin Rules, *supra* note 818, art. 16.

899 Trail Smelter Case, 3 Rep. Int'l Arb. Awards 1905, 1965 (1950) (It is well established "principles of international law [that] no State has the right to use or permit the use of its territory in such a manner as to cause injury by fumes in or to the territory of another or the properties or persons therein when the case is of serious consequence and the injury is established by clear and convincing evidence.") *see* also Lake Lanoux (Fr. v. Spain), 12 R.I.A.A. 281 (Arb. Trib. 1957).

900 J.L. BRIERLY, THE LAW OF NATIONS 204 (1955), as cited in IBRAHIM KAYA, EQUITABLE UTILIZATION: THE LAW OF NON-NAVIGATIONAL USES OF INTERNATIONAL WATERCOURSES 82 (2003).

901 Shih & Stutz, *supra* note 60, 10816; *see* generally Salman M. A. Salman, *Equitable and Reasonable Utilization and the Obligation against Causing Significant Harm—Are They Reconcilable?,* 115 AJIL UNBOUND 183 (2021).

902 *Id*; Shih & Stutz, *supra* note 60, 10816.

903 MCCAFFREY, *supra* note 4, 468.

904 *Id*, 498.

905 U.N. Watercourses Convention, *supra* note 818, art. 7 ¶1.

906 MCCAFFREY, *supra* note 4, 498.

harm.[907] The harm can either be factual in nature or may constitute a legal injury.[908] It can include environmental impacts, like pollution, or "diminution in quantity of water, … increased siltation due to upstream deforestation [or] … erosion of the riverbed resulting from channeling of the river upstream."[909]

The rule also governs upstream harms caused by downstream uses.[910] New uses by "a downstream state may have no factual impact on an upstream state but may so alter the equitable balance of uses that they in effect constrain the scope of subsequent new uses the upstream state can make without breaching its obligation of equitable utilization."[911] The no significant harm rule, therefore, encompasses "not only the paradigm of factual harm caused to a downstream state by activities upstream, but also this effective constriction of development possibilities upstream by unilateral new uses downstream."[912]

Second, not every harm violates the principle. The harm must be significant: it must be more than "trivial," though it does not be "substantial."[913] In the words of the ILC, "[t]here must be a real impairment of use, i.e. a detrimental impact of some consequence upon, for example, public health, industry, property, agriculture or the environment in the affected State."[914]

Then, even if the harm is significant, it must also be inequitable to violate the doctrine.[915] Factual harm, regardless of the magnitude—whether appreciable, significant, or substantial—does not in itself constitute the harm prohibited by the doctrine. "The factual harm caused must be recognized as unreasonable and inequitable when weighed against other countervailing interests."[916] In other words, the principle prohibits "conduct by which one state exceeds its equitable share or deprives another state of its equitable share of the uses and benefits of the watercourse."[917] Understood this way, the no significant harm rule complements that of equitable and reasonable utilization. It therefore "neither embodies an absolute standard nor supersedes the doctrine of equitable utilization where the two appear to conflict with each

907 *Id*, 495.
908 *Id*, 448, 470–72.
909 *Id*, 470.
910 *Id*, 471.
911 *Id*.
912 *Id*.
913 *Id*, 496.
914 1988 Y.B. INT'L L. COMM'N, v. 2, pt. 2, at 36.
915 MCCAFFREY, *supra* note 4, 496–97.
916 Shih & Stutz, *supra* note 60, 10816.
917 *See* Second Report, *supra* note 850, 134; MCCAFFREY, *supra* note 4, 496–97.

other."[918] Professor Stephen McCaffrey, in his treatise on the law international watercourses, explains the interplay between two doctrines as follows:

> It is not the causing of significant harm per se, but the unreasonable causing of such harm that is prohibited. In other words, conduct of a state that results in some harm—even significant harm—may be reasonable under the circumstances, and thus the harm may have to be tolerated by the harmed state. Analytically, this is equivalent to treating harm as but one factor in an equitable utilization determination: significant harm may have to be tolerated in order to achieve an overall regime of equitable and reasonable utilization. It is thus the flexibility of the no-harm rule that makes it compatible, even if not entirely identical, with the principle of equitable utilization ... There is therefore no need to "reconcile" the no-harm and equitable utilization principles. They are, in reality, two sides of the same coin.[919]

In the Nile Basin context, prioritizing the no-harm rule over equitable utilization tantamount to be categorically prohibiting the upstream states from using the Nile watercourse. Given the current level of Egyptian and Sudanese use of the Nile,[920] any new upstream use by Ethiopia or other upstream states will significantly affect these existing uses and would therefore be prohibited under this principle.[921] For this reason, Ethiopia consistently maintained that the principle of equitable and reasonable utilization should take precedence over the no-harm rule.[922] Egypt, on the other hand, asserts the reverse.[923]

The relationship between these two fundamental principles was the subject of significant controversy when the U.N. Watercourses Convention was drafted. While abstaining from the vote on the draft U.N. Watercourses Convention in the General Assembly, Egypt expressed "reservations on the final version

---

918 MCCAFFREY, *supra* note 4, at 496.

919 *Id*, 496–97.

920 UN. FOOD & AGRIC., AQUASTAT COUNTRY PROFILE—EGYPT 7–9 (2016); Salman, *supra* note 89, 90.

921 Bulto, *supra* note 843, 314.

922 Elias N. Stebek, *Eastern Nile at Crossroads: Preservation and Utilization Concerns in Focus*, 1 MIZAN L. REV. 33, 52 (2007). ("Both prior to and after 1993, Ethiopia has consistently expressed its right to equitable utilization of its transboundary water resources, and in effect, the no-harm rule cannot be the governing principle in Ethio-Egyptian relations").

923 Mohammed S. Helal, *Sharing Blue Gold: The 1997 UN Convention on the Law of the Non-Navigational Uses of International Watercourses Ten Years On*, 18 COLO. J. INT'L ENVT'L. L. & POL'Y, 337, 366 (2007).

of article 5 [the principle of equitable and reasonable utilization] of the Convention," and stressed "the need to link this principle with the obligations ... not to cause significant harm."[924] It also expressed its understanding that "the wording of article 7 [the no significant harm rule] should not be construed as undermining the established principle of *sic utere tuo* ... and ... that this principle remains the cornerstone of any regime to be established by watercourse States."[925] Ethiopia, on the other hand, expressed its desire "to see the primacy of Article 5 [equitable and reasonable utilization] clearly established in the Convention."[926] And, though the final text of the U.N. Watercourses Convention does afford the principle of equitable and reasonable utilization priority over the no-harm rule,[927] Ethiopia still abstained from the vote from the U.N. General Assembly due to a perceived "lack of clear-cut distinction and balance" between the two principles.[928]

Egypt often uses the no-harm doctrine to justify perpetuating the status quo. It offers various versions of the "prior appropriation" or "historical rights" arguments, and advocates for absolute prohibition of harms.[929] Egypt rejects the significant harm threshold, arguing that the causing of any harm should be prohibited.[930] It also tried to insert an absolute prohibition of harm rule in the CFA under the guise of "water security."[931] In its attempt to perpetuate the status quo, Egypt proposed that the CFA prohibit the Nile Basin States from "not to adversely affect[ing] the water security *and current uses and rights* of any other Nile Basin State."[932]

But despite Egypt's arguments, upstream uses that adversely affect Egypt's current and existing use of the Nile would not *per se* violate the principle. To breach the principle, the conduct of upstream States or the use resulting in harm to Egypt must be unreasonable and inequitable given the circumstances. Considering upstream states ever increasing demand for water to satisfy vital

924 United Nations General Assembly, Official Records Fifty-first Session, 99th plenary meeting, at 10–11 (1997) (hereinafter Official Records Fifty-first Session).

925 Helal, *supra* note 923, 366.

926 Official Records Fifty-first Session, *supra* note 924, at 10.

927 Salman, *supra* note 901, 186. The notion that principle of equitable and reasonable utilization trumps over the no-harm rule is supported by the ICJ, which shortly after the adoption of the U.N. Watercourses Convention in 1997, confirmed equitable and reasonable utilization principle in both the Gabčíkovo-Nagymaros Project case and the Pulp Mills cases as the fundamental norm of international watercourses law. *Id.*

928 *See* also Official Records Fifty-first Session, *supra* note 924, at 10.

929 Shih & Stutz, *supra* note 60, 10818.

930 *Id.*

931 *See* discussion *infra* section 6.1.

932 CFA, *supra* note 132, Annex on Article 14(b) (emphasis added).

human needs, new upstream utilization affecting the lopsided pattern of water utilization would arguably not be unreasonable (or inequitable),[933] and would therefore be allowed under international law.

4.2.2.3 Procedural Obligations

Given their general nature, the principle of equitable and reasonable utilization and no significant harm rule can only be pragmatically implemented through procedural rules.[934] There are currently four procedural obligations that are recognized under international watercourses law. These include (1) general obligation to cooperate, (2) obligation to consult with other riparian states, (3) obligation to exchange data and information on a regular basis, and (4) obligation of prior notification of planned measures.

While a detailed analysis of each of the procedural obligations is beyond the scope of this section, the following general remarks can be made to provide context for the subsequent parts of this book. First, it is widely accepted that water-sharing states should cooperate in good faith over transboundary watercourses.[935] Cooperation is a *sine qua non* for equitable and sustainable utilization of the transboundary water resources.[936] Without cooperation, the principle of equitable utilization and no significant harm rule cannot be practically applied,[937] and water-sharing states cannot discharge their procedural obligations.[938]

In the Gabčíkovo-Nagymaros Project case, the ICJ underscored the necessity of cooperation between states sharing the Danube, stating that "[t]he Danube has always played a vital part in the commercial and economic development of its [ten] riparian States, and has underlined and reinforced their

933 Shih & Stutz, *supra* note 60, 10818.

934 Schachter has succinctly described the importance of procedural rules as follow: "[P]rocedural requirements should be regarded as essential to the equitable sharing of water resources. They have particular importance because of the breadth and flexibility of the formulae for equitable use and appropriation. In the absence of hard and precise rules for allocation, there is a relatively greater need for specifying requirements for advance notice, consultation, and decision procedures. Such requirements are, in fact, commonly found in agreements by neighboring States concerning common lakes and rivers." OSCAR SCHACHTER, SHARING THE WORLD'S RESOURCES 69 (1977), cited in MCCAFFREY, *supra* note 4, 527.

935 MCCAFFREY, *supra* note 4, 527–28.

936 *Id.*

937 *Id*, 528 & 531.

938 *Id.*

interdependence, *making international cooperation essential*."[939] The court also considered "international cooperation" as the only option to "alleviate problems [of navigation, flood control, and environmental protection]."[940] The U.N. Watercourses Convention also recognizes the general obligation to cooperate,[941] recommending "watercourse States [to] consider the establishment of joint mechanisms or commissions, as [they] deemed necessary."[942]

Second, consultation, although does not serve as a means of dispute settlement, plays a significant role in the use and allocation of international watercourses.[943] International watercourses law contemplates consultation in various circumstances.[944] For instance, regular consultations between

---

939 Gabčíkovo-Nagymaros Project (Hung./Slovk.), Judgment, 1997 I.C.J. 7, ¶ 17 (Sept. 25) (emphasis added).

940 *See* MCCAFFREY, *supra* note 4, 529–30 (citing Gabčíkovo-Nagymaros Project (Hung./Slovk.), Judgment, 1997 I.C.J. 7, ¶ 17 (Sept. 25)).

941 U.N. Watercourses Convention, supra note 818, art 8. It should be noted that the nature of the obligation depends on the specific context. For example, cooperation with co-riparian states is required to achieve an equitable allocation of uses and benefits of a watercourse or to prevent pollution or protect the ecosystem of international watercourses. MCCAFFREY, *supra* note 4, 531–32. "These situations (as well as others) all require cooperation between riparian states. And in each of them, failure to cooperate would likely result in the non-fulfillment of one or more other obligations." *Id*, 532. Examples of failure to cooperate could also be those conducts "identified by the *Lake Lanoux* tribunal: unjustified delay, systematic refusal to consider the proposals or interests of co-riparian states", and "more generally, lack of good faith in the conduct of relations with other riparian states." *Id*. In the latter situations, failure to cooperate would "constitute an independent internationally wrongful act, engaging the responsibility of the non-cooperating state." *Id*.

942 U.N. Watercourses Convention, *supra* note 818, art 8, ¶ 2.

943 MCCAFFREY, *supra* note, 538.

944 *Id*. The U.N. Watercourses Convention, for instance, refers to riparian states' obligation to consult in several of its provisions. The Convention, in ¶ 5 of Article 3, provides: "Where a watercourse State considers that adjustment and application of the provisions of the present Convention is required because of the characteristics and uses of a particular international watercourse, watercourse States shall consult with a view to negotiating in good faith for the purpose of concluding a watercourse agreement or agreements." U.N. Watercourses Convention, *supra* note 818, art 3, ¶5. Article 6 ¶2 of the Convention provides that in implementing the principle of equitable and reasonable utilization, watercourse states "shall, when the need arises, enter into consultations in a spirit of cooperation." *Id*, art 6 ¶ 2. Article 7 ¶ 2 also requires watercourse states whose use causes significant harm to consult with the affected state concerning the elimination or mitigation of the harm. *Id*, art 7 ¶ 2. Part 3 of the Convention further imposes an obligation to consult with potentially affected riparian states when planned measures may have significant adverse effects upon their interests. *Id*, arts 11–19. Finally, per Article 17(1), watercourse states are required to "enter into consultations and, if necessary, negotiations with a view to arriving at an equitable resolution of the situation." *Id*, 17 ¶ 1.

riparian countries are extremely imperative "to ensure that a fair balance between their respective uses is maintained—especially in view of the usual changes not only in uses of the water but also in the natural factors affecting it."[945] Although the rules regarding consultation are not crystalized as customary international law,[946] there are two instances where consultations are required under international law. McCaffrey has aptly described these instances as follows:

> [I]t is likely that consultations are required in at least two of the instances ... where a state believes they are necessary to achieve or maintain equitable and reasonable utilization of shared water resources; and where a state believes implementation of measures planned in another state would be inconsistent with the latter's obligations to utilize a watercourse in an equitable and reasonable manner, and to prevent the causing of significant harm. In both of these cases, consultations are a key element of the processes that maintain a fair balance of uses and prevent unreasonable harm.[947]

The third obligation, regular exchange of data and information, is also necessary "adjunct to the obligations of equitable utilization and prevention of significant harm."[948] Indeed, it is only through the regular exchange of data and information that water-sharing states can "make informed decisions as to reasonable and equitable water sharing and to introduce resource conservation and protection measures whenever necessary in order to prevent significant harm."[949] Without such an obligation, it would be extremely difficult, if at all possible, for a riparian state not only to regulate the uses of the watercourse within its territory but also "to ensure that its utilization [remains] equitable and reasonable vis-à-vis other states sharing the watercourse."[950] Perhaps because of these reasons, the obligation to regularly exchange data and information has been included in several international instruments,[951] including in the U.N. Watercourses Convention, which, *inter alia*, requires watercourse

945 MCCAFFREY, *supra* note 4, 539.
946 *Id.*
947 *Id.*
948 *Id*, 540.
949 DANTE A CAPONERA, PRINCIPLES OF WATER LAW AND ADMINISTRATION: NATIONAL AND INTERNATIONAL 219 (2007).
950 MCCAFFREY, *supra* note 4, 540.
951 For the list of international instruments, *see Id*, 540–41.

states to "exchange readily available data and information on the condition of the watercourses."[952]

The last, and perhaps the most controversial, obligation relates to prior notification of planned measures. According to this principle, a state planning to undertake measures—or asked to issue a permit for planned measures—on a transboundary watercourse that could result in "significant adverse effects" on other riparian states should provide advance notification.[953] The main objective of this rule is the prevention of significant harm and the avoidance of disputes, "by requiring notification ... even before there is an indication that legally significant harm may result from the proposed use."[954] A State planning new measure is expected to provide not only timely notification but also any available "technical information and data ... that will enable the notified State to assess whether [and to what extent] the planned infrastructure affects its interests."[955]

To satisfy this obligation, the State planning the new impactful measures may undertake an environmental impact assessment (EIA) and provide its outcome to those watercourse states that may be significantly affected.[956] In supporting this assertion in the *Pulp Mills* case, the ICJ observed: "[I]t may now be considered a requirement under general international law to undertake an ... [EIA] where there is a risk that the proposed industrial activity may have a significant adverse impact in a transboundary context, in particular, on a shared resource."[957]

Reinforcing the general acceptance of the principle, the U.N. Watercourses Convention "devotes an entire section, Part 3, to detailed rules on notification, consultation, and negotiation concerning planned measures that may have a significant adverse effect on other riparian states."[958] While the obligation to provide prior notification of planned measures is generally accepted as

952 U.N. Watercourses Convention, *supra* note 818, art 9, ¶ 1.

953 MCCAFFREY, *supra* note 4, 534.

954 *Id.*

955 LAURENCE DE CHAZOURNES, FRESH WATER IN INTERNATIONAL LAW 70 (2013).

956 *Id*, 69–70; MCCAFFREY, *supra* note 4, 537.

957 Pulp Mills on the River Uruguay (Arg. v. Uru.), Judgment, 2010 I.C.J. p 83, ¶ 224 (Apr. 20).

958 MCCAFFREY, *supra* note 4, 533. *See* also U.N. Watercourses Convention, *supra* note 818, Part 3, arts 11–19. McCaffrey made the following comments regarding Part 3 of the U.N. Watercourses Convention: "The first two provisions of Part 3, Articles 11 and 12, capture the essential principles involved. Article 11 is a highly general provision that sums up the entire process of notification, consultation, and negotiation concerning planned measures, serving as a chapeau for the provisions to follow. Article 12 introduces the detailed regime of Part 3 by setting forth rules concerning when notification must be provided and what kinds of information must accompany it. Other recent instruments contain similar obligations. The Convention goes on to lay down procedures for replying to the

customary international law,[959] there is no state practice supporting the principle in the Nile Basin. Almost all Nile Basin projects are unilateral, and neither the upstream nor downstream states tend to notify their neighbors prior to undertaking their respective projects.[960] Ethiopia rejected the principle during the negotiation of the U.N. Watercourses Convention.[961] As discussed in Chapters 6 and 7, Ethiopia also managed to exclude the principle from the CFA and the DoP.[962]

Ethiopia and other upstream states reject this principle based in part on the belief that it is only "the upstream state that will be harming (adversely affecting) the downstream state, and thus it is the upstream state which will always have to notify and consult with its downstream neighbor, rather than vice versa."[963] This, according to Professor McCaffrey, has lead Ethiopia to "maintain, albeit incorrectly, that the Convention's prior notification regime is really a prior *consent* regime, effectively giving the potentially affected state a 'veto.'"[964] But in fact, prior notification does not equate to prior consent. The former does not condition the development of water projects on eventual agreement by affected states.[965]

---

notification, consultations, and negotiations concerning the planned measures, obligations in the absence of notification, and the like." MCCAFFREY, *supra* note 4, 533–34.

959 DE CHAZOURNES, *supra* note 955, 68–69 (Stating "[t]he obligation to notify those watercourse States that are potentially adversely affected to a significant extent by planned infrastructure development is today considered to form part of customary international law.") MCCAFFREY, *supra* note 4, 535. (Concluding that "prior notification is required by customary international law").

960 *See* the above discussion in sections 2.2 & 2.3. For the post-cold war developments, *see* the discussion *infra* sections 5.1 & 7.1.

961 Official Records Fifty-first Session, *supra* note 924, at 9. ("Although there was considerable opposition to part 3 [notifications of planed measures] and a number of amendments were suggested to create a balance and lessen the obligations to be assumed by upper riparian States, there was no serious desire to accommodate such suggestions. As a result, we have been forced to register our reservations on the whole of part 3 and some of its specific provisions").

962 *See* the discussion *infra* sections 6.2.2 & 7.2.

963 MCCAFFREY, *supra* note 4, 535.

964 *Id.* McCaffrey, articulating the two-way nature of the obligation, concluded that "it is incumbent upon downstream states to notify their upstream co-riparians when they contemplate water development projects that may affect the equitable balance of uses, possibly foreclosing future upstream uses, just as it is for upstream countries to notify those downstream." *Id*, 536.

965 *Id.*

Conclusion

This chapter has scrutinized the principal legal arguments of Nile Basin States based on the 1959 Agreement and customs. Based on this review, it is possible to draw several conclusions. First, the contents of the 1959 Agreement violate basic principles of international watercourses law, including, *inter alia*, equality of rights of Nile Basin States, the principle of equitable and reasonable utilization, and the no significant harm rule. Moreover, although it is prized as "a model International River' water-sharing agreement"[966] by some, the 1959 Agreement is just simply a means for creating a downstream hydro-hegemonic alliance.

Second, when South Sudan declared its independence in 2011, it did not inherit the 1959 Agreement. South Sudan did not conclude a devolution agreement with Sudan, and the 1959 Agreement does not create a territorial regime as envisioned in article 12 of VCSSRT. Thus, South Sudan is not bound by the 1959 Agreement.

Third, while treaty rules can transform into customary law, there is neither consistent state practice nor *opinio juris* justifying the water allocation provided in the 1959 Agreement. The upstream states did not exercise forbearance in exploiting the Nile watercourse and constructing large-scale dams dam earlier out of any sense of legal obligation. They have guarded against the establishment of regional customs in the Nile Basin by objecting to the development of the existing status quo. Therefore, they are not bound by the allocation provided in the 1959 Agreement.

Finally, although upstream and downstream states of the Nile Basin occasionally invoked the absolutist conflicting doctrines, "there is virtually no support, in either state practice, judicial decisions, or the writings of commentators, for the isolationist and unilateralist theories of absolute territorial sovereignty and absolute territorial integrity."[967] In the absence of an all-inclusive treaty, the doctrine of limited territorial sovereignty, and its customary international principles such as equitable and reasonable utilization and no significant harm should be the governing rubric of the Nile watercourse.

966 Ahmed, *supra* note 480, 357.
967 MCCAFFREY, *supra* note 4, 157.

PART 2

Post-Cold War Attempts to Change or Maintain the Status Quo

CHAPTER 5

Between Unilateralism and Cooperation: the Nile Basin in the Post-Cold War Era

Introduction

Part 1 of this book has reconstructed the legal and hydro-political history of the Nile Basin. The pre-colonial myths that Ethiopia would block the Nile waters, the colonial legacies that established inequitable utilization in the basin, and the Cold War rivalries that made unilateralism the *modus operandi* of the Nile Basin have all been investigated there. This chapter now scrutinizes the post–Cold War unilateral, bilateral, and multilateral developments in the Nile Basin. It begins by analyzing bilateral cooperative initiatives after the Cold War. After scrutinizing the legal and hydro-political implications of the Ethiopia-Sudan Peace and Friendship Declaration[968] (hereinafter Khartoum Declaration) and the Framework for General Cooperation between Ethiopia and the Arab Republic of Egypt[969] (hereinafter Framework Instrument), the chapter then examines the multilateral initiatives including, *inter alia*, the Technical Cooperation Committee for the Promotion of the Development and Environmental Protection of the Nile (TECCONILE), the NBI and the CFA. Finally, the chapter provides a brief overview of unilateral projects and indicates how unilateralism is still the *modus operandi* of the Nile Basin.

5.1 Bilateral Cooperative Initiatives

As indicated in section 4.1, Egypt and Sudan established a downstream hydro-hegemonic alliance through the 1959 Agreement and agreed to address as one unit any issue regarding the Nile watercourse with other Nile Basin States.[970] Despite this commitment, however, Sudan and Egypt respectively signed the 1991 Khartoum declaration and the 1993 Framework for Cooperation with Ethiopia. This section analyzes both instruments.

968 1991 Khartoum Declaration, *supra* note 175.
969 1993 Framework Instrument, *supra* note 176.
970 1959 Agreement, *supra* note 106, art V, ¶ 1; *see* also Salman, *supra* note 89, at 85–89.

 | DOI:10.1163/9789004549869_006

5.1.1 *The 1991 Khartoum Declaration*

Shortly after the downfall of the Mengistu regime in May 1991, the new transitional government of Ethiopia started a rapprochement with the Bashir regime in Sudan.[971] Meles Zenawi, the leader of the transitional government, visited Khartoum in December 1991 and signed the Ethiopia-Sudan Peace and Friendship Declaration with Sudan.[972]

Paragraph 4.1 of the Declaration, entitled "Minutes of Appreciation of Principles and Needs for Uses of the Nile Waters,"[973] affirmed that "the Nile is a common resource of the co-basin states, a vital resource, one of which our lives, and respective cultures are intimately tied to it forever."[974] The paragraph further reiterated that "the two sides believe in, and affirm equitable entitlements to the uses of the Nile waters without causing appreciable harm to one another."[975] In light of international law, this paragraph recognized the foundation of international watercourses law of the equality of all watercourse states and codified the two customary principles of international watercourses law, namely equitable and reasonable utilization and no significant harm.[976]

In paragraph 4.1.5, the two countries recalled the absence of Ethiopia from the previous Nile Basin cooperative initiatives,[977] and agreed that "Ethiopia will now declare upgraded participation at a full membership level to contribute to the regional and international initiatives that tend to forge cooperation among the basin countries."[978] Paragraph 4.1.6 further affirmed the need for "establish[ing] a joint technical committee with multi-discipline composition of experts who would pave the way for prior consultations; exchange of data and information, and explore areas of cooperation."[979] Envisioning basin-wide cooperation, Sudan and Ethiopia considered this committee as a first step "towards the objective of achieving the formation of the Nile Basin Organization taking the interests of all riparian countries into account, and with their universal consent."[980]

971 Salman M. A. Salman, *The Nile Basin Cooperative Framework Agreement: Disentangling the Gordian Knot, in* GERD IMPLICATIONS, *supra* note 169, 22.
972 1991 Khartoum Declaration, *supra* note 175.
973 *Id*, ¶ 4.1.
974 *Id*. ¶ 4.1.1.
975 *Id*.
976 Salman, *supra* note 971, 22.
977 1991 Khartoum Declaration, *supra* note 175, ¶ 4.1.5.
978 *Id*.
979 *Id*, ¶ 4.1.6.
980 *Id*. ¶ 4.1.7.

The 1991 Khartoum Declaration has various implications for the legal regime governing the Nile watercourse. First, amongst all, the Declaration incorporates Sudan's acceptance of the basic principles of international watercourses law.[981] Through the declaration Sudan—the state that signed the 1959 Agreement and apportioned the entire flow of the Nile with Egypt—recognized Ethiopia's right to equitable entitlement to the Nile watercourse. Second, considering "the Nile [as] a common resource of the co-basin states,"[982] the Declaration endorsed the notion of equality of rights of all basin states.[983] In addition to explicitly codifying the principle of equitable and reasonable utilization and the obligation not to cause significant harm,[984] the Declaration also reflects the modern notion of transboundary water resource governance by underscoring the need for basin-wide institutional cooperation between all Nile Basin States.[985] In sum, the Declaration represents the first step towards changing the status quo established by colonial and immediate post-colonial treaties (existing Nile Waters Agreements).

5.1.2 *The 1993 Framework for Cooperation*

Two years after the Khartoum Declaration, Ethiopia and Egypt also signed the 1993 Framework Instrument, "desirous of the realization of their full economic and resource potential."[986] Underscoring the two parties' "mutual interest" over the Nile watercourse,[987] the Framework Instrument laid out general principles including good neighborliness, peaceful settlement of disputes, and noninterference in internal affairs.[988] It also underlined the necessity of consolidating "mutual trust and understanding between the two countries,"[989] and recognized "cooperation as an essential means to promote their economic and political interests as well as stability of the region."[990]

Following these general principles, the Framework Instrument also provided substantive and procedural provisions regarding the Nile watercourse. The procedural provisions include the establishment of "appropriate mechanisms

981 Salman, *supra* note 971, 22.
982 1991 Khartoum Declaration, *supra* note 175, ¶ 4.1.
983 Salman, *supra* note 971, 22.
984 1991 Khartoum Declaration, *supra* note 175, ¶ 4.1.
985 Salman, *supra* note 971, 22.
986 1993 Framework Instrument, *supra* note 176, preamble, ¶ 3.
987 *Id*, preamble ¶ 4.
988 *Id*, art 1.
989 *Id*, art 2.
990 *Id*, art 3.

for periodic consultations" and cooperation.[991] Moreover, the Instrument stipulated in Article 4 that "the issue of the use of the Nile waters shall be worked out in detail through discussions by experts from both sides, on the basis of the *rules and principles of international law*."[992] This article has both procedural and substantive aspects:[993] while the procedural aspect of the provision required the two countries to cooperate and resolve "the issue of [the] use of the Nile waters" through detailed expert study, the substantive aspect simply refers to "rules and principles of international law."[994] Ethiopia and Egypt have different interpretations of this phrase. Egyptian scholars argue that the phrase refers to the rules and principles codified in the existing Nile Waters Agreements,[995] whereas Ethiopia interprets the phrase as customary international watercourses law principles such as equitable and reasonable utilization and the obligation not to cause significant harm.[996]

Ethiopia's approach seems to be supported by the customary rules of interpretation provided in the VCLT. Per Article 31 of the VCLT, the 1993 Framework Instrument should be interpreted in "*good faith* in accordance with the *ordinary meaning* to be given to the terms of the treaty in their *context* and in the light of its *object and purpose*."[997] Here the procedural aspect of the provision, which requires the two countries to resolve the Nile issue through detailed expert study, provides a useful context to understand that the ordinary meaning of the phrase "rules and principles of international law" does not refer to the existing Nile Waters Agreements. If the phrase is interpreted as endorsing these agreements, there would be no Nile issue to be resolved through a detailed expert study. As these agreements gave veto power to Egypt and allocated the entire flow of the Nile waters between the two downstream countries, Egypt and Ethiopia would not need to undertake any expert study. If, however, the phrase is interpreted as the basic principles of customary international watercourses law, Ethiopia and Egypt would be required to undertake comprehensive studies and cooperate in good faith to apply them in the Nile Basin. They would, for instance, be required to consider all relevant objective

991 *Id*, art 7.

992 *Id*, art 4 (emphasis added).

993 YIHDEGO, *supra* note 172, 33.

994 1993 Framework Instrument, *supra* note 176, art. 4.

995 Mosaad Shetewy, *Legal Commitments Regulating the Establishment of Water Projects on International Rivers Application Study over the Nile Basin,* 11 (39) AFRICAN PERSPECTIVES 35 (2013). ("Ethiopia had ratified the General Framework Agreement for Cooperation with Egypt, upon which Ethiopia pledged not to violate Egypt's historical rights.")

996 YIHDEGO, *supra* note 172, 33.

997 VCLT, *supra* note 520, 31, ¶ 1 (emphasis added).

factors and conduct detailed studies to implement the principle of equitable and reasonable utilization in the Nile Basin.[998]

Moreover, given Ethiopia's persistent objections discussed above, it would be contrary to good faith to use this phrase as a pretext to impose the ramifications of the existing Nile Waters Agreements on Ethiopia. The endorsement of those agreements would also hinder Ethiopia from realizing its "full economic and resource potential," and thereby defeat the object and purpose of the 1993 Framework Instrument.[999]

Indeed, the precise nature of the "rules and principles of international [watercourses] law" was controversial during the conclusion of the 1993 Framework Instrument. The U.N. Watercourses Convention was adopted four years after the instrument. As such, Ethiopia's position *may* be challenged based on the principle of intertemporal law. It is possible, for instance, to argue that the current basic principles of international watercourses law were not the contemporary law of the time, and therefore cannot be considered as the "rules and principles [of] international law" referred to by the Framework Instrument. However, this argument is still problematic and cannot pass the test of international law. First, while it is true that international watercourses law has been controversial during the conclusion of the Framework Instrument, the current basic principles, and more specifically the principle of equitable and reasonable utilization and no significant harm rule, were in fact the contemporary customary law of the time.[1000] The U.N. Watercourses Convention largely reflects the codification of rules and principles of customary international watercourses law.[1001] Four months after its adoption, the ICJ referred to the Convention and confirmed the customary status of the principle of equitable and reasonable utilization in its judgment in the case involving the Gabčíkovo-Nagymaros Project.[1002]

Second, assuming, *arguendo*, that the principle of equitable and reasonable utilization is not the contemporary customary law of the time, the principle is still relevant for interpreting the Framework Instrument. Pursuant to the VCLT, any relevant rules of international law applicable between Ethiopia and Egypt need to be taken into account while interpreting the Framework

---

998 *See* the discussion in section 4.2.2.1.

999 1993 Framework Instrument, *supra* note 176, preamble, ¶ 3.

1000 MCCAFFREY, *supra* note 4, 445.

1001 *Id*, 422. ("[T]he Convention reflects in large measure rules and principles of customary international law on international watercourses, and it is indeed generally taken as such").

1002 Gabčíkovo-Nagymaros Project (Hung./Slovk.), Judgment, 1997 I.C.J. 7, ¶ 78 (Sept. 25).

Instrument.[1003] In this regard, the ICJ also requires any "international instrument…to be interpreted and applied within the framework of the entire legal system prevailing at the time of the interpretation."[1004] Currently, customary international law principles such as equitable and reasonable utilization and the obligation not to cause significant harm are applicable between Ethiopia and Egypt.[1005] Therefore, the ordinary meaning of the phrase "rules and principles of international law" should be construed to mean customary international watercourses laws, not the existing Nile Waters Treaties.

Ethiopia and Egypt also agreed under Article 5 "to refrain from engaging in any activity related to the Nile waters that may cause *appreciable harm* to the interests of the other party."[1006] Surprisingly, while mentioning the no-harm principle, the Framework Instrument omitted the overriding principle of international watercourses law, that is, the principle of equitable and reasonable utilization. As a result, some Ethiopian scholars criticized the Framework Instrument as favoring Egypt and compromising Ethiopia's national interests over the Nile.[1007] However, even if no-harm rule is explicitly mentioned in the Instrument, it is not the only rule governing the use and allocation of the Nile watercourse. Ethiopia's interests can still be protected by the Instrument as the principle of equitable and reasonable utilization is implicitly included in Article 4.[1008]

Fasil Amdetsion, considering the Instrument as unfavorable to Ethiopia, argued against Article 5 based on several grounds. "First, it does not reflect … the higher threshold posed by the more common injunction against *significant* harm. Second, it does not counterbalance the notion of significant harm by mandating use which is equitable. Also troubling is the broadness in [the] scope of what is circumscribed—*any* activity which is merely *related* to *interests*."[1009] Given the stipulations of the U.N. Watercourses Convention that impose the duty to "take all appropriate measures to prevent the causing of significant harm"[1010] rather than "to refrain from engaging in any activities"

1003 VCLT, *supra* note 520, art. 31, ¶ 1 (c).
1004 *See* Legal Consequences for States of the Continued Presence of South Africa in Namibia (South-West Africa) Advisory Opinion, 1971 I.C.J. 16, ¶ 53 (June 21).
1005 *See* the discussion in section 4.2.
1006 1993 Framework Instrument, *supra* note 176, art 5.
1007 Fasil Amdetsion, *Time to Think about Ethiopia's Post-GERD Nile Policy*, COOPERATIVE WATERS MAGAZINE, https://www.africanidea.org/Nile_Coop_Waters.pdf.
1008 1993 Framework Instrument, *supra* note 176, art 4.
1009 Amdestion, *supra* note 1007.
1010 U.N. Watercourses Convention, *supra* note 818, art. 7 ¶1.

and that may even permit infliction of significant harm,[1011] one may concur with Amdetsion, and consider the 1993 Framework Instrument more prohibitive and restrictive. However, the argument that the Instrument benefits Egypt while compromising the interests of Ethiopia is based on an erroneous assumption that harm can only be caused by upstream riparian states to the downstream ones. As noted in section 4.2.2.2, harm is a two-way street; and just as upstream riparian states can harm downstream riparian states, downstream riparian states can also cause harm to upstream ones.[1012] Professor McCaffrey succinctly articulated such harm as follows:

> By implementing a water development project, a downstream state is creating "facts on the ground" which could alter the equitable balance of uses between the upstream and downstream states and could thus effectively foreclose, or limit, future uses by the upstream state. That is, the upstream state's options for development would be restricted by the equitable utilization and no-harm rules because it would have a narrower margin for development before its compliance with those obligations could be called into question due to the fact that the water available to the downstream state was being fully, or largely, utilized there. This is clearly an "adverse effect" and also qualifies as "harm," as Ronald Coase has shown, and as the U.S. Supreme Court has recognized in its interstate apportionment decisions.[1013]

Therefore, as the Instrument imposed an obligation on Ethiopia not to cause applicable harm to Egypt, it also equally obliged Egypt not to cause appreciable harm to Ethiopia through foreclosure of future uses.[1014] However, Egypt, in what seems a flagrant violation of the Instrument, started undertaking the South Valley Development Project in 1997.[1015] The project requires a minimum of 5 BCM of Nile waters annually and is now causing significant harm to the interests of Ethiopia, effectively foreclosing its future uses of the Nile waters.[1016] In light of this reality, Ethiopia protested the project through its *Note Verbale* of

1011 *Id*, art. 7 ¶2. In requiring watercourse states to "take all appropriate measures, having due regard for the provisions of Articles 5 and 6 [principle of equitable and reasonable utilization]" the U.N. Watercourses Convention allowed causing significant harm if it is equitable and reasonable under the circumstance. *Id*.

1012 MCCAFFREY, *supra* note 4, 474.

1013 *Id*, 536.

1014 Salman, *supra* note 971, 23.

1015 WOLDETSADIK, *supra* note 172, 44–55.

1016 *Id*.

March 20, 1997, addressed to Egypt, the UN, the World Bank, and the OAU. The *Note Verbale* stated: "Ethiopia wishes to be on record as having made it unambiguously clear that it will not allow its share to the Nile waters to be affected by a *fait accompli* such as the Toshka project, regarding which it was neither consulted nor alerted."[1017]

Article 6 of the Framework Instrument addressed the necessity of conservation and protection of the Nile waters, and the need to consult and cooperate "in projects that are mutually advantageous, such as projects that would enhance the volume of flow and reduce the loss of Nile Waters through comprehensive and integrated development schemes."[1018] The remaining two provisions further dealt with regular consultation[1019] and regional cooperation as discussed above.[1020]

Diverse views have been reflected regarding the legal status of the Framework Instrument. Mohammed Abdo argues that the Instrument "does not have a binding effect. It is no more than the heralding of a new era of improved relations between the two states with regard to the water of the Nile."[1021] Shetewy, on the other hand, argues that the Instrument is binding and that Ethiopia "pledged not to violate Egypt's historical rights."[1022]

Per international law, the status of the 1993 Framework Instrument should be determined based on the two countries' intention to be bound by it: the ICJ uses "an 'objective test' to determine" the binding nature of a given document and considers "its actual terms and … the particular circumstances in which it was drawn up."[1023] The rub is that the intention of Ethiopia and Egypt cannot be inferred from the 1993 Framework Instrument and the text does not support or reject either Shetewy's or Abdo's arguments.[1024] But, given the general nature of the Instrument and the lack of specific rights and obligations thereto, Abdo's argument seems appropriate.[1025]

Nevertheless, Egypt already registered the Instrument with the UN in 2010, per Article 102 (1) of the UN Charter, which requires every treaty concluded by the UN member states to "as soon as possible be registered with the Secretariat

1017 Ethiopia's 2020 Letter to the UNSC 1, *supra* note 788, annex V.
1018 1993 Framework Instrument, *supra* note 176, art 6.
1019 *Id*, art 7.
1020 *Id*, art 8.
1021 Abdo, *supra* note 835, 52.
1022 Shetewy, *supra* note 995, 35.
1023 YIHDEGO, *supra* note 172, 34–35 (quoting Aegean Sea Continental Shelf (Gr. V. Turkey), Judgment, 1978 I.C.J. ¶ 39 (December 19)).
1024 YIHDEGO, *supra* note 172, 35.
1025 *Id*.

and published by it."[1026] Professor Zeray Yihdego argues that this would not affect the status of the Instrument:

> Unlike the League of Nations Covenant ..., [the] nonregistration of an agreement does not determine its binding or non-binding nature. The ICJ and other UN organs do not consider registration of an instrument when dealing with legal cases involving agreements concluded between states. It follows that the UN Secretariat generally registers an agreement when it is submitted by any of the parties without making a judgment on the nature of that instrument. ... The move to register the instrument by Egypt after the lapse of 17 years arguably poses questions of good faith and might not be in compliance with the "as soon as possible" precondition of Article 102 (1) of the Charter.[1027]

Generally, it can be stated that the 1993 Framework Instrument is an "unfinished and vague law-making endeavor, which has been selectively relied upon by the parties to blame each other for making use of Nile waters."[1028] Notwithstanding its dubious legal status, the instrument is an important commitment that codified the basic principles of international water law, significantly varying from the existing Nile Waters Agreements.[1029] It is the foundation for the beginning of other multilateral cooperative initiatives in which Ethiopia upgraded its status from an observer to a full membership level.[1030]

5.2 Multilateral Cooperative Initiatives

In addition to these bilateral cooperative initiatives, the decades following the end of the Cold War also witnessed several multilateral cooperative initiatives. With the support of the international community and donor countries, the Nile Basin States made progressive attempts to develop basin-wide programs, including the hydrometeorological project (Hydromet project) the Undugu group, the TECCONILE, the NBI, and the CFA. This section focuses on these multilateral initiatives.

1026 U.N. Charter, art. 102, ¶ 1.

1027 YIHDEGO, *supra* note 172, 35.

1028 *Id*, 36.

1029 *Id*.

1030 Salman, *supra* note 971, 24.

5.2.1 *Overlapping Initiatives: from Hydromet to the Nile Basin Initiative*

Ever since the late 1960s, the Equatorial Lake states have had institutional cooperation with Egypt and Sudan in the area of data and information exchange.[1031] Based on the 1967 Agreement between Egypt, Sudan, Kenya, Tanzania, and Uganda, and with the support of the UNDP as well as the World Meteorological Organization (WMO),[1032] several hydrometeorological studies (Hydromet Project) were re-initiated in the early 1980s.[1033] The goal was to facilitate data and information exchange between the five member states[1034] and to identify baseline measurements for determining "water availability and future needs affecting the White Nile in and around lakes Victoria, Kyoga, and Albert."[1035]

The project "consisted in the elaboration of a mathematical model of the precipitation and runoff regimes, and data analysis … [It] undertook basic training of technicians and technocrats in several of the newly independent riparians."[1036] It was hoped that Hydromet Project data would promote joint planning; however, this desire has not materialized because of political unrest in some basin states.[1037] Although the project was limited to technical cooperation in the Equatorial Lake sub-basin,[1038] it facilitated conversations for the establishment of a basin-wide cooperation mechanism,[1039] Ethiopia joining as an observer in 1971.[1040] It also served as a foundation for the conclusion of the

1031 Arsano & Tamrat, *supra* note 100, 19.

1032 *Report of the Hydrometeorological Survey of the Catchments of Lakes Victoria, Kyoga, and Albert (Burundi, Egypt, Kenya, Rwanda, Sudan, United Republic of Tanzania, and Uganda)* 1 METEOROLOGY AND HYDROLOGY OF THE BASIN PART 1, at 9 (1974) (UNDP and WMO, RAL 66–025 Tech. Report No. 1) [hereinafter Hydrometeorological Survey].

1033 Jutta Brunne & Stephen Toope, *The Changing Nile Basin Regime: Does Law Matter?*, 43 HARV. INT'L L.J. 105, 132 (2002). Explaining the first phase of Hydromet project, WATERBUR stated: "Between 1961 and 1964, the level of Lake Victoria and other equatorial lakes rose dramatically, in the case of Victoria by some 2.5. meters (over eight feet), leading to extensive coastal flooding and displacement of populations … The causes were not known, prompting the World Meteorological Organization, with Egyptian backing, to undertake a survey of rainfall in the affected regions of the upper Nile. The project, known as Hydromet (the Hydrometeorological Survey), was begun in 1967, and the first phase of catchment survey ended in 1974." WATERBURY, *supra* note 302, 76–77.

1034 Arsano & Tamrat, *supra* note 100, 19.

1035 *Id*, Brunne & Toope, *supra* note 1033, 132.

1036 WATERBURY, *supra* note 302, 77.

1037 *Id*, Brunne & Toope, *supra* note 1033, 132. For instance, it was impossible to "undertake necessary follow-up activities in Uganda" and "the meteorological service came close to collapse during the dark years of Amin and Obote." *Id.*

1038 WATERBURY, *supra* note 302, 76–77.

1039 GODANA, *supra* note 477, 260.

1040 WATERBURY, *supra* note 302, 76–77.

agreement between Rwanda, Burundi and Tanzania on the establishment of the Kagera Basin Organization in 1977.[1041] The project finally ended in 1992.[1042]

In 1983, Egypt, Sudan, Uganda, DRC (then Zaire), and the Central African Republic, created an ambitious informal initiative with annual ministerial meetings called UNDUGU—meaning "brotherhood" in Swahili.[1043] Founded at Egypt's behest and subsequently joined by Burundi, Rwanda, and Tanzania, UNDUGU brought all the Nile Basin States together, except Ethiopia and Kenya, which participated only as observers.[1044] This initiative aimed to facilitate discussions on "such issues as the Nile waters, agriculture and resource development, and the promotion of economic, technical, and scientific cooperation among the riparians."[1045]

Given its functions as a forum for data and information exchange, UNDUGU had been praised "as an institutional locus for sharing expertise and as a group accustomed to treating the Nile as a whole, not as less than the sum of its national parts."[1046] It also undertook fact-finding activities designed to facilitate the formation of a "comprehensive joint economic planning, including planning for water resource development."[1047] Notwithstanding these modest contributions, UNDUGU was generally perceived as a failed drive toward "self-reliance and African interdependence."[1048] It was also criticized for its failure to establish meaningful basin-wide cooperation, mainly due to a lack of political will from Egypt,[1049] which considered the initiative only "as an exercise in hegemonic influence."[1050] Moreover, the initiative was also significantly undermined by Egypt's large-scale, unilateral land reclamation projects.[1051]

1041 Agreement for the Establishment of the Organization for the Management and Development of the Kagera River Basin., August 24, 1977, 171 UNTS 1089. *See* also John Waterbury, *Legal and Institutional Arrangements for Managing Water Resources in the Nile Basin,* 3(2) INT. J. WATER RESOUR. DEV., 97 (1987). (Mentioning how Hydromet facilitated the conclusion of the agreement).

1042 Arsano & Tamrat, *supra* note 100, 19.

1043 *Id*; WATERBURY, *supra* note 302, 77; Brunne & Toope, *supra* note 1033, 132.

1044 *Id*; WATERBURY, *supra* note 302, 77–78 (Stating that "Ethiopia saw it as another Egyptian Trojan horse and opposed it from the outset.") *See* also Brunne & Toope, *supra* note 1033, 133.

1045 Brunne & Toope, *supra* note 1033, 133.

1046 *Id.*

1047 *Id.*

1048 *Id.*

1049 Mekonnen, *supra* note 135, 426.

1050 Brunne & Toope, *supra* note 1033, 133.

1051 COLLINS, *supra* note 64, at 225.

"Perhaps in [an] attempt to circumvent the effects of the perceived political dominance of Egypt in UNDUGU,"[1052] the Technical Cooperation Committee for the Promotion of the Development and Environmental Protection of the Nile (TECCONILE) was established in 1992, by Egypt, Rwanda, Sudan, Tanzania, Uganda, and Zaire (DRC).[1053] "Even with the strong technical focus, Ethiopia and Kenya again refused to join as members because they deemed the framework for the organization to be inadequate since it did not address the fundamental equitable concerns of water apportionment."[1054] Still skeptical of the initiative, Ethiopia, Kenya, Burundi, and Eritrea joined TECCONILE only as observers.[1055]

The structure of the initiative encompassed (1) the Council of Ministers of Water Affairs (Nile COM), (2) the Technical Committee (TC), and (3) the Secretariat.[1056] The Nile COM, which agreed to meet annually, was the highest decision-making body of the initiative, while the TC was a steering committee for the initiative that would meet three times per year.[1057] The Secretariat, located in Entebbe, Uganda, would execute the day-to-day activities of the Initiative.[1058] In 1993, TECCONILE started its activities after getting financial and technical support from the Canadian International Development Agency (CIDA).[1059] The Nile-COM and TC had several meetings from 1993 to 1995 and developed the Nile River Basin Action Plan (NBRAP).[1060] All the Nile Basin States were involved in the development of the action plan.[1061]

1052 Brunne & Toope, *supra* note 1033, 133. Mekonnen disagrees with Brunne & Toope and asserts that "TECCONILE was in fact an offshoot of Hydromet." Mekonnen, *supra* note 135, 427.

1053 *Id*, 426; Brunne & Toope, *supra* note 1033, 133–4; WATERBURY, *supra* note 302, 78; Arsano & Tamrat, *supra* note 100, 19.

1054 Brunne & Toope, *supra* note 1033, 133–4.

1055 NILE RIVER BASIN DRAFT ACTION PLAN, TECCONILE 4 (1994), https://www.ircwash.org/sites/default/files/824-AAF94-14893.pdf (hereinafter ACTION PLAN). Ethiopia constantly refused to join those initiatives as a member because of the fear that Egypt would use them to exert hydro-hegemonic influence. Amdetsion, *supra* note 72, at 39. "The series of cooperative ventures serving as a precursor to the NBI, for instance, were often sabotaged in one way or another. Egypt and Sudan tried repeatedly to establish a Nile Commission prior to the Hydromet Project, and before the establishment of TECCONILE. According to upper riparian states who rebuffed the efforts, the goal was to furtively pass measures that were advantageous to lower riparians by taking advantage of the lower technical skills and scant resources of East African states." *Id.*

1056 ACTION PLAN, *supra* note 1055, 4.

1057 *Id.*

1058 *Id.*

1059 PRISCOLI & WOLF, *supra* note 48, 235.

1060 ACTION PLAN, *supra* note 1055. *See also* Brunne & Toope, *supra* note 1033, 134.

1061 *Id. See* also Elemam, *supra* note 81, 227.

The plan provided for 22 projects[1062] with 5 components: (a) integrated water resources planning, (b) capacity building, (c) training, (d) regional cooperation, and (e) environmental protection.[1063] In February 1995, the NBRAP was approved by the Council of Ministers for Water Affairs of all Nile Basin States with an estimated total cost of US$100 million.[1064] Within the "component D" or "regional cooperation," the NBRAP contemplated "the establishment of a basin-wide, multidisciplinary framework for legal and institutional arrangements," also known as Project D3.[1065]

As was the case with the previous initiatives, "very little implementation occurred under the Action Plan … in part because of resource constraints, and in part because of continuing competitive behavior among the basin states."[1066] Regarding the latter, for instance, Egypt was interested in cooperating only on non-consumptive water projects, while Ethiopia insisted on the determination of the states' equitable entitlement to Nile waters through the development of a multilateral legal and institutional framework.[1067] Ethiopia further asserted that "the elaboration of a framework for cooperation that would have to *precede* any action plan. Action can be taken, the Ethiopians argued, only after we have agreed on a users' code, preferably based on principles of equitable use."[1068] Despite these challenges, and perhaps because of Ethiopia's insistence,[1069] the multilateral works continued under the supervision of the Nile COM through two different, but parallel tracks: (1) the Cooperative Framework Agreement Project (Project D3) and (2) developing other joint technical projects.[1070]

The short-term objective of the first track, Project D3, was to establish a basin-wide legal and institutional cooperative framework acceptable to all Nile Basin States.[1071] The project also sought "to determine the equitable entitlements [of] each country for consumptive and non-consumptive use

1062 WATERBURY, *supra* note 302, 78.

1063 ACTION PLAN, *supra* note 1055, 15.

1064 WATERBURY, *supra* note 302, 78; Brunne & Toope, *supra* note 10, 134.

1065 Abdel Fattah Metawie, *History of Co-operation in the Nile Basin*, 20 (1) WATER RESOUR. DEV. 54 (2004).

1066 Brunne & Toope, *supra* note 1033, 135.

1067 SAMAAN, *supra* note 188, 138; WATERBURY, *supra* note 302, 78.

1068 *Id*, 79.

1069 *Id.*

1070 McCaffrey Interview, *supra* note 135; SAMAAN, *supra* note 188, 138; Emmanuel Kasimbazi, *Developing a Cooperative Framework Agreement for a Transboundary River: Lessons from a Comparative Analysis of the Mekong and Nile Rivers Basins*, 8 US-CHINA LAW REVIEW 748 (2011).

1071 DIANA KARYABWITE, WATER SHARING IN THE NILE RIVER VALLEY 48 (1998), https://hcil.umd.edu/media/simple/nilereport.pdf.

of Nile waters [and] for optimum sustainable socio-economic benefits of the inhabitants of the basin."[1072] To that end, all ministers of Water Affairs of the Nile Basin States nominated three experts and with the support of UNDP, the Panel of Experts (POE) was formed in 1997.[1073] The POE subsequently adopted a Strategic Work Plan and developed a Project Document in 1997.[1074] It also formed two POE groups, one working as a legal and institutional team and another as a data and information (technical resources) team, and assigned two international consultants to work with two POE groups.[1075] The POE visited the Mekong river (Thailand and Cambodia) and the Senegal river to gain practical experience in transboundary water resource governance.[1076] It submitted the first draft of the CFA in 2000 to the Nile-COM.[1077] The Nile-COM, however, acknowledging the existence of substantive outstanding issues,[1078] formed a Joint Negotiation Committee (JNC) that negotiated the CFA for about 10 years until it was rejected by Egypt and Sudan in 2010.[1079]

While undertaking the multilateral works under the first track, the Nile Basin States also followed the second track. In 1998, they reviewed the NBRAP adopted in 1995 and developed a new Nile River Basin Strategic Action Program (NRBSAP) based on the recommendations of the World Bank.[1080] It was recommended that the Nile COM should form "a new transitional institutional mechanism with all riparian states as equal members to succeed TECCONILE until [the works on Project D3 were finalized and] the permanent institutional and legal framework of co-operation was formed."[1081] Thus, with the support from the World Bank, UNDP and CIDA, the Nile Basin Initiative (NBI) was established in 1999.[1082] The NBI brought all Nile Basin States together as members, except Eritrea, which has participated only as an observer.[1083]

Regarding the relationship between the NBI and the CFA, it is important to recall that the overwhelming Nile literature erroneously asserts that the

1072 Tafesse, *supra* note 529, at 75 (internal citation omitted).
1073 Metawie, *supra* note 1065, 62.
1074 *Id.*
1075 *Id.*
1076 *Id.*
1077 *Id.*
1078 *Id*, 63.
1079 MCCAFFREY, *supra* note 4, 319.
1080 *Id*; Brunne & Toope, *supra* note 1033, 135 & 137–38.
1081 Metawie, *supra* note 1065, 54.
1082 Brunne & Toope, *supra* note 1033, 138.
1083 *See* the NBI website, https://nilebasin.org/index.php/nbi/who-we-are, for information on the membership of NBI.

CFA was negotiated under the auspices of the NBI.[1084] However, as this section demonstrates, the CFA, which predated the NBI itself, was conceived in the TECCONILE[1085] and negotiated as an independent and separate track after TECCONILE was superseded by the NBI in 1999.[1086] The next section examines the NBI in detail.

5.2.2 *The Nile Basin Initiative: Structure, Programs, and Hydro-political Implications*

The NBI was conceived in 1998 as a strategic program for the Nile Basin, with the initiation and support of the World Bank.[1087] It was formally launched on 22 February 1999 in Dar es Salaam at the Nile COM meeting[1088] with the objectives to develop the Nile waters in a cooperative, sustainable, and equitable manner, to eradicate poverty and enhance economic integration, and to promote peace, security, and prosperity in the region.[1089] The NBI does not have a conventional constitutive treaty and was established by the minute of the Nile COM meeting.[1090] All Nile Basin States at the time, except Eritrea—which participates an observer—became members of the NBI.[1091] After its independence, South Sudan acceded to the Initiative in 2012.[1092]

1084 *E.g.*, ARSANO, *supra* note 169, 217; Helal, *supra* note 86, 932; Mekonnen, *supra* note 525, 233; Salman, *supra* note 172, 20.

1085 Brunne & Toope, *supra* note 1033, 135 & 137–38; Metawie, *supra* note 1065, 54.

1086 McCaffrey Interview, *supra* note 135.

1087 Brunne & Toope, *supra* note 1033, 137–38.

1088 Metawie, *supra* note 1065, 47; NBI, *supra* note 1083.

1089 *Id.*

1090 SERGEI VINOGRADOV ET AL, TRANSFORMING POTENTIAL CONFLICT INTO COOPERATION POTENTIAL: THE ROLE OF INTERNATIONAL WATER LAW (2003), https://www.semanticscholar.org/paper/Transforming-potential-conflict-into-cooperation-of-VinogradovWouters/e1faef020e5e2da65f0d83b02f8c3ed4e799656f. Explaining the peculiar feature of this arrangement VINOGRADOV ET AL remarked: "One unique feature of the NBI, which distinguishes it from similar institutional mechanisms on other watercourses, is that it was launched by the Nile basin countries without any formal treaty. Rather than trying to conclude an agreement, which seemed very unlikely given the range of unresolved contentious issues separating them, the basin states established the NBI at the 1999 meeting of the Ministers of Water Affairs by simply adopting and signing the Minutes." *Id.*

1091 NBI, *supra* note 1083.

1092 *See* the NBI website, https://nilebasin.org/index.php/south-sudan, for information on the accession of South Sudan to the NBI. "The Republic of South Sudan was admitted to the NBI by the Council of Minsters during their 20 regular meeting held on 5 July, 2012 in Kigali, Rwanda."

Guided by a shared vision "to achieve sustainable socio-economic development through equitable utilization of, and benefit from, the common Nile Basin water resources,"[1093] the NBI is structured in a way that "provide a forum for consultation and coordination among the Nile Basin States."[1094] The organizational structure of the NBI encompasses the Nile Basin Council of Ministers (Nile COM), the Nile Technical Advisory Committee (Nile-TAC), the NBI Secretariat (Nile-SEC),[1095] and two Subsidiary Action Programs (SAPs) offices, one in Kigali and another in Addis Ababa.[1096]

The Nile-COM is composed of "ministers in charge of Water Affairs each NBI Member State."[1097] As the highest decision-making organ of the initiative, the Nile COM is responsible for ensuring the implementation of all activities, making "policy and political decisions," and approving "the annual work plan and budget [of the NBI]."[1098] The Nile COM is to be supported by the Nile-TAC, which consists of two senior officials from each member state of the NBI.[1099] The Nile-TAC "provide[s] oversight for ... [all] programmatic activities," and offers "technical assistance and advice to [the Nile COM] on matters related to the management and development of Nile waters."[1100] It also "act[s] as an interface between the Nile COM and developmental partners [as well as] the Secretariat," which executes the day-to-day activities of the Initiative.[1101]

The NBI facilitates cooperation among the Basin States through structured programs. In 1999, the first Strategic Action Program was developed, comprising a Shared Vision Program (SVP) at the basin level and Subsidiary Action Programs (SAPs) at the sub-basin level.[1102] The SVP is comprised of a range of basin-wide projects aimed at creating an "enabling environment for cooperative management and development in the Nile basin."[1103] These projects include, *inter alia*, water resource planning and management, environmental protection, confidence-building and stakeholder engagement, regional power trade, and efficient use of water for agricultural production.[1104] The projects

1093 *See* the NBI website https://www.nilebasin.org/ for information on the shared vision.
1094 NBI, *supra* note 1083.
1095 *Id.*
1096 *Id*; Salman, *supra* note 172, 20.
1097 NBI, *supra* note 1083.
1098 *See* the NBI website, https://nilebasin.org/index.php/nbi/governance, for the role and responsibility of Nile-COM.
1099 *Id*; NBI, *supra* note 1083.
1100 *See* NBI, *supra* note 1098.
1101 *Id*; NBI, *supra* note 1193.
1102 Arsano & Tamrat, *supra* note 100, 19–20; Metawie, *supra* note 1065, 54–61.
1103 *Id*, 55.
1104 *Id.*

were completed by the end of 2012,[1105] and currently the Basin Cooperation Program administered by the NBI Secretariat is the only platform facilitating basin-wide collaboration among riparian states.[1106]

Regarding the SAPs, the NBI established the Eastern Nile Subsidiary Action Program (ENSAP) and the Nile Equatorial Lake Subsidiary Action Program (NELSAP), which are managed respectively by the Eastern Nile Technical Regional Office (ENTRO) at Addis Ababa and the Nile Equatorial Lake Subsidiary Action Program Coordination Unit (NELSAPCU) at Kigali.[1107] Burundi, DR Congo, Egypt, Kenya, Rwanda, Sudan, Tanzania, and Uganda participate in NELSAP.[1108] The program facilitates jointly agreed-upon "water resource management and development sub programs" and promotes "power development and trade" in the Nile Equatorial Lake sub-basin.[1109] ENSAP, on the other hand, facilitates cooperation between Ethiopia, Sudan, and Egypt on projects related to "flood preparedness and early warning" systems.[1110] Other projects include the eastern Nile regional power trading, energy transmission between Ethiopia and Sudan, irrigation programs, and watershed management.[1111]

As noted previously, the NBI was conceived as a transitional cooperative mechanism[1112] until the Nile River Basin Commission (NRBC) was established through CFA.[1113] As of now, the NRBC has not been established, and the Nile Basin does not have an organization for all-inclusive basin-wide institutional cooperation.[1114] Egypt has withdrawn from the NBI, opposing the adoption of the CFA.[1115] Nevertheless, the NBI had enormous hydro-political implications on the Nile Basin. First, "[i]n what may be considered a clean break from the past, [it] managed to bring all riparian States together"[1116] and provide forums to resolve the Nile questions through cooperation. In so doing, it offered the upstream states the opportunity to articulate their interests "as

1105 *See* Nile Basin Initiative, *The NBI Secretariat Strategic Plan 2012–2016*, 3, https://nilesec.nilebasin.org/images/docs/Nile_sec_strategicplan_final.pdf.

1106 *See* the NBI website, http://nilesec.nilebasin.org/index.php/what-we-do/basin-cooperation-program.

1107 Salman, *supra* note 172, 20; Elemam, *supra* note 81, 230.

1108 *Id.*

1109 *See* the NBI website, http://nelsap.nilebasin.org/index.php/en/, for the NELSAP projects.

1110 *See* the NBI website, http://entro.nilebasin.org/index.php/our-projects, ENSAP projects.

1111 *Id.*

1112 VINOGRADOV ET AL, *supra* note 1090, 60; Brunne & Toope, *supra* note 1033, 108.

1113 CFA, *supra* note 132, art 31.

1114 *See* discussion *infra* Chapter 6.

1115 Hend Kortam, *Egypt Meets with Nile Basin Countries*, DAILY NEWS EGYPT (June. 28, 2012), https://dailynewsegypt.com/2012/06/28/egypt-meets-nile-basin-countries/.

1116 Mekonnen, *supra* note 525, 233.

a united upstream block," which in effect increased their bargaining power, while enabling them to set the agenda and influence decisions.[1117]

Second, the NBI also furnished the upstream states with the opportunity to refute the Egyptian narrative "which portrays the Nile waters as a veritable life-blood even a slight reduction of which would bring mortal harm to Egypt"[1118] and craft a counter-narrative that the Nile originates in their territory and that they have right to use it to ensure food and energy security.[1119] Third, the NBI facilitated funding for upstream states to develop the Nile waters. Owing to the World Bank's operational policy, which requires the support or non-objection of all riparians to fund projects on transboundary water resources,[1120] Egypt has been blocking international funding for upstream development projects on the Nile River.[1121] Nevertheless, as the NBI was supported and funded by the World Bank, the access to international funding, which otherwise would only be available to, and contingent upon the consent of, Egypt, became more open to the upstream states.[1122]

The NBI also served the lower riparian States as a tool for maintaining the status quo. Egypt used the NBI for sanctioning "the discourse as cooperative."[1123] Egypt accepted the shared vision of the NBI, which calls, *inter alia*, for equitable and reasonable utilization of the Nile watercourse, to impose "a discourse of cooperation in order to prevent the upstream riparians from taking unilateral action on the Nile."[1124] Furthermore, following such an "*active stalling* [tactic] wherein a hydro-hegemon agrees to a process, which can then be drawn out for years,"[1125] Egypt was buying time and managing the tension regarding the inequitable utilization of the Nile watercourse. Although the principle of equitable utilization of the Nile watercourse, as stipulated in the shared vision of the NBI,[1126] allows upstream states to undertake consumptive projects, Egypt

1117 Nielsen, *supra* note 168, at 41.

1118 Mekonnen, *supra* note 525, 237.

1119 The former Ethiopian Prime Minister Meles Zenawi, for instance, stated: "while Egypt is taking the Nile water to transform the Sahara into something green, we in Ethiopia are denied the possibility to feed ourselves. And we are being forced to beg for food every year." *See* Mike Thomson, *Nile restrictions anger Ethiopia*, BBC NEWS, (Feb. 3, 2005) http://news.bbc.co.uk/2/hi/africa/4232107.stm.

1120 World Bank, *OP 7.50—Projects on International Waterways*, http://web.worldbank.org/archive/website01541/WEB/0_C-137.HTM [hereinafter *Projects on International Waterways*].

1121 *See* Swain, *supra* note 459 and accompanying text.

1122 Nielsen, *supra* note 168, 38.

1123 *Id*; *see* also WATERBURY, *supra* note 302, 76.

1124 Nielsen, *supra* note 168, 38.

1125 *Id*.

1126 NBI, *supra* note 1093.

was willing to cooperate only on non-consumptive water projects which would maintain the hydro-hegemonic status quo. It sought "basin-wide cooperation, but only in the sense of helping other riparians develop alternatives to Nile water."[1127] Egypt was unwilling to cooperate on joint consumptive projects that would affect the flow of the Nile waters.[1128] In other words, Egypt used the NBI to engage in sham cooperation and managed the tension regarding resource utilization, "temporarily satisfying the upstream riparians."[1129]

5.3 Back to Competition: Unilateralism as Post-Cold War Modus Operandi

Apart from bilateral and multilateral cooperation initiatives, the period following the Cold War also witnessed the implementation of several unilateral projects in the Nile Basin. During the Cold War, Egypt started its controversial desert reclamation projects and began building the peace canal to transfer water out of the basin towards the northern Sinai region.[1130] By 1997, it had embarked on undertaking yet another controversial desert reclamation project in southern Egypt.[1131] The South Valley Development Project has three important components along the Toshka, East Oweinat, and the New Valley Oases, and envisaged the creation of a new valley and human settlement outside of the Nile Delta.[1132] The implementation of the project would require diverting 5 BCM of water from the Nile River annually. Woldetsadik made the following remarks regarding the detailed components of the project:

> The Toshka scheme required the interlinking of four canals from pumping stations on the north-western shores of Lake Nasser with the western deserts, ultimately allowing Egypt to divert as much as 4–5bcm of overflowing water from the Aswan reservoir annually. It was designed to settle new communities of a large number of people far from the Nile

1127 WATERBURY, *supra* note 302, 76 ("Enjoying, by seniority, a near monopoly in expertise on all the engineering and agronomic issues facing basin-wide development, Egypt offers technical assistance in helping other riparians exploit alternatives.")

1128 *Id.* (Egypt's was willing to cooperative only "in development of watercourses that do not feed into the Nile, improving rainfed agriculture, and implementing sophisticated water harvesting and water reuse programs.")

1129 Nielsen, *supra* note 168, 40.

1130 Othman et al, *supra* note 407, 100.

1131 WOLDETSADIK, *supra* note 172, 44–45.

1132 *Id.*

> valley on 226,800 hectares (540,000 feddans) of agricultural land … The East Oweinat project started in 1998 and would reclaim 107,100 hectares (255,000 feddans) using renewable underground water. The expansion of the oases projected to irrigate up to 187,740 hectares (447,000 feddans) similarly using groundwaters … The strings of schemes are part of the national plan that had hoped to reclaim as much as 15,000sq.km of land by 2017, transforming up to 3200sq.km of central-western desert into agricultural land, and accommodating about six million people. Upon completion of the 25-year planning period, therefore, Egypt would gain between 300,000–500,000 additional hectares of irrigated lands, withdrawing 5–10bcm/yr of waters.[1133]

As discussed above, these projects would significantly affect the interests of upstream countries. Thus, in March 1997, immediately after Egypt started the South Valley Development Project, Ethiopia sent a letter of protest to Egypt, the UN, the World Bank, and the OAU, expressing its "wishes to be on record as having made it unambiguously clear that it will not allow its share to the Nile waters to be affected by a fait accompli such as the Toshka project, regarding which it was neither consulted nor alerted."[1134] In 2005, the then prime minister of Ethiopia, Meles Zenawi condemned Egypt's desert reclamation project in strong terms: "While Egypt is taking the Nile water to transform the Sahara Desert into something green, we in Ethiopia are denied the possibility of using it to feed ourselves. And we are being forced to beg for food every year."[1135]

During the same period, Sudan undertook various unilateral projects on the Nile. Sudan started constructing the Merowe Dam in 2004 to generate electricity and irrigate some 120,000 hectares of land in the Nile.[1136] The dam, which costs about $1.8 billion, can produce 1250 MW of hydroelectricity, and its reservoir can store 12 BCM.[1137] In 2008, Sudan also commissioned the China Water and Electric Corporation to expand the Roseires Dam, which cost about $396 million when it was completed in 2013.[1138] The project increased

---

1133 *Id.*

1134 Ethiopia's 2020 Letter to the UNSC 1, *supra* note 788, annex V.

1135 Thomson, *supra* note 1119.

1136 Nicholas Hildyard, *Neutral? Against What? Bystanders and Human Rights Abuses: The case of Merowe Dam,* THE SUDAN STUDIES SOCIETY OF THE UNITED KINGDOM, 2 (2008).

1137 *Id. See* Taha, *supra* note 90, at 197–98 (The project was completed in 2009 with a total cost of 1.8 billion).

1138 SAMAAN, *supra* note 188, 137; *Sudan, China sign $396mln contract to heighten Roseires Dam,* SUDAN TRIBUNE (April. 27, 2008), https://sudantribune.com/article26929/. *See also* Ulf Laessing, *Sudan Launches Major Dam to Boost Agricultural Production Investment,*

the Roseires Dam by 10 m in height and 25 km in length.[1139] In so doing, the project enabled the dam to store an additional 4 BCM of water and increased the hydropower generation capacity of the Roseires Dam by 600 MW. It also doubled the generation capacity of the Sennar Dam (100% increase).[1140] In 2010, Sudan commissioned the Chinese company to build the Upper Atbara and Setit Dam. This project enabled Sudan to irrigate more than 300,000 hectares of land, generate an additional 320 MW, and reduce the siltation of the Khashm al-Girba.[1141]

Since the mid-1990s, Ethiopia, due to its rapid population growth and increasing food demands, has needed more water for its own use. And, having relative stability and economic progress, it started constructing small dams along the Nile in the early 2000s.[1142] In 2002, Ethiopia commissioned the Chinese National Water Resources and Hydropower Engineering Corporation (Sinohydro) to build the Tekeze Dam on one of the tributaries of the Nile, Atbara.[1143] The dam, which cost $360 million, was officially inaugurated in 2009 and added about 300 MW to the national grid of Ethiopia.[1144] Further, Ethiopia also revived the Tana-Beles project.[1145] In 2005, it commissioned an Italian company, Salini Costruttori, to construct the Tana-Beles multipurpose dam that connects the Beles River, a tributary of the Blue Nile, with Lake Tana.[1146] The cost of the dam was estimated at $500 million. It was officially inaugurated in 2010; it can generate 460 MW and may help Ethiopia to irrigate some 120,000 hectares of land.[1147]

REUTERS (Jan. 1, 2013), https://www.reuters.com/article/us-sudan-dam/sudan-launches-major-dam-to-boost-agricultural-production-investment-idUSBRE9000B320130101.

1139 *Id.* SAMAAN, *supra* note 188, 137; *Work begins to heighten Sudan's 280-MW Roseires Dam*, HYDRO REVIEW (Aug. 29, 2008), https://www.hydroreview.com/world-regions/work-begins-to-heighten-sudans-280-mw-roseires-dam/#gref.

1140 *Id.* SAMAAN, *supra* note 188, 137.

1141 Frank Zoellner et al, *Implementation of the Dam Complex at Upper Atbara, Sudan, in Challenging Site Conditions* (2017), https://www.lahmeyer.de/fileadmin/alle/publikationen/HYDRO_2017__Paper_54_Zoellner_Scheid_Mukthar.pdf.

1142 Salman, *supra* note 146, 515.

1143 *Ethiopia inaugurates Africa's first ever biggest power dam,* SUDAN TRIBUNE (Nov. 15, 2009), https://sudantribune.com/spip.php?article33117.

1144 DEGEFU, *supra* note 117, 212.

1145 SAMAAN, *supra* note 188, 150-54; Kristin Fedeler, *Hydraulic Missions, Ruins and Revival: Politics of Space in the Tana-Beles Basin From 1985 to Today*, PAPER PRESENTED IN INTERNATIONAL CONFERENCE OF ETHIOPIAN STUDIES (2018) (The project "will be redone with national founds to strength power component").

1146 SAMAAN, *supra* note 188, 150-54; *Ethiopia Sees Exporting Power as it Opens New HP Project*, SUDAN TRIBUNE (May 15, 2010), https://sudantribune.com/article34868/.

1147 *Id.*

In December 2010, Ethiopia also started constructing the GERD that has "caused a tectonic shift in Nile water relations,"[1148] as discussed in Part 3. The GERD is a giant hydrologic project on one of the Nile River's main tributaries—the Blue Nile in Ethiopia—designed to generate 5,150 megawatts of electricity from 13 turbines.[1149] Ever since the commencement of its construction, the GERD has been a point of serious contention between Ethiopia and its downstream neighbors—Egypt and Sudan.[1150] Although Ethiopia, Sudan, and Egypt managed to sign a declaration of principle on the dam,[1151] the three states are disputing over the filling and annual operation of the dam. As discussed in Part 3, the dispute, which is mainly related to the colonial and immediate post-colonial Nile treaties (the existing Nile Waters Treaties), is threatening the peace and security of Northeast Africa.

Conclusion

The Nile Basin saw several developments in the decades following the Cold War. First, the Basin States emerged from the Cold War attempting to cease their acrimonious relationships and to forge a new chapter of bilateral and multilateral cooperation. Ethiopia, for instance, signed the 1991 Khartoum Declaration with Sudan and the 1993 Framework Instrument with Egypt, and undermined the downstream hydro-hegemonic alliance established through the 1959 Agreement. Those bilateral instruments codified the principle of equitable use and no significant harm rule and thereby recognized the equality of rights of the eastern Nile Basin States over the Nile watercourse.

During the same period, the Nile Basin States also participated in several multilateral cooperative arrangements supported by international organizations. While upstream States attempted to use some of the arrangements, especially the NBI and the CFA, to change the existing status quo through the development of joint upstream projects, and the conclusion of an all-inclusive basin-wide agreement, downstream states used the same arrangements to maintain its hydro-hegemonic status quo by rejecting the CFA[1152] and refusing

1148 MCCAFFREY, *supra* note 4, at 308.

1149 *Power Generation Capacity of the GERD Slashed to 5150 MW—Ethiopian Minister*, EZEGA NEWS (Oct. 17, 2019) (Hereinafter *Power Generation Capacity of the GERD*) https://www.ezega.com/News/NewsDetails/7331/Power-Generation-Capacity-of-GERD-Slashed-to-5150MW-Ethiopian-Minister.

1150 *See* discussion *infra* Part 3.

1151 DoP, *supra* note 152.

1152 *See* the discussion *infra* section 6.1.

to cooperate on joint consumptive projects that would affect the flow the Nile waters.[1153] Therefore, the Nile Basin has not witnessed significant change during the post-Cold War era in terms of basin-wide institutional cooperation. The regime governing the Nile watercourse has continued to be purely competitive,[1154] and unilateralism is still the *modus operandi* of the Nile Basin. Several factors hinder cooperation in the Nile Basin. Some of these factors include increasing demand for the Nile waters due to alarming population growth, high dependency on the river, acrimonious inter riparian relationship between the Nile Basin States, characterized by historical baggage of animosity, and military confrontations, coercive hydro-hegemonic policy, and on top of it all, the dispute over the validity of the existing Nile Waters Treaties that reached its apex during the negotiation of the CFA.

1153 WATERBURY, *supra* note 302, 76.
1154 Brunne & Toope, *supra* note 1033, 129.

CHAPTER 6

The Cooperative Framework Agreement

Introduction

As noted previously, the CFA was conceived as one of the TECCONILE projects (Project D3) in 1995. At the time, all riparian Nile states[1155]—except for Eritrea, which participated in the project as an observer—negotiated the CFA for about 13 years. In 2010, the CFA was open for signature, and since then the agreement has been signed by six upstream states and subsequently ratified by four states.[1156] Adopted to promote integrated management and sustainable utilization of the Nile watercourse,[1157] the CFA has six parts along with a preamble, definitions, and annex. The first part of the CFA provides for 15 general principles governing the use and conservation of the Nile watercourse.[1158] The second part, entitled "rights and obligations" of the Nile Basin States, encompasses the substantive and procedural rules of the CFA.[1159] The remaining four parts, respectively, deal with institutional structure, subsidiary institutions, miscellaneous provisions, and final clauses.[1160]

The present chapter critically scrutinizes the legal and hydro-political implications of the CFA. It begins by examining the drafting and negotiating history of the agreement, focusing primarily on the sticking points that comprise the principal obstacle to the adoption of an agreement acceptable to all Nile Basin States. The chapter then turns to analyzing the basic substantive and procedural principles of the CFA vis-à-vis international watercourses law and examines the institutional structure, dispute settlement, and other miscellaneous issues contemplated in the CFA. Since the legal discipline is not enough to explain the significance of the CFA, this chapter goes beyond legal analysis and critically scrutinizes the hydro-political implications of the CFA in the last section.

1155 *See supra* note 134 and accompanying text.
1156 *See supra* note 142 and accompanying text.
1157 *See* CFA, *supra* note 132, preamble ¶ 4.
1158 *Id*, part 1, art 3.
1159 *Id*, part 2 arts 4–14.
1160 *Id*, part 3, arts 15–30, part IV, arts 31–32, part V, arts 33–34 & part VI, arts 35–44.

 | DOI:10.1163/9789004549869_007

6.1 Drafting and Negotiations of the CFA: Sisyphean Endeavors?

The CFA was the result of the riparian states' attempt to create a basin-wide legal and institutional framework to regulate the interstate utilization and management of the Nile River. The CFA negotiations began in the early 1990s under the auspices of TECCONILE and were formalized in the CFA Project in 1995.[1161] All Nile riparian states at the time—except Eritrea which was only an observer—participated in the project, and with financial and technical support from UNDP, the project provided for high-level legal and political negotiations in order to conclude a basin-wide agreement. A separate but parallel track, the NBI, focused on development, was supported by the World Bank beginning in 1999 and was participated in by the same nine Nile Basin States that participated in the CFA.[1162]

Work on the first draft of the CFA began after the Panel of Experts (POE) was established by the Nile COM in 1997.[1163] Following its establishment, the POE assigned two international consultants to prepare the draft CFA based on the terms of reference elaborated by the Nile-COM.[1164] Immediately, the Sudanese member of the POE suggested that the POE should use the U.N. Watercourses Convention as a starting point, and this was accepted by the full POE.[1165] Then, by 1999, the international consultants developed the first draft of the CFA that attempted to apply the Convention's provisions to the Nile Basin[1166] and submitted it to the POE for discussion and revision.[1167] The POE negotiated on every provision of the draft agreement and produced a revised version that included the positions (i.e., reservations and counter-reservations on each provision of the draft) of the Nile Basin States.[1168] In 2000, the POE submitted the revised CFA to the Nile COM.[1169] Recognizing that "substantive issues in the cooperative framework remain[ed] unresolved,"[1170] the Nile COM formed

1161 McCaffrey Interview, *supra* note 135.

1162 *Id.*

1163 Metawie, *supra* note 1065, 62.

1164 Tafesse, *supra* note 529, 75. The terms of reference include, *inter alia*, assessing international watercourses law, reviewing the legal and institutional frameworks of other watercourses, identifying relevant and applicable the principles to the Nile Basin, determining the quantity and quality of the water supply within the Nile Basin, and prioritize the existing uses and needs, while examining the development potential in the basin. *Id.*

1165 McCaffrey Interview, *supra* note 135.

1166 *Id.*

1167 Tafesse, *supra* note 529, 75.

1168 *Id.* 76.

1169 Metawie, *supra* note 1065, 63; Tafesse, *supra* note 529, 76.

1170 Tafesse, *supra* note 529, 76.

a Joint Negotiation Committee (JNC)—composed of two experts from each state—to overcome the impasses and find amicable solutions for the outstanding issues.[1171] The JNC continued meeting regularly but failed to strike a deal acceptable to all of the Nile Basin States. The principal sticking points include, *inter alia*, (1) determining the shared water resources, (2) the principle of prior notification of planned measures, (3) the interplay between the principle of equable and reasonable utilization and the obligation to prevent significant harm, and (4) the fate of existing Nile Waters Agreements.[1172]

Regarding the first issue, the Egyptian delegation, advocating for the notion of a drainage basin as recognized by the Helsinki Rules, proposed that the waters of the Nile should include not only the amount of water flowing in the river (that is, the average 84 BCM water measured at Aswan High Dam (AHD)) but also the water falling on the entire basin (green water) which is estimated by Egypt to be about 1660 BCM.[1173] Delegates from the upstream countries, particularly Ethiopia, on the other hand, rejected the concept of the drainage basin and proposed that only the amount of water flowing in the river (blue water) should be shared by the Nile Basin States.[1174] Advocating for the notion of "international watercourse" recognized in the U.N. Watercourses Convention,[1175] upstream states asserted that the waters that fall on the Basin but do not reach a common terminus should be excluded from the scope of shared water resources.[1176]

In an attempt to reconcile this disagreement, delegates of the Nile Basin States adopted the two concepts in the final text of the CFA. The first is the concept of the "Nile River Basin," which is defined in Article 2(a) as "the geographical area determined by the watershed limits of the Nile River System of waters."[1177] This definition is based on the drainage basin approach, which includes not only the actual waters flowing in the river, but all waters available in the entire basin.[1178] However, Article 2(a) stipulates that this approach is to be followed only "where there is [a] reference to environmental protection,

1171 *Id.* ("Nile-COM formed a Joint Negotiation in August 2000 that was made up of two experts from each of the Nile riparian states").

1172 Salman, *supra* note 172, 21–23.

1173 *Id*, 23; Hesham Hamid, *A Study on the Concept of International River in International Water Law and Its Applications in Nile Basin Agreements*, 11 (39) AFRICAN PERSPECTIVES 44–46 (2013).

1174 *Id*; Salman, *supra* note 172, 23.

1175 U.N. Watercourses Convention, *supra* note 818, art. 2 (b).

1176 *Id*; Salman, *supra* note 172, 23.

1177 CFA, *supra* note 132, art. 2 (a).

1178 Hamid, *supra* note 1173, 44–46.

conservation or development."[1179] But, "where there is [a] reference to utilization of water" in the Agreement, the second concept, "Nile River System," applies.[1180] Article 2(b) defines this concept as "the Nile River and the surface waters and groundwaters which are related to the Nile River."[1181] Therefore, the CFA includes both surface and groundwater as shared resources of the Nile Basin States, provided that they are related to the Nile watercourse, while excluding the green water in the basin.[1182]

As for the second sticking point, the Ethiopian delegation vehemently objected to the provisions on prior notifications of planed measures on the Nile Basin, alleging that such provisions may be construed as recognition of the 1902 Anglo-Ethiopian Treaty based on which Egypt claims veto power over upstream projects in Ethiopia.[1183] They further asserted that Egypt and Sudan did not notify Ethiopia while undertaking all of their projects on the Nile, and so Ethiopia is not obliged to notify them.[1184] Egypt and Sudan, on the other hand, strongly advocated for the principle of prior notifications of planned measures on the Nile Basin, and demanded that the CFA should include the provisions of the U.N. Watercourses Convention governing the obligation of prior notification of planned measures.[1185] The final text of the CFA reconciled the two extreme positions: It requires the Nile Basin States to exchange information on planned measures through the Nile River Basin Commission (NRBC), without providing detailed explicit provisions on prior notification between the Nile Basin States.[1186]

The disagreement over the interplay between equitable and reasonable utilization and the no significant harm rule is similar to the controversies witnessed during the negotiation of the U.N. Watercourses Convention. The upstream states favored the equitable and reasonable utilization principle that would provide more scope to harness the Nile watercourse, and allow harm to downstream states.[1187] The Ethiopian delegation, for instance, expressed reservations on the obligation "not [to] cause significant harm to downstream users."[1188] Conversely, the downstream states strongly supported the no-harm

1179 CFA, *supra* note 132, art. 2 (a).
1180 *Id*, 2 (b).
1181 *Id.*
1182 *Id*; Salman, *supra* note 172, 23.
1183 *Id*, 22; Tafesse, *supra* note 529, 76.
1184 Salman, *supra* note 172, 22.
1185 *Id.*
1186 Salman, *supra* note 172, 22; Tafesse, *supra* note 529, 76. *See* also CFA, *supra* note 132, art. 8.
1187 Salman, *supra* note 172, 21.
1188 Tafesse, *supra* note 529, 76.

rule and proposed a provision that would protect their existing uses against any harm resulting from activities undertaken by upstream states.[1189] The delegations from Egypt and Sudan, for instance, objected to articles that refer to "environmental audits of existing projects" and "taking appropriate measures to prevent the causing of significant harm to other basin states."[1190] Regarding the latter, the delegates wanted to impose an obligation of result—not due diligence—on the Nile Basin States "to refrain from and prevent the causing of *harm* to [the] other Basin States."[1191]

According to the proposals of the downstream states, which at times envisioned absolute prohibition of harm, priority should be given to the no-harm rule over the principle of equitable and reasonable utilization in case of conflict between the two principles.[1192] However, since Egypt and Sudan are already over-exploiting the Nile watercourses, any new upstream use would significantly affect these existing uses, and prioritizing the no-harm rule would prohibit the upstream states from using the Nile watercourse.[1193] As such, upstream states maintained that the principle of equitable and reasonable utilization should be seen as the fundamental principle which takes precedence over the no-harm rule.[1194] The final text of the CFA, which followed the approach in the U.N. Watercourses Convention, supported Ethiopia's position and gave priority to the principle of equitable and reasonable utilization over the no-harm rule.[1195]

The final and certainly the most controversial sticking point revolved around the need to change or maintain the Egyptian hydro-hegemonic status quo. As victims of the status quo, the upstream states insisted that the new CFA should replace all colonial and immediate post-colonial Nile agreements which were referred to as existing agreements, and proposed to explicitly declare them void whenever incompatible with the provisions of the CFA.[1196] Egypt and Sudan, on the other hand, argued that the CFA should be supplementary to

1189 *Id.*
1190 *Id.*
1191 *Id* (emphasis added).
1192 Salman, *supra* note 172, 21.
1193 *Id.*
1194 *Id.* MCCAFFREY, *supra* note 4, 474.
1195 Salman, *supra* note 172, 21. This approach is supported by the ICJ, which shortly after the adoption of the U.N. Watercourses Convention in 1997, confirmed equitable and reasonable utilization principle in both the Gabčíkovo-Nagymaros Project case and the Pulp Mills cases as the fundamental norm of international watercourses law. Salman, *supra* note 901, 186.
1196 Taha, *supra* note 90, 216; Arsano & Tamrat, *supra* note 100, 23.

the existing agreements that guarantee their historical rights.[1197] They specifically proposed that the CFA is without prejudice to the colonial and immediate post-colonial agreements.[1198]

In an attempt to bridge this gap, the negotiators of the CFA introduced the new, non-legal concept of "water security"[1199] to replace the provision governing the relationship between the CFA and the existing agreements, on which no agreement could be reached.[1200] The idea was that Egypt, concerned about water security, could be protected through a new provision and the relationship between the CFA and the "existing agreements" (whether the former supersedes the latter or vice versa) could be governed by the general rules of international law.[1201]

However, the Nile Basin States were not able to agree on the draft provision on water security contained in Article 14 of the draft CFA.[1202] Specifically, the lower riparian states opposed the part of Article 14 providing that the parties "agree, in a spirit of cooperation not to significantly affect the water security of any other Nile Basin State."[1203] The lower riparian states insisted that the language should obligate all Nile Basin States "*not to adversely affect the water security and current uses and rights* of any other Nile Basin State."[1204] The position of lower riparian states brought the long-standing dispute over the colonial and immediate post-colonial agreements (existing Nile Waters Agreements) back as a request for unequivocal recognition of their validity against upstream states. The upstream states rejected that proposal and proposed removing the principle of water security from the document.[1205] This proposal was, in turn, rejected by the downstream states, which were not willing to accept any agreement without explicit recognition of the existing Nile Waters Agreements.[1206]

The negotiating committee, which agreed on all provisions of the CFA except for water security, submitted the draft agreement to the Nile COM at its

---

1197 *Id.*

1198 *Id* ("The Egyptian and Sudanese delegations registered reservations and proposed an amendment to read: 'The principles and framework are without prejudice to existing agreements'").

1199 McCaffrey Interview, *supra* note 135.

1200 *Id.*

1201 *Id.*

1202 *Id.*

1203 CFA, *supra* note 132, Annex on Article 14(b).

1204 *Id* (emphasis added).

1205 McCaffrey Interview, *supra* note 135.

1206 *Id.*

meeting in Entebbe in June 2007.[1207] The Nile COM also found it impossible to reach a consensus on the principle of water security.[1208] Two years later, the draft was renegotiated at the Extra-Ordinary Meeting of the Nile COM Ministers, in Kinshasa.[1209] An agreement could not, however, be reached on the principle of water security.[1210] As a result, the delegates from upstream states proposed adopting the CFA, with a stipulation that the NRBC would decide on the annexed Article 14 (b) within six months of its establishment through the CFA.[1211] Egypt and Sudan, on the other hand, demanded that the parties should continue negotiating the CFA and that the NRBC should be established through a presidential decree.[1212] After a heated debate, the Nile COM decided to "open the CFA for signature at a designated date."[1213]

To finalize the process of adopting the Agreement, the Nile COM and the negotiating committee held another meeting in April 2010 in Sharm El Sheikh.[1214] Still, the Nile Basin States could not agree on the principle of water security.[1215] As a result, the upstream states decided to open the Agreement for signature.[1216] The downstream states vehemently opposed the adoption of the Agreement and suspended their participation in the NBI altogether.[1217] Egypt in particular proclaimed that it "will not sign any deal" that does not recognize "its share of 55.5 billion cubic meters of water from the river that was apportioned to it by the 1959 Agreement."[1218] Despite such opposition, however, the CFA was open for signature on May 14, 2010.[1219] The CFA has been signed by six upstream states and subsequently ratified by four states.[1220] By its terms, the CFA requires six ratifications to enter into force and, consequently, the CFA

1207 *Id. See* also Tafesse, *supra* note 529, 76–77.

1208 *Id.*

1209 Tadesse Woldetsadik, *The Nile Basin Initiative and the Cooperative Framework Agreement: Failing Institutional Enterprises*, 11 MIZAN L. REV. 201–202 (2017).

1210 *Id. See* also Tafesse, *supra* note 529, 77.

1211 *Id.*

1212 *Id.*

1213 Woldetsadik, *supra* note 1209, 201.

1214 Tafesse, *supra* note 529, 77.

1215 *Id*; Woldetsadik, *supra* note 1209, 203.

1216 *Id*; Tafesse, *supra* note 529, 77; Kasimbazi, *supra* note 1070, 753; Salman, *supra* note 172, 21.

1217 *Dispute over Water in the Nile Basin*, CLIMATE DIPLOMACY https://climate-diplomacy.org/case-studies/dispute-over-water-nile-basin.

1218 Tafesse, *supra* note 529, 78.

1219 *Id*, 77; Woldetsadik, *supra* note 1209, 203; Kasimbazi, *supra* note 1070, 753; Salman, *supra* note 172, 20.

1220 *See supra* note 142 and accompanying text.

neither binds the lower riparian states nor governs the uses and allocation of the entire Nile watercourse.[1221]

6.2 Basic Principles of the Cooperative Framework Agreement

The CFA included several general principles including, *inter alia*, cooperation, sustainable development, subsidiarity, equitable and reasonable utilization, no significant harm rule, protection and conservation of the Nile Basin, community of interest, information concerning planned measures, exchange of data and information, and water security.[1222] This section addresses the basic substantive and procedural principles of the CFA.

6.2.1 *Substantive Principles*

The CFA has several substantive principles governing the use and conservation of the Nile watercourse.[1223] This part focuses on the basic principles such as the doctrine of community of interest, the principle of equitable and reasonable utilization, the no significant harm rule, and the obligation to protect the Nile Basin.

6.2.1.1 Community of Interest

The doctrine of community of interest, which goes beyond the doctrine of limited territorial sovereignty, is considered as "not only the optimal, but also the necessary approach to dealing with future water problems."[1224] Amazingly, this doctrine is recognized in the Nile Basin: the CFA incorporates "the community of interest of the Nile Basin States in the Nile River System" as one of its general principles.[1225] However, unlike other principles, it neither defined the term "community of interest," nor provided any substantive right and obligation that the principle bestow on the Nile Basin States. Yet, the recognition of the principle itself has several "powerful" implications.[1226] First, it confirms that all Nile Basin States share an interest in the Nile watercourse.[1227] It also underlines that the Nile Basin States "form a community" due to this shared

1221 CFA, *supra* note 132, art 42.
1222 *Id*, art 3.
1223 *Id*, part 2 arts 4–14.
1224 MCCAFFREY, *supra* note 4, 99.
1225 CFA, *supra* note 132, art 3, ¶9.
1226 McCaffrey, *supra* note 860, 87.
1227 *Id* (commenting on the doctrine generally).

interest.[1228] More importantly, it underscores the "perfect equality" of rights of all Nile Basin States in the use of the Nile watercourse as well as the "exclusion of any preferential privilege of any one riparian State in relation to the others."[1229]

In other words, the CFA recognizes that both the upstream and downstream Nile Basin States have "equal rights" in the use of the Nile watercourse. Later developing states like Ethiopia have an equal right to the use of the Nile watercourse, even if it had previously been fully developed by the downstream states.[1230] Such previous development does not confer a "preferential privilege" on Egypt or Sudan, any more than Ethiopia would enjoy such a privilege by virtue of its position on the Nile watercourse.[1231] As equality of rights does not entitle equal shares to all Nile Basin States, the actual apportionment of the Nile watercourse would be governed by the principle of equitable and reasonable utilization as discussed below.

6.2.1.2 Equitable and Reasonable Utilization

The CFA recognized the principle of equitable and reasonable utilization in accordance with international watercourses law.[1232] The CFA, in the relevant part, stipulates:

> Nile Basin States shall in their respective territories utilize the water resources of the Nile River system and the Nile River Basin in an equitable and reasonable manner. In particular, those water resources shall be used and developed by Nile Basin States with a view to attaining optimal and sustainable utilization thereof and benefits therefrom, taking into account the interests of the Basin States concerned, consistent with adequate protection of those water resources. Each Basin State is entitled to an equitable and reasonable share in the beneficial uses of the water resources of the Nile River system and the Nile River Basin.[1233]

The first sentence of the principle is directly incorporated from the U.N. Watercourses Convention, which entitles each riparian state to make use of transboundary watercourses based on the principle of sovereign equality, or

1228 *Id* (commenting on the doctrine generally).
1229 *Id* (commenting on the doctrine generally).
1230 *Id* (commenting on the doctrine generally).
1231 *Id* (commenting on the doctrine generally).
1232 CFA, *supra* note 132, art 4.
1233 *Id*, art 4, ¶ 1.

equality of right.[1234] The principle of sovereign equality or equality of rights, in turn, entitles each Basin State equal rights to the utilization of transboundary watercourse.[1235] Although the principle of equality of rights is the foundation of international watercourses law, it does not mean an equal share of the uses and benefits of an international watercourse; nor does it imply the equal appropriation of the water resource itself in quantity terms.[1236] Since the underlining notion of the sentence is equity and reasonableness, it demands the weighing and balancing of various competing interests of states, while taking into account all relevant factors and circumstances provided below.[1237]

The second sentence of the principle, which is almost identical to the U.N. Watercourses Convention,[1238] elaborates upon the concept of equitable and reasonable utilization, stipulating that the Nile Basin States shall develop the Nile River System "with a view to attaining optimal and sustainable utilization thereof and benefits therefrom, taking into account the interests of the Basin States concerned, consistent with adequate protection of those water resources."[1239] The term "with a view to" implies that the ultimate objective of the Nile Basin States should be optimal utilization and benefit from the Nile River System.[1240] The term "optimal utilization" neither indicates an objective to "achieve the 'maximum,' the most efficient, or even the most (economically) valuable use,"[1241] nor does it imply that the Nile Basin State in the position of utilizing the Nile River System "most efficiently should have a superior claim to the use of the waters."[1242] Instead, it signifies attaining "maximum possible benefits" for all Nile Basin States, while mitigating potential adverse effects.[1243] The term "sustainable use" underscores the necessity to balance socioeconomic and environmental values while using the Nile River System and to consider the ecosystem in line with the principle of sustainable development.[1244]

The term "benefits therefrom" signifies the notion of benefit sharing as part of the principle of equitable and reasonable utilization. Conceptually,

1234 U.N. Watercourses Convention, *supra* note 818, art. 5, ¶ 1.
1235 CFA, *supra* note 132, art 4 ¶ 1; MCCAFFREY, *supra* note 4, 451.
1236 *Id.*
1237 U.N. Watercourses Convention, *supra* note 818, art. 6.
1238 *Id*, art 5, ¶ 1.
1239 CFA, *supra* note 132, art 4, ¶1.
1240 ALISTAIR RIEU-CLARKE ET AL, UN WATERCOURSES CONVENTION: USER'S GUIDE 107 (2012) (Commenting on the U.N. Watercourses Convention).
1241 *Id.* (Commenting on the U.N. Watercourses Convention).
1242 *Id.* (Commenting on the U.N. Watercourses Convention).
1243 *Id.* (Commenting on the U.N. Watercourses Convention).
1244 *Id.* (Commenting on the U.N. Watercourses Convention).

the notion of benefit sharing focuses on maximizing potential benefits from transboundary watercourses through basin-wide institutional cooperation.[1245] It assumes sharing all benefits of the Nile River System including, *inter alia*, ecological, economic, social, and political gains, instead of simply allocating the water resources.[1246] Remarkably, the CFA goes beyond the recognition of benefit sharing and empowers the Council of Minsters (Nile-COM) to decide on "formulas for cost and benefit-sharing by the Nile Basin States in respect of particular joint projects within the Nile River Basin."[1247] In so doing, the CFA establishes the foundation for the pragmatic implementation of benefit sharing in the Nile Basin through the Nile-COM.[1248]

The CFA illustrates the relevant factors for determining equitable and reasonable utilization of the Nile River System.[1249] Requiring all Nile Basin States to "take into account all relevant factors and circumstances," and to ensure equitable and reasonable utilization of the Nile River System,[1250] the CFA provides the following factors:

a. Geographic, hydrographic, hydrological, climatic, ecological and other factors of a natural character;
b. The social and economic needs of the Basin States concerned;
c. The population dependent on the water resources in each Basin State;
d. The effects of the use or uses of the water resources in one Basin State on other Basin States;
e. Existing and potential uses of the water resources;
f. Conservation, protection, development and economy of use of the water resources and the costs of measures taken to that effect;
g. The availability of alternatives, of comparable value, to a particular planned or existing use;
h. The contribution of each Basin State to the waters of the Nile River System;
i. The extent and proportion of the drainage area in the territory of each Basin State.[1251]

1245 *See* generally, David Grey & Claudia Sadoff, *Beyond the River: The Benefits of Cooperation on International Rivers,* 4 WATER POLICY (2002).
1246 *Id.*
1247 CFA, *supra* note 132, art 24, ¶ 16.
1248 *Id.*
1249 *Id,* art 4, ¶ 2.
1250 *Id,* art 4, ¶ 2.
1251 *Id.*

The CFA enumerates all the factors provided in Article 6 of the U.N. Watercourses Convention[1252] and has added two additional factors: (1) the contribution of each Basin State to the waters of the Nile River System, and (2) the extent and proportions of the drainage area in the territory of each Basin State.[1253] The first additional factor may seem beneficial to the upstream states that have long been adversely affected by the colonial treaties as they contribute almost all of the Nile Waters.[1254] However, in what may resemble the "one hand giveth the other taketh away" scenario, the parallel inclusion of the second factor diminishes the value of the first factor because significant parts of the drainage area is in the lower riparian states.[1255]

The CFA, like the U.N. Watercourses Convention and Berlin Rules, does not recognize any hierarchy between any kind of uses,[1256] and treats both existing use and potential use of the Nile Water System equally.[1257] Like the U.N. Watercourses Convention, the CFA requires the Nile Basin States to consider "all relevant factors… together" and determine equitable and reasonable utilization of the Nile River System "on the basis of the whole."[1258] Unlike the U.N. Watercourses Convention, the CFA requires the Nile Basin States to "keep the status of their water utilization under review in light of substantial changes in relevant factors and circumstances."[1259] As noted below, the inclusion of this provision in the CFA is important for ensuring flexible application of the principle while addressing changing conditions, including the aforementioned factors.[1260]

The CFA does not contain a provision governing the interplay between various types uses. It does not include Article 10 of the U.N. Watercourses Convention, which stipulates that no use of an international watercourse (e.g., irrigation, hydroelectric power production, industrial uses) enjoys inherent priority over other uses unless there is an agreement or custom to the

1252 U.N. Watercourses Convention, *supra* note 818, art. 6. It should be noted that the CFA does not include two additional factors, i.e., sustainability of proposed or existing uses and minimization of environmental harm, mentioned in the Berlin Rules. Berlin Rules, *supra* note 818, art. 13 ¶ 2 h & I.

1253 CFA, *supra* note 132, art 4, ¶ 2.

1254 NILE BASIN INITIATIVE, *supra* note 52, at 36.

1255 NBI 2016, *supra* note 58, 19.

1256 CFA, *supra* note 132, art 4, ¶ 2.

1257 U.N. Watercourses Convention, *supra* note 818, art. 6 ¶ 1 (e); Berlin Rules, *supra* note 818, art. 13, ¶ 2 (e) and CFA, *supra* note 132, art 4, ¶ 2 (e).

1258 CFA, *supra* note 132, art 4, ¶ 4.

1259 *Id*, art 4, ¶ 5.

1260 *See* the discussion *infra* section 9.2.

contrary.[1261] Despite such a nod to equality of uses, the article recognizes that "special regard" is to be given to the requirements of "vital human needs" in cases of conflict with other uses.[1262] Given the looming water crisis in the Nile Basin, and the necessity of the Nile waters for ensuring "vital human needs" in each of the Nile Basin States, the inclusion of a similar provision into the CFA is extremely necessary.

6.2.1.3 No Significant Harm Rule

The no significant harm rule prohibits riparian states from using shared watercourses in such a way as to cause significant harm to other watercourse states or their environment.[1263] The CFA included the obligation "not to cause significant harm" in accordance with the general principle of international watercourses law.[1264] In the relevant part, it stipulates that the "Nile Basin States shall, in utilizing Nile River System water resources in their territories, take all appropriate measures to prevent the causing of significant harm to other Basin States."[1265]

As noted previously, the nature of this obligation is one of conduct, rather than one of result, requiring states only to expend reasonable effort under the circumstances to avoid harm.[1266] Thus, the Nile Basin States are under obligation to take "all appropriate measures" to ensure that any measure undertaken in their jurisdiction does not cause significant harm to the territory of other riparian States.[1267] Taking "all appropriate measures," is an obligation of due diligence that "would be expected of a reasonable government in similar circumstances" including, *inter alia*, "enacting necessary legislation, enforcing laws, preventing or terminating an illegal activity, and punishing the person responsible for it."[1268] Therefore, a Nile Basin State can be considered to have violated this principle not only when it has caused significant harm by itself, but also when it has failed to "prevent others in its territory from causing it."[1269]

As noted above, the level of harm, in order to qualify as "significant," has to be higher than merely trivial but could be less than severe or substantial.[1270]

1261 U.N. Watercourses Convention, *supra* note 818, art. 10 ¶ 1.

1262 *Id*, 10 ¶ 2.

1263 U.N. Watercourses Convention, *supra* note 818, art 7.

1264 CFA, *supra* note 132, art 5.

1265 *Id*, art 5, ¶1.

1266 RIEU-CLARKE ET AL, *supra* note 1240, 119 (Commenting on the U.N. Watercourses Convention).

1267 *Id.* (Commenting on the U.N. Watercourses Convention).

1268 *Id.* (Commenting on the U.N. Watercourses Convention).

1269 *Id.* (Commenting on the U.N. Watercourses Convention).

1270 MCCAFFREY, *supra* note 4, 498.

However, the "harm" has to be more than just an "adverse effect," and should constitute "a real impairment of use, [with] a detrimental impact of some consequence upon" the environment or the interests of the affected state (e.g., public health, industry, property, agriculture).[1271]

Approached from such a threshold required for violating the principle, the proposal submitted by the downstream states for the principle of water security provided in Article 14(b) of the CFA deviates from the no harm rule jurisprudence under international law. According to the downstream states' proposal, the Nile riparian states would be required "not to adversely affect the water security and current uses and rights of any other Nile Basin State."[1272] Although the interplay between this proposal and the principle of no significant harm enshrined in Article 5 is absurd, the proposal does not provide any room for affecting current uses. It assumes absolute prohibition of harms against downstream countries.[1273] Yet, as indicated above, "the no-harm principle is not, and has never been, conceived as absolutely prohibiting the causing of significant harm in all circumstances."[1274]

Concerning the interplay between the principle of equitable and reasonable utilization and the rule of no significant harm, the CFA mimicked the approach followed by the U.N. Watercourses Convention. The CFA, in the relevant part, requires a Nile Basin State whose use causes significant harm to another basin state to "take all appropriate measures, having due regard for the provisions of Article 4 above [equitable and reasonable utilization], in consultation with the affected State, to eliminate or mitigate such harm and, where appropriate, to discuss the question of compensation."[1275] In line with the U.N. Watercourses Convention, this provision considers significant harm simply as one factor for determining equitable and reasonable utilization of the Nile watercourse.[1276] The reference to the principle of equitable and reasonable utilization (Article 4) in this provision means that the Nile Basin States are not legally responsible for causing significant harm if they can show that they have taken all appropriate measures to prevent such harm, and their use of the Nile watercourse is equitable and reasonable.

1271 1988 Y.B. INT'L L. COMM'N, v. 2, pt. 2, at 36.

1272 CFA, *supra* note 132, Annex on Article 14(b).

1273 Shih & Stutz, *supra* note 60, 10818.

1274 MCCAFFREY, *supra* note 4, 468.

1275 CFA, *supra* note 132, art 5 ¶ 2.

1276 U.N. Watercourses Convention, *supra* note 818, art 7.

6.2.1.4 Protection and Conservation of the Nile Basin

The CFA has several provisions geared toward the protection and conservation of the Nile Basin and its ecosystem. Under Article 3 (2), the CFA stipulates sustainable development as one of the general principles for the use of the Nile River System.[1277] The 1987 Bruntland Commission Report defines sustainable development as "development that meets the needs of the present generation without compromising the ability of future generations to meet their needs."[1278]

Article 3(2) of the CFA provides for the principle of subsidiarity and requires the Nile Basin States to plan and implement the development and protection of the Nile Basin at the lowest appropriate level.[1279] The CFA further requires the Nile Basin States to promote integrated water resource management in the Basin. Article 3 (13) stipulates that the Nile watercourse is "a finite and vulnerable resource, essential to sustain life, development and the environment, and must be managed in an integrated and holistic manner, linking social and economic development with protection and conservation of natural ecosystems."[1280] The inclusion of the principle of subsidiarity and integrated water resources management into the CFA is in line with the most recent international environmental law practice, which increasingly gives special emphasis to the regulation of the environment.[1281] It should be noted that the U.N.

1277 CFA, *supra* note 132, art 3 ¶ 2. Following the 1992 United Nations Conference on Environment and Development in Rio de Janeiro, the principle of sustainable development is included in various international watercourse agreements. *See* generally, REPORT OF THE UNITED NATIONS CONFERENCE ON ENVIRONMENT AND DEVELOPMENT, UN Doc. A/CONF.15/26/Rev.1 (Vol. I), p. 275 (1993); *see* also MCCAFFREY, *supra* note 4, 516. In this respect, McCaffrey remarked: "Virtually all recent multilateral agreements of a framework nature dealing with the non-navigational uses of international watercourses take into account these imperatives and the resulting need to use and develop international watercourse systems in a sustainable manner. In addition to the U.N. Watercourses Convention, prominent examples include the 1992 ECE Convention on the Protection and Use of Transboundary Watercourses and International Lakes, the 1994 Convention on Cooperation for the Protection and Sustainable Use of the Danube River, the 1995 Agreement on the Cooperation for the Sustainable Development of the Mekong River Basin, and the 1995 Protocol on Shared Watercourse Systems in the Southern African Development Community (SADC) Region." *Id.*

1278 OUR COMMON FUTURE, *supra* note 26, ¶ 1.

1279 CFA, *supra* note 132, art 3 ¶ 2.

1280 CFA, *supra* note 132, art 3 ¶ 13.

1281 MCCAFFREY, *supra* note 4, 516 ("Virtually all recent multilateral agreements of a framework nature dealing with the non-navigational uses of international watercourses take into account … [environmental protection] and the resulting need to use and develop international watercourse systems in a sustainable manner.")

Watercourses Convention, unlike the Berlin Rules,[1282] did not explicitly follow this approach.

More specifically, the CFA, under Article 3(7), requires the Nile Basin States to undertake "all appropriate measures… for the protection and conservation of the Nile River Basin and its ecosystems."[1283] Article 6 of the CFA further elaborates this principle, requiring all Nile Basin States to take "all appropriate measures, individually and, where appropriate, jointly, to protect, conserve and, where necessary, rehabilitate the Nile River Basin and its ecosystems."[1284] This article recognizes the emerging obligation to protect the ecosystem under international law.[1285] The obligation is also included in Article 20 of the U.N. Watercourses Convention under which water-sharing states are required to "individually and, where appropriate, jointly, protect and preserve the ecosystems of international watercourses."[1286] Virtually all recent multilateral watercourse agreements and several ICJ decisions also underscore the obligation to protect the ecosystem and sustainably use freshwater resources.[1287] Therefore, the inclusion of obligations to protect, preserve, and rehabilitate the Nile Basin and its ecosystem into the CFA represents the Nile Basin States' endorsement of the emerging trends that take holistic approaches to the solution of environment-related problems.

Furthermore, Article 6 imposes particular obligations including, *inter alia*, the obligation to (1) protect and improve the water quality of the Basin, (2) prevent the introduction of alien or new species into the Nile River System which may have detrimental effects to the ecosystems of the Nile River Basin, and (3) protect and conserve wetlands within the Nile River Basin.[1288]

To take these obligations in turn: the first seems to address water pollution. Pollution, which causes negative impacts on human health, food products such as fisheries, and inland and coastal ecosystems,[1289] is one of the most significant problems affecting various international watercourses, including the Nile. In an attempt to address this problem, Article 21 of the U.N. Watercourses Convention provides detailed obligations regarding the "prevention,

1282 Berlin Rules, *supra* note 818, art 6.
1283 CFA, *supra* note 132, art 3 ¶ 7.
1284 *Id*, art 6.
1285 MCCAFFREY, *supra* note 4, 509–14.
1286 U.N. Watercourses Convention, *supra* note 818, art. 20.
1287 MCCAFFREY, *supra* note 4, 516–520.
1288 CFA, *supra* note 132, art 6 ¶ 1.
1289 RIEU-CLARKE ET AL, *supra* note 1240, 173 (Commenting on the U.N. Watercourses Convention).

reduction and control of pollution."[1290] After generally defining pollution as "any detrimental alteration in the composition or quality of the waters of an international watercourse which results directly or indirectly from human conduct,"[1291] the article establishes the core obligations, requiring the Watercourse States to "prevent, reduce and control pollution of an international watercourse that may cause significant harm to other watercourse States or to their environment."[1292]

1290 U.N. Watercourses Convention, *supra* note 818, art 21; *see* also Berlin Rules, *supra* note 818, art. 27.

1291 U.N. Watercourses Convention, *supra* note 818, art 21.

1292 *Id.* Critical questions that can be raised as to the obligation not to cause significant pollution harm includes: Is there an "equitable right to pollute" under international law? Or does a pollution that causes significant harm inherently inequitable? What is the nature of the obligation not to cause significant pollution-harm? Is it strict or one of due diligence? Regarding the first two questions, Professor McCaffrey states: "Since significant harm is the only standard contained in paragraph 2, and equitable utilization is not mentioned, it seems reasonable to conclude that what the ILC intended was that a use becomes inequitable and unreasonable to the extent that it causes significant pollution harm to other watercourse states. This interpretation is supported by the ILC's commentary to Article 7, according to which: "A use which causes significant harm to human health and safety is understood to be inherently inequitable and unreasonable." Significant pollution harm to a state or its environment would usually entail "significant harm to human health and safety," and would therefore be "inherently inequitable and unreasonable." MCCAFFREY, *supra* note 4, 511–12. He then suggested the possibility of an "equitable right to pollute," and made the following argument in favor of such a right: "[P]ollution that does not rise to the level of causing significant harm to other watercourse states is not addressed by Article 21(2). Therefore, such pollution of an international watercourse would not be governed by the rule of general international law prohibiting significant pollution harm. However, like any other use, it would nevertheless be governed by the principle of equitable and reasonable utilization, which would allow a state an equitable share of the assimilative capacity of an international watercourse. But by the same token, the state of origin of the pollution would have an obligation to ensure that the polluting use was both equitable and reasonable vis-à-vis other watercourse states under the circumstances ... So, while there might be said to be an "equitable right to pollute" under Article 21(2) in the sense just described, the norm in question would more properly be characterized as an *obligation* to utilize the watercourse in an equitable and reasonable manner, which would include uses that result in pollution of the watercourse." *Id*, 512. As for the last question, McCaffrey, invoking the "statement of understanding" of the Working Group that drafted the Convention, argued that obligation "impose[s] a due diligence standard on watercourse States." *Id.* He further states that this due diligence standard, which is consistent with the no significant harm rule, is "appropriate, and has been supported by the International Court of Justice (ICJ)." However, he warned that "as polluting substances become more dangerous, the level of the required diligence increases. At some point, the level of danger will be so great as to make the obligation, for all practical purposes, a strict one." *Id.*

Unlike the U.N. Watercourses Convention, the CFA does not have a detailed provision regarding the obligation not to cause significant pollution harm. However, as the above definition of pollution reveals, the obligation to protect and improve the water quality of the Nile River Basin includes an obligation not to cause significant pollution harm.[1293] Moreover, the ICJ in the 2010 *Pulp Mills* case holds: "A State is obliged … to use all the means at its disposal in order to avoid activities which take place in its territory, or in any area under its jurisdiction, causing significant damage to the environment of another State. This Court has established that this obligation 'is now part of the corpus of international law relating to the environment.'"[1294] Therefore, the obligation not to cause significant pollution harm binds the Nile Basin States, as a matter of customary international law, regardless of the general nature of the obligation in the CFA.

The second obligation is incorporated from Article 22 of the U.N. Watercourses Convention which requires watercourse States to "take all measures necessary to prevent the introduction of species, alien or new, into an international watercourse which may have effects detrimental to the ecosystem of the watercourse resulting in significant harm to other watercourse States."[1295] Like the Convention, the CFA does not completely ban the introduction of alien or new species. Instead, it requires the Nile Basin States to prevent the introduction of alien or new species into the Nile River System that may have detrimental effects on the ecosystems of the Nile River Basin.[1296] Thus, the obligation provided in the CFA not only incorporates a precautionary approach[1297] but also sets the threshold at "detrimental effects resulting in significant harm to other watercourse states."[1298] Furthermore, as with the obligation contained in Article 6, this obligation is also one of due diligence, requiring the Nile Basin states to "take all appropriate" measures necessary to prevent the introduction of alien or new species.[1299]

The third obligation, which requires protecting "wetlands within the Nile River Basin,"[1300] seems incompatible with the 1959 Agreement, since the latter

1293 CFA, *supra* note 132, art 6 ¶ 1 (a).
1294 *Pulp Mills*, 2010 I.C.J. ¶ 101.
1295 U.N. Watercourses Convention, *supra* note 818, art. 22; *see* also Berlin Rules, *supra* note 818, art. 25.
1296 CFA, *supra* note 132, art 6 ¶ 1 (b).
1297 Berlin Rules, *supra* note 818, art. 23.
1298 RIEU-CLARKE ET AL, *supra* note 1240, 181 (Commenting on the U.N. Watercourses Convention).
1299 *Id* (Commenting on the U.N. Watercourses Convention).
1300 CFA, *supra* note 132, art 6 ¶ 1 (d).

contemplates various projects that would drain the wetlands in the South Sudan to increase the Nile water flowing to Egypt.[1301] However, given the importance of wetlands for the Nile Basin and its ecosystem, the inclusion of the obligation in the CFA is very commendable and is in line with the current trend towards robust environmental protection.[1302]

The CFA also included other provisions relevant to environmental protection. In addition to the procedural obligations such as environmental impact assessments and audits discussed below,[1303] Article 11 of the CFA requires the Nile Basin States to "make every effort to take all appropriate measures to prevent or mitigate conditions related to the Nile River System that may be harmful to [the] other Nile Basin States, whether resulting from human conduct or natural causes, such as flood conditions, invasive water weeds, water-borne diseases, siltation (silting), erosion, drought or desertification."[1304] Article 12 of the CFA further requires the Nile Basin States to immediately take all practicable measures to prevent, mitigate, and eliminate harmful effects that result suddenly from natural causes, such as floods, landslides, or earthquakes, or from human conduct, such as industrial accidents.[1305]

Furthermore, the CFA contemplates the protection of the Nile River System in times of war. Article 13 stipulates: "The Nile River System and related installations, facilities and other works, as well as installations containing dangerous forces in the Nile River Basin, shall enjoy the protection accorded by the principles and rules… international humanitarian law, and shall not be used in violation of those principles and rules."[1306]

Indeed, all the aforementioned provisions demonstrate that the CFA gives special emphasis to environmental protection. This is especially true when compared with the existing Nile Waters Agreements, which merely focus on water allocation. Given the ever-increasing environmental problems in the Nile Basin,[1307] the inclusion of such detailed provisions in the CFA is extremely important for robust protection of the environment.

1301 1959 Agreement, *supra* note 106 at art. III.

1302 MCCAFFREY, *supra* note 4, 514–20 (Underlining the emerging obligations toward protecting the ecosystem).

1303 CFA, *supra* note 132, art 9; *see* Berlin Rules, *supra* note 818, art. 29.

1304 CFA, *supra* note 132, art. 11.

1305 *Id*, art. 12.

1306 *Id*, 13.

1307 *See* the discussion in section 1.2.

6.2.2 *Procedural Principles*

The CFA also included several procedural principles essential for pragmatic applications of the substantive rights and obligations in the Nile Basin. Some of these principles include, *inter alia*, the general obligation to cooperate,[1308] regular exchange of data and information,[1309] and prior notifications of planned measures.[1310] Article 3(1) sets forth the principle of cooperation, requiring the Nile Basin States to cooperate "on the basis of sovereign equality, territorial integrity, mutual benefit and good faith in order to attain optimal utilization and adequate protection and conservation of the Nile River Basin and to promote joint efforts to achieve social and economic development."[1311]

The article directly incorporated three terms from the U.N. Watercourses Convention: sovereign equality, territorial integrity, and mutual benefit.[1312] As the pillar of the existing international legal order, sovereign equality provides the foundation for the rights and duties of the Nile Basin States.[1313] It contains two basic premises: (1) The Nile Basin States jurisdiction over their respective territories and population living there; and (2) non-intervention in the affairs of other Nile Basin States.[1314] It is also the cornerstone of other important principles including, *inter alia*, the right to independence and the prohibition of the use of force.[1315] Since international law is influenced by hegemonic powers, sovereign equality—as a legal concept—does not ensure political and economic equality, and can therefore be described as only equality of opportunities of all Nile Basin States.[1316]

The notion of territorial integrity is a well-recognized principle under international law. It is included in Article 2(4) of the UN Charter where all member states are required to "refrain ... from the threat or use of force against the *territorial integrity* or political independence of any state."[1317] Although not defined by the charter, the principle of territorial integrity reflects "the fundamental international objective in the stability of boundaries."[1318] The last

1308 CFA, *supra* note 132, art 3¶ 1.

1309 *Id*, art. 7.

1310 *Id*, art. 8.

1311 CFA, *supra* note 132, art 3¶ 1.

1312 U.N. Watercourses Convention, *supra* note 818, art. 8 ¶ 1.

1313 RIEU-CLARKE ET AL, *supra* note 1240, 124 (Commenting on the U.N. Watercourses Convention).

1314 *Id* (Commenting on the U.N. Watercourses Convention).

1315 *Id* (Commenting on the U.N. Watercourses Convention).

1316 *Id* (Commenting on the U.N. Watercourses Convention).

1317 U.N. Charter, art. 2, ¶ 4.

1318 RIEU-CLARKE ET AL, *supra* note 1240, 124 (Commenting on the U.N. Watercourses Convention).

term, "mutual benefit," entails that the Nile Basin States should not engage in zero-sum games and that cooperation should lead to "win-win" outcomes for all of them.[1319]

The CFA, further expanding the general obligation to cooperate, provides a specific obligation to regularly exchange data and information. In this regard, Article 7 of the CFA stipulates:

> 1. In pursuance of their cooperation concerning the use, development and protection of the Nile River Basin and its water resources, Nile Basin States shall on a regular basis exchange readily available and relevant data and information on existing measures and on the condition of water resources of the Basin, where possible in a form that facilitates its utilization by the States to which it is communicated.
> 2. If a Nile Basin State is requested by another Basin State to provide data or information that is not readily available, it shall employ its best efforts to comply with the request but may condition its compliance upon payment by the requesting State of the reasonable costs of collecting and, where appropriate, processing such data or information.
> 3. In the implementation of their obligations under Paragraph 1 and 2, Nile Basin States Nile Basin States agree to observe procedures to be developed by the Nile River Basin Commission.[1320]

The significance of this provision is obvious, as regular exchange of data and information is the first step in the process of cooperation between the Nile Basin States, and in the determination of the relevant factors for equitable and reasonable utilization of the Nile Water System.[1321] It is also important for the Nile Basin States to take all appropriate actions and fulfill their due diligence obligation not to cause significant harm.[1322]

In requiring a "regular" exchange of data and information, the CFA contemplates a continuous systematic process, which fundamentally differs from the

1319 *Id.* (Commenting on the U.N. Watercourses Convention).

1320 CFA, *supra* note 132, art 7.

1321 RIEU-CLARKE ET AL, *supra* note 1240, 126 (Commenting on the U.N. Watercourses Convention).

1322 MCCAFFREY, *supra* note 4, 540 (Stating that data and information exchange is part of principle of equitable and reasonable utilization and the obligation to prevent significant harm). CAPONERA, *supra* note 949, 219. (Explaining the significance data and information exchange for determining equitable and reasonable utilization and preventing significant harm).

provisional obligation of prior notification of planned measures.[1323] The use of the term "readily available" also restricts the legal obligation of the Nile Basin State only to the data and information that is already at their disposal or is easily accessible.[1324] The data and information should be transmitted when it concerns "existing measures and on the condition of water resources of the Basin."[1325] In other words, the data and information should include existing use and infrastructures as well as hydrological, meteorological, hydrogeological, and ecological conditions. Data and information should not only be about the current conditions but "may also include forecasts—e.g., changing weather patterns with long-term effects on present uses."[1326]

Article 7(2) requires that a Nile Basin State that has been asked to provide data or information that is not readily available "employ its best efforts to comply with the request."[1327] Here the state is required to act in good faith and in the spirit of the general obligation to cooperate, which, *inter alia*, includes not causing unnecessary delay in the transmission of the information and not overwhelming the requesting state with data irrelevant to the request.[1328]

While regularly exchanging data and information, the Nile Basin States should also "observe procedures to be developed" by the NRBC.[1329] In addition to the power to develop procedures for data and information exchange, the NRBC is also tasked "to compile available data and information and coordinate ... monitoring of information relating to the Nile Basin, including the environment, review ... and synthesize ... the information with a view to integrating it into basin-wide databases and establishing standards, and develop ... mechanisms for the regular exchange of information where needed."[1330]

Regarding prior notification of planned measures, Article 8 of the CFA stipulates that the Nile Basin States should exchange information through the NRBC and that they should observe the rules and procedures established by the NRBC for exchanging information concerning planned measures.[1331] Article 9

1323 RIEU-CLARKE ET AL, *supra* note 1240, 126 (Commenting on the U.N. Watercourses Convention).

1324 *Id* (Commenting on the U.N. Watercourses Convention).

1325 CFA, *supra* note 132, art 7, ¶ 1.

1326 RIEU-CLARKE ET AL, *supra* note 1240, 127 (Commenting on the U.N. Watercourses Convention).

1327 CFA, *supra* note 132, art 7, ¶ 2.

1328 RIEU-CLARKE ET AL, *supra* note 1240, 127 (Commenting on the U.N. Watercourses Convention).

1329 CFA, *supra* note 132, art 7, ¶ 3.

1330 *Id*, art. 30 ¶ 9.

1331 *Id*, art. 8.

further requires an environmental impact assessment and audits for planned measures.[1332] Unlike the U.N. Watercourses Convention, the CFA does not include detailed rules regarding the notification of planned measures. The provisions governing prior notifications of planned measures as provided in part III (Articles 11 to 19) of the U.N. Watercourses Convention were not included in the CFA.[1333] This was because the principle of prior notification was one of the most controversial issues between the Nile Basin States during the negotiations of the CFA. Ethiopia persistently objected to the inclusion of this principle, due to its fear that the principle will amount to a prior consent regime, effectively imposing the existing Nile Waters Agreements on upstream countries.[1334] Accordingly, the CFA reconciles the positions of the Nile Basin States, requiring exchange of information on planned measures through the NRBC.[1335]

Public participation is the other significant characteristic of the CFA. Article 3(3) establishes as a general principle that the "development and protection of the Nile River Basin water resources is planned and implemented at the lowest appropriate level."[1336] Article 10(a) further elaborates this principle and requires the Nile Basin States to "allow all those within a State who will or may be affected by the project in that State to participate in an appropriate way in the planning and implementation process."[1337] The inclusion of this principle in the CFA reflects the recent trends of international environmental law that "promote public participation in environmental decision-making."[1338]

6.2.3 *Institutional Structure, Dispute Settlement, and Amendment and Termination of the CFA*

The CFA also contains several provisions regarding institutional structure, dispute settlement, amendment procedure, and termination. The following section briefly addresses these provisions.

6.2.3.1 Institutional Structure

Sustainable water resource management is inextricably linked with River Basin Organizations (RBOs). Developing an institutional structure for joint management of international watercourses is essential for the pragmatic application

1332 *Id*, art. 9.
1333 *Id*, art. 8; *see* also U.N. Watercourses Convention, *supra* note 818, arts. 9–19.
1334 Official Records Fifty-first Session, *supra* note 924, at 9–10.
1335 CFA, *supra* note 132, art 8.
1336 *Id*, art. 3 ¶ 3.
1337 *Id*, art. 10 (a).
1338 CHAZOURNES, *supra* note 955, 142. *See* also Berlin Rules, *supra* note 818, arts. 4, and 17–21.

of both substantive and procedural principles governing transboundary watercourses.[1339] Although international watercourses law does not require the establishment of RBOs, state practice shows an increasing tendency to create such organizations.[1340] While the U.N. Watercourses Convention recommends the establishment of RBOs,[1341] the Berlin Rules provide the minimum requirements for such institutional mechanisms.[1342] Among others, the RBO should have the authority to coordinate scientific and technical research programs and to establish harmonized, coordinated, or unified networks for permanent observation and control.[1343] The constitutive act of the RBO should also expressly stipulate the objectives and purposes, nature and composition, form and duration, legal status, area of operation, functions, and powers, and financial arrangements of the organization.[1344]

Drawing on the Berlin Rules that delineate a model for RBOs, the CFA envisions the establishment of the Nile River Basin Commission (NRBC) as a joint body for the management and sustainable development of the Nile River Basin.[1345] Part 3 of the CFA determines the legal status and objectives of the NRBC.[1346] It also enumerates constituting organs, and their composition, powers, functions and decision-making procedures.[1347] The NRBC will become operational, if and when the CFA enters into force, and permanently replace the NBI.[1348]

The CFA envisioned the NRBC as an intergovernmental organization with an international legal personality.[1349] It will "serve as an institutional framework for cooperation among the Nile Basin States in the use, development,

1339 *See* Glen Hearns & Richard Kyle Paisley, *Lawyers Write Treaties, Engineers Build Dikes, Gods of Weather Ignore Both: Making Transboundary Waters Agreements Relevant, Flexible, and Resilient in a Time of Global Climate Change*, 6 GOLDEN GATE U. ENV'T L.J. 259, 274–75 (2013).

1340 Christina Leb, *Implementation of the general duty to cooperate*, *in* RESEARCH HANDBOOK, *supra* note 42, 105.

1341 U.N. Watercourses Convention, *supra* note 818, art. 24 ¶1 ("Watercourse States shall, at the request of any of them, enter into consultations concerning the management of an international watercourse, which *may* include the establishment of a joint management mechanism") (emphasis added).

1342 Berlin Rules, *supra* note 818, arts. 64–67.

1343 *Id*, art. 65.

1344 *Id.*

1345 CFA, *supra* note 132, art 15.

1346 *Id*, part 3, arts 15–30.

1347 *Id.*

1348 *Id*, art. 30.

1349 *Id*, art 19.

protection, conservation, and management of the Nile Basin and its waters."[1350] The purpose and objective of the Commission are "to promote the implementation of the principles, rights, and obligations provided" in the CFA, and "to facilitate closer cooperation among the Nile Basin States in social, economic, and cultural fields."[1351]

The NRBC institutional structure includes five organs: (1) Conference of Heads of State and Government; (2) Council of Ministers (COM); (3) Technical Advisory Committee (TAC); (4) Sectoral Advisory Committees (SAC); and (5) the Secretariat.[1352] As the name implies, "the Conference of Heads of State and Government … is composed of the Heads of States and Governments of the Nile Basin States [and] establishes its own rules and procedures."[1353] The COM is made up of the water ministers of all Nile Basin States, "establish[es] its own rules and procedures [and] convene[s] once a year in a regular session."[1354] The COM approves the rule and procedure of the TAC, which is "composed of two members from each Nile Basin States [and] convene[s] twice a year in regular session."[1355] The COM may also establish SAC composed of one member from each Nile Basin State.[1356] Finally, the COM appoints the head of the Secretariat (Executive Secretary) for a three years term.[1357]

The CFA also provides detailed provisions regarding the functions and decision-making procedures of the NRBC. While the Conference of Heads of State and Government is "the supreme policy-making organ,"[1358] the COM is "the governing body" of the NRBC.[1359] The CFA contemplates that the COM should make its decisions by consensus and that the "decisions … are binding on all Nile Basin States."[1360] In terms of function, the COM "approves the annual work programs of [the NRBC], the rules and procedures governing the operations of [the TAC, SAC], and the Secretariat as well as its work program and financial and staff regulations."[1361] The COM "appoints the Executive Secretary and other senior staff" of the NRBC and determines "the staffing and

1350 *Id*, art. 16.
1351 *Id*.
1352 *Id*, art. 17.
1353 *Id*, art. 20.
1354 *Id*, art, 22 & 23 ¶¶ 1 &2.
1355 *Id*, art 25 ¶¶¶ 1, 3 & 4.
1356 *Id*, art 27.
1357 *Id*, art. 29.
1358 *Id*, art. 21.
1359 *Id*, art 24 ¶ 1.
1360 *Id*, art. 23 ¶ ¶ 5 & 6.
1361 *Id*, art. 24 ¶ 8.

organizational structure of the Secretariat."[1362] It "adopts, keeps under review, and revises as necessary the plans for the coordinated, integrated, and sustainable management and development of the Nile River Basin."[1363] It supervises the implementation of the CFA and adopts rules, procedures, guidelines, and criteria for its implementation.[1364] It also investigates and "makes decisions regarding the determination of equitable and reasonable use of water in each Basin State, taking into consideration the factors listed" in Article 4 (2) of the CFA.[1365] Moreover, the COM serves as a discussion forum for all "matters within the scope of its function and [the CFA]."[1366]

The TAC assists the COM in discharging its functions.[1367] In particular, it prepares "cooperative programs for the sustainable management and development of the Nile River Basin" and submits them to the COM for consideration.[1368] It provides recommendations to the COM on "the implementation of the provisions" of the CFA,[1369] and "regarding the determination of equitable and reasonable use of water" in each Basin State.[1370] It advises the COM on "technical matters regarding the use, development, protection, conservation, and management of the Nile River Basin."[1371] It "supervises the Secretariat," submits proposals to the COM regarding "the appointment of the Executive Secretary and senior technical staff of the Secretariat," and provides recommendations to the COM "concerning the rules and procedures governing the operations of the Secretariat."[1372]

The last organ, the Secretariat, represents the NRBC "in its relations with international and bilateral assistance institutions and with any Nile sub-basin institutions or arrangements."[1373] Headed by the Executive Secretary,[1374] the secretariat is also "responsible for the administration and finances of [the NRBC],"[1375] and assisting all organs of the NRBC in discharging their

1362 *Id*, ¶ 9–10.
1363 *Id*, ¶ 5.
1364 *Id*, ¶ 3 & 11.
1365 *Id*, ¶ 12.
1366 *Id*, ¶ 2.
1367 *Id*, art. 26.
1368 *Id* ¶ 1.
1369 *Id*, art 26 ¶ 4.
1370 *Id*, ¶ 5.
1371 *Id*, ¶ 6.
1372 *Id*, ¶ 7 & 8.
1373 *Id*, art. 30, ¶ 1.
1374 *Id*, art. 29 ¶ 1.
1375 *Id*, art. 30, ¶ 3.

functions.[1376] It is also tasked with compiling "available data and information and coordinates monitoring of information relating to the Nile Basin," and developing "mechanisms for the regular exchange of information."[1377]

According to Article 30 of the CFA, the NRBC will succeed to all rights, obligations, and assets of the NBI as soon as the Agreement enters into force.[1378] As indicated above, Egypt and Sudan refuse to sign the CFA.[1379] The upstream states, on the other hand, are still committed to enter the CFA into force and establish the NRBC, even without the involvement of the downstream States.[1380] If the CFA enters into force, "[w]hat will happen to the rights and obligations under the NBI of the States that are not parties (and do not plan to be parties) to the CFA?"[1381] Salman, anticipating that "[t]his situation ... will raise some difficult legal issues and exacerbate the existing disputes over the CFA,"[1382] suggested that "the mediators and drafters of the CFA neither took into account nor anticipated the occurrence of this situation."[1383]

Although the establishment of the NRBC without the downstream states could exacerbate the existing disputes over the CFA, the legal ramifications of the situation are clear. Under international law, states can conclude an agreement to liquidate an international organization and transfer its powers and functions to a successor organization.[1384] However, this rule applies only when "the membership of the predecessor organization and of the successor organization is identical."[1385] If the membership is not identical, an agreement is required among all members of the predecessor and the successor organizations.[1386] Therefore, the ramifications of Article 30 are restricted only between these states that are parties to the CFA and NBI. As for the downstream states that are not parties to the CFA, Article 30 is irrelevant, and another agreement would be necessary between the future members of the NRBC and downstream states to transfer the rights, obligations, and assets of the NBI to the

1376 *Id*, ¶ 8.
1377 *Id*, ¶ 9.
1378 *Id*, art 30.
1379 *See* the discussion in sections 6.1. & 6.2.
1380 *Id.*
1381 Salman, *supra* note 172, 23.
1382 *Id.*
1383 *Id.*
1384 Kirsten Schmalenbach, *International Organizations or Institutions, Succession, in* MAX PLANCK ENCYCLOPEDIA OF PUBLIC INTERNATIONAL LAW, (Rüdiger Wolfrum, ed., 2017).
1385 *Id.*
1386 *Id.*

NRBC. Confirming this, the legal consultant of the CFA project, Professor McCaffery, stated: "The legal situation seems clear enough. How it will play out is another question. As between states that are not parties to a CFA in force, the old regime will govern their relations. The same is true for relations between those States and States that are parties to the CFA. It is only as between States, all of which are parties to a CFA in force that will govern their relations."[1387]

6.2.3.2 Dispute Settlement, and Amendment and Termination of the CFA

The CFA also provided several provisions regarding dispute settlement, amendment, and termination of the agreement. Part V of the CFA provided detailed provisions regarding the settlement of disputes arising out of interpretation or implementation the Agreement.[1388] These provisions, directly incorporated from the U.N. Watercourses Convention, include negotiations, mediation, conciliation and submission of the dispute to arbitration or the ICJ, as means for dispute settlement.[1389] If the dispute cannot resolved by any of these means within six months, it should "be submitted, at the request of any of the parties to the dispute, to impartial fact-finding in accordance with the Annex on the factfinding Commission."[1390]

Regarding amendment, Article 35 sets forth two distinct rules for approving proposed amendments, one requiring consensus and another requiring a two-thirds majority vote.[1391] The articles of the CFA that can only be amended by consensus include, *inter alia*, Articles 3, 4, 5, 8, 9, and 14.[1392] The CFA also explicitly stipulates that the two rules should govern annexes to the agreement or to any protocol, and that "any annex relating to one of the articles ... which may be amended only by consensus, must be adopted by consensus."[1393] As for termination, the CFA allows the Basin States to withdraw from the Agreement at any time after two years from the date of its entry into force. The only requirement is that the State terminating its treaty obligation shall give written notifications to the depositary.[1394] "The withdrawal shall take place upon expiry of one year after the date of its receipt by the Depositary."[1395] The other

1387 McCaffrey Interview, *supra* note 135.
1388 CFA, *supra* note 132, part V, arts 33–34.
1389 *Id*, art 33, ¶ 1 (a).
1390 *Id*, art 33, ¶ 1 (b).
1391 *Id*, art. 35¶ 3.
1392 *Id.*
1393 *Id*, art, 36.
1394 *Id*, art 39, ¶ 1.
1395 *Id*, ¶ 2.

provisions govern the signature of the CFA,[1396] its ratification,[1397] and entry into force, which would take place on "the sixtieth day following the date of the deposit of the sixth instrument of ratification or accession with the African Union."[1398]

6.3 Hydro-political Implications

As noted previously, the fate of the colonial and immediate post-colonial Nile Waters Agreements ("existing Nile Waters Agreements") was the subject of controversy between the Nile Basin States during the negotiation of the CFA. The upstream states believed that the purpose of the CFA Project was to produce an inclusive agreement that would replace and supersede these agreements.[1399] The lower riparian states—Egypt and Sudan—insisted that the new agreement must explicitly recognize the existing Nile Waters Agreements and continue to be binding upon all riparian states.[1400] The principle of water security, which was deliberately introduced as a means of inserting constructive ambiguity and a compromising technique,[1401] did not bridge the negotiation gap and resolve the dispute over these agreements.[1402] The upstream states opened the CFA for signature after 13 years of negotiation on May 14, 2010. So far, the CFA has been signed by six upstream states and subsequently ratified by four states.[1403]

Given the fact that the final text of the CFA does not address the fate of the existing Nile Waters Agreements, and considering the principle of privity of a treaty, one may wonder why the upstream states went ahead with the signature process, despite the downstream states' unequivocal denunciation of the CFA and withdrawal from the NBI.[1404] From a legal perspective, there

1396 *Id*, art. 40.
1397 *Id*, art. 41.
1398 *Id*, art. 42.
1399 Taha, *supra* note 90, 216; Arsano & Tamrat, *supra* note 100, 23.
1400 *Id*; McCaffrey Interview, *supra* note 135; *see also* Mekonnen, *supra* note 135, 421.
1401 *Id*, 429–31.
1402 *Id*. McCaffrey Interview, *supra* note 135.
1403 *See supra* note 142 and accompanying texts.
1404 For Egypt, the CFA tantamount to asking Egyptians to "leave their culture and go and live in the desert." Barry Malone, *Ethiopian PM warns Egypt off Nile war*, REUTERS (Nov. 23, 2010), https://www.reuters.com/article/us-ethiopia-egypt-meles/ethiopian-pm-warns-egypt-off-nile-war-idUSTRE6AM5V820101123. Ambassador Hossam Zaki a spokesperson for the Ministry of Foreign Affairs of Egypt is quoted to have said, "Egypt will not join or sign any agreement that affects its share." *East Africa seeks more Nile water from Egypt*, BBC NEWS (May 14, 2010), http://news.bbc.co.uk/2/hi/8682387.stm. Sudan still

seems to be no sensible reason justifying why the upstream states alone should sign the CFA because the whole point of having a basin-wide agreement on the Nile Basin is to govern upper and downstream states' interests on the use, allocation, and management of the Nile watercourse.[1405] "Except for the states on the Lake Victoria basin, whose water use can affect each other's rights and interests, there is no reason for upper riparian states on the Blue Nile and the White Nile to be concerned about each other's water use."[1406]

The fact that six upper riparian states signed, and four ratified, an agreement that has no legal ramifications means that the CFA should have some hydro-political or tactical significance to the upstream states.[1407] Although upstream states attempted to justify their decision, portraying that consensus has already been reached in almost all aspects of the agreement and that the outstanding issue will be resolved in due time,[1408] a closer examination of the situation reveals that the CFA is more a counter hydro-hegemonic strategy "to diplomatically corner the lower riparian states."[1409] In the past, Ethiopia and Kenya had been following a strategy of "aggressive silence" and had boycotted several cooperative initiatives (participating as mere observers on some) to express their resentment at the existing hydro-hegemonic status quo.[1410] However, as this "aggressive silence strategy" was not effective,[1411] they seem to have shifted into a policy of politically isolating the downstream states[1412] and portraying Egypt "as unwilling to cooperate and recognize an agreement that harms none and benefits all."[1413] Therefore the question is, to what extent is the CFA effective as a counter hydro-hegemonic tool for isolating and pressuring Egypt?

The CFA alone would not change the hydro-political dynamics of the Nile Basin. Given its status as the hegemon of the basin,[1414] and its geopolitical

---

opposes the agreement, albeit its flexibility in resuming cooperation with upstream States through the NBI since 2013. Hanne Knaepen & Bruce Byiers, *Understanding The Nile Basin Initiative Balancing Historical Rights, National Needs and Regional Interests*, EUROPEAN CENTER FOR DEVELOPMENT 7 (2017), https://ecdpm.org/wp-content/uploads/NBI-Background-Paper-PEDRO-Political-Economy-Dynamics-Regional-Organisations-Africa-ECDPM-2017.pdf.

1405 Ibrahim, *supra* note 189, at 304.

1406 *Id*, 304–305.

1407 *Id*, 305.

1408 *Id.*

1409 *Id.*

1410 *Id*, 307.

1411 *Id.*

1412 *Id.*

1413 Nielsen, *supra* note 168, 45.

1414 Ibrahim, *supra* note 189, at 307.

strategic advantages to the western countries,[1415] "Egypt will not lose its diplomatic influence over potential donors and lenders such as the World Bank and Western governments, which means that the upper riparian states will not be better off in garnering funds for significantly large projects."[1416] As such, for the CFA to have a significant impact, the upstream states had to succeed on two fronts: (1) They should use the agreement to create a new counter-hegemonic narrative, and (2) develop the ability to undertake unilateral projects that would affect the flow of the Nile to Egypt.[1417] The upstream states' success on the two fronts, along with "their geographic position (i.e., the fact that the water passes through their territory before it reaches Egypt) should significantly weaken the hegemonic position of Egypt."[1418]

The hegemonic narrative of the Nile Basin "portrays the Nile waters as a veritable lifeblood even a slight reduction of which would bring mortal harm to Egypt,"[1419] and that such interfering with the status quo will threaten the national security of Egypt. It also asserts that "Egypt is the Nile, and the Nile is Egypt" and that "any gain in water to the upstream riparians is a loss to Egypt."[1420] The upstream states have recognized the need to counter these narratives. By signing the CFA, they have formulated "a non-securitized and morally laden counter-narrative."[1421] They also developed a well-articulated benefit-sharing counter-narrative, that the utilization of the Nile based on the CFA is not a zero-sum game. Depicting the inclusion of win-win solutions in the CFA, the late Ethiopian prime minister, Meles Zenawi, once stated that the utilization of the Nile watercourse through the CFA "does not mean [that] if the upper riparian countries benefit, Egypt and Sudan should lose. It doesn't mean that if Egypt and Sudan benefit, the upper riparian countries should lose."[1422]

Indeed, scientific evidence demonstrates that downstream states would benefit more from a basin-wide cooperative framework.[1423] The upstream states should, therefore, exert more efforts to exploit such evidence to de-securitize the Nile issue and convince the decision-makers and the public in downstream states that such a cooperative arrangement would not be "a lose-lose situation.

1415 *Id.*

1416 *Id.*

1417 *Id*, 308.

1418 *Id.*

1419 Mekonnen, *supra* note 525, 237.

1420 *Id.*

1421 Ibrahim, *supra* note 189, at 309.

1422 Interview by Egyptian TV with Meles Zenawi, the Prime Minister of Ethiopia (July 2010), https://www.youtube.com/watch?v=2zzXLFKUoHM.

1423 Ibrahim, *supra* note 189, at 310.

Since such a framework would be more beneficial to the Sudan than Egypt, a big part of the upper riparian states' effort ... should involve bringing South Sudan into their camp. This would ... be easier with ... South Sudan than North, but the effort should be aimed at both."[1424]

It should also be remembered that formulating a counter-hegemonic narrative by itself is not sufficient to "bring about significant changes in the hydro-politics of the Nile if the upper riparian states are not able to create and implement projects that can threaten Egypt's negotiating power."[1425] Ethiopia, realizing this reality, raised enough funds by itself and embarked upon a unilateral project, the GERD, that would affect the amount of water flowing downstream.[1426] The GERD, under construction since 2011, had enormous implications on the hydro-politics of the Nile Basin, effectively serving as a counter hydro-hegemonic to Ethiopia. While GERD did not force the downstream states to accede to the CFA, it does force Egypt and Sudan to agree on the Declaration of Principles in 2015, which incorporates the basic principles of the CFA.[1427]

Conclusion

This chapter has demonstrated that the drafting and negotiation history of the CFA signifies a fundamental change in the previous treaty-making practice of the Nile Basin. Unlike the existing Nile Waters Agreements and other bilateral instruments, the CFA was the first multilateral attempt for developing an all-inclusive basin-wide legal and institutional framework in the Nile Basin. Although the CFA was intended to change the *modus operandi* of the Nile Basin from unilateralism into basin-wide institutional cooperation, the upstream and downstream states' attempt to change and maintain the status quo, and their disputes over the validity of the existing Nile Waters Agreements, have significantly frustrated all cooperative efforts.

The CFA, which closely follows the U.N. Watercourses Convention in terms of content, is a modern and "forward-looking agreement."[1428] It establishes NRBC for basin-wide institutional cooperation, codifies modern customary international watercourses law principles including the principle of equitable

1424 *Id.*

1425 *Id.*

1426 *See* the discussion *infra* Chapter 7.

1427 *Id.*

1428 MCCAFFREY, *supra* note 4, 319.

and reasonable utilization and the obligation to prevent significant harm, and gives special emphasis on the protection and conservation of the Nile Basin and its ecosystem. Furthermore, the CFA, albeit theoretically, treats the Nile Basin as a single unit for the use and development of the Nile watercourse. In this regard, it includes the principle of a community of interest between the Nile Basin States and facilitates the actual implementation of the notion of benefit sharing by empowering the Nile COM to decide upon "formulas for cost and benefit sharing by the Nile Basin States in respect of particular joint projects within the Nile River Basin."[1429]

While the CFA represents a significant step towards institutional basin-wide cooperation, the adoption of the agreement by only the upstream states, despite its unequivocal denunciation by the downstream states, and the principle of privity of treaty signify that the CFA is "intended to be a counter-hegemonic move disguised as a treaty."[1430] As a counter hydro-hegemonic tool, the CFA not only helped the upstream states to change the preexisting narrative and develop their own counter-narrative, but it also enabled them to isolate and pressure Egypt in their attempts to change the status quo.

Given Egypt's status as the hegemon of the basin, and its geopolitical strategic advantages in its relationship to the western countries, the CFA alone would not change the hydro-political dynamics of the Nile Basin. For the CFA to have pragmatic effects, upstream states had to develop the ability "to create and implement projects that can threaten Egypt's negotiating power."[1431] Ethiopia, realizing this reality, raised enough funds by itself and embarked upon a unilateral project, the GERD, that would affect the amount of water flowing downstream.[1432] Despite these developments, however, Egypt and Sudan continue vehemently rejecting the CFA. "It remains to be seen whether the shake-up in the hydro politics of the Nile set in motion by the GERD, discussed below, will soften Egypt's and Sudan's stands on the CFA."[1433]

1429 CFA, *supra* note 132, art 24, ¶ 16.
1430 Ibrahim, *supra* note 189, at 312.
1431 *Id*, 310.
1432 *See* the discussion *infra* Chapter 7.
1433 MCCAFFREY, *supra* note 4, 320.

PART 3

The Grand Ethiopian Renaissance Dam and the Current Dispute over the Existing Nile Water Agreements

CHAPTER 7

The Grand Ethiopian Renaissance Dam and Declaration of Principles

Introduction

As demonstrated in Part 1 and 2, Egypt has long been the principal hegemon in the Nile Basin. Through a myriad of mechanisms, including a series of colonial treaties, Egypt has established an effective hydro-hegemony in the Nile Basin. This has prevented upstream countries, like Ethiopia, from utilizing the waters of the Nile.[1434] Further, Egypt has used its strategic position in the Middle East as leverage to block international funds intended to help Ethiopia develop the Nile.[1435] For a long time, Ethiopia lacked funds to develop irrigation projects.[1436] This resulted in "one of Africa's cruelest ironies: the land that feeds the Nile is unable to feed itself."[1437]

Eventually, Ethiopia decided to change the game by constructing the Grand Ethiopian Renaissance Dam ("GERD"). The GERD is a giant hydrologic project on one of the Nile River's main tributaries—the Blue Nile in Ethiopia—designed to generate 5,150 megawatts of electricity from thirteen turbines.[1438] The GERD reservoir will cover an area of 1,874 square kilometers and can hold seventy-four billion cubic meters ("BCM") of water.[1439] Solely financed by Ethiopia, the GERD is expected to provide electricity access for an estimated sixty-five million Ethiopians.[1440] It will also support Ethiopia's development endeavors through income from energy exports and serve to lift millions of

1434 Tekuya, *supra* note 785, 10.

1435 *See* Swain, *supra* note 459 and accompanying text.

1436 Thurow, *supra* note 105.

1437 *Id.*

1438 *Power Generation Capacity of the GERD, supra* note 1149.

1439 IPOE FINAL REPORT, *supra* note 111, 7.

1440 Letter dated 14 May 2020 from the Permanent Rep. of Eth. to the United Nations addressed to the President of the Security Council, U.N. Doc. S/2020/409 (May 14, 2020) [hereinafter Ethiopia's 2020 Letter to the UNSC 2] (underscoring that the GERD is "a national project built solely through the direct contributions of all Ethiopians because Egypt persistently blocked international financial institutions from supporting the construction of the Dam"). *See* Permanent Rep. of Ethiopia to the U.N., Letter dated 23 June 2021 from the Permanent Rep. of Ethiopia to the United Nations addressed to the President of the Security Council, U.N. Doc. S/2021/600, 7 ¶ 4 (June 23, 2021) (hereinafter Ethiopia's

 | DOI:10.1163/9789004549869_008

people out of poverty.[1441] Despite the fact that eighty-six per cent of the Nile waters reaching Egypt originates in Ethiopia,[1442] the GERD is the second major dam on any of the Nile tributaries flowing from Ethiopian territory.[1443]

Ethiopia maintains that the dam will not have a significant adverse impact on the two downstream states—Egypt and Sudan. On the contrary, Ethiopia contends the GERD confers enormous benefits to Egypt and Sudan, including a more regular flow of water, better siltation prevention, a reduction in evaporation, and cheaper electricity.[1444] In a historic break with its past practice of moving in lockstep with Egypt, Sudan has since 2012 become more receptive to the GERD because of these benefits.[1445] Egypt, on the other hand, maintains its view that any upstream dam on the Nile River poses an existential threat.[1446]

Egypt initially rejected the project entirely, but later demanded Ethiopia conduct an independent transboundary impact study before continuing with the construction of the GERD.[1447] When Ethiopia refused to halt the construction of the GERD, Egypt requested a reduction in the size of the dam.[1448] In 2015, after painstaking negotiations,[1449] Egypt, Sudan, and Ethiopia signed the Declaration of Principles ("DoP") on the GERD.[1450] The DoP provides a framework for further negotiation on the filling and annual operation of the dam and reflects Egypt's recognition of the importance of the Nile River to Ethiopia's development.[1451]

2021 Letter to UNSC 1) (stating that GERD will provide electricity for sixty-five million Ethiopians); Yihdego, *supra* note 150, 0–3.

1441 Mahmoud Aziz, *Ethiopia Demands 'Fair and Serious' Talks to Return to Negotiating Table Over Disputed Nile Dam: Ethiopian FM*, AHRAMONLINE (Mar. 17, 2020), http://english.ahram.org.eg/News/365426.aspx.

1442 NILE BASIN INITIATIVE, *supra* note 52, at 36.

1443 Salman, *supra* note 146, 515–16. Ethiopia's first major dam, the Tekeze Dam, sits on the Atbara River and was completed in 2010. *Id.* The Tekeze dam can store up to four BCM of water and has the capacity to produce more than 360 megawatts of electricity. *Id.*

1444 Tawfik, *supra* note 145, 576.

1445 Tawfik, *supra* note 146, 24. (describing Sudan's position as "a turning point" in the hydro-political relations between the two downstream countries—Sudan and Egypt); *see also* Salman, *supra* note 146, at 516–19. Sudanese support for the project, however, has not been unwavering. *See* Kate Ng, *Sudan Boycotts Talks Over Controversial Mega-Dam in Ethiopia*, INDEP. (Nov. 24, 2020), https://www.independent.co.uk/news/world/africa/sudan-ethiopia-boycott-talks-mega-dam-b1759672.

1446 *See* Salman, *supra* note 146, at 516–17; Tawfik, *supra* note 145, at 574; *see also* Tawfik, *supra* note 146, at 24.

1447 *See* Tawfik, *supra* note 146, at 22.

1448 Yihdego, *supra* note 150, 0.

1449 *See generally* Salman, *supra* note 146 (reviewing the negotiation process).

1450 DoP, *supra* note 152.

1451 *Id*, preamble.

This chapter analyzes the legal and hydro-political implications of the GERD, and the DoP. The next section provides a brief overview of the GERD and the downstream states' initial reactions to the project. Demonstrating the factors that forced Egypt and Sudan to accept the GERD and sign the DoP, the section submits that the GERD represents the beginning of the *de facto* change in the Egyptian hydro-hegemonic status quo. Section 7.2. critically scrutinizes the legal status of the DoP and its relationship with the colonial and immediate post-colonial treaties. After analyzing the basic principles of the document, this section submits that the DoP, which contains important international watercourses law principles, neither abrogates the past treaties nor brought about a *de jure* change in the Egyptian hydro-hegemonic status quo.

7.1 The Grand Ethiopian Renaissance Dam: the Beginning of De-Facto Change in the Status Quo?

This section provides a brief overview of the GERD and analyzes Egyptian and Sudanese initial reactions to the project. After encapsulating the negotiation history of the DoP, it then reflects on the overall hydro-political ramifications of the GERD.

7.1.1 *The Grand Ethiopian Renaissance Dam: Non-consumptive Hydroelectric Project*

The origin of the GERD can be traced back to the studies of the U.S. Bureau of Reclamation (USBR) discussed in section 2.3.2.[1452] The report of USBR identified hydropower "projects capable of producing 8,660,000 kilowatts to add to the present limited supply."[1453] The report recommended several dam projects on the Blue Nile, including the Border Dam about 20 km from Sudanese borders.[1454] Ethiopia, updating the USBR study on this dam, commenced, in December 2010, constructing a hydroelectric dam on the Blue Nile, some 20 km upstream from the border with Sudan.[1455]

The dam, initially known as the Millennium Dam, and later changed into the GERD,[1456] is being constructed at a site that has seven times lesser evaporation

1452 *See* the discussion in section 2.3.2.

1453 U.S.B.R BLUE NILE REPORT A, *supra* note 360, 40–41.

1454 U.S.B.R, LAND AND WATER RESOURCES OF THE BLUE NILE BASIN, ETHIOPIA, 2 (1964 B) (hereinafter U.S.B.R BLUE NILE REPORT B).

1455 Ethiopia's 2021 Letter to UNSC 1, *supra* note 1440, 7 ¶ 4.

1456 Salman, *supra* note 146, 515.

than Aswan High Dam (AHD).[1457] As opposed to the original plan of the border dam which had a storage capacity of 15.5 BCM,[1458] the GERD is a large dam, with a height of 145 m, and a storage capacity of 74 BCM.[1459] The reservoir of the dam, which extends about 1,874 square kilometers,[1460] is more than twice the size of Lake Tana,[1461] or two and half times smaller than AHD's reservoir, Lake Nassir.[1462] The GERD, which is supplemented by a saddle dam with a length of 5 km, and a height of 245 m,[1463] has an installed capacity of 5150 megawatts of hydropower.[1464] It is expected to generate "fifteen thousand seven hundred gigawatt hours per year clean energy" from thirteen turbines.[1465]

The cost of the project is estimated at US $5 billion. Since the commencement of the project, Ethiopia has been financing "the GERD from its own resources and through the issuance of bonds to Ethiopians and interested foreign nationals, with no resort to foreign borrowing."[1466] The construction of the dam, now completed by more than 80 percent,[1467] created a great sense of euphoria in Ethiopia. The dam, being the product of the blood, sweat, and tears of Ethiopians, is expected to provide electricity access for an estimated sixty-five million Ethiopians.[1468] It will also support Ethiopia's development endeavors through income from energy exports and serve to lift millions of people out of poverty.[1469]

Ethiopia has made it abundantly clear that the sole purpose of the dam is generation of electricity, and that it does not intend to use the dam for irrigation.[1470] Thus, the GERD, being a hydroelectric dam, will not consume water (except for minor evaporation losses) and will release the inflow of water to Sudan and Egypt after hitting turbines to generate electricity. It is expected that, the GERD when completed, will be "a source of clean and renewable energy that puts East Africa in [a] clean energy pathway that advances sustainable

1457 Ethiopia's 2021 Letter to UNSC 1, *supra* note 1440, 9 ¶ 10.
1458 U.S.B.R BLUE NILE REPORT B, *supra* note 1454, 2.
1459 Salman, *supra* note 146, 516.
1460 *Id.*
1461 *Id.*
1462 Ethiopia's 2021 Letter to UNSC 1, *supra* note 1440, 9 ¶ 10.
1463 Salman, *supra* note 146, 516.
1464 *Power Generation Capacity of the GERD*, *supra* note 1149.
1465 *Id.* Ethiopia's 2021 Letter to UNSC 1, *supra* note 1440, 7 ¶ 3.
1466 Salman, *supra* note 146, 516.
1467 Getahun Legesse, *GERD Construction Reaches Over 80 Percent Completion*, THE ETHIOPIAN HERALD (May 21, 2021), https://www.press.et/english/?p=35147.
1468 Ethiopia's 2021 Letter to UNSC 1, *supra* note 1440, 9 ¶ 10; Yihdego, *supra* note 150, 0–3.
1469 Aziz, *supra* note 1441.
1470 Salman, *supra* note 146, 516.

development goals. It enhances water availability and better management in the Nile Basin."[1471]

Ethiopia maintains that the GERD will not have a significant adverse impact on the two downstream states—Egypt and Sudan. On the contrary, Ethiopia contends the GERD confers enormous benefits to Egypt and Sudan, including a more regular flow of water, better siltation prevention, a reduction in evaporation, and cheaper electricity.[1472] Egypt and Sudan initially opposed the GERD, alleging that it would significantly and adversely affect their interests and violate the rules regulating the Nile watercourse.[1473] Considering the numerous benefits conferred by the GERD, Sudan latter changed its position to support the construction of the dam.[1474] Gradually, after painstaking negotiations,[1475] Egypt accepted the importance of the dam and the three states signed the Declarations of Principles on the GERD Project ("DoP") on March 23, 2015.[1476] The next section briefly encapsulates the downstream states' preliminary reactions and the negotiation leading toward the DoP and recognition of the project.

7.1.2 *Downstream States' Preliminary Positions and Reactions*

Following the commencement of the dam, Egypt and Sudan denounced Ethiopia's decision and vehemently opposed the GERD. Both States alleged that the GERD would have a significant adverse impact on their interests, substantially decreasing the flow of the Blue Nile reaching to their respective territories.[1477] "Egypt further claimed that the GERD will turn a large tract of its irrigated lands into the desert, and will result in a considerable decrease of the hydropower generated by the AHD."[1478] Sudan, on the other hand, expressed its concerns "about the safety of the GERD, and the extensive harm Sudan could suffer if the GERD were to crack, fail or collapse."[1479] Both States also requested Ethiopia to furnish them with the studies conducted on the GERD to assess the potential adverse impacts of the dam on each of them.[1480]

1471 Ethiopia's 2020 Letter to the UNSC 1, *supra* note 788, 1, ¶ 1.
1472 Tawfik, *supra* note 146, 576.
1473 Salman, *supra* note 144, 23.
1474 Salman, *supra* note 146, at 516–18; Tawfik, *supra* note 146, at 21, 23–24.
1475 For a description of the negotiation process, *see* Salman, *supra* note 146.
1476 DoP, *supra* note 152.
1477 Salman, *supra* note 146, 516.
1478 *Id.*
1479 *Id.*
1480 *Id.*

Despite its initial opposition, Sudan changed its position and started to support the GERD since 2012.[1481] This, according to Salman, was mainly because of the scientific understanding that "Sudan will actually benefit from the GERD."[1482] In this regard, Salman identified several benefits Sudan would get from the dam. First, the GERD would increase the lifespan of the Sennar and Roseiris dams by retaining the huge Blue Nile sediments.[1483] Second, the GERD would regulate the flow of the Nile waters, and thereby prevent "the recurrent flooding, and the destruction to property and crops, caused by the seasonal flow of the Blue Nile."[1484] It is worth mentioning that regulation of the flow of the Nile water would increase water availability during the dry season, thereby enable Sudan to have two or three crop seasons as oppose to the current single crop season.[1485] It would also "refill groundwater throughout the year."[1486]

Third, Sudan is one of the countries with the lowest storage capacity, storing only about 10 BCM in its four dams.[1487] The GERD's reservoir will help Sudan to store the Nile waters. Currently, Egypt is using around 61 BCM of the Nile waters annually (more than its 55.5 BCM water "share" in the 1959 Agreement), while Sudan uses around 12 BCM from its 18.5 BCM "share" in the Agreement.[1488] In ensuring the regular flow of the Nile, the GERD will, therefore, increase the irrigation potential of Sudan, and enable Khartoum to use more water from the Nile (even more than its 18.5 BCM "share").[1489]

Furthermore, the GERD will provide cheaper electricity to Sudan, and Egypt, which is more cost-efficient than the electricity generated by either country.[1490]

1481 *Id.*

1482 *Id.*

1483 Letter dated 2 June 2020 from the Permanent Rep. of the Sudan to the United Nations addressed to the President of the Security Council, U.N. Doc. S/2020/480 7 (June 2, 2020) (hereinafter Sudan's 2020 Letter to UNSC). *See* also Salman, *supra* note 146, 516–17 (Stating that the Blue Nile sediments "have caused the Sennar and Roseiris dams to lose more than half their storage.")

1484 *Id*, 517.

1485 Sudan's 2020 Letter to UNSC, *supra* note 1483, at 7; *See* also Salman, *supra* note 146, 517.

1486 *Id.*

1487 *Id.*

1488 *Id.*

1489 Permanent Rep. of Ethiopia to the U.N., Letter dated 28 June 2021 from the Permanent Rep. of Ethiopia to the United Nations addressed to the President of the Security Council, U.N. Doc. S/2021/613, 8 ¶ 17 (June 28, 2021) (hereinafter Ethiopia's 2021 Letter to UNSC 2).

1490 Because of the GERD, "the Sudan will be able to expand … its electricity generation will be increased by 2,700 megawatts per year." Permanent Rep. of Ethiopia to the U.N., Letter dated 16 April 2021 from the Permanent Rep. of Ethiopia to the United Nations addressed to the President of the Security Council, U.N. Doc. S/2021/376, 11–12 (April 16, 2021) (hereinafter Ethiopia's 2021 Letter to UNSC 3).

Considering all the benefits, Sudanese officials stated: "the GERD is for Sudan what the Aswan High Dam is for Egypt."[1491] In March 2012, President Omar Albshir of Sudan also reiterated that the GERD has significant advantages for Sudan and that his government would provide any support for the completion of the project.[1492] Since then, Sudan, albeit with some safety-related concerns, supports GERD.[1493]

Notwithstanding the Sudanese change in position, Egypt maintained its view that any upstream dam on the Nile River poses an existential threat.[1494] It responded with belligerent rhetoric, expressing the possibility of even bombing the dam.[1495] Egypt further demanded that Ethiopia should "formally notify" the downstream states of the dam, furnish "them with all available information, and allows time for their responses before it continues with the construction of the GERD."[1496] Ethiopia, on the other hand, rejected Egypt's demand for notification, alleging that it will amount to recognizing a prior consent regime, effectively imposing the 1902 Anglo-Ethiopian Treaty on Ethiopia.[1497] Ethiopia also invoked the notion of reciprocity and insisted that "Egypt and Sudan never notified Ethiopia of any of their projects on the Nile."[1498]

However, committed to accommodating the interest of Egypt, Ethiopia made an unprecedented decision in the Nile Basin and initiated the establishment of an international Panel of Experts (IPoE), comprising ten members, six from the three states (two from each), and four international experts.[1499] The IPoE was establish in November 2011 to determine whether the GERD will cause a significant impact to the downstream states.[1500] Soon after its establishment

1491 Ethiopia's 2021 Letter to UNSC 2, *supra* note 1489, at 8 ¶ 17.

1492 Tawfik, *supra* note 146, 24 (describing Sudan's position as "a turning point" in the hydropolitical relations between the two downstream countries—Sudan and Egypt).

1493 *Id. See* also Salman M.A. Salman, *The Declaration of Principles on the Grand Ethiopian Renaissance Dam: An Analytical Overview, in* ETHIOPIAN YEARBOOK OF INTERNATIONAL LAW 203, 210 (Zeray Yihdego et al, eds., 2017); Salman, *supra* note 146, at 516–17; Tawfik, *supra* note 146, 24. Sudanese support for the project, however, has not been unwavering. Ng, *supra* note 1445.

1494 Tawfik, *supra* note 145, at 574; *see also* Tawfik, *supra* note 146, 24; Salman, *supra* note 146, at 516–17.

1495 *Id*, 517.

1496 *Id.*

1497 *Id.*

1498 *Id.*

1499 Ethiopia's 2021 Letter to UNSC 2, *supra* note 1489 at 17 ¶ 24; *see* also generally, IPOE FINAL REPORT, *supra* note 111.

1500 Salman, *supra* note 146, at 517.

in November 2011, Ethiopia submitted all 153 design and study documents of the GERD and the IPoE commenced its work.[1501]

Meanwhile, Ethiopia continued the construction of the dam unabated, and eventually "diverted the Blue Nile from its main and natural course of flow so it could commence construction of the GERD."[1502] Egypt vehemently opposed the diversion of the Blue Nile and contended that "Ethiopia should have waited for the issuance of the panel report before making any drastic decisions on the GERD."[1503] In early June 2013, the Egyptian government and the opposition parties held a meeting where participants openly and in lively broadcast, "called for a military attack on the GERD, as well as arming and funding opposition groups in Ethiopia to carry out that task."[1504]

The IPoE issued its report in May 2013 and recommended that more thorough studies should be conducted regarding the effects of the GERD on the downstream states.[1505] Egypt subsequently requested that Ethiopia should halt "the construction of the GERD until the studies were completed."[1506] Ethiopia rejected this request, arguing that IPoE did not recommend such a suspension and that the construction of the dam and the studies should occur simultaneously.[1507] "Another impasse ensued, but the three parties continued to talk to each other and agreed to meet at the ministers of water resources level to discuss their differences."[1508] As noted below, they undertook seven meetings to agree on a general framework for GERD.

7.1.3 *Negotiation History of the Declaration of Principles*

The first meeting was held in Khartoum on November 4, 2013. In this meeting, Egypt continued insisting that Ethiopia should stop GERD's construction until the studies recommended by the IPoE were completed.[1509] Following Ethiopia's rejection of this demand, another disagreement erupted between Ethiopia and Egypt. Egypt insisted that international experts should conduct the studies, while Ethiopia asserted that studies should be conducted only by

1501 Ethiopia's 2021 Letter to UNSC 1, *supra* note 1440, 20, annex 2.
1502 Salman, *supra* note 146, at 517.
1503 *Id.*
1504 *Id.*
1505 *Id*; IPOE FINAL REPORT, *supra* note 111.
1506 Salman, *supra* note 146, at 518.
1507 *Id.*
1508 *Id.*
1509 *Id.*

"Ethiopian experts. Thus, the first ministerial meeting ended in failure, but the three parties agreed to meet again in December 2013."[1510]

At the second tripartite ministerial meeting, Egypt insisted that Ethiopia should suspend the construction of the GERD until the studies are completed and international experts should conduct the studies.[1511] Again, unprecedented in the history of the basin, Ethiopia showed some willingness to compromise and conceded that the studies could be conducted by experts from the three states instead of just Ethiopian experts.[1512] However, the meeting was not successful in resolving the two outstanding issues as the concession was rejected by Egypt.[1513] Despite this, the three states agreed to meet again within a month time.

In the third tripartite meeting, held in January 2014 in Khartoum, neither of the States was willing to change its position or discuss the possibility of convening another meeting.[1514] Yet, as highlighted by Salman, the parties had their own calculations.[1515] Ethiopia, committed to making the GERD a *fait accompli* project, and continued construction of the dam unabated. On the other hand, Egypt was a bit reluctant, assuming that Ethiopia will not finance the dam by itself and that it would not get any funds from donor countries or international financial institutions.[1516] In its part, Sudan seemed to assume that it will continue facilitating the talks between the two countries.[1517] Evidently, Ethiopia's commitment bear fruit, and the GERD eventually became a *fait accompli* project.[1518]

After five months, the President of Egypt, Abdel Fattah El-Sisi, and Ethiopian Prime Minister Hailemariam Desalegn met in person[1519] and agreed that their countries should resume the tripartite negotiations on the GERD.[1520] Accordingly, in the fourth meeting held on 25–26 August 2014 in Khartoum, the three states addressed the two outstanding issues[1521] and agreed that the two studies recommended by the IPoE would be conducted by international

1510 *Id.*
1511 *Id.*
1512 *Id.*
1513 *Id.*
1514 *Id.*
1515 *Id.*
1516 *Id*, 519.
1517 *Id.*
1518 *Id.*
1519 *Id.*
1520 *Id.*
1521 *Id.*

consultants under the supervision of the Technical National Committee (TNC), comprising of four members from each of the States.[1522] As for the construction, Ethiopia was not required to suspend the construction of the GERD. This clearly indicated "the Egyptian acceptance of the fact that the GERD had indeed become a reality, and that the GERD construction will continue unabated."[1523]

At the fifth meeting, held on 22–23 September 2014 in Addis Ababa, the three states agreed that the international consultants would be selected by the TNC,[1524] and that the TNC would have its chairmanship, as well as its meetings, by rotation amongst the three countries."[1525] During this meeting, the three ministers visited the GERD site. Although the Egyptian minister stated that the purpose of "the visit was technical," Ethiopian officials seemed to have felt relieved as "Egypt could no longer deny the fact that it has accepted the GERD."[1526]

In the sixth meeting, held on 16 October 2014 in Cairo, the three states "agreed that international consultants would be selected and that the studies would be completed within six months."[1527] Finally, at the last meeting, held on 3–5 March 2015 in Khartoum, the three states announced that "they had reached an agreement on the GERD."[1528] Then, on March 23, 2015, the three states' heads of States signed the Agreement on the Declaration of Principles on the Grand Ethiopian Renaissance Dam Project (DoP).[1529] In signing the DoP, Egypt recognized Ethiopia's right to a fairer share of the Nile waters.[1530] It also officially accepted the GERD and the importance of the Nile watercourse for Ethiopian development.[1531] Therefore, effect-wise, it can be concluded that the construction of GERD transformed the hydro-political configuration of the Nile Basin from challenging the Egyptian hegemony into pragmatically changing the *status quo*.

1522 *Id.*
1523 *Id.*
1524 *Id.*
1525 *Id.*
1526 *Id.*
1527 *Id.*
1528 *Id.*
1529 DoP, *supra* note 152.
1530 *Id*, preamble.
1531 *Id*, art, 11.

7.2 The Declaration of Principles on GERD: a New Paradigm?

The DoP contains important principles that consider the interest of Ethiopia[1532] and recognize the significance of the Nile watercourses as the source of livelihood and development to its people.[1533] This section analyzes these principles in light of international law. It also critically scrutinizes the interplay between the existing Nile Waters Agreements and the DoP and determines the legal status of the latter under international law.

7.2.1 *The Declaration of Principles vis-à-vis the Existing Nile Waters Agreements*

The DoP, signed due to Ethiopia's unprecedented initiatives to accommodate the interest of downstream states, is a unique addition to the legal regime governing the use of the Nile watercourse. Unlike the existing Nile Waters Agreements, the DoP expressly considers Ethiopia's interests and recognizes the significance of the Nile River for the sustainable development of its people. It also codifies some fundamental principles of international watercourses law—including the principle of equitable and reasonable utilization, and the "no significant harm" rule—as the governing rubric of the Blue Nile.[1534] However, the legal effect of the DoP vis-à-vis the existing Nile Waters Agreements is unclear. There are two questions worth asking: Is the DoP binding? And, if so, does it supersede the colonial and immediate post-colonial Nile treaties?

First, the DoP may be a soft law instrument that does not bind Ethiopia, Sudan, and Egypt. This assertion is supported by the nomenclature of the document; declarations are not typically binding under international law.[1535] Moreover, the DoP does not include final clauses governing signature, ratification, entry into force, or deposit of the document pursuant to Article 24(4) of the VCLT[1536] and, as such, it indicates the parties did not intend the DoP to be a binding instrument.[1537] If the DoP is in fact soft law, the issue of the

1532 *Id*, arts. III & IV.

1533 *Id*, preamble.

1534 *Id.* arts. III–IV.

1535 Arnold N. Pronto, *Understanding the Hard/Soft Distinction in International Law*, 48 VAND. J. TRANSNAT'L L. 941, 951 (2015) ("The legal value of instruments adopted as 'declarations' or statements of principle is constrained by the limited authority of the adopting entity. Such instruments are legally indistinguishable from simple recommendatory texts.")

1536 VCLT, *supra* note 520, art 24 ¶4.

1537 The DoP has not been ratified by the three countries in accordance with their respective constitutions. In Ethiopia, the executive organ is empowered to negotiate

relationship between the DoP and the existing Nile Waters Agreements disappears. Nonetheless, the DoP is still important for the three states as it provides guidelines for the GERD negotiations. Ethiopia, Sudan, and Egypt may prefer the soft law nature of the DoP because it offers more flexibility in the GERD negotiations and facilitates compromise without significantly affecting their respective interests.

Second, it can be argued that the DoP is a legally binding instrument that must be enforced in good faith. While declarations are generally considered soft law, the title of a document is not wholly dispositive of its legal effect.[1538] "Treaties are known by a variety of differing names, ranging from Conventions, International Agreements, Pacts, General Acts, Charters, through to Statutes, Declarations, and Covenants."[1539] Rather, "the intent of the parties, as reflected in the language and context of the document, the circumstances of its conclusion, and the explanations given by the parties"[1540] determines its legal effect.[1541] Further, the DoP does not necessarily need to be ratified by Ethiopia, Sudan, and Egypt in order to have legal effect, because establishing the intention to be bound by a treaty is "governed by international law."[1542] Several aspects of the DoP suggest that it was intended to bind the three states. For instance, phrases including: the three states "*respect* the final outcomes

international agreements, but such agreements must be ratified by the House of Peoples' Representatives to be fully binding and have the force of law. CONSTITUTION OF THE FEDERAL DEMOCRATIC REPUBLIC OF ETHIOPIA, Aug. 21, 1995, art. 55 ¶ 12. In Egypt, the constitution empowers the president to "conclude treaties and ratify them after the approval of the House of Representatives." CONSTITUTION OF THE ARAB REPUBLIC OF EGYPT, Jan. 18, 2014, *as amended* Apr. 23, 2019, art. 151. Under Omar al-Bashir, Sudan's constitution structured treaty ratification in the same manner. NATIONAL CONSTITUTION OF THE REPUBLIC OF SUDAN, July 6, 2005, art. 58, ¶ 1(k) (repealed 2019). Sudan's new, provisional constitution brings it in line with Ethiopia's approach. DRAFT CONSTITUTIONAL CHARTER FOR THE 2019 TRANSITIONAL PERIOD, Aug. 17, 2019, arts. 16 ¶ 2, 25 ¶ 1(e) (Sudan).

1538 VCLT, *supra* note 520, art. 2.

1539 SHAW, *supra* note 668, 93 (citation omitted).

1540 Marian Nash (Leich), *Contemporary Practice of the United States Relating to International Law*, 88 AM. J. INT'L L. 515, 515 (1994) (quoting a memorandum from Robert E. Dalton, U.S. Department of State Assistant Legal Adviser for Treaty Affairs).

1541 *See, e.g.*, Maritime Delimitation and Territorial Questions Between Qatar and Bahrain (Qatar v. Bahr.), Judgment, 1994 I.C.J. 112, ¶ 30 (July 1) (finding the Minutes, like the exchanges of letters, "constitute an international agreement creating rights and obligations for the Parties"); *see also* Gabčíkovo-Nagymaros Project (Hung./Slovk.), Judgment, 1997 I.C.J. 7, ¶ 78 (Sept. 25).

1542 Sir Humphrey Waldock, *First Report on the Law of Treaties*, [1962] 2 Y.B. INT'L L. COMM'N 27, 32, U.N. Doc. A/CN.4/144.

of the Technical National Committee,"[1543] "the three countries have *committed to* …,"[1544] and "the three countries *shall take*"[1545] imply the DoP is binding. Hence, the agreement does not seem to be merely a "gentlemen's agreement." Subsequent state practice also appears to suggest that the three states intended to be bound by the DoP. In December 2015, Ethiopia, Sudan, and Egypt signed the 2015 Khartoum Document, agreeing to implement the DoP.[1546]

Even if the DoP is hard law, the issue of the relationship between the DoP and the existing Nile Waters Agreements becomes less crucial if the two legal regimes govern different subject matters or are found to be compatible with each other. For the reasons explained below, the DoP cannot supersede the existing Nile Waters Agreements simply because it is binding upon the three states.

The third, and perhaps the most convincing, argument would consider the DoP as a reflection of customary international law governing watercourses. The DoP binds the three states as an endorsement of existing international customs regulating transboundary watercourses. Confirming this, the International Court of Justice (ICJ) in *Military and Paramilitary Activities in and Against Nicaragua* stated that "the effect of consent to the text of such resolutions cannot be understood as merely that of reiteration or elucidation … it may be understood as an acceptance of the validity of the rule or set of rules declared by the resolutions themselves."[1547] Even if the DoP is non-binding, the two customary principles—equitable utilization and no significant harm—are binding on Ethiopia, Sudan, and Egypt by virtue of being rules of customary international law.[1548] The inclusion of these principles in the DoP indicates

1543 DoP, *supra* note 152, art V (emphasis added).

1544 *Id.* pmbl. (emphasis added).

1545 *Id.* arts. III–IV, VII & IX (emphasis added).

1546 *See* Salman, *supra* note 146, at 523–24. The relevant part of this document states that the three countries "reiterated their full commitment to implement the provisions of the Agreement on DoP signed in Khartoum on 23 March 2015." Summary and Outcomes of the 4th Tripartite Meeting of Ministers of Foreign and Water Affairs on the Grand Ethiopian Renaissance Dam Project art. iii, ¶ 1, Dec. 29, 2015, INT'L WATER L. PROJECT, https://www.internationalwaterlaw.org/documents/regionaldocs/Khartoum_Document_29_Dec_2015.pdf.

1547 Military and Paramilitary Activities in and Against Nicaragua (Nicar. v. U.S.), Judgment, 1986 I.C.J. 14, ¶ 188 (June 27) (internal quotations omitted).

1548 *See* MCCAFFREY, *supra* note 4, at 445 (considering the two principles as customary international law); Dellapenna, *supra* note 49, 269–72.

the three states' willingness to govern the Blue Nile based on contemporary international watercourses law.[1549]

The DoP is silent as to whether it supersedes the existing Nile Waters Agreements and does not address the present applicability or legal status of these agreements. Salman considers this omission an indirect nullification and contends that the decision to omit references to the rights flowing from either the 1902 Anglo-Ethiopian Treaty or the 1959 Agreement was demonstrative of Egyptian and Sudanese acceptance of "the new legal order established by and resulting from the DoP."[1550] Hence, this new order would replace the 1902 Treaty and the 1959 Agreement.[1551] Although he does not provide any legal ground for this assertion, Salman appears to rely on the *lex posterior* doctrine and assumes that the DoP is binding.

The later-in-time, or *lex posterior*, principle under international law permits states to supersede past treaties by concluding a new treaty governing the same matter. However, the assertion that the DoP has replaced the colonial and immediate post-colonial agreements is questionable. First, per Article 59 of the VCLT, the later-in-time treaty supersedes the prior treaty when the two conflict on an analogous point of international law.[1552] As indicated above, the legal status of the DoP is unclear and may not be considered as a legally-binding treaty capable of abrogating a pre-existing treaty. As Professor Stephen McCaffrey rightly described it, the DoP is a "quasi-legal document" that merely rearticulates established principles under international watercourses law.[1553]

Even if we assume that the DoP is a treaty, it falls short of fulfilling the requirements provided in the VCLT. The *lex posterior* doctrine applies when (1) both the former and new treaties relate to the same subject matter, and (2) the parties intended the later treaty to govern the same matter, or the two

1549 Recent developments in the GERD negotiations further support this assertion. Egypt formally submitted letters to the United Nations Security Council requesting its intervention in the GERD dispute, after which Ethiopia and Sudan each submitted their own letters. In their respective documents, all three states invoked and subscribed to, *inter alia*, the equitable and reasonable utilization and no significant harm rule as customary international law governing the Nile Basin. *See* Permanent Rep. of Egypt to the U.N., Letter dated 19 June 2020 from the Permanent Rep. of Egypt to the United Nations addressed to the President of the Security Council, U.N. Doc. S/2020/566, annex 1, 3 (June 19, 2020) [hereinafter Egypt's 2020 Letter to the UNSC 2]; *see generally* Ethiopia's 2020 Letter to the UNSC 2, *supra* note 1440; *see* generally Sudan's 2020 Letter to UNSC, *supra* note 1483.

1550 Salman, *supra* note 1493, 219.

1551 *See* Salman, *supra* note 146, at 52.

1552 VCLT, *supra* note 520, art. 59.

1553 MCCAFFREY, *supra* note 4, at 322.

treaties are "incompatible" and cannot be applied together.[1554] The DoP does not satisfy the first and most important test because it regulates a different matter than the 1902 Anglo-Ethiopian Treaty. While the former provides a framework for the GERD negotiations and, to some extent, for the use of the Blue Nile, the latter only addresses whether Ethiopia is required to obtain prior authorization from Britain (Sudan) before undertaking projects along the Nile tributaries.

With respect to the second requirement, the DoP is arguably a special agreement governing the GERD that can be applied concurrently with the existing Nile Waters Agreements. As noted, the DoP and the 1902 Anglo-Ethiopian Treaty establish distinct regimes that do not conflict. As for the other Nile Waters Agreements, the DoP is a narrow agreement that has no relevance to other Nile tributaries such as White Nile, Sobat (Baro), and the Atbara (Tekeze and Angereb) rivers. To the extent that it does not address these Nile tributaries, the DoP does not replace the existing Nile Waters Agreements.

If, however, Salman is correct in asserting that the DoP replaced the 1959 Agreement, the latter treaty does not govern the Nile River as between Egypt and Sudan, who are parties to both instruments. But, as discussed below, Egypt and Sudan heavily relied on the 1959 Agreement during the GERD negotiations.[1555] This has two potential implications. The first and least plausible is that the DoP supersedes the 1959 Agreement and Egypt and Sudan's subsequent reliance was erroneous. Second, and more plausibly, the DoP did not supersede the 1959 Agreement, in which case Egypt and Sudan properly relied upon it.[1556]

7.2.2 *Analysis of the Basic Principles*

The DoP has a preamble and ten articles, four of which specifically address the GERD, while the others focus on the Blue Nile, reiterating the general principles of international watercourses law.[1557] The following section analyzes these articles, addressing first the general principles, before moving on to discuss the special provisions governing the GERD.

1554 VCLT, *supra* note 520, art. 59.

1555 *See* the discussion *infra*-sections 8.1, 8.2. and 8.3.

1556 If the DoP does not establish a new legal order, the question is whether the colonial and immediate post-colonial Nile Treaties remain valid. Chapters 3 and 4 address this and indicate various grounds for invalidating the treaties.

1557 DoP, *supra* note 152.

7.2.2.1 General Principles

The DoP, which recognizes the significance of the Blue Nile as the source of livelihood and development to Ethiopia, Sudan, and Egypt,[1558] is developed based on the very foundation of international watercourses law, i.e., equality of rights of all riparian states in the use and allocation of an international watercourse.[1559] It contains the basic principles of international watercourses law including, *inter alia*, the principles of cooperation,[1560] no significant harm,[1561] equitable and reasonable utilization,[1562] and peaceful settlement of disputes.[1563] It should be noted that these general principles extend the scope of the DoP, albeit its title specifically deals with the GERD, to the Blue Nile. As indicated above, this may have implications in terms of creating a new legal regime governing the Blue Nile by reaffirming the cardinal principles of international watercourses law.

Regarding cooperation, Article I of the DoP stipulates that Ethiopia, Sudan, and Egypt are committed "to cooperate based on common understanding, mutual benefit, good faith, win-win and principles of international law."[1564] The general obligation to cooperate has also been cited in articles V and IX and forms the steppingstone for ensuring the realization of the needs of the three states.[1565] The latter principle, for instance, requires the three states to "cooperate on the basis of sovereign equality, territorial integrity, mutual benefit and good faith in order to attain optimal utilization and adequate protection of the River."[1566]

The obligation to cooperate is a well-established rule of international watercourses law.[1567] Hence, the inclusion of this principle into the DoP, in legal terms, is nothing more than the reaffirmation of what has already been recognized under international law. However, the issue of cooperation has not been practiced in the Nile basin except for some bilateral and multilateral efforts discussed in Chapter 5.[1568] The downstream states were not ready to act in the

---

1558 *Id*, preamble. This recognition especially important when contrast with the colonial and immediate post-colonial Nile Waters Treaties, which exclusively allocated the entire flow of the Nile watercourse between the two downstream States.

1559 *See* Salman, *supra* note 146, at 521.

1560 DoP, *supra* note 152, art. I, V & IX.

1561 *Id*, III.

1562 *Id*, IV.

1563 *Id*, X.

1564 *Id*, art. I.

1565 *Id*, art. V and IX.

1566 *Id*, IX.

1567 U.N. Watercourses Convention, *supra* note 818, art. 8.

1568 *See* the discussion in Chapter 5.

spirit of cooperation, attributing the Nile watercourse to their very existence and national security. Simply put, unilateralism has long been the *modus operandi* of the Nile Basin.[1569]

Despite such competitive practice, it is generally understood that the Nile Basin States would benefit more from cooperation than unilateral measures. In this regard, Ethiopia's commitment to break away from the unilateral practice and accommodate the interests of the downstream states is very commendable. The move by the downstream states to cooperate with Ethiopia on the GERD could also be taken as a positive step. Hence, the principle which intends to set aside the conformational strategies inherent in actions of the parties is an applauded one.

Concerning the no significant harm rule, Article III of the DoP requires the three states to take "all appropriate measures to avoid causing significant damage while using the Blue Nile."[1570] The principle also requires a state whose use causes significant harm to another state to "take all appropriate measures in consultations with the affected state to eliminate or mitigate such harm and, where appropriate, to discuss the question of compensation."[1571] It is to be noted this principle is largely incorporated from Article 7 of the U.N. Watercourses Convention and Article 5 of the CFA.[1572] Like the U.N. Watercourses Convention and CFA, the nature of the obligation in Article III is one of due diligence, requiring the three states only to undertake reasonable effort under the circumstances to avoid harm. Similarly, the harm required to violate the principle should be "significant," which is higher than merely trivial but could be less than severe or substantial.[1573]

However, it is also important to note that Article III of the DoP differs from both the U.N. Watercourses Convention and the CFA in three aspects. First, unlike the DoP, the U.N. Watercourses Convention and the CFA include the phrase in utilizing an international watercourse or the Nile River System "in their territories."[1574] This has been excluded from Article III of the DoP but kept in the principle of equitable and reasonable utilization.[1575] Second, the principle left out reference to the equitable and reasonable utilization incorporated under Articles 7 (2) of the U.N. Watercourses Convention and 5(2) of

1569 *Id.*
1570 DoP, *supra* note 152, art. III.
1571 *Id.*
1572 U.N. Watercourses Convention, *supra* note 818, art. 7; CFA, *supra* note 132, art 5.
1573 MCCAFFREY, *supra* note 4, 498.
1574 U.N. Watercourses Convention, *supra* note 818, art. 7; CFA, *supra* note 132, art 5.
1575 DoP, *supra* note 152, art. III.

the CFA.[1576] The latter instruments provided that "significant harm" is to be measured having due regard for the principle of equitable and reasonable utilization (Articles 5 and 6 of the Convention or 4 of the CFA) in consultation with the affected State.[1577] Third, unlike the U.N. Watercourses Convention and the CFA, Article III of the DoP addresses the obligation not to cause significant harm, before dealing with the principle of equitable and reasonable utilization, which is addressed in Article IV.

These deviations pose a critical issue: Does the DoP change the existing international law jurisprudence regarding the interplay between the two principles? Or does it make the principle of equitable and reasonable utilization subordinate to the no significant harm rule? Answering the question in negative, Salman concluded that under the DoP "the obligation not to cause significant harm has been subordinated to the principle of equitable and reasonable utilization, in line with the U.N. Watercourses Convention and the CFA."[1578] Two grounds can justify this argument. First, the DoP does not provide a clear indication that the principle of equitable and reasonable utilization is subordinate to the no significant harm rule. Neither the exclusion of reference to the equitable and reasonable utilization in Article III, nor the reversal of the order of the two articles in the DoP, alters the fact that under international law, equitable and reasonable utilization trumps the no significant harm rule.[1579] Besides, as indicated above, Article III of the DoP requires a state whose use causes significant harm to another state to "take all appropriate measures in consultations with the affected state to eliminate or mitigate such harm and, where appropriate, to discuss the question of compensation."[1580] This shows that the DoP, although it does not require giving due regard to the principle of equitable and reasonable utilization, tolerates the causing of significant harm when the harm can be mitigated, and the possibility of compensation may be considered.[1581]

Article IV dealt with equitable and reasonable utilization.[1582] Like other principles, this principle is based on the U.N. Watercourses Convention and the CFA. But, it left out the rules under Article 6 (2) and (3) of the U.N. Watercourses Convention.[1583] The U.N. Watercourses Convention stipulates

1576 U.N. Watercourses Convention, *supra* note 818, art. 7 ¶ 2; CFA, *supra* note 132, art 5 ¶ 2.
1577 U.N. Watercourses Convention, *supra* note 818, art. 7(2).
1578 Salman, *supra* note 1493, 213.
1579 *Id.*
1580 DoP, *supra* note 152, art. III, ¶ 2.
1581 Salman, *supra* note 1493, 213.
1582 DoP, *supra* note 152, art. IV.
1583 U.N. Watercourses Convention, supra note 818, art. 6 ¶ 2 & 3.

that "watercourse States concerned shall, when the need arises, enter into consultation" (i.e. in all other scenarios states operate independently).[1584] But this principle does not show this freedom for Ethiopia in particular.

Moreover, this principle, unlike the CFA and U.N. Watercourses Convention, fails short of determining the waters shared by the three countries. Both the U.N. Watercourses Convention and the CFA, which respectively use the expression of *watercourses* and the *Nile River System*, excluded the waters that fall on the basin but do not reach a common terminus from the scope of shared water resources.[1585] Article IV of the DoP, on the other hand, simply uses the term "shared water resource" without defining what it is.[1586] In so doing, it fails to settle the issue whether the unquantified waters falling on Ethiopian highlands (green water) are part of the "shared water resource."

Like the U.N. Watercourses Convention and the CFA, this principle lays down illustrative factors to ensure equitable and reasonable utilization.[1587] A noticeable inclusion under this principle that can be taken as a good achievement for Ethiopia is setting a guideline that calls for considering the *contribution* of states to the Nile waters.[1588] But, in what may resemble the "one hand giveth the other taketh away" scenario, the parallel inclusion of "the extent and proportion of the drainage area in the territory of each basin state"[1589] as a factor diminishes the value of the contribution factor for significant parts of the drainage area is in the lower riparian states.[1590]

The last provision, Article X, deals with the peaceful settlement of disputes. It recommends the three states to "amicably settle disputes, arising out of the interpretation or implementation of the [DoP] ... through consultation or negotiation in accordance with the principle of good faith."[1591] If the parties fail "to resolve the dispute through consultation or negotiation, they may jointly request for conciliation, mediation *or* refer the matter for the consideration of the Heads of State/Head of Government."[1592]

Although this article does not include arbitration and ICJ as dispute settlement mechanisms, it is one of the sticking points between Ethiopia and Egypt in the GERD negotiation. Egypt has demonstrated its amenability to

1584 *Id*, art. 6 ¶ 2.
1585 U.N. Watercourses Convention, *supra* note 818, art. 2(a); CFA, *supra* note 132, art 2(b).
1586 DoP, *supra* note 152, art. IV.
1587 *Id*, IV ¶ 2.
1588 *Id*, IV ¶ 2 (h).
1589 *Id*, IV ¶ 2 (i).
1590 NBI 2016, *supra* note 58, 19.
1591 DoP, *supra* note 152, art. X.
1592 *Id*.

third-party mediation and even formally requested the UNSC to intervene in the GERD negotiation.[1593] Ethiopia does not accept third-party mediation on the GERD, arguing that the three states should resolve their dispute by themselves through consultation or negotiation, with the engagement of the AU as an observer.

7.2.2.2 Principles on the GERD

The DoP includes four principles that specifically address GERD. Article II deals with development, regional integration, and sustainability.[1594] Per this article, the three states recognize the purpose of GERD as power generation, contribution to economic development, promotion of transboundary cooperation, and regional integration through the generation of sustainable and reliable clean energy supply.[1595] In so doing, the downstream states—especially Egypt—practically acknowledged Ethiopia's right to utilize the Nile watercourse. The acknowledgment, if considered vis-à-vis Egypt's longstanding position that views any upstream dam as an existential threat, is indeed a new paradigm and a breakthrough development in the Nile Basin history.

However, given that the purpose of the GERD is for power generation, one may wonder if Ethiopia can use the dam for other consumptive purposes. This should be governed by the no significant harm rule provided in Article III of the DoP. As noted above, the harm required to violate this article should be "significant," which is higher than merely trivial but could be less than severe or substantial.[1596] Accordingly, Ethiopia is allowed to use the dam for fishing, recreation, and small-scale industrial projects which may have trivial effects on the downstream states. Moreover, as the GERD is located some 20 km from the Sudanese border, other consumptive and irrigation projects around the dam would not cause significant harm to the downstream states and thus are allowed under the DoP.

Article VI is about confidence-building between the three states. The principle, which is not well-established under international watercourses law, stipulates that "priority *will* be given to downstream countries to purchase power generated from GERD."[1597] Though the use of 'will' remains to be vague (whether it makes a binding, directory provision, or optional stipulation) in the legal lexicon, one can argue that contextually it puts an obligation on

1593 Egypt's 2020 Letter to the UNSC 1, *supra* note 163.
1594 DoP, *supra* note 152, art. II.
1595 *Id.* art. III.
1596 MCCAFFREY, *supra* note 4, 498.
1597 DoP, *supra* note 152, art. VI.

Ethiopia to give priority to the two states, compromises the right to choose freely, and affects the long term economic interest of Ethiopia which is part of its sovereignty.

Article VII deals with the issue of dam safety. As noted above, dam safety is one of the main concerns of Sudan. Under international law, concerns regarding the safety of the GERD can be addressed under Ethiopia's due diligence obligation.[1598] Since 2010, Ethiopia has taken various measures in accordance with its international obligations to prevent harm to the downstream states. Ethiopia conducted transboundary impact studies, initiated a tripartite committee,[1599] and established an International Panel of Experts ("IPoE") which confirmed that the design and construction process of the dam was in line with "a number of international Standards, Codes, and Guidelines."[1600] Egypt, Sudan, and Ethiopia recognized all of these measures in Article VIII of the DoP.[1601] Given that ensuring the GERD's safety is a continuous process, Ethiopia should in good faith continue taking all dam safety-related measures.

Article V deals with the first filling and annual operation of the GERD. The article, in the relevant part, requires the three states to implement the recommendations of the IPoE[1602] and respect the final outcomes of the TNC's report on the joint studies recommended by the IPoE.[1603] It also suggests the three states utilize the outcome of these studies, and agree on rules and guidelines of the first filling and annual operation of GERD, in parallel with the construction of the dam, which the owner of the dam may adjust from time to time.[1604]

Article V further provides the framework for the three states' negotiation over the first filling and annual operation of the GERD. After signing the DoP, the three states have undertaken tripartite negotiations for more than five years but failed to strike a deal acceptable to them all. Considering the first filling and testing of the GERD as dam construction, Ethiopia has already started filling the dam without an agreement with Egypt and Sudan.[1605] Egypt rejected this, claiming that by filling and testing the dam Ethiopia was in violation of

1598 *See* the discussion *infra* section 8.3.1.

1599 Wondyifraw Qerenso, *Egypt: Better to Unshackle the Nile*, REPORTER (May 12, 2018), https://www.thereporterethiopia.com/article/egypt-better-unshackle-nile.

1600 IPOE FINAL REPORT, *supra* note 111, 21.

1601 DoP, *supra* note 152, art. VIII.

1602 *Id*, art. V ¶ 1.

1603 *Id.*

1604 *Id*, art. V ¶ 2 (a) and (b).

1605 Ethiopia's 2021 Letter to UNSC 2, *supra* note 1489.

Article V of the DoP, which—according to Egypt—requires all three states to reach an agreement on the rules of filling and operating the dam before such process can begin.[1606] These exchanges raise a fundamental issue as to whether Ethiopia is required to conclude an agreement with Sudan and Egypt before beginning filling the GERD.[1607] This issue is specifically addressed in the next chapter. Suffice to say that international law principles and precedents allow Ethiopia to fill and test the GERD without a preliminary agreement with Egypt and Sudan.

Conclusion

The launching of the GERD, after the failure of the Nile Basin States to forge an all-inclusive institutional cooperation, is a significant counter-hegemonic measure that brought about a *de facto* change in the Egyptian hydro-hegemonic *status quo*. It forced the downstream states that walked away from the CFA to come to the negotiating table and sign the DoP with Ethiopia, recognizing Ethiopia's right to a fairer share of the Nile waters.[1608] It also forced Egypt to officially acknowledge the importance of the Nile watercourse for Ethiopia's development.[1609]

While such recognitions make the DoP a breakthrough development, the context in which the instrument was negotiated and its failure to abrogate the existing Nile Waters Agreements pose serious challenges to the prospect of change. Instead of undertaking tripartite negotiation and adopting the DoP, Ethiopia should follow a basin-wide approach and use the GERD as a bargaining chip to incentivize Egypt and Sudan to accept the CFA. This approach would be "consistent with an emerging international consensus that projects undertaken to develop international water basins should meet metrics for efficiency and environmental sustainability which are basin-wide in scope."[1610] It would also be in line with "the letter and spirit" of the CFA, which explicitly endorses the community of interest approach.[1611] More

1606 Samar Samir, *Egypt Slams Ethiopia for Renaissance Dam Remark*, EGYPT TODAY (Mar. 1, 2020)https://www.egypttoday.com/Article/2/82175/Egypt-slams-Ethiopia-for-Renaissance-dam-remarks.

1607 *See* the discussion *infra* section 8.3.

1608 DoP, *supra* note 152, preamble.

1609 *Id*, II.

1610 Amdetsion, *supra* note 1007.

1611 *Id.*

importantly, it would significantly increase the GERD's counter-hegemonic value in terms of bringing *a de-jure* change in the *status quo* and address the three states' concerns regarding the filling, and operation of the GERD as demonstrated below.

CHAPTER 8

Sink or Swim: Unlocking the Grand Ethiopian Renaissance Dam Dispute

Introduction

Following the adoption of the DoP, Ethiopia, Sudan, and Egypt have been negotiating the filling and annual operation of the GERD but failed to strike a deal acceptable to them all. At first, the three states disputed over the modalities of the two studies—transboundary impact study and hydrological modeling study—recommended by IPoE.[1612] Egypt insisted that the baseline data to determine the impact should be its current use of the Nile waters.[1613] Sudan demanded the 1959 Agreement water allocation serve as the baseline, while Ethiopia rejected both positions.[1614]

As the dispute persists, Egypt has demanded the GERD's reservoir be filled over a long period, lasting about twenty years,[1615] and that it should have a say in the operational management of the dam.[1616] Ethiopia does not recognize Egypt's claim of "existing use" or "historic rights" regarding the Nile but has offered to fill the reservoir over a period of four to seven years despite the ability of the Blue Nile to support a fill period of three years.[1617] Since the GERD is a national project, wholly within Ethiopian territory,

1612 Salman, *supra* note 89, 95.

1613 *Id.*

1614 *Id.*

1615 Meseret, *supra* note 160.

1616 Bart Hilhorst, *Water Management in the Nile Basin: A Fragmented but Effective Cooperative Regime* 1 (Georgetown University Ctr. for Int'l & Reg'l Stud. Occasional Paper No. 17, 2016) https://ssrn.com/abstract=3447020; Telephone Interview with Zerihun Abebe Yigzaw, Diplomat, Ministry of Foreign Affairs of Ethiopia (Apr. 13, 2020) [hereinafter Yigzaw Interview]. Yigzaw was a member of the Ethiopian GERD negotiating team.

1617 Aidan Lewis, *Ethiopia Says Egypt Trying to Maintain "Colonial Era" Grip Over Nile*, REUTERS (Oct. 8, 2019) https://www.reuters.com/article/us-ethiopia-dam/ethiopia-says-egypt-trying-to-maintain-colonial-era-grip-over-nile-idUSKBN1WN1OG.

 | DOI:10.1163/9789004549869_009

Ethiopia insists on exclusive management of the dam and its operations.[1618] Apart from some safety-related concerns, Sudan supports the GERD.[1619]

For over five years, the three states have failed to resolve these outstanding issues. In August 2019, Egypt submitted proposals on the filling and operation of the dam[1620] and later effectively internationalized the GERD negotiations[1621] by involving the United States government and the World Bank as observers.[1622] The three states have held meetings with the U.S. Department of Treasury and the World Bank's representatives in both Africa and Washington, D.C.[1623]

The Washington talks, which were progressing well at first,[1624] took a turn for the worse in January 2020, resulting in a stalemate.[1625] The United States, evidently going beyond its status as an observer in the talks, proposed an agreement that Ethiopia considered adverse to its national interest.[1626] Ethiopia rejected the proposal and withdrew from the last meeting in Washington, D.C.[1627] The U.S. Department of the Treasury requested that Ethiopia sign the proposed agreement and cautioned Ethiopia to refrain from testing and filling the GERD without an agreement with Egypt and Sudan.[1628] Ethiopia expressed its disappointment with the statement and announced that it would proceed with filling the reservoir in parallel with the construction of the dam as agreed

1618 It is worth mentioning that Ethiopia's approach to its exclusive management of the dam does not exclude providing Egypt and Sudan with data and information concerning the dam's annual operation. Article V of the DoP recommends "cooperation and coordination on the annual operation of GERD with downstream reservoirs." DoP, *supra* note 152, art. V, ¶ 3.

1619 Salman, *supra* note 1493, 210; *see also* Salman, *supra* note 146, at 516–17; Tawfik, *supra* note 146, 24; and Ng, *supra* note 1445.

1620 *Ethiopia Rejects Egypt Proposal 1*, *supra* note 157; *Ethiopia Rejects Egypt Proposal 2*, *supra* note 157.

1621 *Egypt Seeks International Support*, *supra* note 158; *Egypt Calls on the U.S*, *supra* note 158.

1622 Joint Statement 1, *supra* note 159.

1623 Declan Walsh & Somini Sengupta, *For Thousands of Years, Egypt Controlled the Nile. A New Dam Threatens That*, N.Y. TIMES (Feb. 9, 2020), https://www.nytimes.com/interactive/2020/02/09/world/africa/nile-river-dam.html.

1624 Jacob Wirtschafter, *U.S.-Led Talks Lead to Breakthrough as African Rivals Inch Closer to War Over Nile*, WASH. TIMES (Nov. 11, 2019), https://www.washingtontimes.com/news/2019/nov/11/steven-mnuchin-mediated-talks-see-grand-ethiopian-/.

1625 Patsy Widakuswara, *No Deal from US-Brokered Nile Dam Talks*, VOICE AMERICA (Feb. 29, 2020), https://www.voanews.com/africa/no-deal-us-brokered-nile-dam-talks; Benita van Eyssen, *Trouble as Trump Dives into the Dispute Over Ethiopia's Nile Mega-Dam*, DEUTSCHE WELLE (Mar. 6, 2020), https://www.dw.com/en/trouble-as-trump-dives-into-the-dispute-over-ethiopias-nile-mega-dam/a-52663126.

1626 Meseret, *supra* note 160.

1627 *Id; US Being 'Undiplomatic'*, *supra* note 161.

1628 Treasury Statement, *supra* note 162.

in the DoP.[1629] Egypt, on the other hand, signed the United States' proposal and vowed to protect its interests in the Nile River "by all available means."[1630]

Egypt subsequently formally requested the UNSC to intervene in the GERD dispute.[1631] The UNSC made an unprecedented move and held an open session on the GERD dispute where most of the members encouraged the three states to resolve their dispute through the African Union (AU).[1632] After an intermittent tripartite negotiation under the auspices of the AU, Ethiopia announced that it is preparing to conduct the second-year filling of the GERD.[1633] Egypt, daring Ethiopia to "take a single drop of water from Egypt," warned of "inconceivable instability in the region" if Ethiopia filled the dam without a binding agreement.[1634] It then brought the GERD dispute to the UNSC for the second time.[1635] The UNSC, after holding yet another session on the GERD dispute, encouraged the three states to resolve their dispute through the AU.[1636]

Although disguised in talks over the GERD's filling and operation, the current tension between the three states is principally related to their longstanding disagreement over the validity of the 1902 Anglo-Ethiopian Treaty, the 1929 Anglo-Egyptian Treaty, and the 1959 Agreement between Egypt and Sudan (collectively, the "existing Nile Waters Agreement"). This disagreement—which reached an apex during the negotiation of the CFA[1637]—is adversely impacting the GERD negotiations.

1629 Press Release, Embassy of Eth., London, Statement of Ethiopia on the Negotiations on the Grand Ethiopian Renaissance Dam (Feb. 29, 2020), https://www.ethioembassy.org.uk/statement-of-ethiopia-on-the-negotiations-on-the-grand-ethiopian-renaissance-dam/ [hereinafter Statement of Ethiopia on the GERD] (responding to the Treasury Statement, *supra* note 162).

1630 *Egypt Vows to Use 'All Means' to Defend Nile Interests After Ethiopia Skips U.S. Talks*, HAARETZ (Feb. 29, 2020), https://www.haaretz.com/middle-east-news/egypt/egypt-vows-to-use-all-means-to-defend-nile-interests-after-ethiopia-skips-talks-1.8600505.

1631 Egypt's 2020 Letter to the UNSC 1, *supra* note 163.

1632 *Egypt Warns of 'Existential Threat'*, *supra* note 164.

1633 Tara Kavaler, *Khartoum says no to Planned 2nd Filling of Ethiopian Mega-Dam*, THE JERUSALEM POST (June 30, 2021), https://www.jpost.com/international/khartoum-says-no-to-planned-2nd-filling-of-ethiopian-mega-dam-672403.

1634 El-Din, *supra* note 113.

1635 *See* Permanent Rep. of Egypt to the U.N., Letter dated 15 April 2021 from the Permanent Rep. of Egypt to the United Nations addressed to the President of the Security Council, U.N. Doc. A/75/858 (April 15, 2021).

1636 Michelle Nichols, *U.N. Security Council Backs AU Bid to Broker Ethiopia Dam Deal*, REUTERS (July 9, 2021), https://www.reuters.com/world/un-security-council-backs-au-bid-broker-ethiopia-dam-deal-2021-07-08/.

1637 *See* the discussion in section 6.1.

This chapter analyzes the implications of the existing Nile Waters Agreements for the ongoing GERD dispute between Ethiopia, Sudan, and Egypt. The next section analyzes the post-DoP talks on the filling and operation of the GERD. Section 8.2. discusses the justifications for the involvement of the United States and the World Bank, and explores recent sticking points in the GERD talks. Section 8.3 examines whether—as the U.S. Treasury has suggested—a preliminary agreement is required to fill and test the GERD. It further probes the legitimacy under international law of the United States' involvement in the GERD. Section 8.4 addresses the post-Washington negotiations, while Section 8.5 provides the way forward for resolving the GERD dispute. Finally, the chapter offers its concluding remarks and a call for Egypt, Ethiopia, and Sudan, *inter alia*, to stop approaching the Nile watercourse as a zero-sum game and cooperate for their mutual benefit.

8.1 First Filling and Annual Operation of the GERD

As indicated above, Ethiopia, Sudan, and Egypt participated in negotiations before adopting the DoP. The three states also established an IPoE, which consists of ten members, two from each of the three states, and four members from outside the Nile Basin.[1638] The IPoE, after studying the GERD and its potential impacts on the two downstream states, found GERD would not cause significant harm.[1639] It also recommended the three states conduct two studies: a transboundary impact study and a hydrological modeling study.[1640] The three states agreed, in Article V of the DoP, to use the outcome of these studies to determine the guidelines and rules on the GERD's first filling, and annual operation.[1641]

8.1.1 *The Two Studies on the GERD*

Following the adoption of the DoP, Ethiopia, Sudan and Egypt agreed that international consultants would conduct the studies under the supervision of the Technical National Committee ("TNC").[1642] In September 2016, the TNC

1638 Salman, *supra* note 89, at 95.

1639 *Id.*; *see also* IPOE FINAL REPORT, *supra* note 111.

1640 Salman, *supra* note 89, at 95. Note that Salman mistakenly describes the TNC as the "Tripartite National Committee" while the DoP in actuality establishes a "Technical National Committee." DoP, *supra* note 152, art. V.

1641 *Id.*

1642 Salman, *supra* note 89, at 98.

hired two French firms, BRLi Group and Artelia, to conduct the studies.[1643] However, the initiation of the studies reignited the dispute over the existing Nile Waters Agreements. Egypt insisted that the baseline data to determine the impact should be its current use of the Nile waters.[1644] In other words, Egypt claimed every drop of water that currently flows into the Lake Nasser reservoir of the AHD, including the waters that Sudan fails to use.[1645] Sudan demanded the 1959 Agreement water allocation serve as the baseline. Ethiopia rejected both positions, reiterating that it is not a party to the 1959 Agreement and the baseline for the studies will not create rights to the three states.[1646] Later, Egypt attempted to include the World Bank as a mediator[1647] and even sought to exclude Sudan from the GERD negotiations.[1648] Ethiopia rejected Egypt's proposals, on the grounds that "[t]here is an opportunity for the three countries to resolve possible disputes by themselves."[1649] They ultimately agreed to

1643 *Id.* at 100.

1644 *Id.*

1645 As noted in section 5.1.1, Sudan currently uses only 12 BCM from its 18.5 BCM annual "share" under the 1959 Agreement while Egypt uses around 61 BCM—approximately 5 BCM of which is water from Sudan's "share" under the 1959 Agreement.

1646 *See* Salman, *supra* note 89, at 103.

1647 Mu Xuequan, *Egypt Seeks World Bank as Technical Mediator in Ethiopia's Dam Issue*, XINHUA (Dec. 26, 2017), http://www.xinhuanet.com/english/2017-12/27/c_136853702.htm.

1648 *See* Fasika Tadesse, *Egypt Proposes to Exclude Sudan from Dam Talks*, ADDIS FORTUNE (Dec. 30, 2017), https://addisfortune.net/articles/egypt-proposes-to-exclude-sudan-from-dam-talks/ Considering tripartite cooperation as the *modus operandi* of the DoP, Salam indicated how Egypt's proposal to exclude Sudan from the GERD negotiation violated articles 1, 5, 9 and 10 of the DoP. "Article 1 of the DoP deals with the principle of cooperation, which should be based on common understanding, mutual benefits, good faith, and the principles of international law, as well as understanding upstream and downstream water needs in its various aspects. Moreover, Article 9 of the DoP requires the three countries to cooperate on the basis of sovereign equality, territorial integrity, mutual benefit, and good faith in order to attain optimal utilization and adequate protection of the Nile. Article 5 confirms the agreement of the three countries to respect the final outcomes of the Tripartite National Committee (TNC) final report on the joint studies recommended by the International Panel of Experts. As clarified earlier, the TNC consists of two experts from each of the three countries. Additionally, Article 10 on peaceful settlement of disputes states that the three countries will settle disputes arising out of interpretation or implementation of the DoP amicably, through consultation or negotiation, in accordance with the principle of good faith. The article goes on to state that if the parties are unable to resolve the dispute through consultation or negotiation, they may jointly request conciliation or mediation or refer the matter for the consideration of the heads of state/head of government." *See* Salman, *supra* note 89, at 103.

1649 Elias Meseret, *Ethiopia Refuses World Bank Arbitration over Nile River Dam*, ASSOCIATED PRESS (Jan. 21, 2018), https://apnews.com/42dba7a51c0b4d0c90829d0c2c4e596b.

establish a new National Independent Scientific Research Group ("NISRG") to study scenarios for filling and annual operation of the GERD.[1650]

However, instead of refining and agreeing on the work of the NISRG, Egypt shortly thereafter reopened negotiations by submitting its own plan. In August 2019, Egypt proposed the GERD's first filling "be conducted over a seven-year period, with a minimum release of forty billion meter cubic ("BMC") of water annually and a guarantee to ensure that the AHD remained at 165 meters above sea level."[1651] Moreover, the proposals would require Ethiopia to obtain approval from Egypt at various stages of the filling[1652] and to release the entire average annual flow of the Blue Nile (forty-nine BMC) once the GERD becomes operational.[1653] Egypt also proposed that it be allowed to open an office at the GERD site.[1654]

Ethiopia outright rejected the proposals and considered them to be an Egyptian "effort to maintain a self-claimed colonial era-based water allocation and veto power on any project in the Nile system."[1655] Egypt, in return, claimed that the talks had reached a deadlock[1656] and called upon the United States to mediate in order to overcome the impasse.[1657] Ethiopia, in the beginning, considered Egypt's claim "an unwarranted denial of the progress" made in

---

1650 *See* Fred Oluoch, *Joint Team to Study Likely Effects of Ethiopian Dam on Nile Waters*, EAST AFRICAN (May 19, 2018), https://www.theeastafrican.co.ke/news/africa/Joint-study-effects-Ethiopian-dam-on-Nile/4552902-4570178-05ju7nz/index.html.

1651 *Cooperation is Imperative for an Agreement on Filling, and Operation of GERD*, WALTA (Sept. 23, 2019), https://waltainfo.com/51842/.

1652 Salem Solomon & Mohamed Elshinnawi, *Ethiopia Condemns Egyptian Proposal for Nile Water Usage*, VOICE AMERICA (Oct. 10, 2019), https://www.voanews.com/africa/ethiopia-condemns-egyptian-proposal-nile-water-usage.

1653 Addisu Lashitew, *Why Ethiopia, Egypt, and Sudan Should Ditch a Rushed Washington-Brokered Nile Treaty*, BROOKINGS INST. (Feb. 18, 2020), https://www.brookings.edu/blog/africa-in-focus/2020/02/18/why-ethiopia-egypt-and-sudan-should-ditch-a-rushed-washington-brokered-nile-treaty/; *Ethiopia Rejects Egypt Proposal 2*, *supra* note 157.

1654 Yigzaw Interview, *supra* note 1616. It is worth mentioning that there is a precedent for this arrangement in the Nile Basin where Egypt has on-site office rights on the White Nile where the river leaves Lake Victoria. Exchange of Notes Constituting an Agreement Regarding Co-Operation in Meteorological, and Hydrological Surveys in Certain Areas of the Nile Basin, Egypt-U.K., art. 1, ¶ 3, Jan. 19–Mar. 20, 1950, 226 U.N.T.S. 287 [hereinafter Owen Falls Dam Treaty] ("The Resident Egyptian Engineer at the Owen Falls Dam … shall have access to all the Posts which are in Uganda in order to undertake periodical inspections to assure themselves that the posts are being satisfactorily maintained and the observations regularly collected.")

1655 Lewis, *supra* note 1617.

1656 *Egypt Seeks International Support*, *supra* note 158 (discussing Egyptian President Abdel Fattah el-Sisi's speech in the U.N. General Assembly).

1657 *Egypt Calls on the U.S.*, *supra* note 158.

the negotiations and hoped that the three states could resolve their disputes without intervention.[1658] But later, Ethiopian Prime Minister Abiy Ahmed Ali met with the Egyptian President in Russia, and the two leaders agreed "to resume talks" on the GERD.[1659] Ethiopia accepted the United States' invitation and came to Washington DC, where delegates of the three states met with the U.S. Secretary of the Treasury and the President of the World Bank.[1660] They agreed to resume talks with the United States and the World Bank serving as observers.[1661]

8.1.2 *Egypt's Bid to Preserve the Status Quo—and Its Hegemony*

Egypt's 2019 proposal outlines the following five requirements: (1) that Ethiopia fills the GERD slowly while releasing forty BCM of water every year; (2) that Egypt maintains its water surplus in the AHD reservoir (165 meters above sea level); (3) that Ethiopia obtains approval from Egypt at various stages of the filling and operation of the dam; (4) that Ethiopia releases the entire flow of the Nile waters after the filling of the GERD; and (5) that Egypt's on-site-office right on the upper White Nile at the Owen Falls Dam in Uganda is replicated in Ethiopia at the GERD.[1662] The proposal is extremely advantageous to Egypt.[1663]

The effect of Egypt's proposal would be to directly or indirectly impose the existing Nile Waters Agreements on Ethiopia and preserve the status quo and Egypt's hydro-hegemony. The third requirement, for instance, would, in effect, impose Egypt's understanding of the 1902 Anglo-Ethiopian Treaty on Ethiopia by giving Egypt veto power over upstream projects. The fourth requirement also presupposes the validity of the 1959 Agreement, to which Ethiopia is not a party and thus not bound to respect. Although the GERD is limited to electricity production, agreeing to release the entire flow of the Nile after the completion of the GERD will foreclose Ethiopia's existing and future right under

1658 *Egypt Says 'Deadlock' in Nile Dam Talks with Ethiopia*, AL JAZEERA (Oct. 6, 2019), https://www.aljazeera.com/news/2019/10/egypt-deadlock-nile-dam-talks-ethiopia-191006070043565.html.

1659 *Egypt, Ethiopia 'Agree' to Resume Talks on Massive Nile Dam*, AL JAZEERA (Oct. 24, 2019), https://www.aljazeera.com/news/2019/10/egypt-ethiopia-agree-resume-talks-massive-nile-dam-191024140822273.html.

1660 *See* Joint Statement 1, *supra* note 159.

1661 *Id.*

1662 Yigzaw Interview, *supra* note 1616; *see* Owen Falls Dam Treaty, *supra* note 1654, for a similar arrangement in Uganda.

1663 *Why Ethiopia Rejected the U.S.-Drafted GERD Deal*, ETHIOPIAN INSIGHT (Apr. 2, 2020), https://www.ethiopia-insight.com/2020/04/02/why-ethiopia-rejected-the-u-s-drafted-gerd-deal/ [hereinafter *Why Ethiopia Rejected the U.S. Deal*].

international law to use the Nile waters for other essential consumptive purposes. The standard should not be the 1959 Agreement, but rather the customary international norm of equitable and reasonable utilization.[1664] The ICJ has underscored the foundational nature of this principle, recognizing that both upstream and downstream riparian states have a "basic right to an equitable and reasonable sharing of the resources of an international watercourse."[1665] This norm thus requires a balanced use of the Nile waters by each of the Nile Basin States.

In practice, Egypt's requirements would prevent Ethiopia from using its reasonable and equitable share of the riparian rights. First, they would delay the production of electricity and prevent Ethiopia from getting the expected returns from the GERD. As a result, Ethiopia would be less able to eliminate extreme poverty, which is the GERD's main purpose.[1666] Second, the requirement that Egypt maintains current water levels in the AHD reservoir may unreasonably require Ethiopia to subsidize Egyptian water rights based on events beyond its control. For one, Egypt could use or export the Nile waters, perpetually making the water stored in the AHD below 165 meters above sea level ("MASL"). Ethiopia would then be forced to compensate Egypt for the loss from its own share of the water. Moreover, maintaining the AHD at 165 MASL will be difficult in the future because of global climate change. The Nile Basin is experiencing droughts that are increasing both in frequency and magnitude.[1667] Therefore, arguably, the GERD will end up being a second reservoir for Egypt.

Finally, agreeing to the last proposal would require nothing short of the surrender of Ethiopian sovereignty. While past practice shows that joint or transnational projects require shared management, strictly national projects should be independently managed.[1668] The GERD is an Ethiopian project whose

---

1664 *Report of the Commission to the General Assembly on the Work of its Forty-Sixth Session*, [1994] 2 Y.B. INT'L L. COMM'N, 96–97, U.N. Doc. A/CN.4/SER.A/1994/Add.l (Part 2) [hereinafter *46th ILC Report*]; U.N. Watercourses Convention, *supra* note 818, art. 5; *see also* MCCAFFREY, *supra* note 4, 445; Gabčíkovo-Nagymaros Project (Hung./Slovk.), Judgment, 1997 I.C.J. 7, ¶ 78 (Sept. 25); *see generally*, Dellapenna, *supra* note 49 (describing equitable and reasonable utilization as customary law).

1665 *Id.*

1666 DoP, *supra* note 152, art. II.

1667 Schiffler, *supra* note 69, at 137, 146. (predicting the Nile's flow will decrease by up to 78%).

1668 For instance, the Manantali Dam on the Senegal River and the Kariba Dam on the Zambezi River are joint projects run together. *See* Robert Rangeley et al., *International River Basin Organizations in Sub-Saharan Africa*, 7–8 (World Bank, Technical Paper No. 250, 1994). Chinese unilateral dams on the Mekong River, on the other hand, are managed independently. *See generally* Madeleine De Simone, *On the Forecast: Easing Tension Over Hydraulic Power Along the Mekong* (Project on Int'l Peace & Sec., Student Policy Brief No.

operation should be left solely to Ethiopia. Ethiopia would, of course, remain obligated under general international law to use the Nile waters equitably and reasonably,[1669] exercise due diligence to avoid causing significant harm to the lower riparian states,[1670] and regularly share data and information.[1671]

8.2 The GERD Washington Talks: Illuminating the Sticking Points

Once Ethiopia rejected Egypt's proposal, Egypt sought to internationalize the negotiations and convince the international community that the tripartite talks failed to deliver the expected result and that the dispute could not be resolved absent third-party involvement. The President of Egypt, Abdel Fattah el-Sisi, in his speech at the U.N. General Assembly, stated that the GERD "negotiations have not yielded the desired results" and called for international interventions to break the deadlock.[1672] Egypt further requested that the United States and World Bank join the negotiation process to resolve the impasse.[1673]

In complex multilateral talks, like those around GERD, it is important to scrutinize the relationship between the negotiating parties and third parties as such relationships influence the third parties' neutrality. Egypt has a close relationship with the World Bank, as its nationals have occupied high positions within the World Bank and Egypt has benefitted from its development programs.[1674] The same can be said of Egypt's relationship with the United States. For example, President el-Sisi met with President Donald Trump in April 2019 and has received high praise from President Trump.[1675] Ethiopia does not

---

5.2, 2013). Furthermore, all the dams and reservoirs built in Egypt and Sudan are unilateral projects managed independently without the involvement of Ethiopia or other upstream states.

1669 U.N. Watercourses Convention, *supra* note 818, arts. 5–6; CFA, *supra* note 132, art 4; *see also* DoP, *supra* note 152, art. IV. *See* also MCCAFFREY, *supra* note 4, 445 and 477 (considering the two principles of equable and reasonable utilization and the no significant harm rule as customary international law).

1670 U.N. Watercourses Convention, *supra* note 818, art. 7; CFA, *supra* note 132, art. 5; DoP, *supra* note 152, art. III.

1671 Ethiopia also promised to share data and information in the CFA and DoP. *See* CFA, *supra* note 132, arts. 7 ¶ 2–3, 8, 30 ¶ 9; DoP, *supra* note 152, art. VII.

1672 *Egypt Seeks International Support, supra* note 158.

1673 *Egypt Calls on the U.S., supra* note 158; Xuequan, *supra* note 1647.

1674 Amdetsion, *supra* note 72, at 12.

1675 Clark Mindock, *'Where's My Favorite Dictator?' Trump Comment on Egyptian President 'Met with Stunned Silence', Report Says*, INDEPENDENT (Sept. 13, 2019), https://www.independent.co.uk/news/world/americas/us-politics/trump-egypt-president-sisi-favorite-dictator-meeting-a9104951.html.

maintain close relationships with either the World Bank or the United States. As such, Ethiopia was warranted in its concern that the Washington D.C. talks were not on a level playing field.

In January 2020, Ethiopia's fears were realized when the United States assumed the role of a mediator as opposed to a mere observer,[1676] submitting proposals on the GERD's filling and operation. The United States then pressured Ethiopia to accept its proposals, which Ethiopia rejected.[1677] The principal sticking points related to how Ethiopia should fill and operate the GERD during drought or prolonged dry years[1678] and what mechanisms for dispute resolution would be available.[1679]

8.2.1 *Sticking Points: The Three Drought Mitigation Mechanisms*

In a joint statement issued on January 15, 2020 Egypt, Sudan, and Ethiopia underscored the necessity of developing drought mitigation mechanisms for three kinds of situations: (1) drought, (2) prolonged drought, and (3) prolonged dry years during the filling and operation of the GERD.[1680] The proposal from the United States and the World Bank detailed drought mitigation mechanisms applicable in such situations.[1681]

8.2.1.1 Filling of the GERD

According to the proposals submitted by the United States and World Bank, a "drought" occurs when the GERD's release is below thirty-seven BCM. If a drought coincides with the filling years, Ethiopia is expected to release the "flow" of the Nile River and supplemental water from the GERD. "Prolonged drought" is when the release from the GERD is below thirty-nine BCM for four years. During the filling period, a prolonged drought requires Ethiopia to release the river flow and 62.5 per cent of the water above 603 MAS of the GERD for the following four years. "Prolonged dry years" occur when the GERD's release is below forty BCM for four consecutive years. Ethiopia must release the flow and

1676 Kifle Worku, *"Egypt Is Sailing Against the Wind, Squandering Its Opportunity," Diplomat Zerihun Abebe*, ETHIOPIAN PRESS AGENCY (Mar. 26, 2020), https://www.press.et/english/?p=20054#.

1677 *Id.*

1678 *Why Ethiopia Rejected the U.S. Deal*, *supra* note 1663.

1679 Yigzaw Interview, *supra* note 1616.

1680 Press Release, U.S. Dep't of the Treasury, Joint Statement of Egypt, Ethiopia, Sudan, the United States and the World Bank, (Jan. 15, 2020), https://home.treasury.gov/news/press-releases/sm875 [hereinafter Joint Statement 2].

1681 Yigzaw Interview, *supra* note 1628.

50 per cent of the GERD storage above 603 MASL for the next four consecutive years in the event of prolonged dry years during the dam's filling.[1682]

The U.S. and Egyptian proposals have two common features: (1) Ethiopia is expected to release the "flow" of the Blue Nile to the downstream states, which constitutes all of the Blue Nile's water that reaches the GERD reservoir, and (2) Ethiopia can incur certain quantities of water debt that must be paid from the reservoir of GERD. The first feature forecloses Ethiopia's right to use the Blue Nile's flow—which includes the waters of its tributaries—prohibiting Ethiopia from using the waters above the GERD equitably and reasonably.

The second feature is similarly adverse to Ethiopia's interests. Analogous international practice shows that upstream states are allowed to deliver below the minimum quantity of water during severe drought seasons and repay the water during normal seasons.[1683] However, water debt and repayment are relevant only when there is a water-sharing arrangement between riparian states. Here, there is neither a water-sharing arrangement nor a minimum water quantity allocated to Egypt and Sudan. Therefore, the concept of water debt is inappropriate. International treaty law demonstrates that the riparian states must help shoulder the burden caused by drought. The proposals for the GERD's filling and operation impose the burden of drought solely on Ethiopia.

The implication of agreeing to release water from the GERD's reservoir is nothing short of recognizing the inequitable water-sharing scheme under the 1959 Agreement. In other words, if Ethiopia is required to release water from its own reservoir, it does not have any share from the Nile waters. The proposals on the long-term operation of the dam support this conclusion.

And, if Egypt does indeed have "established rights" in the flow of the Blue Nile, against whom are such rights enforceable? Egypt does not have a treaty right vis-à-vis Ethiopia; under the 1959 Agreement, Egypt only has such a right against Sudan. Therefore, any right Egypt has against Ethiopia must derive from customary international law. Ethiopia did not exercise forbearance in constructing a GERD-type dam earlier out of any sense of legal obligation

1682 Egypt's 2020 Letter to the UNSC 2, *supra* note 1549, annex II.

1683 For instance, the 1944 agreement between the United States and Mexico on the Rio Grande and Colorado Rivers has provisions governing possible problems resulting from drought. With respect to both the Rio Grande and Colorado Rivers, the treaty allows upstream countries to deliver below the minimum quantity of the water during severe drought seasons and repay the water during the normal seasons. *See* Utilization of the Waters of the Colorado and Tijuana Rivers and of the Rio Grande, Mex.-U.S., arts. 4.B(c)–(d), 10(a)–(b), Feb. 3, 1944, 59 Stat. 1219 [hereinafter 1944 Colorado Treaty].

(*opinio juris*).[1684] Any such forbearance was due to a combination of other factors, including threats from Egypt[1685] and a lack of funding from international financial institutions.[1686] Thus, any Egyptian right to a given flow of the Blue Nile is enforceable only against Sudan.

8.2.1.2 "Long-Term" Operation of the GERD

The definitions of drought, prolonged drought, and prolonged dry years in the long-term operation are similar to the definitions provided in the filling period. The only difference is the amount of water to be released from the GERD. During the drought period, Ethiopia must release the flow and more waters, the amount of which is to be agreed upon by the parties, from the GERD. During prolonged drought periods and dry years, Ethiopia must release the flow and all available water above 603 MASL of the GERD within four (five in case of prolonged dry years) years.[1687]

All the concerns raised above as to the filling of the GERD apply here. Further, agreeing on the long-term operation of the GERD has two additional and devastating consequences for Ethiopia. First, since the "flow" includes the entire quantity of water that is naturally available, Ethiopia, which contributes all Blue Nile waters, would not have a share of water allocation from the Blue Nile. In sum, Ethiopia would be prohibited from using the Blue Nile's tributaries for irrigation or hydroelectric power generation. Second, it would recognize Egypt's claim to established rights (55.5 BCM) and, consequently, impose the 1959 Agreement on Ethiopia.

In light of increased water scarcity and severe droughts in the Nile Basin due to global climate change,[1688] it will be impossible for Ethiopia to release forty BCM from the GERD, let alone get a share of the Blue Nile. Even worse, Ethiopia will be in perpetual water debt and, thus, forced to release more waters from the GERD. In effect, this will make the GERD an Egyptian storage facility—the GERD reservoir's evaporation rates will be lower than those of Lake Nasser, the Aswan High Dam's ("AHD") reservoir.[1689] But this is an incidental benefit. It would be unrealistic to expect Egypt to plan its entire project around this goal.

1684 *See* North Sea Continental Shelf Cases (Ger. v. Den.; Ger. v. Neth.), Advisory Opinions, 1969 I.C.J. 44, ¶ 77 (Feb. 20) (discussing the two elements of customary international law, state practice and *opinio juris*).

1685 *See* Tekuya, *supra* note 785 and accompanying texts.

1686 *See* Swain, *supra* note 459 and accompanying texts.

1687 Egypt's 2020 Letter to the UNSC 2, *supra* note 1549, annex II.

1688 Schiffler, *supra* note 69, at 137, 146 (predicting the Nile's flow will decrease by up to 78%).

1689 *See* Salman, *supra* note 146, at 516 tbl.1. Studies by British engineers in the early 20th century had shown already that dams at the African Great Lakes and Lake Tana would be the

The DoP provides the framework for the GERD talks and, as such, the forthcoming GERD Treaty should be in line with the DoP. The scope of the GERD Treaty envisaged in Article V of the DoP is limited to the GERD.[1690] Ethiopia should, therefore, agree to release only the inflow of the GERD (i.e., the water that enters the GERD reservoir minus normal evaporation).

Given that the proposals proffered by Egypt and the United States did not address obligations when the GERD's release is above forty BCM, Ethiopia would likely have a water share during normal operation of the GERD when the Blue Nile's average flow is forty-nine BCM. Egypt already requested that Ethiopia release the entire flow of the Blue Nile during the GERD's normal operations, but Ethiopia rejected the proposal outright.[1691] Even if we assume that Egypt, Ethiopia, and Sudan share the remaining nine BCM of water, it seems that Ethiopia would not get much water from the Blue Nile. Given the increase in average global temperature due to climate change, the GERD's reservoir is projected to evaporate at an annual rate of two BCM.[1692] This is much less than the ten to fifteen BCM annual evaporation in Egypt from Lake Nasser,[1693] but it still affects the water share. That means the net water the three states must share will be less than seven BCM. Considering this, one may wonder how much Ethiopia would get from the Blue Nile.

Generally, it can be said that drought is a natural phenomenon that should be addressed collectively.[1694] The burden of drought mitigation is not solely Ethiopia's to bear. Egypt, Sudan, and Ethiopia should support one another in mitigating drought, without placing the entire burden on any one state.

8.2.2 *Disagreement over Dispute Resolution*

Although the above-discussed proposals by Egypt effectively impose the existing Nile Waters Agreement on Ethiopia, Egypt sought additional means to safeguard its status quo. To that end, Egypt proposed and included a binding arbitration clause in the U.S. draft agreement. Ethiopia rejected this provision,

---

most suitable locations for storing water with minimal evaporation. *See* the discussion in section 2.2.

1690 DoP, *supra* note 152, art. V.

1691 Yigzaw Interview, *supra* note 1616.

1692 *See* Salman, *supra* note 146, at 516 tbl.1.

1693 The 1959 Agreement already allocated ten BCM towards water for evaporation. 1959 Agreement, *supra* note 106, art. 2, ¶ 4.

1694 Kaori Tembata & Kenji Takeuchi, *Collective Action and Cooperation in Drought Response*, GLOB. WATER F. (June 18, 2018), https://globalwaterforum.org/2018/06/18/collective-action-and-cooperation-in-drought-response/.

demanding instead that the three states resolve disputes by themselves and resort to mediation only when necessary.[1695]

Ethiopia's approach seems appropriate for several reasons. First, the DoP does not require compulsory and binding dispute resolution. Article X of the DoP contemplates disputes arising from the GERD and indicates that they should be resolved through the consultation of the national ministries tasked with water management. If the dispute cannot be resolved, the matter is referred to the respective heads of state, who *may* resolve the dispute or refer it to mediation.[1696]

Moreover, imposing compulsory resolution mechanisms for disputes arising from the GERD is contrary to the principle of reciprocity.[1697] In the past, Egypt and Sudan constructed several dams and reservoirs without consulting—and even over objections from—Ethiopia.[1698] These dams and reservoirs significantly harmed Ethiopia by foreclosing its future use of Nile waters,[1699] and yet Ethiopia did not have recourse to compulsory dispute resolution. An approach that subjects the GERD to compulsory dispute resolution and leaves other downstream dams and reservoirs without any analogous recourse is rather problematic. Currently, there is no structure in place to ensure accountability in the use and activities of downstream states. Ethiopia is unable to challenge Egypt's possible exportation of water from AHD in the absence of any mechanism for dispute resolution. By parity of reasoning, the GERD should also not

1695 Yigzaw Interview, *supra* note 1616.

1696 DoP, *supra* note 152, art. X.

1697 Reciprocity is the relationship between two states when each of them gives the subjects of the other certain privileges on the condition that its subjects enjoy similar privileges in the other state. *Reciprocity*, BLACK'S LAW DICTIONARY (5th ed. 1979). As there is no centralized enforcement mechanism under international law, the principle of reciprocity plays an extremely significant role in relations between sovereign nations and the pragmatic application of existing international law. *See generally* Francesco Paris & Nita Ghei, *The Role of Reciprocity in International Law*, 36 CORNELL INT'L L.J. 93 (2003); *see also* Robert O. Keohane *Reciprocity in International Relations*, 40 INT'L ORG. 1, 5–6 (1986).

1698 For instance, Ethiopia objected to the construction Toshka Project and the Peace Canal, and stating that it "in the most categorical manner, [does] not recognize ... [them] as having any consequence to what is and will always be its fair, legitimate and equitable share of the Nile waters." Ethiopia's 2020 Letter to the UNSC 1, *supra* note 788, annex V.

1699 For the discussion regarding upstream harm and foreclosure of Ethiopia's future use, *see* sections in 4.1.2.2. and 5.1.2. *See* also Salman M.A. Salman, *Downstream Riparians Can Also Harm Upstream Riparians: The Concept of Foreclosure of Future Uses*, 35 WATER INT'L 350, 352 (2010) (quoting Ethiopia's Note Verbale of 20 March 1997, "Ethiopia wishes to be on record as having made it unambiguously clear that it will not allow its share to the Nile waters to be affected by a fait accompli such as the Toshka project, regarding which it was neither consulted nor alerted").

be subject to binding dispute resolution. One possible compromise, however, might be to subject the GERD to compulsory dispute resolution with the other downstream dams and reservoirs through a basin-wide legal and institutional framework as suggested below.

8.3 The Role of the United States in the GERD Talks under International Law

Following the disagreement over the United States' proposal, and after the parties attempted to prepare the final agreement, the U.S. Treasury, with technical support from the World Bank, drafted an agreement open for signature by the parties.[1700] Egypt endorsed the agreement, while Ethiopia requested more time for national consultation.[1701] Ethiopia duly notified all parties of this request,[1702] reminded the U.S. Treasury of its observer status,[1703] and demanded that the United States not send the draft agreement to Addis Ababa.[1704] The U.S. Treasury disregarded Ethiopia's request by undertaking separate bilateral meetings with Egypt and Sudan.[1705] The U.S. Treasury then issued a surprising statement requesting Ethiopia sign the agreement and warned Ethiopia to refrain from filling and testing the GERD without an agreement with Egypt and Sudan.[1706]

These exchanges raise a fundamental issue as to whether it was legitimate for the U.S. government to involve itself when, formally, it was merely an observer to the negotiations. Assuming, *arguendo*, the legitimacy of U.S. participation, there remains the question of whether Ethiopia is required to conclude an agreement with Sudan and Egypt before beginning filling the GERD. The following section addresses both issues, addressing first the constraints on Ethiopia's rights to fill the dam prior to reaching an agreement, before moving on to discuss the question of U.S. involvement in the negotiation process.

1700 Press Release, U.S. Dep't of the Treasury, Joint Statement of Egypt, Ethiopia, Sudan, the United States, and the World Bank, (Feb. 13, 2020), https://home.treasury.gov/news/press-releases/sm907 [hereinafter Joint Statement 3].

1701 Meseret, *supra* note 160.

1702 *Id.*

1703 *Id.*

1704 *Id.*

1705 *Id.*

1706 Treasury Statement, *supra* note 162.

8.3.1 *The U.S. Treasury Statement: Is a Preliminary Agreement Necessary to Fill the GERD Reservoir?*

In an apparent fit of pique at Ethiopia's refusal to accept its terms, on February 28 2020 the U.S. Treasury made a statement which includes the following: "Consistent with the principles set out in the [DoP], and in particular the principles of not causing significant harm to downstream countries, final testing and filling should not take place without an agreement."[1707] Considering the first filling and testing of the GERD as dam construction, Ethiopia stated that it will start filling and testing the dam regardless of an agreement as it is permitted in the DoP.[1708] Egypt rejected this, claiming that by filling and testing the dam Ethiopia was in violation of Article V of the DoP, which—according to Egypt—requires all three states to reach an agreement on the rules of filling and operating the dam before such process can begin.[1709] However, Egypt's position contravenes the DoP. The DoP does not require the parties to reach an agreement prior to Ethiopia's initial filling the GERD, but rather states that "[t]he three countries ... will utilize the final outcomes of the joint studies ... to [a]gree on guidelines and rules on the first filling of GERD ... in parallel with the construction of GERD."[1710]

One may dispute Ethiopia's position and argue that the first filling and the construction of the dam are two different things that are treated separately in the DoP. Assuming this argument is true, Ethiopia could still legally fill the dam without an agreement. First, per Article 31 of the VCLT, "[a] treaty shall be interpreted in good faith in accordance with the ordinary meaning to be given to the terms of the treaty in their context and in the light of its object and purpose."[1711] "[I]t would be contrary to good faith to use the failure to cooperate as an excuse to deny a fundamental right of a state, to develop and make an equitable use of its shared resource" because the GERD is a project within Ethiopia's shared watercourse.[1712]

In addition, if a preliminary agreement was required, Egypt would have the "veto power" it already claims under the colonial Nile Waters Treaties. Giving Egypt this veto power would further contravene international law governing due diligence obligations of transboundary harm.[1713] Egypt's veto power

1707 *Id.*
1708 Statement of Ethiopia on the GERD, *supra* note 1629.
1709 Samir, *supra* note 1606.
1710 DoP, *supra* note 152, art. V, ¶ 2(a).
1711 VCLT, *supra* note 520, art. 31.
1712 Yihdego, *supra* note 150, at 7.
1713 *Gabčíkovo-Nagymaros Project* (Hung./Slovk.), Judgment, 1997 I.C.J. 7, ¶ 88 (Sept. 25).

would also impose the colonial Nile Waters Treaties on Ethiopia, defeating the DoP's purpose of ensuring equal rights to the three states to use the Nile watercourse.[1714] Moreover, Egypt's veto power would undermine the GERD's purpose of generating hydroelectric power, boosting the economic development of Ethiopia, and promoting transboundary cooperation and regional integration through the generation and supply of sustainable and reliable clean energy on financially attractive terms.[1715]

The silence of the DoP similarly justifies why Ethiopia can legally fill the GERD without an agreement. The DoP requires only that the three states use studies to agree on the first filling and annual operation of the dam.[1716] There is an obligation to negotiate in good faith and use the studies to strike a deal establishing the filling and annual operation of the dam. But what if they fail to reach an agreement? The DoP does not address this scenario, and the DoP does not prohibit Ethiopia from filling and testing the GERD without an agreement. And, per the Permanent Court of International Justice in *Lotus*, it is a longstanding principle of international law that "everything which is not prohibited is permitted."[1717] As such, Ethiopia is permitted under international law to fill the GERD without an agreement.

It is true that states are required to take all appropriate measures to prevent and mitigate significant transboundary environmental harm. However, the nature of this obligation is one of due diligence, requiring states only to expend reasonable effort under the circumstances to avoid harm.[1718] The due diligence standard is evident from Article 7(2) of the U.N. Watercourses Convention which sets forth a process to be followed "[w]here significant harm … is caused to another watercourse State"[1719] despite the taking of "all appropriate measures to prevent the causing of significant harm to other

1714 DoP, *supra* note 152, preamble.

1715 *Id.* art. II.

1716 *Id.* art. V ¶¶ 2–3.

1717 S.S. Lotus (Fr. v. Turk.), Judgment, 1927 P.C.I.J. (ser. A) No. 10 (Sept. 7). Indeed, with the introduction of *erga omnes* and *jus cogens* norms, and recent human rights developments, part of the *Lotus* principle, which considers states' consent as the sole source of international law, challenged by proponents of natural law theory. But, the argument in this article would not be affected by this as it recognizes both state consent and these new norms as sources of international law. The argument here is that no international law, regardless of its source, whether state consent or other norms, prohibits Ethiopia from filling and testing the dam without an agreement with Sudan and Egypt.

1718 *See* MCCAFFREY, *supra* note 4, at 437–40.

1719 U.N. Watercourses Convention, *supra* note 818, art. 7 ¶2.

watercourse States."[1720] Due diligence is an obligation of conduct, rather than one of result.[1721]

The *Lake Lanoux* case between France and Spain[1722] provides a useful illustration of this due diligence obligation. The tribunal denied the Spanish claim that the French project's execution required the preliminary agreement of both states, absent which France could not freely undertake the planned works, including a complex inter-basin transfer of water from Lake Lanoux.[1723] The tribunal ultimately concluded it was neither a customary rule nor a general principle of law that states may only exploit the hydraulic power of international waterways where there is a *preliminary agreement* between concerned states.[1724]

The ICJ reaffirmed this principle in its 2010 *Pulp Mills on the River Uruguay* judgment.[1725] One of the core issues before the Court was whether Uruguay was entitled to proceed with the construction of a pulp mill on the Uruguay River after having failed to reach an agreement with Argentina,[1726] with whom it had a treaty governing the use of the shared River Uruguay.[1727] Argentina asserted that Uruguay could not continue the works without a favorable ruling from the Court,[1728] as the treaty provided for ICJ adjudication in the event of a dispute surrounding the treaty.[1729] The Court, however, allowed Uruguay to proceed with the construction "at its own risk," concluding that nothing prohibited Uruguay from proceeding with construction absent treaty terms requiring—rather than permitting—parties to submit the matter before a court.[1730] The Court further explained the mechanisms for dispute resolution

1720 *Id*, 7 ¶ 1.

1721 The ILC's articles formed the basis of the negotiations leading to the adoption of the U.N. Watercourses Convention. The ILC's commentary on Article 7 is relevant and it begins as follows: "The Commission, in this article, is setting forth a process aimed at avoiding significant harm as far as possible while reaching an equitable result in each concrete case." *46th ILC Report, supra* note 1664, at 103. This is hardly an absolute prohibition of harm.

1722 Lake Lanoux (Fr. v. Spain), 12 R.I.A.A. 281 (Arb. Trib. 1957).

1723 *Id.* ¶¶ 10–11.

1724 *Id.* ¶ 12 (emphasis added).

1725 Pulp Mills on the River Uruguay (Arg. v. Uru.), Judgment, 2010 I.C.J. 14 (Apr. 20).

1726 *Id.* ¶¶ 46–47.

1727 Statute of the River Uruguay, Arg.-Uru., Feb. 26, 1975, 1295 U.N.T.S. 340.

1728 *Pulp Mills*, 2010 I.C.J. ¶ 153.

1729 In the event of a disputed project on the River Uruguay on which no agreement is reached after 180 days, Article 12 directs parties to Article 60, which states: "[a]ny dispute concerning the interpretation or application of the Treaty and the Statute which cannot be settled by direct negotiations may be submitted by either party to the International Court of Justice." Statute of the River Uruguay, *supra* note 1724, arts. 12, 60.

1730 *Pulp Mills*, 2010 I.C.J. ¶¶ 154–55.

in question did nothing to alter the rights and obligations of the parties "as long as the Court has not ruled finally on them" and that such rights included "that of implementing the project, on the sole responsibility of that party, since the period for negotiation has expired."[1731]

In both cases, the court declined to compel a preliminary agreement prior to project-commencement, motivated by the fact that such requirement otherwise hinders what the tribunal in *Lake Lanoux* called the state's "right to act alone as a consequence of unconditional and arbitrary opposition of another state." Thus, ruling otherwise, the tribunal explained, would tantamount "to admit a 'right of consent,' a 'right of veto,' which at the discretion of one state paralyzes another state's exercise of its territorial competence."[1732]

Concerns regarding the safety of the GERD can be addressed under Ethiopia's due diligence obligation. Since 2010, Ethiopia has taken various measures in accordance with its international obligations to prevent harm to the downstream states. Ethiopia conducted transboundary impact studies, initiated a tripartite committee,[1733] and established an International Panel of Experts ("IPoE") which confirmed that the design and construction process of the dam was in line with "a number of international Standards, Codes, and Guidelines."[1734] Egypt, Sudan, and Ethiopia recognized all of these measures in Article VIII of the DoP.[1735] Given that ensuring the GERD's safety is a continuous process, Ethiopia should in good faith continue to take all dam safety-related measures.

It can thus be concluded that the U.S. Treasury Department's statement requiring a preliminary agreement for filling and testing the GERD goes beyond the requirements of international law governing transboundary watercourses. Ethiopia can begin filling and testing the GERD without an agreement with Sudan and Egypt.

1731 *Id.* ¶ 155.

1732 *See* Lake Lanoux (Fr. v. Spain), 12 R.I.A.A. 281 (Arb. Trib. 1957), ¶ 11. This reasoning is also supported by the general international law as reflected in the 2001 Draft articles of the International Law Commission on Prevention of Transboundary Harm from Hazardous Activities, Article 9 of which states that "[i]f the consultations ... fail to produce an agreed solution, the State of origin shall nevertheless take into account the interests of the State likely to be affected in case it decides to authorize the activity to be pursued." Int'l L. Comm'n Rep. on the Work of Its Fifty-Third Session, U.N. Doc. A/56/10, at 160 (2001). In explaining the purpose of this article, the International Law Commission stated that "the State of origin is permitted to go ahead with the activity, for the absence of such an alternative would, in effect, create a right of veto for the States likely to be affected." *Id.* at 161.

1733 Qerenso, *supra* note 1599.

1734 IPOE FINAL REPORT, *supra* note 111, 21.

1735 DoP, *supra* note 152, VIII.

8.3.2 *The U.S. and the GERD Talks: from Observer to Self-proclaimed Mediator?*

Diplomatic avenues such as consultation, mediation, and conciliation are recognized peaceful dispute settlement mechanisms under international law.[1736] In accordance with state sovereignty, these mechanisms afford disputing states the opportunity to control the process. The DoP recognizes these mechanisms in Article X, and urges the parties to resolve disputes through consultation, negotiation, and only as a last resort to "jointly request for conciliation [or] mediation."[1737]

Consequently, in order for the United States' participation to be legitimate, the three states must have jointly requested its active engagement and consented to its proposed solutions. There is, however, no available evidence supporting an assertion that either Ethiopia or Sudan consented to the United States' or World Bank's mediation. There are only statements by Ethiopia accepting the United States and the World Bank as observers to the negotiations, not mediators.[1738] Therefore, it can be argued that the United States and the World Bank acted contrary to Article X of the DoP by actively participating in the GERD negotiations as a mediator without obtaining Ethiopia's consent.

While the Trump Administration expressed its willingness "to facilitate the preparation of the final agreement,"[1739] reports indicate that Ethiopia did not consent to the United States' preparation of a final agreement.[1740] When U.S. Secretary of the Treasury Steven T. Mnuchin stated that the U.S. had "agreed" to facilitate, he was only speaking on behalf of the United States. But, even if we assume for the sake of the argument that the United States was tacitly authorized "to facilitate the preparation of the agreement," the draft agreement is still illegitimate. This is because facilitating the preparation of the agreement is vastly different from drafting the agreement without the consent or input from Egypt, Sudan, or Ethiopia. There is no possible construction of the Mnuchin statement or its provenance that would authorize the United States to unilaterally (or jointly with Egypt) draft an agreement and impose it on the parties.[1741]

1736 U.N. Charter art. 33, ¶ 1.

1737 DoP, *supra* note 152, X.

1738 *See, e.g.*, Joint Statement 1, *supra* note 159; Joint Statement 2, *supra* note 1680; Joint Statement 3, *supra* note 1700. All the joint statements issued by the U.S. Department of the Treasury refer to the United States and World Bank as observers.

1739 Joint Statement 3, *supra* note 1700.

1740 Meseret, *supra* note 160.

1741 Yihdego, *supra* note 150, at 14.

Moreover, Ethiopia officially demanded the U.S. Treasury Department not draft and send an agreement to Addis Ababa.[1742] The U.S. Treasury Department ignored this instruction and urged Ethiopia to sign the agreement. It also, without any mandate, interpreted the DoP and warned Ethiopia to refrain from filling or testing the dam without an agreement with Sudan and Egypt. In so doing, it interfered with Ethiopia's foreign affairs in violation of its sovereignty and restricted its use of the Nile waters. This course of conduct suggests the U.S. "violated the rules of non-intervention and the principles of sovereignty and sovereign equality."[1743] Further, because the U.S. acted through the Treasury Secretary,[1744] it is responsible for such infringements and, under Article 30 of the Articles of the International Law on State Responsibility, must cease its course of conduct, and offer appropriate assurances that it will adjust its actions accordingly.[1745]

8.4 Post-Washington Negotiations

After undertaking the national consultation, Ethiopia rejected the agreement proposed by the United States. On April 10, 2020, Ethiopian Prime Minister Abiy Ahmed proposed an interim agreement governing the initial stage of the first filling (over two years) of the GERD up to 595 m above sea level and retaining 4.9 BCM and 13.5 BCM in the first and second years of filling, respectively.[1746] Although the filling schedule was agreed upon by the three states in the Washington negotiations, Sudan and Egypt did not accept the proposed interim agreement, alleging that "[a]ny agreement on the GERD must, as per the DoP, be comprehensive, and must regulate the complete process of filling the dam and its operation after the completion of the filling."[1747]

To overcome the impasses, Sudanese Prime Mister Abdalla Hamdok initiated a round of trilateral talks through a virtual video conference that lasted

1742 Meseret, *supra* note 160.

1743 Yihdego, *supra* note 150, at 16.

1744 *Id.*

1745 *Id.*

1746 *Sudan rejects Ethiopian proposal of "partial agreement" on GERD*, EGYPT TODAY (May 12, 2020), https://www.egypttoday.com/Article/1/86699/Sudan-rejects-Ethiopian-proposal-of-%E2%80%9Cpartial agreement%E2%80%9D-on-GERD [hereinafter *Sudan rejects Ethiopian proposal*]; Ethiopia's 2020 Letter to the UNSC 2, *supra* note 1440, 10 ¶ 17.

1747 Egypt's 2020 Letter to the UNSC 1, *supra* note 163, 7 ¶ 10.

for about two months.[1748] Initially, the talks, which were observed by the Republic of South Africa, the European Union (EU), and the USA, resulted in the three states' common understanding on the first filling of the GERD.[1749] However, the dispute over the outstanding issues persisted, and Egypt, alleging consensus is reached on none of the discussion points, expressed its skepticism that no breakthrough or progress will be expected from the trilateral talks "due to Ethiopia's continues intransigent" position.[1750] Sudan, on the contrary, viewed the negotiation process constructively and asserted that the three states agreed on more than 90% of issues regarding the GERD except for a few outstanding legal matters.[1751] In its part, Ethiopia, criticizing Egypt's skepticism on the latest round of talks, expressed that the three states agreed to many important matters. It also urged Egypt not to issue belligerent and confusing statements, and to stop its diplomatic pressures while undertaking the tripartite negotiation.[1752]

Subsequently, Egypt formally submitted letters to the UNSC requesting its intervention in the GERD dispute, after which Ethiopia and Sudan each submitted their own letters articulating their positions.[1753] In response, UN Secretary-General António Guterres encouraged the three states to resolve outstanding issues and "achieve a mutually beneficial agreement."[1754] The UNSC made an unprecedented move and held an open session on the GERD dispute where most of the members encouraged the three states to resolve their dispute through the AU. After a year of intermittent tripartite negotiation

1748 *Egypt ready to resume talks on Ethiopia's Renaissance Dam*, EGYPT TODAY (May 22, 2020), https://www.egypttoday.com/Article/1/87964/Egypt-ready-to-resume-talks-on-Ethiopia-s-Renaissance-dam; Al-Masry Al-Youm, *Sudan-Mediated GERD Talks Stalling Due to Ethiopia's Intransigence: Egypt*, EGYPT INDEPENDENT (June 13, 2020), https://egyptindependent.com/sudan-mediated-gerd-talks-stalling-due-to-ethiopias-intransigence-egypt/.

1749 *Id.*

1750 *Id.*

1751 *Sudan, Egypt, Ethiopia Agree on 90% of Controversial GERD Points*, EGYPT INDEPENDENT (June 23, 2020), https://egyptindependent.com/sudan-egypt-ethiopia-agrees-on-90-percent-of-controversial-points-regarding-gerd/.

1752 Addis Getachew, *Ethiopia, Sudan and Egypt Reach Understanding on Nile Dam*, ANADOLU AGENCY (June 14, 2020), https://www.aa.com.tr/en/africa/ethiopia-sudan-egypt-reach-understanding-on-nile-dam/1876641.

1753 Egypt's 2020 Letter to the UNSC 1, *supra* note 163; Ethiopia's 2020 Letter to the UNSC 2, *supra* note 1440; Sudan's 2020 Letter to UNSC, *supra* note 1483.

1754 Press Release, Sec'y-Gen., Secretary-General Encouraged by Good Progress in Trilateral Talks to Reach Agreement over Grand Ethiopian Renaissance Dam, U.N. Press Release SG/SM/20088 (May 19, 2020) [Press Release of the Sec'y-Gen] https://www.un.org/press/en/2020/sgsm20088.doc.htm.

under the auspices of the AU,[1755] Egypt brought the GERD dispute to the UNSC for the second time.[1756] The UNSC, after holding yet another open session on the GERD dispute, encouraged the three states to resolve their dispute through the AU. This section addresses the post-Washington GERD negotiations. 8.4.1. critically analyze the main claims, counterclaims, and requests of the three states in light of international law. Section 8.4.2. briefly encapsulates the AU-led negotiations.

8.4.1 *Letters to United Nations Security Council*

On May 1, 2020, Egypt formally submitted a letter to the UNSC, characterizing the GERD as "a serious threat to peace and security throughout the region."[1757] It also alleged that Ethiopia's decision to fill the GERD without an agreement with Egypt and Sudan would "constitute a material breach of the DoP"[1758] and "cause significant harm to downstream communities."[1759] Accusing Ethiopia of adopting "a policy of obstructionism that undermined [the GERD] negotiations,"[1760] Egypt requested the international community to (1) "[c]all upon Ethiopia to respect its international legal obligations, including the 2015 DoP, and not to undertake any unilateral measures, including the commencement of impoundment and the filling of the dam, without agreement with downstream riparian's,"[1761] and (2) "[e]ncourage Ethiopia to reconsider its position and to accept the agreement on the filling and operation of the GERD that was initia[t]ed by Egypt on February 28th, 2020."[1762]

In its letter submitted to the UNSC on 14 May 2020, Ethiopia asserted that the "construction of the GERD is based on its sovereign and legitimate rights to use the Nile waters and it is not causing significant harm to downstream countries."[1763] Emphasizing the significance of the GERD as a "non-water consumptive" hydroelectric project aimed at easing its "critical energy deficit, alleviate abject poverty and meet the dire needs of its people,"[1764] Ethiopia reiterated its

1755 Ethiopia's 2021 Letter to UNSC 3, *supra* note 1490, 11–12.
1756 Permanent Rep. of Egypt to the U.N., Letter dated 13 April 2021 from the Permanent Rep. of Egypt to the United Nations addressed to the President of the Security Council, U.N. Doc. S/2021/354 (April 13, 2021) [hereinafter Egypt's 2021 Letter to the UNSC 1].
1757 Egypt's 2020 Letter to the UNSC 1, *supra* note 163, 2.
1758 *Id*, ¶¶ 9–10 & ¶¶ 18–23.
1759 *Id*, 2.
1760 *Id*, ¶ 3.
1761 *Id*, 38.
1762 *Id*.
1763 Ethiopia's 2020 Letter to the UNSC 2, *supra* note 1440, 3.
1764 *Id*, ¶ 2.

position the dam will "provide substantial benefits to Egypt and the Sudan and facilitate regional integration."[1765]

Furthermore, Ethiopia asserted the initial stage-filling of the GERD, which retains about 18.5 BCM over two years (4.9 BCM in the first year and 13.5 BCM in the second year), would not violate the DoP and cause significant harm to the interests of downstream states.[1766] Ethiopia also reiterated its long-standing commitment to multilateralism, listing its role as "the only African member of the League of Nations, a founding member of the United Nations, Organization of the African Unity, African Union [,]....the NBI [and] a state party to the CFA [that] establishes the Nile River Basin Commission (NRBC)."[1767] After listing several initiatives it has taken to accommodate the interests of the downstream states,[1768] Ethiopia condemned Egypt's longstanding unilateral approach to the use of the Nile watercourse, and attributed the failure of the GERD talks to Egypt's attempts "to impose, directly or indirectly, its self-claimed 'historic right and current use' on the Nile riparian countries."[1769]

Ethiopia further asserted its legitimate "right to fill and operate the GERD by complying with the principles of equitable and reasonable utilization and the obligation not to cause significant harm."[1770] It also alleged the first filling of the dam does not require a preliminary agreement as it is "part of the construction," which is explicitly allowed under Article V of the DoP.[1771] Finally, Ethiopia called upon the international community to encourage Egypt to (1) "continue the tripartite negotiation on the guidelines and rules for the first filling and annual operation of the GERD,"[1772] (2) "abandon its insistence to preserve its self-acclaimed 'historic rights and current use' and desist [from] its relentless efforts to politicize and internationalize the remaining technical negotiations,"[1773] and (3) "sign and ratify the CFA in order to forge a genuine cooperation for equitable and reasonable utilization of the Nile waters for the common benefits of all the basin countries."[1774]

In a letter it sent to the UNSC on June 2, 2020, Sudan recognized the significance of the GERD and underlined its potential positive impacts including,

1765 *Id.*
1766 *Id*, ¶¶ 16–18.
1767 *Id*, ¶ 51–55.
1768 *Id.*
1769 *Id*, 3.
1770 *Id*, ¶ 12.
1771 *Id*,¶ 14.
1772 *Id*, ¶ 65.
1773 *Id.*
1774 *Id.*

inter alia, regular flow of water, flood control, cheaper electricity, and increase supply of water for agriculture.[1775] However, for the materialization of these "potential benefits," Sudan submitted, "closer coordination and cooperation is a prerequisite in the way the GERD is operated, otherwise, all the positive impacts will be jeopardized."[1776] Sudan further enumerated its concerns regarding dam safety.[1777]

Although Sudan is not a party to the U.N. Watercourses Convention,[1778] it underlined its understanding that the Convention "reflects and codifies the basic principles of customary international water law, which must be adhered to in order to resolve the remaining differences on the Great Ethiopian Renaissance Dam."[1779] Sudan then specifically recognized the principles of equitable utilization, duty to prevent significant harm, prior notification and information sharing, and peaceful settlement of disputes as codifications of customary international law.[1780] Moreover, emphasizing the need for adhering to the DoP that incorporated such key principles as the way forward to resolving the GERD dispute, Sudan reiterated its commitment to cooperate with both Ethiopia and Egypt in good faith throughout the negotiations.[1781] Finally, after expressing its hope to resolve a few outstanding issues "with a strong political will and commitment from the three parties,"[1782] Sudan called upon the UNSC to encourage all the parties to refrain from (1) "taking unilateral actions including filling the GERD prior to concluding a comprehensive agreement," and (2) "any other action that jeopardizes regional and international peace and security."[1783]

To take the claims and counterclaims of the three states, Egypt, characterizing (1) the GERD as a threat to regional peace and security, claimed that (2) unilateral filling of the GERD would violate international law, including the DoP, and (3) cause significant harm to downstream communities. The issue of whether the GERD is a threat to international peace and security is critically scrutinized in Section 8.5.1.1.[1784] Section 8.3.1 exhaustively examined the

1775 Sudan's 2020 Letter to UNSC, *supra* note 1483, ¶ 8.
1776 *Id*, ¶ 9.
1777 *Id.*
1778 For the list of member states, *see* https://treaties.un.org/Pages/ViewDetails.aspx?src=IND&mtdsg_no=XXVII-12&chapter=27&clang=_en.
1779 Sudan's 2020 Letter to UNSC, *supra* note 1483, ¶ 12.
1780 *Id.*
1781 *Id*, ¶ 34.
1782 *Id*, 6.
1783 *Id.*
1784 *Id.*

second claim and submitted that Ethiopia is allowed—under international law, including the DoP—to fill and test the GERD without an agreement with Sudan and Egypt.[1785] As for the third claim, the Egyptian argument that unilateral filling of the GERD will cause significant harm to downstream communities does not have any legal basis in international watercourses law.[1786]

Indeed, Ethiopia has due diligence obligation to prevent significant harm. However, unlike the Egyptian claim, Ethiopia can still discharge its due diligence obligations and prevent significant harm to the downstream states with, or without, an agreement with the downstream states.[1787] Here, what matters most is the measure Ethiopia would undertake—not the existence or the nonexistence of a preliminary agreement—"to maximize the benefits of the hydro-project while minimizing its negative impacts."[1788] Given that Ethiopia is entitled to equitably use the Nile watercourse, and considering the fact that the filling schedule of the GERD, which has been agreed upon by the three states, is within Ethiopia's legitimate entitlement, one would understand that the initial filling of the GERD would not cause significant harm to Sudan and Egypt. Moreover, there are suggestions that neither state will be immediately affected by the filling as there should be sufficient water in the system to compensate for the amount Ethiopia plans to hold back.[1789]

As previously noted, Egypt accused Ethiopia of adopting "a policy of obstructionism" throughout the GERD negotiation.[1790] Sudan, on the other hand, invoked the principle "notification and exchange of data and information" as a relevant customary international watercourses law principle for resolving the GERD dispute.[1791] In its part, Ethiopia categorically rejected the accusation and attributed the failure of the GERD negotiations to Egypt's reluctance to abide by the principle of equitable and reasonable utilization as demonstrated by its "historical and current use right" claim over the Nile watercourse.[1792] These claims and counterclaims give raise two legal issues: (1) alleged violation of the duty to cooperate in good faith and (2) relevancy of the principle of prior notification of planned measures in the Nile watercourse.

1785 *See* the discussion *infra* section 8.5.1.1.

1786 Zeray Yihdego, *Trilateral Negotiations Over a Dam on the Blue Nile: US Meddling and the 'Role' of the UN Security Council*, *in* ETHIOPIAN YEARBOOK OF INTERNATIONAL LAW 239, 250 (Zeray Yihdego et al. eds., 2019).

1787 *Id.*

1788 *Id.*

1789 *See* Solomon & Elshinnawi, *supra* note 1652.

1790 *See generally* Egypt's 2020 Letter to the UNSC 1, *supra* note 163.

1791 Sudan's 2020 Letter to UNSC, *supra* note 1483, ¶ 12.

1792 Ethiopia's 2020 Letter to the UNSC 2, *supra* note 1440, at 3.

As demonstrated in Section 7.1., Ethiopia took unprecedented cooperative initiatives to accommodate the concerns of downstream states.[1793] Ethiopia conducted transboundary impact studies, initiated a tripartite committee,[1794] established an International Panel of Experts ("IPoE"), and undertook years of comprehensive trilateral technical and political negotiations which lead to the adoption of the DoP.[1795] Ethiopia also agreed to joint studies and established a Tripartite National Committee (TNC) as a mechanism for conducting the two studies recommended by IPoE.[1796] When the two studies could not be conducted because of Egypt's insistence to preserve its current use of the Nile waters,[1797] Ethiopia also agreed to establish NISRG to develop scenarios for the filling and annual operation of GERD.[1798] Ethiopia also undertook several dam safety measures as acknowledged by Sudan and Egypt under Article VIII, which stipulates that "[t]he Three Countries appreciate the efforts undertaken thus far by Ethiopia in implementing the IPoE recommendations pertinent to the GERD safety."[1799] Therefore, Ethiopia did not violate its obligation to cooperate in good faith.

Regarding the second issue, the rules of the U.N. Watercourses Convention on prior notification of planned measures are very controversial in the Nile watercourse. While the obligation of prior notification of planned measures is generally considered customary international law, there is no state practice supporting the principle in the Nile Basin.[1800] Almost all the projects in the Nile Basin are unilateral in nature, and neither the upstream states nor downstream states notified their co-riparian states prior to undertaking their respective projects.[1801] Ethiopia rejected the principle during the negotiation of the U.N. Watercourses Convention[1802] and managed to exclude it from the CFA and the DoP.[1803] Therefore, the principle of prior notification of planned measures is not relevant in the Nile watercourse.

1793 *See* the discussion in section 7.1.

1794 Qerenso, *supra* note 1599.

1795 IPOE FINAL REPORT, *supra* note 111, 21. *See* the discussion in section 7.1.

1796 DoP, *supra* note 152, art. V; Salman, *supra* note 89, at 95.

1797 *Id*, 98–100.

1798 Oluoch, *supra* note 1650.

1799 DoP, *supra* note 152, art. VIII.

1800 *See* the discussion in section 4.1.2.3.

1801 *See* the discussion in sections 2.2., 2.3.& 5.3.

1802 Official Records Fifty-first Session, *supra* note 924, at 9–10.

1803 For the CFA, *see* the discussion in section 6.1. The DoP does not contain an obligation of prior notification planned measures. DoP, *supra* note 152.

Following the submission of the three letters, Ethiopia announced the completion of the first-year filling (4.9 BCM) of the GERD.[1804] Egypt vehemently rejected the filling of the dam and submitted another letter to the UNSC.[1805] Ethiopia and Sudan each submitted their letters articulating their positions. Egypt's letter is relevant to this section. In the letter, Egypt made the following arguments:

(1) Egypt never tried to impose any colonial treaties on Ethiopia because "Ethiopia was never a colony."[1806]

(2) Ethiopia violates the 1902 Anglo-Ethiopian Treaty, and the 1993 framework for cooperation between Ethiopia and Egypt.[1807]

(3) Ethiopia is required to respect the current and existing uses of the Nile watercourse.[1808]

To take those arguments in turn: the first fails to stand on Egypt's practice. As indicated above, Egypt tried to impose the colonial and immediate post-colonial Nile Waters Treaties on Ethiopia in 2019 by submitting a proposal that, *inter alia*, requires Ethiopia to obtain approval from Egypt at various stages of the filling and operation of the dam and release the entire flow of the Nile waters after the filling of the GERD.[1809] Similarly, Egypt, with the help of the United State and the World Bank, tried to impose these agreements on Ethiopia by proposing drought mitigation mechanisms that, *inter alia*, require Ethiopia to release the flow of the Nile and additional supplemental water from the GERD.[1810] Moreover, while it is true that Ethiopia was never a colony, the 1902 Anglo-Ethiopian Treaty is in fact a colonial treaty concluded during colonization between a colonial power, Britain, and Ethiopia. Therefore, Egypt is imposing a colonial treaty on Ethiopia while invoking the 1902 Anglo-Ethiopian Treaty in the UNSC.

The second argument combines a pair of claims: (a) Ethiopia violates the 1902 Anglo-Ethiopian Treaty, and (b) the 1993 framework for cooperation. The first claim is inappropriate because Egypt cannot invoke the 1902 Anglo-Ethiopian Treaty against Ethiopia. Britain concluded the Treaty on behalf of Sudan, not Egypt. While Sudan may arguably inherit the right and obligation in

1804 *River Nile Dam: Reservoir Filling Up, Ethiopia Confirms*, BBC NEWS (July 15, 2020), https://www.bbc.com/news/world-africa-53416277.

1805 Egypt's 2020 Letter to the UNSC 2, *supra* note 1549.

1806 *Id*, 7.

1807 *Id*, 8–9.

1808 *Id*, 9.

1809 *See* the discussion in section 8.1.

1810 *See* the discussion in section 8.2.

the 1902 Anglo-Ethiopian Treaty, there is no legal ground that makes the Treaty opposable to Ethiopia by Egypt.[1811] Moreover, assuming, *arguendo*, that the treaty is opposable, the obligation imposed in the 1902 Anglo-Ethiopian Treaty does not prohibit Ethiopia from using the Nile waters, even without the consent of Britain (now Sudan). What is prohibited in the Treaty is arresting the flow or total blockage of the entire flow of the Nile water.[1812] As a hydroelectric dam, the GERD does not block the water, and it is not therefore prohibited by the 1902 Anglo-Ethiopian Treaty.

The second claim requires proper scrutiny of both Ethiopia and Egypt's practices. Indeed, the 1993 framework for cooperation requires Ethiopia and Egypt to resolve the Nile issues through technical discussion, and to refrain from engaging in "any activity related to the Nile waters that may cause appreciable harm to the interests of the other party."[1813] Ethiopia has always been committed to respecting the framework. Regarding the GERD, for instance, Ethiopia has taken various measures in accordance with its international obligations to prevent harm to the downstream states. Ethiopia conducted transboundary impact studies, initiated a tripartite committee, and established an International Panel of Experts (IPoE) which confirmed that the design and construction process of the dam was in line with "a number of international Standards, Codes, and Guidelines."[1814] Moreover, while Ethiopia can fill the GERD within two years, it extended 4 to 7 years filling period not to significantly affect the interest of downstream states.[1815] On the contrary, Egypt persistently violated the framework by undertaking various unilateral projects including the Toshka Project and the Peace Canal that significantly affect the interest of Ethiopia, foreclosing its current and future uses.[1816]

The third argument, which uses existing usage rates as a baseline, is actually a more severe imposition than a return to the terms of the existing Nile Waters Agreements because Egypt is currently using 61 BCM, preventing Sudan from using the full share to which it is entitled under the 1959 Agreement.[1817] Moreover, the argument is contrary to international watercourses law, which treats both existing and potential use equally as factors for the determination

1811 *See* the discussion in sections 3.2. & 3.3.
1812 See the discussion in section 3.2.1.
1813 1993 Framework Instrument, *supra* note 176, art. 5.
1814 IPOE FINAL REPORT, *supra* note 111, 21.
1815 Ethiopia's 2021 Letter to UNSC 3, *supra* note 1490, 8 ¶ 13.
1816 Salman, *supra* note 1699, 350–2.
1817 Salman, *supra* note 89, 90.

of equitable use.[1818] It is worth noting that as the Nile watercourse is already appropriated by Egypt and Sudan, Ethiopia's future consumptive use may well cause harm, perhaps significant harm, to current and existing uses of the two downstream states. Under international law, such use will be considered a violation of the no-significant-harm principle only when it exceeds Ethiopia's equitable entitlement.[1819] To the extent the harms inflicted upon Sudan and Egypt are within the limit of Ethiopia's exercise of equitable utilization, such exercise should not be regarded as infringing the rights of the downstream states.

After the three states submitted their second letters to the UNSC, the UN Secretary-General António Guterres encouraged the three states to resolve outstanding issues and "achieve a mutually beneficial agreement."[1820] The UNSC also made an unprecedented move and held an open session on the GERD dispute where most of the members encouraged the three states to resolve their dispute through the African Union.[1821]

8.4.2 *African Union and the GERD Negotiations*

Subsequently, the AU started actively involving tripartite negotiation. The chairperson of the AU designated a team of experts to assist the negotiation process.[1822] Other actors such as South Africa, the United States, and European Union (EU) are also involved in the tripartite negotiation as observers.[1823] The three states undertook intermittent tripartite negotiations that were interrupted nine times until Egypt brought the GERD dispute to the UNSC in July 2021.[1824] In addition to the aforementioned two main sticking points (drought mitigation and dispute resolution),[1825] the most controversial issues during the AU-led negotiation include (1) nomenclature of the agreement; (2) scope of the agreement; (3) amendment and termination of the agreement, and (4) roles of the observers.[1826]

1818 U.N. Watercourses Convention, *supra* note 818, art. 6, ¶ 1 (e); DoP, *supra* note 152, art. IV, ¶ II (e).

1819 Second Report, *supra* note 850, 134; MCCAFFREY, *supra* note 4, 496–97.

1820 Press Release of the Sec'y-Gen, *supra* note 1754.

1821 *Egypt Warns of 'Existential Threat', supra* note 164.

1822 Ethiopia's 2021 Letter to UNSC 3, *supra* note 1490, 7 ¶6.

1823 *Id*, 7 ¶7.

1824 *Id*, 11–12.

1825 *See* the discussion in section 8.2.

1826 Permanent Rep. of Egypt to the U.N., Letter dated 11 June 2021 from the Permanent Rep. of Egypt to the United Nations addressed to the President of the Security Council, U.N. Doc. S/2021/565, ¶ 31–43 (June 11, 2021) [hereinafter Egypt's 2021 Letter to the UNSC 2].

Regarding the first issue, Ethiopia insisted that the nomenclature of the forthcoming legal instrument should be "guidelines and rules" on the first filling and annual operation of the GERD.[1827] Sudan, in its part, proposed the nomenclature of the instrument be "Agreement on the Filling and Operation of the Grand Ethiopian Renaissance Dam."[1828] Advancing the Sudanese proposal, Egypt alleged that Ethiopia is "unprepared to accept the conclusion of an instrument that would be unambiguously binding under international law,"[1829] because "[i]t refused to designate the instrument being negotiated as an 'agreement' and propos[ed] labeling it as 'guidelines and rules.'"[1830]

Ethiopia's approach seems appropriate for the following reasons. First, the DoP which provides the framework for the GERD negotiation, contemplates that the forthcoming instrument will be "guidelines and rules."[1831] Article V explicitly states that the three states will agree on "guidelines and rules for the first filling … and annual operation of the GERD."[1832] Therefore, Ethiopia's proposal to designate the instrument being negotiated as "guidelines and rules" is legally justified as it is in line with the DoP.

In contrast, Egypt's argument—that Ethiopia does not need a binding agreement on the GERD because it refused to designate the forthcoming instrument as "agreement"—has no basis under international law. First, Ethiopia did not engage in the GERD negotiations to agree on a soft law instrument that will not bind the three states. It has consistently asserted that forthcoming "guidelines and rules" on the first filling and annual operation of the dam should be binding.[1833] Moreover, contrary to Egypt's claim, labeling the forthcoming instrument as "guidelines and rules" would not diminish its legal status or binding effect under international law.[1834] As noted above, the nomenclature of a given document is irrelevant in determining its legal effect. While states are allowed to agree on soft law instruments that do not have a binding effect, the title of a document is not wholly dispositive of its legal effect.[1835] "Treaties are known by a variety of differing names, ranging from Conventions,

1827 *Id*, ¶ 43.

1828 Letter dated 12 April 2021 from the Chargé d'affaires a.i. of the Permanent Mission of the Sudan to the United Nations addressed to the President of the Security Council, U.N. Doc. S/2021/350, 16 (April 12, 2021) [hereinafter Sudan's 2021 Letter to the UNSC 1].

1829 Egypt's 2021 Letter to the UNSC 2, *supra* note 1826, ¶ 43.

1830 *Id.*

1831 DoP, *supra* note 152, art. V.

1832 *Id*, V, ¶ 2 (a) & (b).

1833 *See* e.g. Ethiopia's 2021 Letter to UNSC 1, *supra* note 1440, 17 ¶ 69.

1834 VCLT, *supra* note 520, art. 2.

1835 *Id.*

International Agreements, Pacts, General Acts, Charters, through to Statutes, Declarations, and Covenants."[1836] With all these various titles possible, "the intent of the parties, as reflected in the language and context of the document, the circumstances of its conclusion, and the explanations given by the parties" rather than the document title determines its legal effect.[1837] In its letter submitted to the UNSC, Ethiopia has already explicitly expressed its intention to be bound by the forthcoming agreement.[1838] Therefore, as a matter of international law, and contrary to Egypt's allegation, the forthcoming instrument on the GERD will be legally binding on the three states, regardless of the nomenclature of the text.

Concerning the scope of the agreement, Ethiopia insisted that the forthcoming "guidelines and rules" should restrict the first filing and annual operation of the GERD.[1839] Egypt and Sudan, on the other hand, demanded that the scope of the agreement should include refilling and long-term operation of the dam.[1840] Ethiopia objected to the downstream states' proposal, and alternatively proposed the piecemeal agreement where the three states would agree on the initial stage of the first filling of the GERD (as per the schedule accepted by the three states in Washington DC),[1841] and continue negotiating other outstanding issues, including refilling and operational rules of the dam in good faith.[1842]

Indeed, Ethiopia's first proposal is a direct replica of the DoP. Article V explicitly provides that the three states will agree on "guidelines and rules for the *first filling* … and *annual operation* of the GERD."[1843] Contrary to the downstream States' proposal, the DoP does not contemplate that the scope of the forthcoming instrument will include the refilling and long-term operation of the dam. It is worth noting that any agreement on the refilling and long-term operation of the dam will have a water allocation effect and may even become a water-sharing agreement. Moreover, given the Nile watercourse is already appropriated by Egypt and Sudan, such an agreement would impose the colonial and immediate post-colonial Nile Waters Treaties on Ethiopia, foreclosing

1836 SHAW, *supra* note 668, 93 (citation omitted).
1837 Nash (Leich), *supra* note 1540, 515 & accompanying texts.
1838 *See* Ethiopia's 2021 Letter to UNSC 1, *supra* note 1440, 17 ¶ 69.
1839 *Id*, 16 ¶ 64.
1840 Egypt's 2021 Letter to the UNSC 2, *supra* note 1826, 23 ¶ 49.
1841 Egypt's 2020 Letter to the UNSC 2, *supra* note 1549, annex II (regarding the schedule accepted by the three States).
1842 *Sudan rejects Ethiopian proposal, supra* note 1746; Ethiopia's 2021 Letter to UNSC 3, *supra* note 1490, 7 ¶ 8.
1843 DoP, *supra* note 152, art. V ¶ 2 (a) & (b).

its right to use the Nile watercourse for consumptive purposes. Therefore, the exclusion of refilling and long-term operation of the dam from the DoP, and the scope of the forthcoming instrument is appropriate.

As for Ethiopia's alternative proposal, Egypt and Sudan opposed a piecemeal agreement on the filling of the dam, alleging that it "place[s] no meaningful obligation on Ethiopia and provide[s] no protection for the interest of downstream states."[1844] Although concluding a comprehensive agreement would better serve the interest of the two downstream states, a piecemeal approach would give the three states the time to build trust and confidence and work out the details on outstanding issues. It will also be an option to avoid unilateral filling of the dam. As noted, Ethiopia is allowed to unilaterally fill the GERD under international law, including the DoP.[1845] Thus, if the three states cannot overcome the impasses, piecemeal agreement would be important for the two downstream states to avoid the unilateral filling of the dam.

Regarding amendment and termination clauses, Ethiopia insisted that it should enjoy the right to unilaterally alter the forthcoming GERD agreement and terminate it within a certain period after its conclusion.[1846] The downstream states outrightly rejected this and asserted that the agreement should not have amendment and termination clauses.[1847] Approach from the DoP, Principle V stipulates that the annual operation guidelines and rules of the GERD can be "adjust[ed] from time to time" by "the owner of the dam."[1848] In so doing, the DoP explicitly gives Ethiopia the discretion to amend the forthcoming GERD agreement and terminate it within a certain period after its conclusion. This is extremely important for treaty flexibility and addressing the uncertainty associated with climate change and population growth in the Nile Basin. As discussed in Chapter 9, the inclusion of amendment and termination clauses into the GERD agreement—as mechanisms for building flexibility—will provide the resilience needed to revise filling and operational guidelines as hydrological and existing conditions change.[1849]

Regarding the last issue, Sudan proposed a quartet of international mediation that includes the AU, the EU, the United Nations, and the United States

1844 Egypt's 2021 Letter to the UNSC 2, *supra* note 1826, 22 ¶ 47.
1845 *See* the discussion in section 8.3.
1846 Egypt's 2021 Letter to the UNSC 2, *supra* note 1826, 21 ¶ 43.
1847 *Id*; Sudan's 2021 Letter to the UNSC 1, *supra* note 1828, 16 (Sudan alternatively proposed the agreement shall not be "amended or terminated without the agreement of all three parties.")
1848 DoP, *supra* note 152, art. V ¶ 2 (a) & (b).
1849 *See* the discussion *infra* chapter sections 9.2 & 9.3.

to overcome the impasse on the GERD talks.[1850] Accepting the Sudanese proposal, Egypt also tried to ostracize "the Republic of South Africa from its role as an observer."[1851] Ethiopia, committed to preserving the "integrity of the AU-led process," urged these third parties to facilitate the tripartite negotiations as observers and share "information and proposal when jointly requested by the Countries."[1852] Per Ethiopia's insistence, South Africa resumed its observer status; the other observers have been given the mandate to propose "solutions when jointly requested by the three countries, and the African Union Chairperson has been allowed to use the African Union Commission and other resources at his disposal in support of his facilitation role."[1853]

Meanwhile, Ethiopia announced that it is preparing to conduct the second-year filling of the GERD, which will impound 13.5 BCM of water from the Blue Nile.[1854] This is 17 percent of the 77 BCM water Ethiopia contributes to the entire Nile Basin,[1855] which constitutes 86 percent of the annual flow of the Nile.[1856] Subsequently, on April 8, 2021, Ethiopia proposed to exchange data and information during the filing of the dam and invited Sudan and Egypt to nominate dam operators.[1857] Egypt and Sudan rejected the proposal, claiming that a "legally binding agreement should precede data sharing on the dam filling."[1858] Egypt, daring Ethiopia to "take a single drop of water from Egypt," warned of "inconceivable instability in the region" if Ethiopia filled the dam without a binding agreement.[1859] It then brought the GERD dispute to the UNSC for the second time.[1860] The UNSC, holding yet another open session on

1850 Sudan's 2021 Letter to the UNSC 1, *supra* note 1828, 7–8.

1851 Ethiopia's 2021 Letter to UNSC 3, *supra* note 1490, 7 ¶ 7.

1852 Press Release, Embassy of Eth., Washington DC, Press Release on the Trilateral Negotiations on the GERD, Kinshasa, Democratic Republic of the Congo (April 6, 2021), https://ethiopianembassy.org/press-release-on-the-trilateral-negotiations-on-the-gerd-kinshasa-democratic-republic-of-the-congo-april-6-2021/ [hereinafter Press Release on the Trilateral Negotiations].

1853 Ethiopia's 2021 Letter to UNSC 3, *supra* note 1490, 7 ¶ 8.

1854 Kavaler, *supra* note 1633.

1855 Ethiopia's 2021 Letter to UNSC 1, *supra* note 1440, 15 ¶ 54.

1856 NILE BASIN INITIATIVE, *supra* note 52, at 36.

1857 Press Release on the Trilateral Negotiations Press Release, Embassy of Eth., Washington DC, Ethiopia invites Sudan and Egypt to nominate dam operators for data exchange before the filling of GERD in upcoming rainy seasons (April 10, 2021), https://ethiopianembassy.org/ethiopia-invites-sudan-and-egypt-to-nominate-dam-operators-for-data-exchange-before-the-filling-of-gerd-in-upcoming-rainy-seasons-april-10-2021/; Egypt's 2021 Letter to the UNSC 2, *supa* note 1826, 22 ¶ 45.

1858 El-Din, *supra* note 113.

1859 *Id.*

1860 Egypt's 2021 Letter to the UNSC 1, *supra* note 1756.

the GERD dispute, issued a statement encouraging the three states to resolve their dispute through the AU.[1861]

8.5 The Way Forward: towards Unlocking the GERD Dispute

The literature on natural resource governance often identifies negotiation, mediation, arbitration, and adjudication as principal mechanisms for resolving transboundary water disputes.[1862] While negotiation and mediation are cooperative and provide a win-win solution, arbitration and adjudication are more competitive and may induce a win-lose solution.[1863] The DoP seems to recognize this fact and excludes arbitration and adjudication from the principle of peaceful settlement of disputes which, as enshrined in article X, urges the three states to resolve disputes through consultation, negotiation, and only as a last resort to "jointly request for conciliation [or] mediation."[1864] Based on the framework provided in this article, the following section investigates the legal and geopolitical ramifications of the involvement of a third party in the GERD negotiation. It also provides substantive proposals for addressing the elephant in the room, i.e., colonial and immediate post-colonial Nile Waters Treaties.

8.5.1 *Procedural Considerations: Involvement of Third Party in the Negotiation*

Egypt has demonstrated its amenability to third-party mediation and even formally requested the UNSC to intervene in the GERD dispute.[1865] Ethiopia, on the other hand, relying on Article X of the DoP, which primarily recommends the three states resolve their dispute through negotiation and conciliation, resisted the involvement of third parties in the GERD negotiation.[1866] In its part, Sudan, changing its previous position that the GERD dispute should be resolved through tripartite negotiation, is now advocating for third-party mediation. Ethiopia, albeit its recent acceptance of the AU as an observer and

1861 United Nations Security Council, Statement by the Pres. of the Security Council, U.N. Doc. S/PRST/2021/18 (Sep. 11, 2021).

1862 *See supra* note 48 and accompanying texts.

1863 STEPHEN J. WARE, PRINCIPLES OF ALTERNATIVE DISPUTE RESOLUTION 12–13 (2016).

1864 DoP, *supra* note 152, art. X.

1865 Egypt's 2020 Letter to the UNSC 1, *supra* note 163.

1866 *See* e.g., Meseret, *supra* note 1649; Press Release on the Trilateral Negotiations, *supra* note 1852.

facilitator of the negotiations, does not consider third-party mediation as a solution for the GERD dispute. These divergent positions raise a fundamental issue as to whether it is legitimate for Ethiopia to reject third-party mediation, including the United States and the World Bank. Assuming, *arguendo*, the legitimacy of Ethiopia's decision, there remains the question of whether the GERD is a threat to international peace and security, warranting the UNSC intervention. The following section addresses both issues, exploring first the possibility of the UNSC intervention in the GERD dispute before moving on to analyzing the legal and geopolitical aspects of third-party mediation.

8.5.1.1 The United Nations Security Council's Intervention in the GERD Dispute: Any Possibility?

As noted above, Egypt has characterized the GERD dispute as a threat to regional peace and security.[1867] Ethiopia vehemently rejected this characterization and indicated how the project will promote "sustainable development, peace and security" in the region.[1868] Sudan, in its part, calls upon UNSC to encourage all the parties to refrain from "*any other action* that jeopardizes regional and international peace and security."[1869] These claims and counterclaims raise a fundamental issue as to whether there is a legal basis for the UNSC to intervene in the GERD dispute.

Two arguments can be made regarding the legal basis of the Egyptian claim. First, it may be argued that Egypt's claim to the UNSC falls under Article 35, Chapter VI, of the UN Charter which allows member states to "bring any dispute or any situation"[1870] that is "likely to endanger the maintenance of international peace and security."[1871] Moreover, per article 24, the UNSC has the primary responsibility for international peace and security, and is obliged to discharge its duties "in accordance with the Purposes and Principles of the United Nations."[1872] Article 2 of the Charter enumerated the principles which, *inter alia,* include sovereign equality, non-intervention in the internal affairs of states, and the need to refrain from the threat or use of force against the territorial integrity and political independence of another state.[1873]

1867 Egypt's 2020 Letter to the UNSC 1, *supra* note 163, 2.
1868 Ethiopia's 2020 Letter to the UNSC 2, *supra* note 1440, at 3.
1869 Sudan's 2020 Letter to UNSC, *supra* note 1483, 6.
1870 U.N. Charter, art. 35.
1871 *Id,* art 34.
1872 *Id,* art 24. *See* also Yihdego, *supra* note 1872, 249.
1873 *Id,* art. 2. *See* also Yihdego, *supra* note 1786, 249.

Approached from these legal grounds, Ethiopia's attempt to make equitable use of the Nile watercourse through the GERD neither constitutes a threat to international peace and security nor does it violate the principles and purposes of the UN Charter.[1874] Ethiopia never used or threatened to use military force against the downstream states.[1875] "In contrast, continuous Egyptian threats, which came in various forms and at different times, may well pose questions of violation of the prohibition on the threat or use of force to secure water or other national interests."[1876] Given the prohibition of the use of force or the threat to use under international law,[1877] Ethiopia "might have sufficient legal grounds to bring a complaint before the UNSC alleging threats to its sovereignty from Egypt."[1878]

However, Ethiopia's letter to the UNSC, which considered tripartite negotiation and basin-wide cooperation as the way forward to resolve the GERD dispute,[1879] did not make such a case,[1880] and simply characterized the Egyptian move as an unwarranted securitization and internationalization of the GERD issue for advancing a self-claimed "historic rights and current use" of Nile watercourse.[1881] Ethiopia also expressed its regret about "the unwarranted escalation of the issues, disinformation campaign and over politicization of what is a technical operation of a single water infrastructure built exclusively through the direct contributions of the poor citizens of Ethiopia with the hope to be uplifted out of an abject poverty."[1882] Accordingly, it can be concluded that Egypt's unprecedented move to bring the GERD dispute to UNSC does not have any legal basis under international law.[1883] Moreover, given the previous two precedents where the UNSC simply encourage the three states to resolve their dispute through the AU and considering the fact that the GERD does not constitute a threat to international peace and security, or violate any provision of the UN Charter,[1884] it is unlikely that the UNSC will directly intervene into the GERD dispute in the future and issue any kind of resolution.

1874 Yihdego, *supra* note 17860, 249.
1875 *Id.*
1876 *Id.*
1877 U.N. Charter, art. 2 ¶ 4.
1878 Yihdego, *supra* note 1786, 249.
1879 *See generally*, Ethiopia's 2020 Letter to the UNSC 2, *supra* note 1440.
1880 Yihdego, *supra* note 1786, 249.
1881 Ethiopia's 2020 Letter to the UNSC 2, *supra* note 1440, ¶ 65.
1882 *Id*, ¶ 14.
1883 Yihdego, *supra* note 1786, 250.
1884 *Id.*

8.5.1.2 Mediation

As of the writing of this book, the three states are undertaking tripartite negotiations under the auspices of the AU. The United States is also still engaged in the negotiations.[1885] As such, if the tripartite negotiations fail, Egypt will likely call upon the United States and the World Bank to continue their active role in mediating the dispute. The U.S. Treasury Department, in its statement issued on February 28th, 2020, signaled that it would "remain engaged with the three countries until they sign the final agreement."[1886]

Although mediation is one of the dispute resolution mechanisms included in Article x of the DoP, it is not mandatory. Article x states that "[i]f the [p]arties are unable to resolve the dispute through consultation or negotiation, they may jointly request for conciliation, mediation *or* refer the matter for the consideration of the Heads of State/Head of Government."[1887] The legal status of the DoP is unclear; only some of its components—namely Articles III and IV on the prevention of significant harm and equitable utilization, respectively[1888]—impose a legal obligation. Article x of the DoP is clear in this regard. Unlike Articles III and IV, which use "shall," Article x uses the term "may" which, in the legal lexicon, makes the whole provision an optional stipulation that has no binding effect.[1889]

Even if Article x were binding, Ethiopia is not obligated to refer the matter to mediation. The Article allows the three parties to request mediation only jointly or refer the matter for the consideration of their leaders. As the word *jointly* indicates, recourse to mediation is impossible if and when one party refuses. Ethiopia retains the ability to refer the matter to its Prime Minister.

Ethiopia may, however, find mediation politically expedient. If so, Ethiopia should oppose the involvement of the United States and the World Bank as mediators. There are several reasons why the United States and the World Bank will not be neutral mediators. Although both Ethiopia and Egypt are strategic partners of the United States in counterterrorism,[1890] Egypt is more

1885 Ethiopia's 2021 Letter to UNSC 3, *supra* note 1490, 7 ¶6.

1886 Treasury Statement, *supra* note 162.

1887 DoP, *supra* note 152, art. X.

1888 *Id.* arts. III–IV.

1889 *May*, BLACK'S LAW DICTIONARY (6th ed. 1990) ("'[M]ay' usually is employed to imply permissive, optional or discretional, and not mandatory action or conduct."). *See* Pronto, *supra* note 1535, at 952.

1890 ROBERT G. BERSCHINSKI, AFRICOM'S DILEMMA: THE "GLOBAL WAR ON TERRORISM," "CAPACITY BUILDING," HUMANITARIANISM, AND THE FUTURE OF U.S. SECURITY POLICY IN AFRICA 42 (2007) (stating "U.S. policy in the Horn of late ... has been exclusively dictated by the GWOT [global war on terror]."). *See also* Mohamed Elmenshawy,

important to the United States than Ethiopia.[1891] Moreover, the intimate relationship between President el-Sisi and President Trump already undermined the United States' neutrality.[1892] President Trump's "deal of the century" to resolve the Palestine-Israel conflict was another source of bias towards Egypt during the negotiation in Washington, DC. The plan was not limited to Palestine and Israel but included other neighboring countries like Jordan, Egypt, and Lebanon.[1893] The Trump Administration, which halted 100 million dollars of foreign assistance destined for Ethiopia as a result of the GERD dispute,[1894] had committed to grant nine billion dollars to Egypt for participating in efforts to resolve the Israel-Palestine conflict.[1895] The United States had further pledged to help Egypt realize its interests relating to the Nile River and the GERD.[1896] Therefore, if Ethiopia accepted the United States as a mediator, the GERD and Ethiopia's rights in the Nile waters would become the "sacrificial

Egypt's War on Terror: ISIS, President Sisi, and the U.S.-led Coalition, Middle East Inst., (Nov. 6, 2014), https://www.mei.edu/publications/egypts-war-terror-isis-president-sisi-and-us-led-coalition.

1891 Mehari Taddele Maru, *The Trump Trap,* ADDIS STANDARD, (Mar. 11, 2020), http://addisstandard.com/commentary-the-trump-trap/ ("All allies are equal, but some are more than equal. Egypt is far strategic an ally [sic] of the United States and Israel that it is difficult to imagine how Washington or any other power close to it can be an impartial arbiter on the Nile. Given that the Camp David agreement is the cornerstone on which the U.S.-Egypt relation is founded, it would be almost impossible for the United States to treat other riparian states equally.")

1892 In addition, Trump is also quoted to have called el-Sisi his "favorite dictator." Mindock, *supra* note 1675.

1893 *See generally* THE WHITE HOUSE, PEACE TO PROSPERITY: A NEW VISION FOR THE PALESTINIAN PEOPLE AND THE MIDDLE EAST REGION (2020), https://www.whitehouse.gov/wp-content/uploads/2020/01/Peace-to-Prosperity-0120.pdf.

1894 Patricia Zengerle, *U.S. to Cut $100 Million in Aid to Ethiopia Over Dam Dispute*, REUTERS (Sept. 15, 2020), https://www.reuters.com/article/usa-ethiopia-int/u-s-to-cut-100-million-in-aid-to-ethiopia-over-dam-dispute-idUSKBN25T2ZD.

1895 *$9 Billion for Egypt in Return for Deal of the Century*, MEMO MIDDLE EAST MONITOR, (June 24, 2019), https://www.middleeastmonitor.com/20190624-9-billion-for-egypt-in-return-for-deal-of-the-century/.

1896 Alula Alemayehu, *Ethiopia and the Nile: Sacrificial Lamb for the "Deal of The Century"?*, ADDIS STANDARD (Feb. 3, 2020), http://addisstandard.com/opinion-ethiopia-and-the-nile-sacrificial-lamb-for-the-deal-of-the-century/; *see also* PEACE TO PROSPERITY: THE ECONOMIC PLAN: PROGRAMS AND PROJECTS 49 (2020), https://www.whitehouse.gov/wp-content/uploads/2019/06/MEP_programsandprojects.pdf (asserting that the U.S. promised to "[s]upport water infrastructure projects in the Sinai to bolster broader economic development"). Recall that Egypt is developing the Peace Canal project to divert the Nile from its natural flow to the Sinai in order to irrigate the desert. Egypt has started the project over Ethiopia's objections and, though it has not yet been finalized, possible assistance from the United States may improve the likelihood of the project's completion.

lamb" for the realization of the "deal of the century."[1897] The pressure during the Washington, D.C. negotiations, the drought mitigation proposals drafted by the United States and World Bank, the statement issued on February 28, the U.S. Treasury Secretary's answer in Congress,[1898] the decision to block foreign aid to Ethiopia, and President Trump's irresponsible statement that "Egypt will blow up the dam"[1899] all attest to the Trump Administration's lack of neutrality.

As for the current administration, it seems that President Biden is following a relatively neutral position regarding the GERD.[1900] However, the damage inflicted by the Trump Administration, the increasingly strained relationship between Ethiopia and the United States government due to the crisis in the northern part of Ethiopia,[1901] and many Ethiopian's perceptions that the Biden administration is working with rebel groups to destabilize Ethiopia[1902] all will make it impossible for the United States to involve in the GERD negotiation as a mediator.

The World Bank is similarly likely to favor Egypt. In the 1980s and 1990s, many Egyptian professionals occupied key political and environmental

---

1897 Alemayehu, *supra* note 1896.

1898 *See* Widakuswara, *supra* note 1625.

1899 *Trump comment on 'blowing up' Nile Dam angers Ethiopia*, BBC NEWS (October 24, 2020), https://www.bbc.com/news/world-africa-54674313.

1900 For instance, the current administration reversed a policy that had linked foreign aid to Ethiopia to the GERD and linked it to the conflict in Northern Ethiopia. *U.S. to De-link Ethiopian Aid Pause From Dam Policy,* REUTERS (Feb. 20. 2021), https://www.reuters.com/article/us-ethiopia-dam-usa/u-s-to-de-link-ethiopian-aid-pause-from-dam-policy-idUSKBN2AK08O.

1901 See e.g., The White House, Executive Order on Imposing Sanctions on Certain Persons with Respect to the Humanitarian and Human Rights Crisis in Ethiopia (Sept. 17, 2021), https://www.whitehouse.gov/briefing-room/presidential-actions/2021/09/17/executive-order-on-imposing-sanctions-on-certain-persons-with-respect-to-the-humanitarian-and-human-rights-crisis-in-ethiopia/; Farouk Chothia, *Tigray crisis: How the West Has Fallen out with Ethiopia's PM,* BBC NEWS (October 25, 2021), https://www.bbc.com/news/world-africa-58967302. It should be noted that Ethiopian officials allege that Sudan is providing military support to Tigray People Liberation Front (TPLF) and fomenting troubles to destabilize Ethiopia, although Sudan categorically denied the allegations. *Sudan denies Ethiopian reports about Khartoum's support to TPLF: Foreign Ministry,* AHRAM ONLINE (Dec. 12, 2021), https://english.ahram.org.eg/News/446317.aspx.

1902 Bronwyn Bruton & Ann Fitz-Gerald, *To End Ethiopia's War, Biden Needs to Correct Course,* FP, (Dec. 28, 2021), https://foreignpolicy.com/2021/12/28/ethiopia-tigray-abiy-tplf-war-biden-needs-to-correct-course/ ("Many Ethiopians even fear that Washington actively backs the insurgency and is seeking a Libya-Iraq-Somalia-style intervention to shatter Ethiopia and the new efforts for regional peace that Abiy, for many, has come to represent.")

positions in the World Bank[1903] and developed the World Bank Operational Directive 7.50.[1904] Like the colonial Nile Waters Treaties, the Directive favors the existing status quo by conditioning funding for projects on the consent of all Basin States. Egypt has repeatedly opposed World Bank funding for several developmental projects in the Nile and Ethiopia.[1905] Moreover, the fact that the World Bank assisted in drafting the U.S. proposal[1906] and actively engaged in the Washington, D.C. negotiations as a mediator without Ethiopia's consent shows that the World Bank is not a neutral mediator.

As indicated above, the AU is already engaged in the GERD negotiations as an observer rather than a mediator. So far, the AU is facilitating talks and the three states are trying to resolve the dispute by themselves. Given the mutual suspicions among the three states and their disagreements over the sticking points, it is unlikely that they will resolve the dispute by themselves. If mediation becomes necessary, it must be initiated in the spirit of "African solutions for African problems" and with neutral mediators. As external parties are biased towards Egypt due to its geopolitical advantages, the AU and the Council of Water Minsters of the Nile Basin States ("Nile-COM") should be more involved and should mediate the GERD dispute. The AU and Nile-COM will likely be neutral because the three states are members of both organizations, which do not have the same vested interests as the United States and the World Bank.

8.5.2 *Substantive Propositions: towards Taming the Elephant in the Room*

The colonial and immediate post-colonial Nile Agreements (existing Nile Waters Agreements) comprise the principal obstacle to the GERD negotiations; however, Egypt, Sudan, and Ethiopia are not openly discussing them. Addressing these agreements is a *sine qua non* for an amicable resolution of the GERD dispute. Regardless of the possibility of third-party mediation, any attempt to resolve the GERD dispute without addressing the ramifications of the existing Nile Waters Agreements will be a Sisyphean endeavor. This is because the existing Nile Waters Agreements have already created a negative bargaining zone where mutual agreement is extremely challenging. In such a

1903 WATERBURY, *supra* note 302, 71.

1904 *Projects on International Waterways, supra* note 1120.

1905 *See* ROBERT G. WIRSING ET AL, INTERNATIONAL CONFLICT OVER WATER RESOURCES IN HIMALAYAN ASIA 145 (2013).

1906 Joint Statement 3, *supra* note 1700. ("The United States, with technical support from the World Bank, has agreed to facilitate the preparation of the final agreement for consideration ...").

scenario, where Egypt continues to rely on the existing Nile Waters Agreements, Ethiopia's highest offer will be lower than Egypt's reservation price—the rights it already has under these accords. Yet, as Ethiopia rejects the validity of the existing Nile Waters Agreements, its highest offer is likely below what Egypt is guaranteed under these agreements. In this situation, there will be no positive overlap between the two countries' reservation points, and reaching an agreement will be unlikely. The three states, with the help of the AU, should, therefore, create a positive bargaining zone by (1) restricting the scope of the ongoing talks to the filling and annual operation of the GERD, and (2) resorting to the CFA for water allocation, future dispute resolution and long-term operation of the GERD.

8.5.2.1 GERD Treaty: First Filling and Annual Operation

Delineating the scope of a possible GERD treaty is the first, and perhaps most important, way of addressing the inequitable ramifications of the existing Nile Waters Agreements. The three states can and should address the problems associated with the colonial Nile Waters Treaties by explicitly stating in the forthcoming treaty:

(1) that nothing in this treaty shall be construed as recognition of the existing Nile Waters Agreements;
(2) that nothing in this treaty shall be construed as allocation of waters between the three countries;
(3) that nothing in this treaty shall prohibit Ethiopia from equitably using the Nile waters upstream of the GERD; and
(4) that this treaty concerns only the GERD and therefore nothing in the treaty shall associate the GERD with the AHD.

The forthcoming treaty should further ensure equitable filling of the GERD reservoir without causing significant harm to the downstream states. The three states must consider the factors provided in Article IV of the DoP, including climatic and hydrological conditions of the river, the effect of the GERD's use on other riparian states, population, existing and potential water uses efficient utilization of water resources, and the water contribution of each state for ensuring equitable filling of the GERD.[1907]

It is worth mentioning that the January 15 2020, joint statement[1908] did not consider all of the factors provided for in the DoP.[1909] The statement was

1907 DoP, *supra* note 152, art. IV.
1908 Joint Statement 2, *supra* note 1680.
1909 DoP, *supra* note 152, art. IV.

selective[1910] in only considering drought mitigation, "the hydrological conditions of the Blue Nile and the *potential impact* of the filling on downstream reservoirs."[1911] This cherry-picking approach, which disregards equitable and reasonable utilization and focuses only on potential impact, is inappropriate and contrary to the cardinal principles of international watercourses law.[1912] The forthcoming treaty should, therefore, consider drought and hydrological conditions "as part of the factors to determine an equitable and reasonable filling of the GERD."[1913]

Under the statement's proposed framework, Ethiopia would further need to fill the dam "during the wet season, generally from July to August ... [while taking] appropriate mitigation measures for Egypt and Sudan during drought, prolonged drought period and prolonged dry years."[1914] Based on this, the U.S. proposal agreement included the three aforementioned drought-mitigation mechanisms. As noted, the mechanisms would compel Ethiopia to release the "flow" of the Blue Nile and more water from the GERD reservoir without any *quid pro quo*. The mechanisms also presuppose the water share allocated in the colonial Nile Waters Treaties and impose all drought mitigation-related burdens on Ethiopia. Hence, such mechanisms should be excluded from the forthcoming treaty. Because there is no water-sharing arrangement between the three states, Ethiopia's obligation to release water from the GERD reservoir should be equitable and reasonable; Ethiopia's drought-related treaty commitment should be limited to releasing the "inflow" of the GERD.

As for the filling period, filling the GERD in a two to four year timeframe may significantly affect the interests of Sudan and Egypt.[1915] Filling the GERD slowly—over the course of ten or more years—will significantly and adversely impact Ethiopian interests.[1916] Therefore, the forthcoming treaty should establish a fair and reasonable filling plan that "considers factors such as the right season, the impact of swift and prolonged filling on all parties, and the attainment of a middle ground that considers filing the dam primarily, but

1910 Yihdego, *supra* note 150, 3–4.

1911 Joint Statement 2, *supra* note 1680 (emphasis added).

1912 The statement imposes much of the drought mitigation burden on Ethiopia and does not adequately address significant principles such as "equitable utilization" or "significant harm." Yihdego, *supra* note 150, 4. It instead makes reference to the "potential impact" of a project and thus—relative to a duty to prevent significant harm—raises the threshold for, and increases the scope of, the harms that must be prevented during filling. *Id.*

1913 *Id.*

1914 Joint Statement 2, *supra* note 1680.

1915 Yihdego, *supra* note 150, 5.

1916 *Id.*

not exclusively, during the wet season between five to seven years."[1917] In so doing, the treaty "will significantly mitigate the impact of filling the dam on downstream states while granting an equitable, reasonable and timely return to Ethiopia's investment and entitlement to produce electricity."[1918]

Concerning the annual operation of the dam, the forthcoming treaty, as envisaged in Article V of the DoP, should establish a coordination mechanism through the three ministries responsible for water. The three states should use this mechanism to exchange data and information. Ethiopia should regularly notify the other parties of its operation plan, and how much water it will release from the GERD. Egypt and Sudan should also notify Ethiopia and one another of how they are using the Nile waters and how much water is stored in their respective reservoirs regularly.

As discussed in chapter 9.3, the treaty should also be flexible and adaptive to address the uncertainty associated with global climate change and population growth in the Nile Basin.[1919] The treaty should include an amendment provision, a review procedure, and a termination or revocation clause. These provisions will give the three states the resilience needed to revise filling and operational guidelines as hydrological and existing conditions change. Concerning the termination clause, it must be noted that revoking a treaty through an abbreviated period of notice—say six months or a year—is inappropriate in a treaty regulating a permanent structure such as the GERD.[1920] So, the treaty must reconcile the flexibility required for adapting to climate change with the certainty required for the proper management of dams by requiring a long period of notice, anywhere between ten to fifteen years, to withdraw from the treaty.[1921]

8.5.2.2 The Cooperative Framework Agreement: Water Allocation and Long-Term Operation

The CFA, if accepted by Sudan and Egypt, will establish a new legal regime governing the use and allocation of the Nile waters. The CFA does not use a

---

1917 *Id.*

1918 *Id.*

1919 *See* the discussion *infra* Chapter 9.

1920 Stephen C. McCaffrey, *The Need for Flexibility in Freshwater Treaty Regimes*, 27 NAT. RES. F., 156, 160 (2003).

1921 For example, the treaty between the United States and Canada governing hydroelectric power production and flood protection (permanent structures) for the Columbia Basin imposes a notice requirement of ten years prior to termination. Treaty Relating to Cooperative Development of the Water Resources of the Columbia River Basin, Can.-U.S., art. XIX, ¶ 2, Jan. 17, 1961, 15 U.S.T. 1555 [hereinafter Columbia River Basin Treaty].

fixed and volumetric strategy for water allocation, which encourages flexibility. Instead, it requires equitable and reasonable utilization as its allocation strategy.[1922]

The CFA also foresees the establishment of the Nile Basin River Commission (NRBC) as an institutional framework for Nile basin governance.[1923] The NRBC would possess a wide range of powers, including the ability to examine and determine optimal water use and distribution among the Nile basin countries.[1924] It would also have a broad scope;[1925] it would be entrusted with rule-making authority[1926] and empowered to resolve disputes within the Nile Basin.[1927] Considering the need for coordinated dam operation and integrated water resource management, the NRBC is best positioned to manage the long-term operation of the GERD. But, for this to happen, Egypt and Sudan must accede to the CFA.

Given both states' previous oppositions, the question would then be why Egypt and Sudan should accede to the CFA now. The current hydro-political context of the Nile Basin is significantly different than it was during the CFA negotiations. The GERD, which has brought about a *de facto* change in the status quo, will affect the Nile's flow during the filling period. Ethiopia can, therefore, use the GERD as a bargaining chip to negotiate concessions from Egypt and Sudan.

As noted, Sudan is aligned with Ethiopia due to the advantage it would get from the GERD. Egypt, on the other hand, is concerned about the GERD's impact on the status quo of the current Nile water allocation. It follows that Egypt will accept the CFA if it regulates the operation of the dam in a way that protects Egyptian interests. Ethiopia should therefore concede that NRBC will manage the GERD's operation. Since Egypt needs some form of input into the operation of GERD and Ethiopia rejected Egypt's demand to maintain an office at the dam site, NRBC management of GERD operations is a good compromise. As the NRBC makes binding decisions by consensus,[1928] Egypt's interests will be protected better.

Egypt may be further incentivized to accept the CFA by the need to avoid unilateral exploitation through cooperative use of the Nile River. Egypt, after

1922 CFA, *supra* note 132, art 4, ¶ 1.
1923 *See id.* art. 15.
1924 *Id.* art. 24, ¶ 12.
1925 *See id.* art. 24.
1926 *Id.*
1927 *Id.* arts. 24, ¶ 13, 33.
1928 *Id.* art. 23, ¶ 5.

all, cannot prevent Ethiopia from constructing the GERD. There is the risk that other riparian states would follow Ethiopia in unilaterally developing the Nile River. Therefore, the CFA would protect Egypt's interests by ensuring cooperative use of the Nile waters.

Upstream states are beginning to assert their right to use the Nile. Given Egypt's geographic and hydrologic vulnerability by virtue of being a downstream state, a legal regime that protects its interest is a necessity. Egypt (and Sudan) should therefore be urged to accept the CFA as it sufficiently safeguards their interests through equitable and reasonable utilization, cooperative utilization, the no significant harm principle, and binding dispute resolution mechanisms. In addition to empowering the NRBC to make binding decisions,[1929] the CFA already contains terms that would allow parties to submit to binding arbitration and judicial settlement through the ICJ.[1930] Since these dispute resolution mechanisms have basin-wide applications, the CFA is a good compromise to resolve the three states' disagreement over the need for including compulsory dispute resolution in the GERD treaty.

Conclusion

At the time of writing this book, Ethiopia, Sudan, and Egypt are undertaking tripartite negotiations under the auspices of the AU. For the negotiations to move forward, the implications of the existing Nile Waters Agreements must be dispensed with. The AU should help the three states to create a positive bargaining zone by (1) restricting the scope of the ongoing talks to the filling and annual operation of the GERD, and (2) encouraging the states to resort to the CFA for water allocation, dispute resolution and long-term operation of the GERD.

Otherwise, Ethiopia will have no option but to continue filling the GERD without an agreement with Sudan and Egypt. Ethiopia will continue the unilateral filling not only because it is permissible under international law, but also because the downstream states' past behavior suggests they cannot be relied upon to come to an agreement and will instead drag out the negotiation in perpetuity. As for Sudan and Egypt, there are suggestions that neither state will be immediately affected by the filling as there should be sufficient water

1929 *Id.* art. 23, ¶ 6.
1930 *Id.* art. 33, ¶ 1(a).

in the system to compensate for the amount Ethiopia plans to hold back.[1931] Moreover, as the GERD is a non-consumptive hydroelectric project, it will not have any adverse impact after the filling is completed. Therefore, regardless of whether AU-facilitated talks become successful or not, the real dispute between the three states will boil down to whether and to what extent Ethiopia can use the Nile waters for consumptive purposes, including irrigation.

As the Nile watercourse is already appropriated by Egypt and Sudan, Ethiopia's future utilization may well cause harm, perhaps significant harm, to current and existing uses of the two downstream states. Under international law, such use will be considered a violation of the no-significant-harm principle only when it exceeds Ethiopia's equitable entitlement.[1932] To the extent the harms inflicted upon Sudan and Egypt are within the limit of Ethiopia's exercise of equitable utilization, such exercise should not be regarded as infringing the rights of the downstream states. Therefore, Ethiopia should go ahead and start equitably utilizing the Nile watercourse for consumptive purposes, including irrigation.

1931 *See* Solomon & Elshinnawi, *supa* note 1652; *see also* Essayas Kaba & Semu Moges, *Why Is Now the Right Time to Start Filling the Grand Ethiopian Renaissance Dam* (GERD)*?*, E.-AFRICANIST (June 1, 2020).

1932 Second Report, *supra* note 850, 134; MCCAFFREY, *supra* note 4, 496–97.

PART 4

Looking into the Future: towards Building a Flexible Legal and Institutional Framework in the Nile Basin

CHAPTER 9

Governing the Nile under Climatic Uncertainty: the Need for Climate-Proofed Basin-wide Treaty

Introduction

Climate change is projected to have catastrophic impacts on the hydrological cycle.[1933] Water availability, quantity, and demand will all be affected by global climate change.[1934] Existing studies show that climate disruption is changing "the timing of water (when water is delivered), quantity (how much water is available) and quality of the water resources."[1935] Even worse, these changes are coming at a time when the sustainability of water resources is severely strained by other non-climatic factors, such as population growth, economic development, and urbanization. All of these factors will decrease water supply or increase demand.[1936]

Responding to such changes requires building flexibility and adaptability into watercourse treaties.[1937] However, the flexibility needed within these treaties to address the ramifications of climate change could impact the predictability and certainty required by water-sharing States that rely on the language of a watercourse treaty.[1938] Thus, developing principles, procedures, and institutions capable of accommodating the ramifications of climate change is challenging, as it requires governing uncertainty, which is at odds with the notion of legal certainty.[1939]

1933 *See generally* Nigel Arnell et al., *Hydrology and Water Resources*, *in* CLIMATE CHANGE 2001: IMPACTS, ADAPTATION, AND VULNERABILITY 191 (James J. McCarthy et al. eds., Cambridge University Press 2001).

1934 *See* Gabriel Eckstein, *Water Scarcity, Conflict, and Security in a Climate Change World: Challenges and Opportunities for International Law and Policy*, 27 WIS. INT'L L.J. 410, 431 (2009).

1935 Tuula Honkonen, *Water Security and Climate Change: The Need for Adaptive Governance*, 20 PER/PELJ 1, 2 (2017).

1936 Arnell et al, *supra* note 36, 234.

1937 McCaffrey, *supra* note 1920, 156.

1938 ALISTAIR RIEU-CLARKE ET AL., UNITED NATIONS TRANSBOUNDARY WATER GOVERNANCE AND CLIMATE CHANGE ADAPTATION: INTERNATIONAL LAW, POLICY GUIDELINES, AND BEST PRACTICE APPLICATION 34 (2015).

1939 Honkonen, *supra* note 1935, at 3; *see also* A. Dan Tarlock, *Four Challenges for International Water Law*, 23 TUL. ENV'T L.J. 369, 383–84 (2009).

 | DOI:10.1163/9789004549869_010

But still, as the law of treaties does not "ordinarily permit unilateral modification or withdrawal when such changes occur,"[1940] parties are "required to work within the framework of existing treaties to respond to changes" associated with global climate change.[1941] Nevertheless, most of the existing watercourse treaties, locked in rigid rules and procedures, are unable to provide the flexibility needed to address the anticipated changes due to global climate change.[1942] Only a few watercourse treaties possess the intrinsic capacity for dealing with the ramifications of climate change.[1943]

This chapter examines treaty flexibility and climate change adaptation in the context of the Nile Basin. This is especially important because climate disruption is bringing new challenges to the management of the Nile watercourse as well as to the GERD dispute. Existing studies and climate change models commonly predict increases in the average annual temperature in the Nile Basin, leading to greater water loss due to evaporation.[1944] There is much less certainty in projections concerning future rainfall, river flows, and water availability in the Nile Basin. Studies on these topics find contradictory results; one predicts increase water availability and possible floods,[1945] and the other predicts decrease water availability and possible droughts.[1946]

1940 McCaffrey, *supra* note 1920, at 159.

1941 *Id.*

1942 Joseph W. Dellapenna, *Adapting the Law of Water Management to Global Climate Change and Other Hydro-Political Stresses*, 35 J. AM. WATER ASS'N 1302 (1999); McCaffrey, *supra* note 1920, at 156; Goldenman, *supra* note 723, 741; A. Dan Tarlock, *How Well Can International Water Allocation Regimes Adapt to Global Climate Change?*, 15 J. LAND USE & ENV'T L. 423, 433–34 (2000); Elizabeth J. Kistin & Peter J. Ashton, *Adapting to Change on Transboundary Rivers: An Analysis of Treaty Flexibility on the Orange-Senqu River Basin*, 24 INT'L J. WATER RES. DEV. 1 (2008); *see also* Itay Fischhendler, *Legal and Institutional Adaptation to Climate Uncertainty: A Study of International Rivers*, 6 WATER POL'Y 281 (2004).

1943 Hearns & Paisley, *supra* note 1339, 262.

1944 EARLE ET AL., *supra* note 62, 130; Conway, *supra* note 68, 106; UNEP, *supra* note 66, 13; Cooley et al, *supra* note 68.

1945 Shih & Stutz, *supra* note 60, 10789; *see* Conway, *supra* note 68; Vivek K. Arora & George J. Boer, *Effects of Simulated Climate Change on the Hydrology of Major River Basins*, 106 J. GEOPHYSICAL RES. 3335, 3335–48 (2001).

1946 Nigel W. Arnell, *Climate Change and Global Water Resources: SRES Emissions and Socio-Economic Scenarios*, 14 GLOBAL ENV'T CHANGE 31, 31–49 (2004); Reinhard Voss et al., *Enhanced Resolution Modelling Study on Anthropogenic Climate Change: Changes in Extremes of the Hydrological Cycle*, 22 INT'L J. CLIMATOLOGY 755, 771–73 (2002). Schiffler, *supra* note 69, at 146 ("Some experts estimate that the Nile's flow will increase by as much as 30%, while others estimate a decrease of up to 78%").

It seems evident that proper governance of the Nile watercourse in the face of these uncertainties demands a response to two contradictory scenarios—either increase in water availability and flooding or water scarcity and drought—each of which requires opposite adaptation strategies.[1947] Building flexible and resilient legal and institutional arrangements will no doubt be at the heart of such adaptation strategies.[1948] If climate change reduces the available water in the Nile Basin, competition for water between Ethiopia, Sudan, and Egypt will only intensify, possibly leading to conflicts. If the available water resources increase due to climate change, this will create a need for new legal responses to flooding. In either case, flexible legal arrangements governing the Nile watercourse and the GERD will be crucial to adapt to climate disruption.

The next section introduces the mechanisms that can provide flexibility in watercourse treaties; it reviews the practice of various water-sharing countries and encapsulates the principal ways of building a climate-proof treaty. 9.2. analyzes treaty flexibility in the Nile Basin and probes the intrinsic capacity of the 1959 Agreement, and the CFA. 9.3. specifically addresses whether the DoP contemplates a flexible legal arrangement for governing the GERD under climatic uncertainty. After answering in the affirmative, the chapter proposes a flexible basin-wide treaty capable of accommodating the ramifications of climate change in Section 9.4. It finally provides concluding remarks, which call upon Nile Basin States and other water-sharing States to set aside their egoistic national interests and address the ramifications of global climate change by developing flexible and climate-proof treaties.

1947 Richard Kyle Paisley, *Why the 11 Countries That Rely on the Nile Need to Reach a River Deal Soon*, CONVERSATION, (Aug. 27, 2017) https://theconversation.com/why-the-11-countries-that-rely-on-the-nile-need-to-reach-a-river-deal-soon-75868 It is worth mentioning that the global climate change discourse has two approaches, mitigation and adaptation, for tackling the problems of climate change. While mitigation focuses on resolving the root causes of climate change by controlling greenhouse gas emissions and mitigating the rise of global temperature, adaptation "accepts the projected increases and seeks to understand both the effects of global climate change and the impacts of those effects in order to adapt to them." *See* Tarlock, *supra* note 1942, at 423–24.

1948 *See also* Eckstein, *supra* note 1934, 432–33. *See generally* McCaffrey, *supra* note 1920; Hearns & Paisley, *supra* note 1339, at 259–60; Fischhendler, *supra* note 1942, at 282; Goldenman, *supra* note 723, at 741; Cooley et al, *supra* note 68, at 14; RIEU-CLARKE ET AL., *supra* note 1938, at 9–11.

9.1 Building Flexibility into Treaty Regimes

A new paradigm of flexibility in water treaties is essential to adapt to global climate disruption. This part encapsulates five mechanisms through which flexibility can be provided in watercourse treaties.[1949] The five principal ways to build a climate-proof treaty are to incorporate (1) flexible allocation strategies; (2) extreme events provisions; (3) amendment-and-review procedures; (4) termination clauses; and (5) river basin organizations (RBOS).[1950] The section examines each mechanism below, beginning with flexible water allocation.

9.1.1 *Flexible Water Allocation*

Water-sharing States may use flexible water allocation strategies in watercourse treaties to achieve a sustainable water supply in the face of global climate disruption. Instead of allocating shared waters based on the assumption of a fixed, and often too optimistic, perpetual water supply, or fixed allocation strategy, parties should allocate their shared water resources in accordance with the social, economic, or climatic changing conditions existing in the Basin States.[1951] There are a couple of ways this can be achieved. A rather simple method is to enter into an agreement that requires upstream states to deliver a minimum flow to a downstream riparian State in order "to maintain human health and basic ecological functions."[1952] The other mechanism is to proportionally "allocate the water based on a percentage of the flow and time of flow, rather than a fixed or minimum amount."[1953] Although this approach "requires flexible infrastructure, effective operating rules, and regular communication and data sharing,"[1954] it "allows flow regimes to respond to both wet and dry conditions."[1955]

9.1.2 *Response Strategy for Extreme Events*

Perhaps the most common mechanism for enhancing treaty flexibility is to include special provisions in watercourse treaties that govern particular kinds

---

1949 *See also* Fischhendler, *supra* note 1942, at 282–83. McCaffrey, *supra* note 1920, at 158–161.

1950 *See generally* Fischhendler, *supra* note 1942, at 282–83; McCaffrey, *supra* note 1920, at 159–161.

1951 *See generally* Fischhendler, *supra* note 1942, at 282–83; McCaffrey, *supra* note 1920, at 158–161.

1952 *See* RIEU-CLARKE ET AL., *supra* note 1938, at 34.

1953 *Id.*

1954 Heather Cooley & Peter H. Gleick, *Climate-Proofing Transboundary Water Agreements*, 56 HYDROLOGICAL SCI. J. 711, 715 (2011).

1955 *Id.*

of exceptional circumstances, such as droughts and floods.[1956] For instance, the 1944 Agreement between the United States and Mexico on the Rio Grande and Colorado Rivers has provisions governing possible problems resulting from drought.[1957] The Agreement allows Mexico to deliver less than the minimum quantity of water to the United States during an "extraordinary drought" for up to five years.[1958] If deficiencies occur during this period, Mexico is to repay by increasing flows during the next five-year cycle.[1959] In the case of the Colorado River, the Agreement guarantees that Mexico receives a certain annual quantity of the Colorado River's water from the United States.[1960] "In the event of extraordinary drought," though, the water allotted to Mexico is to "be reduced in the same proportion as consumptive uses in the United States are reduced."[1961]

Floods, although posing serious risks for lower riparian States, are often ignored in the recent discourse of climate change concerning resilience and adaptability of international watercourse treaties.[1962] Most international watercourses are not governed by regimes with the institutional capacity to address the problem of flooding.[1963] Only a few watercourse treaties include flood management systems. Among such treaties, the Columbia River Basin Treaty stipulates that "Canada (the upstream party) will adjust its operation of hydroelectric dams to mitigate flooding in the United States."[1964] Also, the Agreement on the Cooperation for Sustainable Development of the Mekong River Basin provides maximum river flow rates, requiring "upstream dam operations to be adjusted to meet these requirements."[1965]

9.1.3 *Amendment and Periodic Review*

Amendment and periodic review processes give the riparian States the chance to address unforeseen circumstances, while "resynchroniz[ing] national and

1956 *Id. See also* Fischhendler, *supra* note 1942, at 283–84; McCaffrey, *supra* note 1920, at 160; Goldenman, *supra* note 723; Eckstein, *supra* note 1934, at 457; Cooley et al, *supra* note 68, at 15.

1957 1944 Colorado Treaty, *supra* note 1683, art. 4.

1958 *Id.* art. 4, ¶ B(c).

1959 *Id.* ¶ B(d).

1960 *Id.* art. 10, ¶ a.

1961 *Id.* ¶ b.

1962 *See* Cooley et al, *supra* note 68, at 15.

1963 *Id.*

1964 *Id.*; Columbia River Basin Treaty, *supra* note 1921. It is worth nothing that flood protection is the purpose of this Treaty.

1965 *See* Cooley et al, *supra* note 68, at 15.

basin-wide strategies with new knowledge and changing circumstance."[1966] These processes are crucial for the sustainability of watercourse treaties because, through time, the hydrological and climatic conditions on which such treaties are based will change significantly.[1967] This is particularly true in the era of climate disruption.

Several mechanisms can be used to amend watercourse treaties. In the Colorado River Basin, for instance, modifications of the 1944 Colorado Treaty are made through the "minutes" of meetings of the International Boundary and Water Commission, a joint commission charged with the application of the Treaty and composed of an engineer commissioner from both Parties (the United States and Mexico).[1968] The Mekong River Basin Agreement between Cambodia, Laos, Thailand, and Vietnam also allows the alteration of the Agreement through amendment proposals agreed to by all the Parties.[1969]

Moreover, some international watercourse treaties have provisions dealing with periodic reviews. In the Syr Darya River Basin, for instance, the Framework Agreement requires periodic review of agreements "on water releases, production and transit of electricity, and compensations for energy losses" and calls for the conclusion of new agreements annually.[1970] Another example is the treaty between India and Nepal governing the Mahakali River, which requires a review every 10 years or "earlier as required by either party."[1971]

9.1.4 *Termination Clauses*

The fourth mechanism for enhancing treaty flexibility is to simply include a termination clause in the treaty allowing any riparian State "to terminate it upon a given period of notice, e.g. six months."[1972] In the Syr Darya Basin,

1966 *See* Kistin & Ashton, *supra* note 1942, at 6. Indeed, a review process has been addressed in the *Kishenganga* case between Pakistan and India. The award states that after seven years from the implementation of the project either party may seek reconsideration of the tribunal's minimum flow requirement. *See* In re Indus Waters Kishenganga Arbitration (Pak. v. India), ¶. 119 (2013), https://pcacases.com/web/sendAttach/48 This was because "a degree of uncertainty is inherent in any attempt to predict environmental responses to changing conditions." *See id.* ¶ 117.

1967 Cooley et al, *supra* note 68, at 16.

1968 1944 Colorado Treaty, *supra* note 1683, arts. 2 and 25; *see* McCaffrey, *supra* note 1920, at 161.

1969 Agreement on the Cooperation for the Sustainable Development of the Mekong River Basin, art. 37, Apr. 5, 1995, 34 I.L.M. 864.

1970 *See* McCaffrey, *supra* note 1920, at 159.

1971 Treaty Between His Majesty's Government of Nepal and the Government of India Concerning the Integrated Development of the Mahakali River Including the Sarada Barrage, Tanakpur Barrage, and Pancheshwar Project, India-Nepal, art. 12, Feb. 12, 1996.

1972 Agreement Between the Governments of the Republic of Kazakhstan, the Kyrgyz Republic, and the Republic of Uzbekistan on the Use of Water and Energy Resources of

for instance, the Framework Agreement restricts its validity to five years,[1973] allowing automatic renewal for another five years provided that no termination notice is submitted six months in advance from any Party.[1974] In so doing, the Framework Agreement provides sufficient flexibility for Parties adversely affected by changed circumstances, permitting them to withdraw from what could otherwise be an oppressive treaty.[1975]

It is, however, to be noted that a termination clause would not always be appropriate for all types of treaties. As pointed out by Professor McCaffrey, it would best fit only treaties that do "not involve permanent structures but provide for allocations of water."[1976]

9.1.5 *River Basin Organizations* (*RBOs*)

Sustainable transboundary water management is inextricably linked with RBOs. Developing an institutional structure for joint management of transboundary watercourses is essential for the pragmatic application of both substantive and procedural principles governing transboundary watercourses.[1977] Indeed, RBOs play a significant role in building flexibility into watercourse treaties. RBOs' ability to adapt, amend, and extend the institutional arrangement between riparian States is at the center of developing greater resilience and adaptability to the changing environment. Of the 260 transboundary river basins, about 119 of them have water institutions.[1978] While the roles and authorities of such institutions vary significantly, institutions capable of adapting to the challenges of climate disruption should "have a broad scope, include all riparian nations, and have management and enforcement authority."[1979] Factors that are likely to influence the resilience of the RBOs include

---

the Syr Darya Basin, art. 12, Mar. 17, 1998 [hereinafter Syr Darya Basin Treaty]. *See* also McCaffrey, *supra* note 1920, at 160.

1973 Syr Darya Basin Treaty, *supra* note 1972, art. 12. *See also* McCaffrey, supra note 1920, at 159–60.

1974 Syr Darya Basin Treaty, *supra* note 1972, art. 12; McCaffrey, supra note 1920, at 159–60.

1975 *Id.*

1976 *Id.* at 160.

1977 *See* Hearns & Paisley, *supra* note 1339, at 274–75.

1978 *See* Cooley & Gleick, *supra* note 1954, at 712. (mentioning 260 international river basins) and at 716 (mentioning 106 RBOs). *See also* Susanne Schmeier, *Opening the Black Box of River Basin Organizations*, GLOBAL WATER F., Oct. 16, 2012, http://www.globalwaterforum.org/2012/10/16/opening-the-black-box-of-river-basin-organizations/ (mentioning 119 RBOs).

1979 Cooley et al, *supra* note 68, at 16. It should be noted that the Berlin Rules, which delineate a model for RBOs, requires such organizations, *inter alia*, to have an authority to coordinate scientific and technical research programs and establish harmonized, coordinated, or unified networks for permanent observation and control. It also requires the

> [t]he membership structure of the organization, focusing on whether all riparians in the respective basin are included in joint climate change adaptation activities; the functional scope of the RBO, focusing on the degree of integration of water resources management and climate change adaptation; a decision-making mechanism that ensures the timely and efficient adoption of decisions; the existence and the well-functioning of data and information sharing mechanisms ensuring long-term cooperation; the existence and well-functioning of dispute-resolution/conflict management mechanisms allowing for solving emerging water-related collective action problems; [and] the secured availability of financial resources for climate change adaptation activities in the basin.[1980]

Consequentially, although mechanisms discussed in this section are by no means exhaustive, water-sharing States are recommended to use these mechanisms when building climate-proofing treaties to adapt to climate change. The next part of this chapter specifically analyzes the legal regime governing the Nile Basin using the aforementioned five mechanisms.

9.2 Adapting the Nile Basin to Climate Change: Analysis of Treaty Flexibility

Legal and institutional frameworks are essential for efficient transboundary water management. States are often advised by scholars to regulate the use and allocation of their shared water resources through a basin-wide treaty.[1981] This advice seems to be ignored in the Nile Basin, however. The Nile Basin has no mutually acceptable legal framework applicable to all riparian States.[1982] The legal regime governing the Nile watercourse consists of several legal instruments, none of which involves all Basin States or applies to the Basin as a whole. Despite the fragmented nature of the treaties, the following part of this Article analyzes the flexibility of the most prominent legal instruments, the

---

constitutive act of RBO to expressly stipulate the objective and purpose, nature and composition, form and duration, legal status, area of operation, functions and powers, and financial arrangements the organization. Berlin Rules, *supra* note 818, arts. 64–67.

1980 *See* Sabine Schulze & Susanne Schmeier, *Governing Environmental Change in International River Basins: The Role of River Basin Organizations*, 10 INT'L J. RIVER BASIN MGMT. 229 (2012).

1981 McCaffrey, *supra* note 1920, at 157.

1982 MCCAFFREY, *supra* note 4, 308.

1959 Agreement, the CFA, and the DoP, and assesses their capacity to adapt to climate change.

9.2.1 *The 1959 Agreement*

As Table 1 demonstrates, the 1959 Agreement does not incorporate most of the mechanisms essential for treaty flexibility. The Agreement does not follow a proportion allocation strategy. It also fails to address flooding and does not have provisions regarding the amendment process and periodic review. Moreover, it envisages perpetual applicability and does not allow for termination by the riparian States.

The 1959 Agreement does not allocate any water for the upstream states. It allocates the waters of the Nile only between Egypt and Sudan. As the 1929 Anglo-Egyptian Treaty determined the "established rights" of the two States, the 1959 Agreement allocated only the net benefit generated from the construction of the AHD.[1983] Of the 32 BCM gross gain expected after the construction of the AHD, the Agreement deducts 10 BCM for evaporation and seepage and divides the remaining 22 BCM in a 2:1 ratio in favor of Sudan, or 14.5 BCM for Sudan and 7.5 BCM for Egypt.[1984] Then, by adding the net benefits to the established rights of each State, the Agreement allocates a fixed volumetric quantity of waters between the two States, 55.5 BCM to Egypt and 18.5 BCM to Sudan.[1985] This allocation strategy is very rigid and at odds with the proportional allocation strategy discussed in Section 9.1.1.

As to extreme events, the drought provision of the 1959 Agreement states that, if normal yearly quotas cannot be drawn during the low years,[1986] the Permanent Joint Technical Committee (PJTC) will devise fair arrangements and submit proposals to both governments for approval.[1987] As to the high flow years,[1988] the Agreement requires the two States to divide net benefits equally.[1989] The Agreement, like many watercourse treaties, does not provide for any flood controlling mechanism.[1990] Yet flooding is a real problem

---

1983 *See* 1959 Agreement, *supra* note 106, art. II, ¶¶ 3–4; Goldenman, *supra* note 723, at 753–54.

1984 *See* 1959 Agreement, *supra* note 106, art. II, ¶ 4.

1985 *Id*, art II, ¶ 3–4.

1986 "Low years" are years when the water flows are below the average mean natural river supply at Aswan (84 BCM).

1987 1959 Agreement, *supra* note 106, art. IV, ¶ 1(e).

1988 "High years" are years when the water flows are above the average mean natural river supply at Aswan (84 BCM).

1989 *See* 1959 Agreement, *supra* note 106, art. II, ¶ 4 ("But if the average yield increases, the resulting net benefit from this increase shall be divided between the two Republics, in equal shares.").

1990 Goldenman, *supra* note 723, at 754–55.

TABLE 1 Treaty flexibility in the Nile Basin

Flexibility Mechanisms	1959 Agreement	CFA	DoP
Allocation	Yes, but fixed	Equitable utilization	Equitable utilization
Extreme Events			
I. Drought	Yes	Yes	No
II. Flood	No	Yes	No
Amendment and Review			
I. Amendment	No	Yes, but rigid	No, but contemplates
II. Review	No	No	No, but contemplates
Revoking Clause	No	Yes	No, but contemplates
RBOS	Yes, but nominal	Yes	No, but contemplates

in the Nile Basin, and its frequency is projected to be exacerbated by climate disruption.[1991]

Further, the 1959 Agreement does not have amendment-and-review provisions. It does, however, envisage the revision of the net benefit generated from the AHD.[1992] Both Parties are allowed to revise the net benefit "at reasonable intervals to be agreed upon as from the date of the operation of the complete" AHD.[1993] Although the intended revision is important for building flexibility, it has not been pragmatically applied throughout the Basin's history. Moreover, as the subject of revision is only "the net benefit," but not "the established rights" of the two States, the Agreement's ability to tackle severely diminished river flows due to climate disruption is questionable. Also, the Agreement does not have a termination clause and hence does not permit the riparian States to end their treaty obligations.

1991 *See* UNEP, *supra* note 66, at 13–14. *Compare* Conway, *supra* note 68, at 106 (analyzing climate models that predict drier scenarios), *How Climate Change Might Affect the Nile*, ECONOMIST, Aug. 3, 2017, https://www.economist.com/middle-east-and-africa/2017/08/03/how-climate-change-might-affect-the-nile (analyzing a climate model that predicts wetter scenarios).

1992 1959 Agreement, *supra* note 106, art. II, ¶ 5.

1993 *Id.*

Indeed, the establishment of the PJTC is the most important achievement of the 1959 Agreement.[1994] But the authority given to the Committee is restricted to administrative matters like overseeing construction and storage works, including the AHD.[1995] The PJTC has no authority to adopt, amend, or extend the existing arrangements between riparian States. Moreover, this Agreement neither provides a dispute settlement procedure nor does it give the PJTC authority to resolve regional disputes concerning the Nile watercourse. Additionally, it does not oblige Egypt and Sudan to share hydrological data.[1996] In a nutshell, it can be said that rigidity is the salient feature of the 1959 Agreement and that it lacks the intrinsic capacity for dealing with the ramifications of climate change.

9.2.2 *The Cooperative Framework Agreement*

The CFA does not use the fixed volumetric allocations strategy, does not provide a minimum flow to the downstream states, and does not allocate the Nile waters proportionally. Instead, it uses equitable and reasonable utilization as an allocation strategy. By allowing all riparian States to use the Nile waters equitably,[1997] the CFA illustrates the relevant factors for determining equitable and reasonable utilization of the water resource.[1998]

The climate, hydrology, and other physical characteristics of the Nile River System are among the factors listed for determining equitable and reasonable utilization.[1999] The CFA lists "[c]onservation, protection, development and economy of use of the water resources"[2000] as factors, thus potentially providing the basis for more efficient uses as part of adaptation to decreased flows. Moreover, in recognizing that these factors, including climate, might change over time, it requires riparian States to "keep the status of their water utilization under review in light of substantial changes in relevant factors and circumstances."[2001]

The CFA does not, however, guide how to weigh the various factors, including climate. It simply asserts that the weight to be given to each factor must be

1994 *Id.*

1995 *Id.* art. IV, ¶ 1.

1996 *See* Goldenman, *supra* note 723, at 755 (indicating how "Egypt regards its data on Nile flows and its consumption of those waters to be highly confidential matters of national security"). *See generally* 1959 Agreement, *supra* note 106.

1997 CFA, *supra* note 132, art 4, ¶ 1.

1998 *Id.* art. 4, ¶ 2.

1999 *Id.* art. 4, ¶ 2(a).

2000 *Id.* art. 4, ¶ 2(f).

2001 *Id.* art. 4, ¶ 5.

determined by comparing it to the other factors, all of which must be considered as a whole.[2002] It also empowers the Council of Ministers (COM), one of the organs of the Nile River Basin Commission (NRBC), to determine the equitable utilization of waters in each riparian State.[2003] As discussed below, while empowering the Commission is essential for treaty flexibility, the composition of the COM and the absence of specific review periods under the CFA would hinder the role of the NRBC.

The CFA provides for an amendment process by setting forth procedures that States are to follow. Article 35 of the CFA sets forth two distinct rules for approving proposed amendments, one requiring consensus and another requiring a two-thirds majority vote.[2004] Specifically, proposals to alter Articles 1, 2, 3, 4, 5, 8, 9, 14, 23, 24, 33, and 34 can only be approved by consensus.[2005] All other provisions and any protocol can be amended by a two-thirds majority vote if States cannot reach an agreement by consensus.[2006] However, adopting a new proposal requires consensus.[2007]

The first amendment procedure of the CFA is quite rigid because it requires consensus.[2008] The consensus requirement appears too idealistic and does not consider the hydro-political landscape of the Basin. There are intricacies that would make it hard for the Basin States to arrive at a consensus. Some of these intricacies include issues such as acrimonious inter riparian relationship between the Nile Basin States, generated by historical baggage of animosity and military confrontations; increasing demand for water due to alarming population growth; high dependency on the river, and coercive hydro-hegemonic policy, characterized by, *inter alia*, war rhetoric and securitization of the Nile watercourse. Moreover, reaching a consensus, if at all possible, requires painstakingly lengthy diplomatic negotiations. Yet addressing

---

2002 *Id.* art. 4, ¶ 4.

2003 *Id.* art. 24, ¶ 12.

2004 *Id.* art. 35, ¶ 3.

2005 *Id.*

2006 *Id.*

2007 *Id.* art. 34, ¶ 4.

2008 *Id.* art. 35, ¶ 3. For insistence, due to the threats of climate change, the Nile Basin States may find it appropriate to change the allocation strategy followed in the CFA from equitable utilization (Article 4) to proportional allocation. But because of the requirement of consensus, they may not be able to amend Article 4 of the CFA. Although consensus does not necessarily mean unanimity, it does require at least the non-objection of some Basin countries (Egypt, Sudan, and Ethiopia), giving them the opportunity to hinder the amendment process.

rapid climate disruption may often require prompt responses, which in return requires building more flexibility into the amendment procedures.

Other procedural issues, such as developing new protocols and periodically reviewing existing agreements, are also important mechanisms to deal with future climatic uncertainties. Although Article 34 of the CFA allows the Nile Basin States to adopt new protocols by consensus, no instrument shall be inconsistent with the provisions of the CFA.[2009] Moreover, the CFA does not provide for periodic reviews. It does, however, empower one of its organs, the COM, to "review and revise ... rules, procedures, guidelines and criteria for the implementation of the provisions of" the CFA.[2010] While flexibility is implicit in this provision, the fact that the COM is not empowered to review the CFA itself and the absence of a specified period within which the CFA would be reviewed could render this call for flexibility of limited value.

Concerning extreme events, the CFA has an explicit provision that includes all "steps of the climate change adaptation chain—prevention, preparedness, response, and recovery."[2011] In this respect, Article 12 of the CFA governing emergencies states:

> 1. For the purposes of this provision, "emergency" means a situation that causes, or poses an imminent threat of causing, serious harm to Nile Basin States or other States and that results suddenly from natural causes, such as floods, landslides or earthquakes, or from human conduct, such as industrial accidents.
> 2. A Nile Basin State shall, without delay and by the most expeditious means available, notify other potentially affected States and competent international organizations of any emergency originating in its territory.
> 3. A Nile Basin State within whose territory an emergency originates shall, in cooperation with potentially affected States and, where appropriate, competent international organizations, immediately take all practicable measures necessitated by the circumstances to prevent, mitigate and eliminate harmful effects of the emergency.
> 4. When necessary, Nile Basin States shall jointly develop contingency plans for responding to emergencies, in cooperation, where

2009 CFA, *supra* note 132, art. 34, ¶ 3. To address the ramification of climate change, the Nile Basin States may need to renegotiate the CFA and change some of its principles by adopting a new protocol that reflects current circumstances. Article 34 forecloses this possibility by requiring such a protocol to conform with the principles of the CFA.

2010 *Id.* art. 24, ¶ 11.

2011 EARLE ET AL., *supra* note 62, at 143.

> appropriate, with other potentially affected States and competent international organizations.[2012]

As demonstrated in this Article, the CFA addresses the possible ramifications of climate change by incorporating the most recent "sophisticated global climate change discourse."[2013] The CFA is unique in underscoring that "the response to climate extreme events must be collective, and not only at [a] national level."[2014]

However, Article 12 of the CFA does not include flooding as an emergency. The CFA addresses flooding in Article 11 concerning the prevention and mitigation of harmful conditions.[2015] Article 11, in the relevant part, requires the Nile Basin States "to take all appropriate measures to prevent or mitigate conditions related to the Nile River System that may be harmful to the other Nile Basin States … resulting from … causes, such as … drought or desertification."[2016] While this provision requires the prevention and mitigation of possible harms resulting from drought, it does not guide how the riparian States shall use the Nile water during the time of drought. Nor does it address how the waters of the Nile would be allocated during the low years.

Examining such gaps and considering the failure of the CFA to use a proportional allocation strategy, one may wonder, during the time of drought, what kind of uses, such as domestic and sanitation, irrigation, or generation of hydroelectric power, will be given priority. Another question is how riparian States will share the water deficiencies occurring during the time of drought. There is no doubt that the lack of concrete guidance regarding priorities among such uses along with the absence of a proportional allocation strategy will pose a significant challenge for the NRBC to determine the equitability of the uses in each riparian State.

Concerning termination, the CFA allows the Basin States to withdraw from the Agreement any time after two years from the date of its entry into force.[2017] The only requirement is that the State terminating its treaty obligation shall

2012 CFA, *supra* note 132, art. 12.

2013 EARLE ET AL., *supra* note 62, at 143.

2014 *See Id.* at 121 (Among others, this discourse considers climate change as a cross-border issue, and suggests adaptation measures will be more effective when undertaken in coordination (joint measures) with the neighboring countries.)

2015 CFA, *supra* note 132, art. 11.

2016 *Id.*

2017 *Id.* art. 39, ¶ 1.

give written notifications to the depositary.[2018] "The withdrawal shall take place upon expiry of one year after the date of its receipt by the Depositary."[2019]

The time limit in which States can withdraw from the Agreement is very short. This abbreviated timeline would cause a fundamental funding problem with the overall CFA. One of the considerations behind the negotiations of the CFA was identifying how the Agreement would provide security for international financial institutions and donor countries. Indeed, ensuring financial security would require a great deal of certainty and predictability within the terms of the Agreement. Yet ultimately, the termination clause hinders the needed certainty by enabling any riparian State to terminate its treaty obligations within a year, effectively.

Ironically, it is even difficult to justify the termination clause on the grounds of treaty flexibility. As indicated above, owing to the certainty and predictability required for the operation of dams and reservoirs, building flexibility through a termination clause is found to be inappropriate for watercourse treaties "involv[ing] permanent structures."[2020] The CFA involves permanent structures, dams, and reservoirs, and is therefore unsuitable for such a termination clause.

The CFA would establish, if and when it enters into force, the NRBC as a joint body for the management and sustainable development of the Nile River Basin. The NRBC comprises five organs: (1) Conference of Heads of State and Government; (2) COM; (3) Technical Advisory Committee (TAC); (4) Sectoral Advisory Committees; and (5) secretariat.[2021]

While the Conference of Heads of State and Government is the supreme policymaking organ of the NRBC,[2022] the COM is the governing body of the NRBC.[2023] The COM is empowered to make binding decisions by consensus.[2024] It also has a wide range of powers, which, among others, includes overseeing the implementation of the CFA;[2025] the power to review and reverse rules, procedures, guidelines, and criteria for the implementation of the provisions of the CFA;[2026] the power to examine and decide the determination of equitable utilization in each riparian State in accordance with the factors provided

2018 *Id.*

2019 *Id.* art. 39, ¶ 2.

2020 McCaffrey, *supra* note 1920, at 160.

2021 CFA, *supra* note 132, art. 17.

2022 *Id.* art. 21.

2023 *Id.* art. 24, ¶ 1.

2024 *Id.* art. 23, ¶¶ 5–6.

2025 *Id.* art. 24, ¶¶ 3–4.

2026 *Id.* art. 24 ¶ 11.

under the CFA;[2027] and the power to resolve disputes between the Nile Basin States on the interpretation and application of the CFA.[2028]

The COM makes its decisions based on the recommendations of the TAC.[2029] Relevant to climate change, for instance, the TAC is empowered to "advise the [COM] on technical matters relating to the use, development, protection, conservation and management of the Nile River Basin and the Nile River System, including protection from drought and floods."[2030] Noticeably, the functional scope of the NRBC encompasses multiple issues ranging from promoting the rights and obligations of the Basin States to the development, protection, conservation, and management of the Nile River Basin and its waters. Certainly, such a wide range of authorities will enable the NRBC to ensure integrated river basin management addressing various aspects like environmental protection and water allocation under one institutional umbrella. This will, in turn, give the NRBC the potential to deal with changes in the river basin and address the ramifications of climate change.

Moreover, as indicated above, there is much uncertainty as to future water availability in the Nile Basin and studies are projecting both flooding and water scarcity.[2031] The CFA seems to address this very issue by empowering the TAC to propose, and submit to the COM, various strategies for adapting to the two possible ramifications of climate change: floods and drought.[2032] Also, while determining equitable utilization, it may reduce or increase allocations in response to changing levels of precipitation or flow and consider other changing conditions.

The NRBC is also empowered to control data and information management. It has the power to develop procedures through which the Nile Basin States shall regularly and readily exchange available and relevant data and information on existing measures and the condition of water resources of the Basin.[2033] The Basin States also agree to exchange information concerning planned measures through the NRBC.[2034] Concerning data management, one of its organs, the secretariat, is tasked "to compile available data and information and coordinate ... monitoring of information relating to the Nile Basin, including the

2027 *Id.* art. 24 ¶12.
2028 *Id.* art. 24 ¶13; *see also Id.* art. 33, ¶1(a).
2029 *Id.* art. 26.
2030 *Id.* art. 26 ¶ 6.
2031 *See* Shih & Stutz, *supra* note 60, at 10789.
2032 *See* CFA, *supra* note 132, art. 26, ¶ 6.
2033 *Id.* art. 7, ¶¶ 2–3.
2034 *Id.* art. 8.

environment, review … and synthesize … the information with a view to integrating it into basin-wide databases and establishing standards, and develop … mechanisms for the regular exchange of information where needed."[2035]

The existence of this formal information exchange system in the CFA will bring about more resilience and adjustment to climate disruption by enhancing reliable recordkeeping, honest disclosures and notifications, and good-faith efforts to accommodate the concerns of fellow riparian States.[2036] Certainly, the sharing of data between the Basin States will "give decision-makers the flexibility to continuously review strategies, policies as well as activities and change management if necessary."[2037] This, in turn, will boost the capacity of the NRBC to conduct adaptive water management when environmental and social changes require change.

Additionally, the Commission may serve as a mediator or conciliator to settle disputes between the Nile Basin States on the interpretation and application of the CFA.[2038] It is likely that the ramifications of climate disruption, such as floods and droughts, will exacerbate potential disputes over water resources. Hence, the existence of clear conflict resolution mechanisms in the CFA is highly commendable and important for adaptive transboundary water governance.[2039]

As indicated above, the COM also has rulemaking authority. All decisions of the COM are binding on the Basin States if they are made by consensus.[2040] Since adaptation requires prompt decisions to respond to changing conditions, the COM decision-making procedure, particularly the requirement of consensus, will pose significant challenges to successful adaptation. Although consensus does not necessarily mean unanimity, it does require at least the non-objection of the Nile Basin States. This in effect will allow any of them "to obstruct the majority of actors from passing a decision,"[2041] and thus compromise the COM's ability "to react in a timely manner in cases of urgency such as of abrupt environmental change."[2042]

2035 *Id.* art. 30, ¶ 9.

2036 *See* Goldenman, *supra* note 723, at 801.

2037 *See* Sabine Schulze & Susanne Schmeier, *Governing Environmental Change in International River Basins: The Role of River Basin Organizations*, at 7 (Paper presented in Berlin Conference on the Human Dimensions of Global Environmental Change, 2010), https://papers.ssrn.com/sol3/papers.cfm?abstract_id=1690244&download=yes.

2038 *See* CFA, *supra* note 132, art. 34, ¶ 1(a).

2039 *See* Goldenman, *supra* note 723, at 795.

2040 *See* CFA, *supra* note 132, art. 23, ¶¶ 5–6.

2041 *See* Schulze &Schmeier, *supra* note 2037, at 6.

2042 *Id.*

The composition of the COM, which comprises the minister for water affairs of each Nile Basin State,[2043] will also be a big challenge for the flexibility needed to respond to climate change. This is because the ministers are political appointees who will advance the interests of their respective state and critical decisions need to go through time-consuming diplomatic negotiations. Yet such "ordinary diplomatic mechanisms will be inefficient to deal with the volume of decisions that climate change will bring."[2044] Reaching agreements through diplomacy has proven to be challenging in the Nile Basin and controversial decisions have rarely been made in the Basin's history. This trend will significantly slow down the process of adaptation to climate change. Unless the Basin States are willing to invest the NRBC with authority to make at least provisional decisions, it is unlikely to build the flexibility needed to accommodate climate change successfully.[2045]

Membership is the other significant problem ahead for the NRBC. As indicated above, Egypt and Sudan have not ratified the CFA. When the CFA enters into force, the NRBC will succeed to all rights, obligations, and assets of the NBI upon entry into force of the CFA.[2046] If the CFA enters into force, "[w]hat will happen to the rights and obligations under the NBI of the States that are not parties (and do not plan to be parties) to the CFA?"[2047] As noted, the ramification of this article is restricted only to these states that are parties to the CFA and NBI and does have any legal effect on the downstream states that are not parties to the CFA.[2048] However, it will impede effective adaptation since the lower riparian States are not integrated into the CFA, leaving their actions as to the utilization of the Nile waters and climate change adaptation outside the NRBC. Moreover, the insufficiently developed cooperation between Egypt and upstream states, the absence of commitment concerning the exchange of hydrological data, as well as the disagreement as to the filling and operation of

2043 *See* CFA, *supra* note 132, art. 22.

2044 *See* Goldenman, *supra* note 723, at 801.

2045 This proposal could be considered as an erosion of the Basin States' sovereignty. But in its first judgment, the Permanent Court of International Justice said in the *Wimbledon* case that entering into a treaty is not giving up sovereignty, it is an expression of sovereignty. This should be treated the same way, with regard to conferring the necessary powers on the Commission. Moreover, as responding to the ramifications of climate change requires an urgent decision-making process, activating the Commission's "dormant" authority for the limited purpose of dealing with climate emergencies is imperative.

2046 *See* CFA, *supra* note 132, art. 31.

2047 Salman, *supra* note 172, 23.

2048 *See* the discussion in Section 6.2.3.1.

the GERD are likely to become significant impediments to successful integration in the river basin.

9.2.3 *The Declaration of Principles*

The DoP is the most important legal instrument regarding the use of the Blue Nile and GERD negotiations. Like the CFA, the DoP uses equitable utilization as an allocation strategy. The DoP does not allocate fixed volumetric water for any of the riparian States. Instead, it simply allows the three states to use their shared water resources in their respective territories equitably and reasonably.[2049] It also lists the factors provided in the CFA as the relevant factors to be considered in determining equitable and reasonable utilization.[2050] However, unlike the CFA, the DoP does not establish any organ responsible for assessing these factors and determining what amounts to equitable use in individual cases. Nor does it provide any guidance for the equitable allocation of "the shared water" during the filling and operation of the GERD. The DoP also neither provides an amendment-and-review process nor does it include a revocation clause and establish any institution for data exchange and information. It does, however, provide a framework for the three states to agree on rules and guidelines for the first filling and annual operation of the GERD, which the owner of the dam may adjust from time to time.[2051] It also contemplates the establishment of an appropriate coordination mechanism for data and information exchange.[2052]

Based on the framework, the three states negotiated over the filling and annual operation of the GERD for about five years but failed to strike a way-forward deal acceptable to all of them. Hence, there is currently no mechanism governing the filling and annual operation of the GERD including during times of flood and drought. The next part examines the extent to which flexibility and adaptation to climate change are contemplated in the DoP.

9.3 The GERD Negotiations: towards a Flexible Tripartite Agreement?

In Article V of the DoP, Ethiopia, Sudan and Egypt agreed to agree on rules and guidelines on the first filling and annual operation of the dam and set

2049 DoP, *supra* note 152, art. IV.
2050 *Id.*
2051 *Id.* art. V ¶ 2 (a) & (b).
2052 *Id.* art. V ¶ 3.

up an appropriate coordination mechanism. In the relevant part, the Article stipulates:

1. That the three states "[a]gree on guidelines and rules on the first filling of GERD … in parallel with the construction of GERD."[2053]
2. That the three states "[a]gree on guidelines and rules for the annual operation of GERD, which *the owner of the dam may adjust from time to time*."[2054]
3. That Ethiopia will "[i]nform the downstream countries of any unforeseen or urgent circumstances requiring adjustments in the operation of GERD."[2055]
4. That the three states "set up an appropriate coordination mechanism" through the line ministries responsible for water and coordinate on the annual operation of GERD with downstream reservoirs.[2056]

Approached from the five mechanisms of building flexibility in the watercourse treaty, the Article does not contemplate any water allocation strategy in the forthcoming GERD agreement. As noted, the DoP follows equitable and reasonable utilization as an allocation strategy. Since the forthcoming agreement is about the first filing and annual operation of the GERD, the flexible allocation strategy discussed above may seem inappropriate for the agreement. However, given the need for developing adaptive strategies to respond to the two contradictory scenarios, either increase in water availability and flooding or water scarcity and drought, it will be extremely important that the three states use a proportional filling strategy in the forthcoming instrument. This is especially imperative because the first filling of the dam might occur during a flood or drought time as the Nile watercourse is experiencing an "increase in the flow variation from year to year"—flood in one year, and drought in another.[2057]

Although the proportional filling strategy would enable the three states to respond to the two scenarios and manage both wet and dry conditions by proportionally sharing the possible water deficiencies and surplus, the three states are following the drought mitigation mechanism discussed above. Since there

2053 *Id.* art. v ¶ 2 (a).
2054 *Id*, art. v ¶ 2 (b) (emphasis added).
2055 *Id*, art. v ¶ 2 (c).
2056 *Id.* art. v ¶ 3.
2057 Kavya Balaraman, *A New Dam on the Nile Reveals Threats From Warming*, E&E NEWS (May 5, 2017), https://www.scientificamerican.com/article/a-new-dam-on-the-nile-reveals-threats-from-warming/.

is no water-sharing agreement in the Nile case, drought mitigation is one of the sticking points in the GERD negotiation between Ethiopia, Sudan, and Egypt. The recent proposal tabled by the United States and World Bank, for instance, provides three types of drought mitigation mechanisms such as drought, prolonged drought, and prolonged dry years. As discussed in 8.2, those mechanisms, which impose the burden of drought mitigation solely on Ethiopia, have the potential of recognizing colonial and immediate post-colonial Nile Waters Treaties and foreclosing Ethiopia's existing and future use of the Nile watercourse. Given that drought is a natural phenomenon that should be addressed collectively,[2058] the burden of drought mitigation is not solely Ethiopia's to bear. Egypt, Sudan, and Ethiopia should support one another in mitigating drought, without placing the entire burden on any one State. To that end, they should follow a proportional filling strategy and share the burden or the possible water deficiencies (and surplus) proportionally.

Regarding the amendment-and-review process, Principle V stipulates that the annual operation guidelines and rules of the GERD can be "adjust[ed] from time to time" by "the owner of the dam."[2059] Unlike the CFA, which contemplates the amendment of the important provisions through consensus, the DoP explicitly gives Ethiopia the discretion to amend and review the forthcoming annual operational rules and guidelines of the GERD. As indicated above, the requirement of consensus for amending and reviewing an agreement is not convenient to address the ramifications of climate change, which often require prompt responses. The DoP seems to address this problem by giving Ethiopia the sole authority to amend and review the forthcoming agreement on the GERD. This would enable the forthcoming agreement to address unforeseen circumstances, and have the resilience needed to revise filling and operational guidelines, as hydrological and existing conditions change. As such, the forthcoming agreement should have an explicit provision allowing Ethiopia to amend the operational rules of the GERD. It is also important that the agreement specify the time limit within which Ethiopia would review the operational rules.

Article V also seems to give the discretion for Ethiopia to terminate or withdraw from the forthcoming annual operational rules and guidelines of the GERD. While this is important for the flexibility needed for adapting to climate change, it must be noted that revoking a treaty through an abbreviated period of notice—say six months or a year—is inappropriate in a treaty regulating

2058 Tembata &Takeuchi, *supra* note 1694.

2059 DoP, *supra* note 152, art. V ¶ 2 (b).

a permanent structure such as the GERD.[2060] So the forthcoming agreement must reconcile the flexibility required for adapting to climate change with the certainty required for the proper management of dams by requiring a long period of notice, anywhere between 10 to 15 years, to withdraw from the treaty.

Regarding an RBO, Article V recommends the three states set up an appropriate coordination mechanism through the line ministries responsible for water, and coordinate on the annual operation of the GERD with downstream reservoirs.[2061] While the kind of institutional mechanism, ad hoc or permanent, envisaged is not clear, the article has made it abundantly clear that the three states should exchange data and information.[2062] The power of the institution contemplated in the Principle is limited only to facilitating data and information exchange, which means that the institution will not have other functions including rulemaking authority.

Generally, it can be argued that the DoP contemplates a flexible legal instrument on the first filling and annual operation of the GERD that would be adjusted by Ethiopia from time to time. However, given that the scope of the forthcoming agreement is restricted on the filling and annual operation of the GERD, the other eight Nile Basin States will not be a party to the agreement and their actions as to the utilization of the Nile waters and climate change adaptation will be outside the joint body. This will impede effective adaptation. Effective adaptation to climate change would ultimately require Ethiopia, Sudan, and Egypt (and the other Nile Basin States) to coordinate the long-term operations of their dams and reservoirs, including the GERD and AHD through the CFA and NRBC.

9.4 The Way Forward: towards a Basin-wide Climate-Proofed Treaty

As demonstrated above, the Nile Basin is highly vulnerable to the impacts of climate disruption. The ramifications of climate change, particularly the rising of average temperatures and uncertainty as to the availability of water, pose substantial challenges to the use and management of the Nile watercourse. Building flexibility and adaptability into a Nile treaty or developing a basin-wide climate-proof treaty is imperative to overcome these challenges. However, the Nile Basin does not have an all-inclusive climate-proof treaty. Even the CFA lacks the flexibility needed to adapt to climate change. For the

2060 McCaffrey, *supra* note 1920, at 159.

2061 DoP, *supra* note 152, art. V ¶ 3.

2062 *Id.*

CFA to be a climate-proof treaty, its amendment is a matter of necessity. In this part, the book proposes a revised form of the CFA as a climate-proof treaty, suggesting mechanisms for building more flexibility into the agreement to accommodate climate change.

The allocation strategy followed by the CFA and the governing rule of the Nile watercourse is equitable and reasonable utilization. There is no doubt that flexibility is implicit in this principle. However, with the anticipated impacts of climate change, what is equitable today could very well be inequitable tomorrow. The CFA attempts to address this problem by empowering the COM to determine the equitable utilization of each riparian State by considering the factors provided therein. Given the COM's composition, determining equitable utilization is likely to be highly politicized. In the COM's attempt to arrive at consensus "national interests [would] trump equitable considerations or become disguised in a party's weighting of factors."[2063] An explicit provision governing how to weigh various factors, and determining priorities among uses, therefore, is extremely necessary as it will "greatly ease the process of determining an equitable utilization of a river's waters in the event of climate-related alterations inflow."[2064]

More specifically, since the drought provision of the CFA does not address the allocation or reallocation of the water, ensuring equitable utilization during the low years would be extremely difficult. One possible way out of this problem is to provide a minimum water quantity for lower riparian States and allow the upstream states to deliver below such quantity during drought seasons. However, given Egypt's dependency on the Nile, this approach is unrealistic. Hence, including a percentage allocation strategy in the CFA and sharing the possible water deficiencies, and surplus, proportionally among the Basin States is imperative to build the flexibility needed to accommodate climate change successfully.

The CFA requires the riparian States to prevent and mitigate the problem of flooding. But, neither the DoPs nor the CFA provides guidance regarding the operation of dams at the time of flooding. Moreover, given the recent increase in the flow variation, specific provisions governing how Ethiopia will fill the GERD during times of flood and drought are necessary. Also, to address the problems of flooding and drought, it is imperative that an explicit provision, calling for joint operations of the GERD, AHD, and Sudan's reservoirs, is included in the revised form of CFA.

2063 Goldenman, *supra* note 723, at 785.
2064 *Id.*

Furthermore, as indicated above, to deal with the hardships of the projected extreme drought years, Nile Basin States will need to build more reservoirs and storage capacity. Accordingly, specific provisions specifying the places to build additional joint storage are necessary. The recommendation is to build additional dams and reservoirs in, and taking the existing ones to, the upstream states. Moreover, flexibility in the filling and operation of the dams, and adapting to climate variability would also require continuous and periodic review of the strategies in light of new knowledge and changing circumstances.

The ramifications of climate change can be expected to necessitate the reallocation of the Nile waters. Periodic review is important to ensure equitability in the face of extreme climate uncertainty. The CFA does not provide for periodic review, and thus ensuring equitable allocation of the Nile during extreme climate events is hardly possible. The revised form of the CFA needs to include explicit provisions concerning the adjustment and review of the Agreement in general, and in particular, regarding the equitable allocation of the Nile waters to adapt to the ramifications of climate change. Moreover, it should define what constitutes climate change and specify when adjustments would be necessary. The latter can be done by setting down "triggers" (magnitude of climate change) that would activate treaty adjustments or by merely providing specific periods when the agreement should be reviewed.[2065]

Apart from reviewing, parties also may withdraw from treaty obligations so as to free themselves from an inequitable allocation of the watercourse. The CFA allows any riparian State to withdraw from the treaty upon one year of notice. While this is important for treaty flexibility, it is in strict contrast with the predictability and certainty required for the effective management of the Nile watercourse, especially where infrastructure is involved. This provision defeats the purpose of the CFA as it compromises the security needed by the riparian States and the donor communities. The flexibility required for adapting to climate change and the certainty required for smooth operations of dams would be reconciled if a long period of notice, say 10–15 years, is required to withdraw from the treaty, while at the same time empowering the NRBC to review the equitable allocation of the waters periodically. For instance, the Columbia River Treaty between Canada and the United States, which is focused on hydroelectric power production and flood protection, provides for either party to give 10 years notice of termination, but only beginning some sixty years after the Treaty's entry into force.[2066]

2065 *Id.*, at 798.

2066 Columbia River Basin Treaty, *supra* note 1921, art. XIX, §2.

As per the CFA, the NRBC has rulemaking authority. The requirement of consensus along with the composition of the COM will, however, cause a big challenge for the flexibility needed to respond to climate change. One way out of this problem would be reorganizing the structure and the composition of the NRBC. Instead of the Conference Heads of States, the revised form of the CFA should empower the COM as the supreme policy-making organ of the NRBC. Moreover, it should establish a new Technical Committee with independent authority. The Technical Committee should be composed of experts, not political appointees, and the Committee should be given all powers of the COM under the current CFA. To efficiently respond to the ramifications of climate change, the Committee should be empowered to make provisional binding decisions as to the use and management of the Nile waters, including review and amendments, and its decisions should be effective immediately until and unless disapproved within six months by the COM. Furthermore, as compliance is extremely important for the effectiveness of this kind of institutional arrangement, the Basin States' political commitment to successfully follow through and implement decisions both at the national and Basin level is a matter of necessity. Also, the establishment of a compliance or implementation committee that will review the Nile Basin States' compliance with their obligations under the revised CFA and the institutional arrangement proposed in this article is critical.

Membership is the other problem related to the NRBC. Given the fact that the revised CFA would protect the interests of the lower riparian States, it is expected that they will join it and be members of the organ envisaged in this article. In the event any Basin State refuses to join such a revised CFA, its interest must be protected in that it should retain its membership in the NBI. Accordingly, the provision which requires the transfer of the rights and obligations of the NBI to the NRBC upon the entry into force of the CFA needs to be amended or should be considered as effective between States that are parties to an in-force CFA.

Conclusion

Governing the Nile Basin under climate uncertainty requires responding to two possible contradictory scenarios: increase in water availability or flooding and also water scarcity or drought, each of which requires adaptation strategies that are the opposite of those required of the other. Although flexible and resilient legal and institutional arrangements are at the heart of such adaptation strategies, the legal regime governing the Nile Basin lacks the flexibility needed to adapt to climate change. Of the three most known legal instruments, the CFA is a big step forward for governing the Nile Basin under climatic uncertainty. However, the CFA itself lacks the intrinsic capacity for addressing the ramifications of climate change.

Among others, the CFA falls short of providing a review period and guidance as to how the Nile waters should be allocated in low times or drought seasons. These omissions, along with the need for joint operation of dams in the Basin, render revision of the CFA imperative in order to build the flexibility needed for successful adaptation to climate change. Moreover, the CFA has some features of rigidity in its amendment and decision-making process. Given the hydro-political landscape of the Nile Basin, the rather unrealistic requirement of "consensus," both for altering the agreement and issuing binding decisions, will significantly undermine the CFA's ability to adapt to climate change. It will also foreclose a possible role of the NRBC in building more flexibility into the Agreement. Accordingly, the need for addressing the ramifications of climate change requires the Nile Basin States to reorganize the structure and composition of the NRBC in such a manner as will ensure an expedited decision-making process that is capable of responding to rapid development brought on by climate change. In addition, the Nile Basin States should empower a Commission, comprising of experts, with independent authority to make at least provisionally binding decisions.

For many years, the Nile Basin States have been using the existing fragmented legal regime to protect their narrow self-interests. But now, with the ever-increasing threats of climate disruption, the time seems ripe to set aside such egoistic national interests and address the ramifications of climate change by developing a basin-wide, climate-proof treaty.

CHAPTER 10

Overall Conclusion

This book has investigated the legal and hydro-political trajectories of the Nile Basin. The starting point of the study was the Axumite period when successive Ethiopian rulers started using the Nile watercourse as a bargaining chip in their dealings with Egypt over political and religious issues. Although Ethiopia's historical ability to divert the flow of the Nile was unrealistic, this book demonstrates that the myth was so convincing at the time that it made the Egyptians pursue a hydrological strategy toward controlling the source of the Nile, Ethiopia. As demonstrated in Chapter 2, Egypt invaded Ethiopia in the 19th century and swallowed successive defeats by Ethiopia.

During colonization, Great Britain controlled the White Nile all the way from its source in Lake Victoria to its mouth, the Mediterranean Sea. As the guardian of the Nile, Great Britain sought to secure plenty of water for Egypt both to provide cotton production for its textile industries and safeguard its interest in the Suez Canal. Great Britain developed the Century Storage Plan to increase water availability in Egypt. It also invested in downstream hydraulic works that established inequitable and lopsided water utilization in the basin. Further, it concluded several colonial treaties to safeguard its imperial interest in Egypt, and thereby shaped the institutional practice of the Nile Basin. In this respect, concluding the 1902 Treaty with Ethiopia, and the 1929 Treaty with Egypt, Great Britain was able to define the 'rules of the game,' prohibiting upstream states from utilizing the waters of the Nile without the consent of those downstream. After decolonization, Egypt followed in the footsteps of Great Britain and concluded the 1959 Agreement with Sudan, effectively institutionalizing the *status quo*.

During the Cold War, upstream Nile Basin States challenged the colonial legacy on two fronts. First, they attempted to develop active unilateral projects in their respective territories and change the inequitable and lopsided water utilization in the basin. Nevertheless, the Cold War geopolitics and bipolar rivalry between the U.S. and the Soviet Union helped Egypt to effectively control the Nile water by unilaterally constructing the AHD within its territory. Egypt also attempted to foreclose Ethiopia's future use by establishing facts on the ground through its controversial desert reclamation projects, i.e., the North and South Valley Development Projects.

Moreover, Egypt's military and technical support to the Eritrean and Tigrayan Liberation Fronts, the 1974 revolution, which overthrew Ethiopian

 | DOI:10.1163/9789004549869_011

Emperor Haile Selassie, the 1978 Camp David Accords and the 1979 Peace Agreement that increased Egypt's strategic importance to the United States in the latter's effort to mediate the Israeli-Arab conflict, and the protracted civil wars in Ethiopia all prevented the implementation of upstream projects along the Nile either by forcing Ethiopia to devote its limited resource towards resolving internal turmoil or blocking access to western sources of funding to implement its ambitious projects on the Blue Nile.

In the second front, the upstream states also invoked several legal grounds and argued against the validity of the colonial and immediate post-colonial agreements (existing Nile Waters Agreements). Chapters 3 and 4 of this book evaluated the merits of these arguments and submitted that several international law principles including, *inter alia*, the international law of state succession, the principle of *rebus sic stantibus*, and the principle of privity of treaty make the existing Nile Waters Agreements devoid of any legal relevance to the upstream countries. The book also indicated the absence of consistent state practice and *opinio juris* in the Nile basin transforming the water allocation provided in the 1959 Agreement into a regional custom. Furthermore, indicating the non-existence of support, in either state practice, judicial decisions, or the writings of commentators, for the doctrines of absolute territorial sovereignty and absolute territorial integrity, the book submitted that the doctrine of limited territorial sovereignty and its customary international principles such as equitable and reasonable utilization and no significant harm should be the governing rubric of the Nile watercourse.

The book also reviewed the post-Cold War bilateral, multilateral, and unilateral developments of the Nile Basin. As demonstrated in Chapter 5, Ethiopia signed the 1991 Khartoum declaration with Sudan and the 1993 Framework for Cooperation with Egypt. Those bilateral instruments not only granted the Eastern Nile Basin States (Ethiopia, Sudan, and Egypt) the right for equitable and reasonable utilization of the Nile watercourse, but also codified the very foundation of international watercourses law and recognized the equality of rights of the Nile Basin States over the Nile watercourse.

Furthermore, recognizing the benefits of cooperation for sustainable use and management of the Nile watercourse, the Nile Basin States also participated in several multilateral cooperative arrangements supported by international organizations. While upstream states attempted to use some of the arrangements, especially the NBI and the CFA, to change the existing status quo through the conclusion of an all-inclusive agreement and development of joint upstream projects, downstream states, particularly Egypt, used the same arrangements to maintain its hydro-hegemonic status quo by rejecting the CFA and refusing to cooperate on joint consumptive projects that would affect the flow of the Nile waters. In terms of basin-wide cooperation, therefore, the Nile Basin has not witnessed significant change during the post-Cold War era. The regime governing the Nile watercourse has continued to be purely competitive and unilateralism is still the *modus operandi* of the Nile Basin. While the prevalence of such competition can be attributed to several factors, the dispute over the validity of the existing Nile Waters Agreements that reached in apex during the negotiation of the CFA is the main reason for the lack of basin-wide institutional cooperation in the Nile Basin.

Indeed, the drafting and negotiation history of the CFA signifies a fundamental change in the previous treaty-making practice of the Nile Basin. Unlike existing Nile Waters Agreements and other bilateral instruments, the CFA was the first multilateral attempt for developing an all-inclusive basin-wide legal and institutional framework in the Nile Basin. The CFA, which closely follows the U.N. Watercourses Convention in terms of content, is a modern and "forward-looking agreement."[2067] It establishes NRBC for basin-wide institutional cooperation, codifies modern customary international watercourses law principles including the principle of equitable and reasonable utilization and the obligation to prevent significant harm, and gives special emphasis on the protection and conservation of the Nile Basin, and its ecosystem. Moreover, the CFA, albeit theoretically, treats the Nile Basin as a single unit for the use and development of the Nile watercourse. In this regard, it includes the principle of a community of interest between the Nile Basin States and facilitates the actual implementation of the notion of benefit sharing by empowering the Nile COM to decide upon "formulas for cost and benefit-sharing by the Nile Basin States in respect of particular joint projects within the Nile River Basin."[2068]

While the CFA represents a significant step forward toward basin-wide cooperation, the adoption of the agreement only by the upstream states, despite its unequivocal denunciation by the downstream states, and the principle of privity of treaty signify that the CFA is "intended to be a counter-hegemonic move disguised as a treaty."[2069] As a counter hydro-hegemonic tool, the CFA not only helped the upstream states to challenge the preexisting narrative and develop their own counter-narrative, it also enabled them to isolate and pressure Egypt in their attempts to change the status quo.

Given Egypt's status as the hegemon of the basin, and its geopolitical strategic advantages to the western countries, the CFA alone would not change

2067 MCCAFFREY, *supra* note 4, 319.

2068 CFA, *supra* note 132, art 24, ¶ 16.

2069 Ibrahim, *supra* note 189, at 312.

the hydro-political dynamics of the Nile Basin. For the CFA to have pragmatic effects, upstream states had to develop the ability to implement large-scale unilateral projects capable of affecting the flow of the Nile waters. Ethiopia, realizing this reality, raised enough funds by itself and embarked upon a unilateral project, the GERD. Although the GERD, which brought about *a de facto change* in the *status quo*, forced the downstream states to come to the negotiating table and sign the DoP with Ethiopia, it did not incentivize Egypt and Sudan to accept the CFA. Ethiopia may have made a strategic mistake in undertaking tripartite negotiations and adopting the DoP, instead of following a basin-wide approach that would significantly increase the GERD's counter-hegemonic value in terms of abrogating the colonial and immediate post-colonial agreements and thereby bringing *a de-jure* change in the *status quo.*

There is still an opportunity for Ethiopia to use the GERD as a bargaining chip and incentivize Egypt and Sudan to accept the CFA. At the time of writing this book, Ethiopia, Sudan, and Egypt are disputing over the filling and operation of the GERD. As demonstrated in Part 3 of this book, Sudan is aligned with Ethiopia due to the advantage it would get from the GERD. Egypt, on the other hand, is concerned about the GERD's impact on the status quo of the current Nile water allocation. It follows that Egypt will accept the CFA if it regulates the operation of the dam in a way that protects Egyptian interests. Ethiopia should therefore concede that NRBC will manage the GERD's operation. Since Egypt needs some form of input into the operation of GERD and Ethiopia rejected Egypt's demand to maintain an office at the dam site, NRBC management of GERD operations is a good compromise. As the NRBC makes binding decisions by consensus,[2070] Egypt's interests will be protected better.

Egypt may be further incentivized to accept the CFA by the need to avoid unilateral exploitation through cooperative use of the Nile River. Egypt, after all, cannot prevent Ethiopia from constructing the GERD. There is the risk that other riparian states would follow Ethiopia in unilaterally developing the Nile River. Therefore, the CFA would protect Egypt's interests by ensuring cooperative use of the Nile waters.

Upstream states are beginning to assert their right to use the Nile. Given Egypt's geographic and hydrologic vulnerability by virtue of being a downstream state, a legal regime that protects its interest is a necessity. Egypt (and Sudan) should therefore be urged to accept the CFA as it sufficiently safeguards their interests through equitable and reasonable utilization, cooperative utilization, the no significant harm principle, and binding dispute resolution

2070 CFA, *supra* note 132, art. 23, ¶ 5.

mechanisms. In addition to empowering the NRBC to make binding decisions,[2071] the CFA already contains terms that would allow parties to submit to binding arbitration and judicial settlement through the ICJ.[2072] Since these dispute resolution mechanisms have basin-wide applications, the CFA is a good compromise to resolve the three states' disagreement over the need for including compulsory dispute resolution in the GERD treaty.

If the CFA is to govern the use and allocation of the Nile watercourse, the following adjustments to the CFA would be necessary. First, the principle of water security should be excluded from the CFA altogether as the whole essence of the principle will be addressed by the principle of equitable and reasonable utilization and the no significant harm rule. Second, the Nile Basin States should build more flexibility into the CFA and thereby adapt to the ramifications of climate change. To build the flexibility needed to accommodate climate change successfully, the Nile Basin States should, *inter alia*: include a percentage allocation strategy in the CFA and share the possible water deficiencies, and surplus; include explicit provisions in the CFA concerning the adjustment and review of the Agreement in general, and, in particular, regarding the equitable allocation of the Nile waters; empower the COM as the supreme policymaking organ of the NRBC; and establish a new Technical Committee, composed of experts, not political appointees, with an authority to make provisional binding decisions as to the use and management of the Nile waters, including review and amendments, and its decisions should be effective immediately until and unless disapproved within six months by the COM.

Third, the Nile Basin States should also consider the need for certainty and predictability and amend the provision that allows any riparian State to withdraw from the CFA upon a one-year period of notice. This termination clause, albeit important for treaty flexibility, is in strict contrast with the predictability and certainty required for the effective management of the Nile watercourse, especially where infrastructure is involved. It also defeats the purpose of the CFA as it compromises the security needed by the riparian States and the donor communities. The flexibility required for adapting to climate change and the certainty required for smooth operations of dams would be reconciled if a long period of notice, say 10–15 years, is required to withdraw from the Agreement, while at the same time empowering the NRBC to review the equitable allocation of the waters periodically.

2071 *Id.* art. 23, ¶ 6.
2072 *Id.* art. 33, ¶ 1(a).

If, however, CFA is not to govern the use and allocation of the Nile watercourse, the three states should restrict the scope of the ongoing talks to the filling and annual operation of the GERD and address the inequitable ramifications of the colonial and immediate post-colonial Nile Waters Treaties. They can do so by *inter alia*, explicitly stating in the forthcoming treaty (1) that nothing in this treaty shall be construed as recognition of the existing Nile Waters Agreements; (2) that nothing in this treaty shall be construed as allocation of waters between the three countries; (3) that nothing in this treaty shall prohibit Ethiopia from equitably using the Nile waters upstream of the GERD; and (4) that this treaty concerns only the GERD and therefore nothing in the treaty shall associate the GERD with the AHD.

Furthermore, the forthcoming treaty must be flexible and adaptive to address the uncertainty associated with climate change and population growth in the Nile Basin. The forthcoming treaty should adopt a proportional filling strategy and include an amendment provision, a review procedure, and a termination or revocation clause as contemplated by the DoP. These provisions will give the three states the resilience needed to revise filling and operational guidelines as hydrological and existing conditions change. Concerning the termination clause, it must be noted that revoking a treaty through an abbreviated period of notice—say six months or a year—is inappropriate in a treaty regulating a permanent structure such as the GERD. So, the treaty must reconcile the flexibility required for adapting to climate change with the certainty required for the proper management of dams by requiring a long period of notice, anywhere between ten to fifteen years, to withdraw from the treaty.

Unless the three states follow either of the two options, Ethiopia will have no option but to continue filling the GERD without an agreement with Sudan and Egypt. Ethiopia will continue the unilateral filling not only because it is permissible under international law, but also because the downstream states' past behavior suggests they cannot be relied upon to come to an agreement and will instead drag out the negotiation in perpetuity. The initial filling of the GERD will not have a significant effect on the interest of Sudan and Egypt as there should be sufficient water in the system to compensate for the amount Ethiopia plans to hold back.[2073] Moreover, as the GERD is a non-consumptive hydroelectric project, it will not have any adverse impact after the filling is completed. Therefore, regardless of whether the current negotiations become successful or not, the real dispute between the three states will boil down to

2073 *See* Solomon & Elshinnawi, *supra* note 1652 and Kaba & Moges, *supra* note 1931.

whether and to what extent Ethiopia can use the Nile waters for consumptive purposes, including irrigation.

As the Nile watercourse is already appropriated by Egypt and Sudan, Ethiopia's future utilization will cause harm, perhaps significant, to current and existing uses of the two downstream states. Under international law, such use will be considered a violation of the no-significant-harm principle only when it exceeds Ethiopia's equitable entitlement. To the extent the harms inflicted upon Sudan and Egypt are within the limit of Ethiopia's exercise of equitable utilization, such exercise should not be regarded as infringing the rights of the downstream states. Therefore, Ethiopia should go ahead and start equitably utilizing the Nile watercourse for consumptive purposes, including irrigation.

Ultimately, as the demand for water increases due to population growth, economic development, and urbanization, and climate change threatens the supply, the three states, and the other Nile Basin States will have to stop approaching the Nile watercourse as a zero-sum game and cooperate for their mutual benefit. They will need to think beyond past inequities and capitalize on the "community of interest" created by the Nile watercourse. The Nile Basin States should also stop using the existing fragmented legal regime to protect their narrow self-interests and develop a basin-wide legal and institutional cooperative framework capable of accommodating the ramifications of climate change.

Bibliography

Selected Cases and Legal Documents

Aegean Sea Continental Shelf (Gr. v. Turkey), Judgment, 1978 I.C.J. (December 19).

Agreement between the Governments of the Republic of Kazakhstan, the Kyrgyz Republic, and the Republic of Uzbekistan on the Use of Water and Energy Resources of the Syr Darya Basin, Mar. 17, 1997.

Agreement between the United Kingdom, France, and Italy, Respecting Abyssinia, Dec. 13, 1906. Accessed from Am. J. Int'l L., Apr. 1907, Vol. 1, No. 2, Supplement: Official Documents (1907).

Agreement for the Full Utilization of the Nile Waters, Egypt-Sudan, Nov. 8, 1959, 453 U.N.T.S.51 (1959).

Agreement on Declaration of Principles on the Grand Ethiopian Renaissance Dam Project, Mar. 23, 2015, INT'L WATER L. PROJECT, https://www.internationalwaterlaw.org/documents/regionaldocs/Final_Nile_Agreement_23_March_2015.pdf.

Agreement on the Cooperation for the Sustainable Development of the Mekong River Basin, Apr. 5, 1995, 34 I.L.M. 864.

Agreement on the Cooperation for the Sustainable Development of the Mekong River Basin, art. 20, Apr. 5, 1995, 2069 U.N.T.S. 1–35844.

Agreement on the Nile River Basin Cooperative Framework art 42, *opened for signature* May 14, 2010, INT'L WATER L. PROJECT, http://internationalwaterlaw.org/documents/regionaldocs/Nile_River_Basin_Cooperative_Framework_2010.pdf.

Case Relating to the Territorial Jurisdiction of the International Commission of the River Oder, Judgment, 1929 PICJ (Sept. 10).

Colorado v. New Mexico (Vermejo I), 459 U.S. 176, 184 (1982), *remanded to Spec. Master*, (Vermejo II), 467 U.S. 310 (1984).

Connecticut v. Massachusetts, 282 U.S. 660 (1931).

CONSTITUTION OF THE ARAB REPUBLIC OF EGYPT, Jan. 18, 2014, *as amended* Apr. 23, 2019.

CONSTITUTION OF THE FEDERAL DEMOCRATIC REPUBLIC OF ETHIOPIA, Aug. 21, 1995.

Convention on the Law of the Non-Navigational Uses of International Watercourses, 21 May 1997, entered into force 17 August 2014, G.A. Res. 51/229 (July 8, 1997).

Decision Regarding Delimitation of the Border Between Eritrea & Ethiopia, XXV R.I.A.A. 83 (Eri.-Eth. Boundary Comm'n 2002).

Dispute Regarding Navigational and Related Rights (Costa Rica v. Nicar.), Judgment, 2009 I.C.J. Rep. 213 (July 13).

DRAFT CONSTITUTIONAL CHARTER FOR THE 2019 TRANSITIONAL PERIOD, Aug. 17, 2019.

Exchange of Notes Constituting an Agreement Regarding Co-Operation in Meteorological, and Hydrological Surveys in Certain Areas of the Nile Basin, Egypt-U.K., Jan. 19–Mar. 20, 1950, 226 U.N.T.S. 287.

Exchange of Notes Regarding the Use of the Waters of the River Nile for Irrigation Purposes, Egypt-U.K., May 7, 1929, [1929] U.K.T.S. 17.

Fisheries Jurisdiction (Federal Republic of Germany v. Iceland), Judgment, 1973, I.C.J. (Feb. 2).

Gabčíkovo-Nagymaros Project (Hung./Slovk.), Judgment, 1997 I.C.J. (Sept. 25).

Grisbadarna (Nor. v. Swed.) XI R.I.A.A. 155 (Perm. Ct. Arb. 1909).

ICJ, Territorial Dispute (Libyan Arab Jamahiriya v. Chad), Judgment, ICJ Reports 1994.

Indus Waters Kishenganga Arbitration (Pak. v. India), (2013), https://pcacases.com/web/sendAttach/48.

Island of Palmas (United States v. Neth.), II R.I.A.A. (Perm. Ct. Arb. 1928).

Kansas v. Colorado, 206 U.S. 46, 104 (1907).

Lake Lanoux (Fr. v. Spain), 12 R.I.A.A. 281 (Arb. Trib. 1957).

Legal Status of Eastern Greenland, 1933 P.C.I.J. (Seri. A/B) No. 53.

Maritime Delimitation and Territorial Questions Between Qatar and Bahrain (Qatar v. Bahr.), Judgment, 1994 I.C.J. 112, (July 1).

Mekelle Memorandum of Understanding between the NCP and the SPLM on Post-referendum Issues and Arrangements (2010).

Military and Paramilitary Activities in and Against Nicaragua (Nicar. v. United States), Judgment, 1986 I.C.J. 14 Minquiers and Ecrehos, 1953 I.C.J. Rep.

Nebraska v. Wyoming, 325 U.S. 589, 618 (1945).

New Jersey v. New York, 283 U.S. 336 (1931).

No. 1211—British and Italian Interests in Abyssinia, 50 L.N.T.S. 281 (1925).

North Sea Continental Shelf Cases (Ger. v. Den.; Ger. v. Neth.), Advisory Opinions, 1969 I.C.J. (Feb. 20).

Protocol for the Demarcation of Their Respective Spheres of Influence in East Africa From Ras Kasar to the Blue Nile, Gr. Brit.-Italy, Apr. 15, 1891.

Pulp Mills on the River Uruguay (Arg. v. Uru.), Judgment, 2010 I.C.J. 14 (Apr. 20).

RESTATEMENT OF THE LAW (THIRD) THE FOREIGN RELATIONS LAW OF THE UNITED STATES § 101 (1987).

Rights of Nationals of United States of America in Morocco (Fr. v. United States), Judgment, 1952 I.C.J. Rep. 193 (Aug. 27).

S.S. Lotus (Fr. v. Turk.), Judgment, 1927 P.C.I.J. (ser. A) No. 10 (Sept. 7).

Southern Sudan Referendum (2009).

Southern Sudan Referendum Act (2009).

Summary and Outcomes of the 4th Tripartite Meeting of Ministers of Foreign and Water Affairs on the Grand Ethiopian Renaissance Dam Project, Dec. 29, 2015, INT'L WATER L. PROJECT.

Territorial Jurisdiction of Int'l Comm'n of River Oder (U.K. v. Pol.), Judgment 1929 P.C.I.J.

The Comprehensive Peace Agreement Between the Government of the Republic of Sudan and the Sudan People's Liberation Movement/the Sudan People's Liberation Army, Chapeau, Sud.-SPLM/SPLA (Jan. 7, 2005).

The Corfu Channel Case (United Kingdom v. Albania), Judgment. 1949 ICJ (Apr. 9); Trail Smelter Arbitration (U.S. v. Can.), RIAA III 1949 (April 16).

Trail Smelter Case, 3 Rep. Int'l Arb. Awards 1905 (1950).

Treaties Relative to the Frontiers Between the Soudan, Ethiopia, and Eritrea, Eth.-U.K., May 15, 1902, [1902] U.K.T.S. 16.

Treaty Between His Majesty's Government of Nepal and the Government of India Concerning the Integrated Development of the Mahakali River Including the Sarada Barrage, Tanakpur Barrage, and Pancheshwar Project, India-Nepal, Feb. 12, 1996.

Treaty Relating to Cooperative Development of the Water Resources of the Columbia River Basin, Can.-U.S., Jan. 17, 1961, 15 U.S.T. 1555.

Treaty with Great Britain Relating to Boundary Waters, and Questions Arising Between the United States and Canada, Jan. 11, 1909, 36 Stat. 2448, T.S. No. 548.

U.N. Charter.

United Nations Security Council, Statement by the Pres. of the Security Council, U.N. Doc. S/PRST/2021/18 (Sep. 11, 2021).

Utilization of the Waters of the Colorado and Tijuana Rivers and of the Rio Grande, Mex.-U.S., 1944, 59 Stat. 1219.

Vienna Convention on Succession of States in Respect of State Property, Archives and Debts, Apr. 8, 1983, U.N. Doc. A/CONF.117/14 (1983).

Vienna Convention on the Law of Treaties, May 23, 1969, 1155 U.N.T.S. 331.

Vienna Convention on the Succession of States in Respect of Treaties, Aug. 23, 1978, 1946 U.N.T.S. 3.

Wyoming v. Colorado, 259 U.S. 419 (1922), modified, 260 U.S. 1 (1922), vacated, 353 U.S. 953 (1957).

References

1974 Y.B. INT'L L. COMM'N, vol. 2 (1974).

1983 Y.B. INT'L L. COMM'N, vol. 2 (1997).

1994 Y.B. INT'L L. COMM'N, vol. 2 (1997).

2.1. *Billion People Lack Safe Drinking Water at Home, More Than Twice as Many Lack Safe Sanitation*, WHO/UNICEF (July 2017) https://www.who.int/news/item/12-07-2017-2-1-billion-people-lack-safe-drinking-water-at-home-more-than-twice-as-many-lack-safe-sanitation.

A. Dan Tarlock, *Four Challenges for International Water Law*, 23 TUL. ENV'T L.J. (2009).

A. Dan Tarlock, *How Well Can International Water Allocation Regimes Adapt to Global Climate Change?*, 15 J. LAND USE & ENV'T L. 423, (2000).

Aaron Schwabach, *The United Nations Convention on the Law of Non-Navigational Uses of International Watercourses, Customary International Law, and the Interests of Developing Upper Riparians*, 33 TEX. INT'L L.J. (1998).

Abadir M. Ibrahim, Note, *The Nile Basin Cooperative Framework Agreement: the Beginning of the End of Egyptian Hydro-Political Hegemony*, 18 MO. ENV'T. L. & POL'Y REV. (2011).

Abdel Fattah Metawie, *History of Co-operation in the Nile Basin*, 20 (1) WATER RESOUR. DEV. 54 (2004).

Abeyou Worqlul, *Assessment of Surface Water Irrigation Potential in the Ethiopian Highlands: The Lake Tana Basin*, 129 CATENA 76 (2015).

Addis Getachew, *Ethiopia, Sudan and Egypt Reach Understanding on Nile Dam*, ANADOLU AGENCY (June 14, 2020), https://www.aa.com.tr/en/africa/ethiopia-sudan-egypt-reach-understanding-on-nile-dam/1876641.

Addisu Lashitew & Haim Gebeyehu, *Could the Nile Dispute Be an Opportunity to Boost Freshwater Technology?*, BROOKINGS INST. (June 18, 2020), https://www.brookings.edu/opinions/could-the-nile-dispute-be-an-opportunity-to-boost-freshwater-technology/.

Addisu Lashitew, *Why Ethiopia, Egypt, and Sudan Should Ditch a Rushed Washington-Brokered Nile Treaty*, BROOKINGS INST. (Feb. 18, 2020), https://www.brookings.edu/blog/africa-in-focus/2020/02/18/why-ethiopia-egypt-and-sudan-should-ditch-a-rushed-washington-brokered-nile-treaty/.

Aidan Lewis, *Ethiopia Says Egypt Trying to Maintain "Colonial Era" Grip Over Nile*, REUTERS (Oct. 8, 2019), https://www.reuters.com/article/us-ethiopia-dam/ethiopia-says-egypt-trying-to-maintain-colonial-era-grip-over-nile-idUSKBN1WN1OG.

ALAN MOOREHEAD, THE BLUE NILE (1962).

Albert H. Putney, *Termination of Unequal Treaties*, 21 AM. SOC'Y INT'L L. PROC. (1927).

Alice Shih & Trevor Stutz, *Sink or Swim: Abrogating the Nile Treaties While Upholding the Rule of Law*, 43 ENVT'L L. REP. 10786 (2013).

ALISTAIR RIEU-CLARKE ET AL., UN WATERCOURSES CONVENTION: USER'S GUIDE (2012).

ALISTAIR RIEU-CLARKE ET AL., UNITED NATIONS TRANSBOUNDARY WATER GOVERNANCE AND CLIMATE CHANGE ADAPTATION: INTERNATIONAL LAW, POLICY GUIDELINES, AND BEST PRACTICE APPLICATION (2015).

Al-Masry Al-Youm, *Sudan-Mediated* GERD *Talks Stalling Due to Ethiopia's Intransigence: Egypt,* EGYPT INDEPENDENT (June 13, 2020), https://egyptindependent.com/sudan-mediated-gerd-talks-stalling-due-to-ethiopias-intransigence-egypt/.

Alula Alemayehu, *Ethiopia and the Nile: Sacrificial Lamb for the "Deal of the Century"?,* ADDIS STANDARD (Feb. 3, 2020), http://addisstandard.com/opinion-ethiopia-and-the-nile-sacrificial-lamb-for-the-deal-of-the-century/.

Amal Othman et al., *El-Salam Canal Is a Potential Project Reusing the Nile Delta Drainage Water for Sinai Desert Agriculture: Microbial and Chemical Water Quality,* 3(2) J. ADV. RES. (2012).

Ana Elisa Cascão & Alan Nicol, *Changing Cooperation Dynamics in the Nile Basin and the Role of the* GERD, THE GRAND ETHIOPIAN RENAISSANCE DAM AND THE NILE BASIN: IMPLICATIONS FOR TRANSBOUNDARY WATER COOPERATION 113 (Zeray Yihdego et al. eds. 2018).

Ana Elisa Cascão & Alan Nicol, GERD: *New Norms of Cooperation in the Nile Basin?,* 41 WATER INT'L 550, (2016).

Ana Elisa Cascao, *Changing Power Relations in the Nile River Basin: Unilateralism vs. Cooperation?,* 2 WATER ALTERNATIVES (2009).

Andrew Carlson, *Who Owns the Nile? Egypt, Sudan, and Ethiopia's History-Changing Dam,* 6(6) ORIGINS: CURRENT EVENTS IN HISTORICAL PERSPECTIVE (2013), https://origins.osu.edu/article/who-owns-nile-egypt-sudan-and-ethiopia-s-history-changing-dam.

Andrew King & Paul Block, *An Assessment of Reservoir Filling Policies for the Grand Ethiopian Renaissance Dam,* 5 J. WATER & CLIMATE CHANGE 233 (2014).

ANOUSHIRA EHTESHAMI & EMMA MURPHY, THE INTERNATIONAL POLITICS OF THE RED SEA (2011).

ANTHONY AUST, MODERN TREATY LAW AND PRACTICE (2007).

ANTON EARLE ET AL., TRANSBOUNDARY WATER MANAGEMENT AND THE CLIMATE CHANGE DEBATE (2015).

AFRICA WATCH: A DIVISION OF HUMAN RIGHTS WATCH, EVIL DAYS: 30 YEARS OF WAR AND FAMINE IN ETHIOPIA (1991).

Arnold N. Pronto, *Understanding the Hard/Soft Distinction in International Law,* 48 VAND. J. TRANSNAT'L L. (2015).

ARTHUR OKOTH-OWIRO, THE NILE TREATY: STATE SUCCESSION AND INTERNATIONAL TREATY COMMITMENTS: A CASE STUDY OF THE NILE WATER TREATIES (2004).

Asegdew Mulat & Semu Moges, *Assessment of the Impact of the Grand Ethiopian Renaissance Dam on the Performance of the High Aswan Dam,* 6 J. WATER RES. & PROT. (2014).

ASHOK SWAIN, MANAGING WATER CONFLICT: ASIA, AFRICA, AND THE MIDDLE EAST (2004).

Ashok Swain, *The Nile River Basin Initiative: Too Many Cooks, Too Little Broth,* 22 SAIS REV. 293, (2002).

BAHRU ZEWDE, A HISTORY OF MODERN ETHIOPIA: 1885–1991 (2001).

Bairu Tafla, *The Father of Rivers: The Nile in Ethiopian Literature,* in THE NILE: HISTORIES, CULTURES, MYTHS (Haggai Erlich & Israel Gershoni eds., 2000).

Barbara Crossette, *Severe Water Crisis Ahead for Poorest Nations in Next 2 Decades,* N.Y. TIMES (Aug. 10, 1995), https://www.nytimes.com/1995/08/10/world/severe-water-crisis-ahead-for-poorest-nations-in-next-2-decades.html.

Barry Malone, *Ethiopian PM Warns Egypt of Nile War,* REUTERS (Nov. 23, 2010), https://www.reuters.com/article/us-ethiopia-egypt-meles/ethiopian-pm-warns-egypt-off-nile-war-idUSTRE6AM5V820101123.

Bart Hilhorst, *Water Management in the Nile Basin: A Fragmented but Effective Cooperative Regime* 1 (Georgetown University Ctr. for Int'l & Reg'l Stud. Occasional Paper No. 17, 2016), https://ssrn.com/abstract=3447020.

Benita van Eyssen, *Trouble as Trump Dives into the Dispute Over Ethiopia's Nile Mega-Dam,* DEUTSCHE WELLE (Mar. 6, 2020), https://www.dw.com/en/trouble-as-trump-dives-into-the-dispute-over-ethiopias-nile-mega-dam/a-52663126.

BONAYA ADHI GODANA, AFRICA'S SHARED WATER RESOURCES: LEGAL AND INSTITUTIONAL ASPECTS OF THE NILE, NIGER AND SENEGAL RIVER SYSTEMS (1985).

BRAHMA CHELLANEY, WATER, PEACE, AND WAR: CONFRONTING THE GLOBAL WATER CRISIS XI (2013).

Bronwyn Bruton & Ann Fitz-Gerald, *To End Ethiopia's War, Biden Needs to Correct Course,* FP, (Dec. 28, 2021), https://foreignpolicy.com/2021/12/28/ethiopia-tigray-abiy-tplf-war-biden-needs-to-correct-course/.

C. D' O. Farran, *The Nile Waters Question in International Law,* 41 SUDAN NOTES AND RECORDS (1960).

C. O. Okidi, *History of the Nile Basin and Lake Victoria Basins Through Treaties,* in THE NILE: SHARING A SCARCE RESOURCE (Paul P. Howell & J. Antonio Allan eds., 1994).

C. O. Okidi, *Review of Treaties on Consumptive Utilization of Waters of Lake Victoria and Nile Drainage System,* 22 NAT. RESOURCES J. (1982).

Charles Bourne, *The Primacy of the Principle of Equitable Utilization in the 1997 Watercourses Convention,* 1997 CAN. Y.B. INT'L L. (1997).

CHARLES L. KATZ, *Another Cup at the Nile's Crowded Spigot: South Sudan and Its Nile Water Rights,* 44 GEO. J. INT'L L (2013).

Christina Carroll, *Past and Future Legal Framework of the Nile River Basin,* 12 GEO. INT'L ENVT'L. L. REV. (1999).

CHRISTINA LEB, COOPERATION IN THE LAW OF TRANSBOUNDARY WATER RESOURCES (2013).

Christina Leb, *Implementation of the general duty to cooperate*, *in* RESEARCH HANDBOOK ON INTERNATIONAL WATER LAW (Stephen C. McCaffrey et al. eds., 2019).

CHRISTOPHER SNEDDON, CONCRETE REVOLUTION: LARGE DAMS, COLD WAR GEOPOLITICS, AND THE U.S. BUREAU OF RECLAMATION (2015).

Clark Mindock, *'Where's My Favorite Dictator?' Trump Comment on Egyptian President 'Met with Stunned Silence,' Report Says*, INDEPENDENT (Sept. 13, 2019), https://www.independent.co.uk/news/world/americas/us-politics/trump-egypt-president-sisi-favorite-dictator-meeting-a9104951.html.

Cooperation Is Imperative for an Agreement on Filling, and Operation of GERD, WALTA (Sept. 23, 2019), https://waltainfo.com/51842/.

Czeslaw Jesman, *Egyptian Invasion of Ethiopia*, 58 AFRICAN AFFAIRS, 77 (1959).

D.P. O Connell, *Reflections on the State Succession Convention*, 39 ZEITSCHRIFT FÜR AUSLÄNDISCHES ÖFFENTLICHES RECHT UND VÖLKERRECHT 725, 738 (1979), http://www.zaoerv.de/39_1979/39_1979_4_a_725_739.pdf.

D.P. O CONNELL, STATE SUCCESSION IN MUNICIPAL LAW AND INTERNATIONAL LAW 14–15 (1967).

D.P. O CONNELL, THE LAW OF STATE SUCCESSION (1956).

Dale Whittington, John Waterbury & Marc Jeuland, *The Grand Renaissance Dam and Prospects for Cooperation on the Eastern Nile*, 16 WATER POL'Y (2014).

Daniel Kendie, *Egypt and the Hydro-Politics of the Blue Nile River*, 6 NORTHEAST AFR. STUD. (1999).

DANTE A CAPONERA, PRINCIPLES OF WATER LAW AND ADMINISTRATION: NATIONAL AND INTERNATIONAL (2007).

David B. Ottaway, *Sadat Assassinated at Military Show*, WASH. POST (Oct. 7, 1981), https://www.washingtonpost.com/archive/politics/1981/10/07/sadat-assassinated-at-military-show/604a2b32-408f-4e99-972d-ad6379c880c2/.

DAVID BEDERMAN, INTERNATIONAL LAW FRAMEWORKS (2010).

David Grey & Claudia Sadoff, *Beyond the River: The Benefits of Cooperation on International Rivers*, 4 WATER POLICY (2002).

David L. Chandle, *Solar-Powered System Offers a Route to Inexpensive Desalination*, MIT, Feb. 14. 2022. https://news.mit.edu/2022/solar-desalination-system-inexpensive-0214.

David Malakoff, *Let's Call It "Climate Disruption," White House Science Adviser Suggests (Again)*, SCIENCEINSIDER (May 2, 2014), https://www.science.org/content/article/lets-call-it-climate-disruption-white-house-science-adviser-suggests-again

Declan Conway, *From Headwater Tributaries to International River: Observing and Adapting to Climate Variability and Change in the Nile Basin*, 15 GLOBAL ENVT'L CHANGE (2005).

Declan Walsh & Somini Sengupta, *For Thousands of Years, Egypt Controlled the Nile. A New Dam Threatens That*, N.Y. TIMES (Feb. 9, 2020), https://www.nytimes.com/interactive/2020/02/09/world/africa/nile-river-dam.html.

Dereje Zeleke Mekonnen, *Between the Scylla of Water Security and Charybdis of Benefit Sharing: The Nile Basin Cooperative Framework Agreement—Failed or Just Teetering on the Brink?*, 3 GOETTINGEN J. INT'L L. (2011).

Dereje Zeleke Mekonnen, *From Tenuous Legal Arguments to Securitization and Benefit Sharing: Hegemonic Obstinacy—The Stumbling Block against Resolution of the Nile Waters Question*, 4 MIZAN L. REV. (2010).

Dereje Zeleke Mekonnen, *The Nile Basin Cooperative Framework Agreement Negotiations and the Adoption of a 'Water Security' Paradigm: Flight into Obscurity or a Logical Cul-de-Sac?*, 21 EUR. J. INT'L L. (2010).

Dereje Zeleke Mekonnen, *Declaration of Principles on the Grand Ethiopian Renaissance Dam: Some Issues of Concern*, 11 MIZAN L. REV. (2017).

Dexter Filkins, *A Bigger Problem than ISIS?*, THE NEW YORKER (Jan. 2, 2017), https://www.newyorker.com/magazine/2017/01/02/a-bigger-problem-than-isis.

DIANA KARYABWITE, WATER SHARING IN THE NILE RIVER VALLEY 48 (1998), https://hcil.umd.edu/media/simple/nilereport.pdf.

Dispute over Water in the Nile Basin, CLIMATE DIPLOMACY, https://climate-diplomacy.org/case-studies/dispute-over-water-nile-basin.

DONAL WORSTER, RIVERS OF EMPIRE: WATER, ARIDITY AND THE GROWTH OF THE AMERICAN WEST (1985).

East Africa seeks more Nile water from Egypt, BBC NEWS (May 14, 2010), http://news.bbc.co.uk/2/hi/8682387.stm.

Egypt and Ethiopia Argue Over Dam Project, DEUTSCHE WELLE (June 14, 2013), https://www.dw.com/en/egypt-and-ethiopia-argue-over-dam-project/a-16880722.

Egypt ready to resume talks on Ethiopia's Renaissance Dam, EGYPT TODAY (May 22, 2020), https://www.egypttoday.com/Article/1/87964/Egypt-ready-to-resume-talks-on-Ethiopia-s-Renaissance-dam.

Egypt Says 'Deadlock' in Nile Dam Talks with Ethiopia, AL JAZEERA (Oct. 6, 2019), https://www.aljazeera.com/news/2019/10/egypt-deadlock-nile-dam-talks-ethiopia-191006070043565.html.

Egypt Seeks International Support to End GERD Talks Deadlock, DAILY NEWS EGYPT (Oct. 1, 2019), https://www.dailynewssegypt.com/2019/10/01/egypt-seeks-international-support-to-end-gerd-talks-deadlock/.

Egypt Vows to Use 'All Means' to Defend Nile Interests After Ethiopia Skips U.S. Talks, HAARETZ (Feb. 29, 2020), https://www.haaretz.com/middle-east-news/egypt/egypt-vows-to-use-all-means-to-defend-nile-interests-after-ethiopia-skips-talks-1.8600505.

Egypt Warns Ethiopia Over Nile Dam, AL JAZEERA (June 11, 2013), https://www.aljazeera.com/news/2013/6/11/egypt-warns-ethiopia-over-nile-dam.

Egypt Warns of 'Existential Threat' From Ethiopia Dam, AL JAZEERA, (June 30, 2020), https://www.aljazeera.com/economy/2020/6/30/egypt-warns-of-existential-threat-from-ethiopia-dam.

Egypt, Ethiopia 'Agree' to Resume Talks on Massive Nile Dam, AL JAZEERA (Oct. 24, 2019), https://www.aljazeera.com/news/2019/10/egypt-ethiopia-agree-resume-talks-massive-nile-dam-191024140822273.html.

Egypt, The World Factbook, CENTRAL INTELLIGENCE AGENCY (2021), https://www.cia.gov/the-world factbook/countries/egypt/#economy.

Elias Meseret, *Ethiopia Refuses World Bank Arbitration over Nile River Dam*, ASSOCIATED PRESS (Jan. 21, 2018), https://apnews.com/42dba7a51c0b4d0c90829d0c2c4e596b.

Elias Meseret, *Ethiopia Won't Be Forced by the US on Dam, Foreign Minister Says*, ASSOCIATED PRESS (Mar. 13, 2020), https://apnews.com/39183ccfeed1c0796ad38796d459ff3b.

Elias N. Stebek, *Eastern Nile at Crossroads: Preservation and Utilization Concerns in Focus*, 1 MIZAN L. REV. (2007).

Elizabeth J. Kistin & Peter J. Ashton, *Adapting to Change on Transboundary Rivers: An Analysis of Treaty Flexibility on the Orange-Senqu River Basin*, 24 INT'L J. WATER RES. DEV. (2008).

Emery Van Donzel, *The Legend of Blue Nile in Europe*, in THE NILE: HISTORIES, CULTURES, MYTHS 79, 99 (Haggai Erlich & Israel Gershoni eds., 2000).

Emmanuel Kasimbazi, *Developing a Cooperative Framework Agreement for a Transboundary River: Lessons from a Comparative Analysis of the Mekong and Nile Rivers Basins*, 8 US-CHINA L. REV. 748 (2011).

Essayas Kaba & Semu Moges, *Why Is Now the Right Time to Start Filling the Grand Ethiopian Renaissance Dam (GERD)?*, E.-AFRICANIST (June 1, 2020), https://eastafricanist.com/2020/06/01/why-is-now-the-right-time-to-start-the-filling-of-the-grand-ethiopian-renaissance-dam-gerd/.

Ethiopia Accuses Egypt, N.Y. TIMES (Feb. 17, 1978), https://www.nytimes.com/1978/02/17/archives/ethiopia-accuses-egypt-little-more-than-gesture.html.

Ethiopia inaugurates Africa's first ever biggest power dam, SUDAN TRIBUNE (Nov. 15, 2009), https://sudantribune.com/spip.php?article33117.

Ethiopia Rejects Egypt Proposal on the Nile Dam, AL JAZEERA (Sept. 19, 2019), https://www.aljazeera.com/news/2019/9/19/ethiopia-rejects-egypt-proposal-on-nile-dam-operation.

Ethiopia Rejects Egypt's Proposal on the Filling, Operation of Grand Dam, ADDIS STANDARD (Sept. 18, 2019), https://addisstandard.com/news-ethiopia-outright-rejects-egypts-proposal-on-the-fillingoperation-of-grand-dam/.

Ethiopia: US Being 'Undiplomatic' Over Nile Dam Project, AL JAZEERA (Mar. 4, 2020), https://www.aljazeera.com/news/2020/03/ethiopia-undiplomatic-nile-dam-project-200304060039736.

F. BALTHAZAR TELLEZ, THE TRAVELS OF THE JESUITS IN ETHIOPIA, BOOK I, (1710).

F. Earnest Work, *Italo-Ethiopian Relations*, 20 J. NEGRO HIST. (1935).

Fadwa Taha, *The History of the Nile Waters in the Sudan*, in THE RIVER NILE IN THE POST-COLONIAL AGE: CONFLICT AND COOPERATION AMONG THE NILE BASIN COUNTRIES, (Terje Tvedt ed., 2010).

Farouk Chothia, *Tigray Crisis: How the West Has Fallen Out with Ethiopia's PM*, BBC NEWS (Oct. 25, 2021), https://www.bbc.com/news/world-africa-58967302.

Fasika Tadesse, *Egypt Proposes to Exclude Sudan from Dam Talks*, ADDIS FORTUNE (Dec. 30, 2017), https://addisfortune.net/articles/egypt-proposes-to-exclude-sudan-from-dam-talks/.

Fasika Tadesse, *Egypt Proposes to Exclude Sudan from Dam Talks*, ADDIS FORTUNE (Dec. 30, 2017), https://addisfortune.net/articles/egypt-proposes-to-exclude-sudan-from-dam-talks/.

Fasil Amdetsion, *Scrutinizing the Scorpion Problematique: Arguments in Favor of the Continued Relevance of International Law and a Multidisciplinary Approach to Resolving the Nile Dispute*, 44 TEX. INT'L L.J. 1, 3 (2008).

Fasil Amdetsion, *Time to Think about Ethiopia's Post-GERD Nile Policy*, COOPERATIVE WATERS MAGAZINE, https://www.africanidea.org/Nile_Coop_Waters.pdf.

Frank Zoellner et al., *Implementation of the Dam Complex at Upper Atbara, Sudan, in Challenging Site Conditions* (2017), https://www.lahmeyer.de/fileadmin/alle/publikationen/HYDRO_2017__Paper_54_Zoellner_Scheid_Mukthar.pdf.

Fred Oluoch, *Joint Team to Study Likely Effects of Ethiopian Dam on Nile Waters*, EAST AFRICAN (May 19, 2018), https://www.theeastafrican.co.ke/news/africa/Joint-study-effects-Ethiopian-dam-on-Nile/4552902-4570178-05ju7nz/index.html.

Gabriel Eckstein, *Water Scarcity, Conflict, and Security in a Climate Change World: Challenges and Opportunities for International Law and Policy*, 27 WIS. INT'L L.J. (2009).

GEBRE TSADIK DEGEFU, THE NILE: HISTORICAL, LEGAL AND DEVELOPMENTAL PERSPECTIVES (2013).

GEORGE ANNESLEY, VOYAGES AND TRAVELS IN INDIA, CEYLON, THE RED SEA, ABYSSINIA, AND EGYPT (VOL. 3, 1809).

Gerhard Hafner & Gregor Novak, *State Succession in Respect of Treaties*, in THE OXFORD GUIDE TO TREATIES (Duncan B. Hollis, 2nd ed., 2020).

GETACHEW METAFERIA, ETHIOPIA AND THE UNITED STATES: HISTORY, DIPLOMACY, AND ANALYSIS (2009).

Getahun Legesse, *GERD Construction Reaches Over 80 Percent Completion*, THE ETHIOPIAN HERALD (May 21, 2021), https://www.press.et/english/?p=35147.

Glen Hearns & Richard Kyle Paisley, *Lawyers Write Treaties, Engineers Build Dikes, Gods of Weather Ignore Both: Making Transboundary Waters Agreements Relevant, Flexible, and Resilient in a Time of Global Climate Change*, 6 GOLDEN GATE U. ENV'T L.J. (2013).

GLOBAL HUNGER INDEX 2020: ETHIOPIA, (2020), https://www.globalhungerindex.org/pdf/en/2020/Ethiopia.pdf.

Gretta Goldenman, *Adapting to Climate Change: A Study of International Rivers and Their Legal Arrangements*, 17 ECOLOGY L.Q. (1990).

HAGGAI ERLICH, THE CROSS AND THE RIVER: ETHIOPIA, EGYPT, AND THE NILE (2002).

Haggai Erlich & Israel Gershoni, *Introduction, in* THE NILE: HISTORIES, CULTURES, MYTHS (Haggai Erlich & Israel Gershoni eds., 2000).

HAILE SELLASSIE I, THE AUTOBIOGRAPHY OF EMPEROR HAILE SELLASSIE: MY LIFE AND ETHIOPIA'S PROGRESS, VOL. 1, (Edward Ullendorff, trans., Ann., 1999).

Hala Nasr & Andreas Neef, *Ethiopia's Challenge to Egyptian Hegemony in the Nile River Basin: The Case of the Grand Ethiopian Renaissance Dam*, 21 J. GEOPOLITICS (2016).

Hanne Knaepen & Bruce Byiers, *Understanding The Nile Basin Initiative Balancing Historical Rights, National Needs and Regional Interests*, EUROPEAN CENTER FOR DEVELOPMENT 7 (2017), https://ecdpm.org/wp-content/uploads/NBI-Background-Paper-PEDRO-Political-Economy-Dynamics-Regional-Organisations-Africa-ECDPM-2017.pdf.

Heather Cooley & Peter H. Gleick, *Climate-Proofing Transboundary Water Agreements*, 56 HYDROLOGICAL SCI. J. 711, 715 (2011).

Heather Cooley et al., *Understanding and Reducing the Risks of Climate Change for Transboundary Waters*, PAC. INST. (2009).

Hend Kortam, *Egypt Meets with Nile Basin Countries*, DAILY NEWS EGYPT (June 28, 2012), https://dailynewsegypt.com/2012/06/28/egypt-meets-nile-basin-countries/.

HERBERT SMITH, THE ECONOMIC USES OF INTERNATIONAL RIVERS (1931).

Hesham Hamid, *A Study on the Concept of International River in International Water Law and Its Applications in Nile Basin Agreements*, 11 (39) AFRICAN PERSPECTIVES (2013).

HIOB LUDOLF, A NEW HISTORY OF ETHIOPIA (1684).

Hosam Elemam, *Egypt and Collective Action Mechanisms in the Nile Basin, in* THE RIVER NILE IN THE POST-COLONIAL AGE: CONFLICT AND COOPERATION AMONG THE NILE BASIN COUNTRIES, (Terje Tvedt ed., 2010).

How Climate Change Might Affect the Nile, ECONOMIST, Aug. 3, 2017, https://www.economist.com/middle-east-and-africa/2017/08/03/how-climate-change-might-affect-the-nile.

HUGO GROTIUS, THE RIGHTS OF WAR AND PEACE 684 (Richard Tuck ed., 2005) (1625).

I.H. Abdalla, *The 1959 Nile Waters Agreement in Sudanese-Egyptian Relations*, 7 MIDDLE E. STUD. 331–32 (1971).

IAN BROWNLIE, PRINCIPLES OF PUBLIC INTERNATIONAL LAW 650 (7th ed. 2008).

IBRAHIM KAYA, EQUITABLE UTILIZATION: THE LAW OF NON-NAVIGATIONAL USES OF INTERNATIONAL WATERCOURSES 82 (2003).

Int'l Crisis Grp., *Bridging the Gap in the Nile Waters Dispute*, Africa Report No. 271, (2019).

Int'l L. Ass'n, Comm. on Formation of Customary (Gen.) Int'l L., *Statement of Principles Applicable to the Formation of General Customary International* Law, art 15 (2000).

Int'l L. Comm., United Nations Conference On Succession Of States In Respect Of Treaties: Official Records, (1977).

Int'l L. Comm'n Rep. on the Work of Its Fifty-Third Session, U.N. Doc. A/56/10, (2001).

INT'L PANEL OF EXPERTS [IPOE] ON THE GRAND ETHIOPIAN RENAISSANCE DAM PROJECT [GERDP], FINAL REPORT, (2013).

International Law Association, The Berlin Rules on Water Resources, Berlin Conference: Water Resources Law (2004).

Interview by Egyptian TV with Meles Zenawi, the Prime Minister of Ethiopia (July 2010), https://www.youtube.com/watch?v=2zzXLFKU0HM.

Int'l Law Ass'n 52nd Conference, Helsinki, Fin., Aug. 1966, The Helsinki Rules (1962).

Itay Fischhendler, *Legal and Institutional Adaptation to Climate Uncertainty: A Study of International Rivers*, 6 WATER POL'Y (2004).

J. A.A. Jones, *Threats to Global Water Security: Population Growth, Terrorism, Climate Change, or Commercialization*, in THREATS TO GLOBAL WATER SECURITY (Jones et al. eds., 2009).

J. P. TAYLOR, THE ORIGINS OF THE SECOND WORLD WAR (1961).

J.N. Blashford-Snell, *Conquest of the Blue Nile*, 136 GEOGRAPHICAL J. (1970).

Jacob Wirtschafter, *U.S.-Led Talks Lead to Breakthrough as African Rivals Inch Closer to War Over Nile*, WASH. TIMES (Nov. 11, 2019), https://www.washingtontimes.com/news/2019/nov/11/steven-mnuchin-mediated-talks-see-grand-ethiopian-/.

JAMES BRUCE, TRAVELS TO DISCOVER THE SOURCE OF THE NILE (VOL. 2, 1790).

JAMES BRUCE, TRAVELS TO DISCOVER THE SOURCE OF THE NILE, (VOL. 1, 1790).

James McCann, *Ethiopia, Britain, and Negotiations for the Lake Tana Dam*, 14 INT'L J. AFR. HIST. STUD. (1981).

JAMES R. CRAWFORD, BROWNLIES PRINCIPLES OF PUBLIC INTERNATIONAL LAW (8th ed. 2012).

Jeffrey Azarva *Conflict on the Nile: International Watercourse Law and the Elusive Effort to Create a Transboundary Water Regime in the Nile Basin*, 25 TEMP. INT'L & COMP. L.J. (2011).

JEROME DELLI PRISCOLI & AARON T. WOLF, MANAGING AND TRANSFORMING WATER CONFLICTS (2009).

Jessica Barnes, *The Future of the Nile: Climate Change, Land Use, Infrastructure Management, and Treaty Negotiations in a Transboundary River Basin*, 8 WIRES CLIM. CHANGE 2 (2017).

John Anthony Allan, *Nile Basin Asymmetries: A Closed Fresh Water Resource, Soil Water Potential, The Political Economy And Nile Transboundary Hydropolitics*, *in* THE NILE: ORIGIN, ENVIRONMENTS, LIMNOLOGY AND HUMAN USE, 749 (Henri J. Dumont, ed. 2019)

John Gallagher & Ronald Robinson, *The Imperialism of Free Trade*, 6 ECON. HIST. 1, 15 (1953).

John Holdern, *Global Climate Disruption: What Do We Know About It and What Should We Do?* (November 6, 2007), https://www.belfercenter.org/sites/default/files/legacy/files/uploads/2007_11-6_Forum_(NXPowerLite).pdf.

JOHN TRIMINGHAM, ISLAM IN ETHIOPIA (1952).

JOHN WATERBURY, HYDROPOLITICS OF THE NILE VALLEY (1979).

John Waterbury, *Is the Status Quo in the Nile Basin Viable?*, 4 BROWN J. OF WORLD AFF. (1997).

John Waterbury, *Legal and Institutional Arrangements for Managing Water Resources in the Nile Basin*, 3(2) INT. J. WATER RESOUR. DEV. (1987).

JOHN WATERBURY, NILE BASIN: NATIONAL DETERMINANTS OF COLLECTIVE ACTION 61 (2002).

Joseph Dellapenna & Joyeeta Gupta, *The Evolution of Global Water Law*, in THE EVOLUTION OF THE LAW AND POLITICS OF WATER 1 (Joseph Dellapenna & Joyeeta Gupta eds., 2009).

Joseph Dellapenna, *International Water Law in a Climate of Disruption*, 17 MICH. ST. J. INT'L L. (2008).

Joseph Dellapenna, *The Customary International Law of Transboundary Fresh Waters*, 1 INT'L J. GLOB. ENV'T ISSUES (2001).

Joseph Dellapenna, *The Nile as a Legal and Political Structure*, *in* THE SCARCITY OF WATER (Edward H.P. Brans et al. eds., 1997).

Joseph W. Dellapenna, *Adapting the Law of Water Management to Global Climate Change and Other Hydro-Political Stresses*, 35 J. AM. WATER ASS'N (1999).

Joseph W. Dellapenna, *International Law's Lessons for the Law of the Lakes*, 40 U. MICH. J.L. REFORM 747, (2007).

Joseph W. Dellapenna, *The Work of International Legal Expert Bodies*, in RESEARCH HANDBOOK ON INTERNATIONAL WATER LAW (Stephen C. McCaffrey et al. eds., 2019).

Jutta Brunne & Stephen Toope, *The Changing Nile Basin Regime: Does Law Matter?*, 43 HARV. INT'L L.J. (2002).

Kaori Tembata & Kenji Takeuchi, *Collective Action and Cooperation in Drought Response*, GLOB. WATER F. (June 18, 2018), https://globalwaterforum.org/2018/06/18/collective-action-and-cooperation-in-drought-response/.

Kate Ng, *Sudan Boycotts Talks Over Controversial Mega-Dam in Ethiopia*, INDEP. (Nov. 24, 2020), https://www.independent.co.uk/news/world/africa/sudan-ethiopia-boycott-talks-mega-dam-b1759672.

Kathryn Reid, *1980s Ethiopia Famine: Facts, FAQs, and How to Help*, WORLD VISION (June 8, 2018), https://www.worldvision.org/disaster-relief-news-stories/1980s-ethiopia-famine-facts.

Kavya Balaraman, *A New Dam on the Nile Reveals Threats from Warming*, E&E NEWS (May 5, 2017), https://www.scientificamerican.com/article/a-new-dam-on-the-nile-reveals-threats-from-warming/.

Kayla Ritter, *Egypt's Nile River Pressured by Population Growth, Rising Sea Level*, CIRCLE OF BLUE (March 21, 2018), https://www.circleofblue.org/2018/africa/egypts-nile-river-pressured-by-population-growth-rising-sea-level/.

Kevin G. Wheeler, *Cooperative Filling Approaches for the Grand Ethiopian Renaissance Dam*, 41 WATER INT'L (2016).

Kifle Worku, *"Egypt Is Sailing Against the Wind, Squandering Its Opportunity," Diplomat Zerihun Abebe*, ETHIOPIAN PRESS AGENCY (Mar. 26, 2020), https://www.press.et/english/?p=20054#.

Kirsten Schmalenbach, *International Organizations or Institutions, Succession*, in MAX PLANCK ENCYCLOPEDIA OF PUBLIC INTERNATIONAL LAW, (Rüdiger Wolfrum ed., 2017).

Kristin Fedeler, *Hydraulic Missions, Ruins and Revival: Politics of Space in the Tana-Beles Basin from 1985 to Today*, PAPER PRESENTED IN INTERNATIONAL CONFERENCE OF ETHIOPIAN STUDIES (2018).

Kristin Wiebe, *The Nile River: Potential for Conflict and Cooperation in the Face of Water Degradation*, 41 NAT. RESOURCES. J. (2001).

LAURENCE DE CHAZOURNES, FRESH WATER IN INTERNATIONAL LAW 70 (2013).

Law of Treaties, 1966 U.N.Y.B. Int'l L. Comm'n 1, (1966).

Letter dated 12 April 2021 from the Chargé d'affaires a.i. of the Permanent Mission of the Sudan to the United Nations addressed to the President of the Security Council, U.N. Doc. S/2021/350, 16 (April 12, 2021).

Letter dated 14 May 2020 from the Permanent Rep. of Eth. to the United Nations addressed to the President of the Security Council, U.N. Doc. S/2020/409 (May 14, 2020).

Letter dated 2 June 2020 from the Permanent Rep. of the Sudan to the United Nations addressed to the President of the Security Council, U.N. Doc. S/2020/480 (June 2, 2020).

Letter dated 22 June 2020 from the Permanent Rep. of Eth. to the United Nations addressed to the President of the Security Council, U.N. Doc. S/2020/567 (June 22, 2020).

LORD MCNAIR, THE LAW OF TREATIES (1961).

Lucius Caflisch, *Unequal Treaties*, 35 GERMAN Y.B. INT'L L. (1992).

LUNA LEOPOLD & KENNETH DAVIS, WATER (1966).

LUNG-CHU CHEN, AN INTRODUCTION TO CONTEMPORARY INTERNATIONAL LAW: A POLICY-ORIENTED PERSPECTIVE 488 (2015)

Madeleine De Simone, *On the Forecast: Easing Tension Over Hydraulic Power Along the Mekong* (Project on Int'l Peace & Sec., Student Policy Brief No. 5.2, 2013).

Mahemud Eshtu Tekuya, *The Egyptian Hydro-Hegemony in the Nile Basin: The Quest for Changing the Status Quo*, 26 J. WATER L. (2018).

Mahmoud Aziz, *Ethiopia Demands 'Fair and Serious' Talks to Return to Negotiating Table Over Disputed Nile Dam: Ethiopian FM*, AHRAMONLINE (Mar. 17, 2020), http://english.ahram.org.eg/News/365426.aspx.

MALCOLM N. SHAW, INTERNATIONAL LAW, (6TH ed.. 2008).

Manuel Schiffler, *Conflicts Over the Nile or Conflicts on the Nile?*, in WATER IN THE MIDDLE EAST: POTENTIAL FOR CONFLICTS AND PROSPECT FOR COOPERATION (Waltina Scheumann & Manuel Schiffler eds., 1998).

Margaret J. Vick, *The Law of International Waters: Reasonable Utilization*, 12 CHI.-KENT J. INT''L & COMP. L. (2012).

Marian Nash (Leich), *Contemporary Practice of the United States Relating to International Law*, 88 AM. J. INT'L L. (1994).

MARK E. VILLIGER, COMMENTARY ON THE 1969 VIENNA CONVENTION ON THE LAW OF TREATIES (2009).

Mark Zeitoun & Jeroen Warner, *Hydro-Hegemony: A Framework for Analysis of Transboundary Water Conflicts*, 8 WATER POLICY (2006).

Mary Morton, *Ancient Water Underlies Arid Egypt: A Hidden Trove of Groundwater Is Left Over from the Last Ice Age*, EOS (June 18, 2019), https://eos.org/articles/ancient-water-underlies-arid-egypt.

Mathias Devi Nielsen, *The Waters of the Nile: Ethiopia Challenging Regional Hydro-Hegemony*, UNIV. OF COPENHAGEN, 41 (2015) (unpublished MA Thesis).

Matthew C.R. Craven, *The Problem of State Succession and the Identity of States under International Law*, 9 EURO. J. INT'L L. (1998).

Matthew G. Maloney, *Succession of States in Respect of Treaties: The Vienna Convention of 1978*, 19 VA. J. INT'L L. (1979).

Meeting on the Grand Ethiopian Renaissance Dam and Regional Relations, SECURITY COUNCIL REPORT (July 7, 2021), https://www.securitycouncilreport.org/whatsinblue/2021/07/meeting-on-the-grand-ethiopian-renaissance-dam-and-regional-relations-2.php.

Mehari Taddele Maru, *The Trump Trap*, ADDIS STANDARD, (Mar. 11, 2020), http://addisstandard.com/commentary-the-trump-trap/.

Menna Alaa El-Din, *'No One Can Take a Drop of Water from Egypt,' Sisi Says on GERD Dispute*, AHRAMONLINE (Mar. 30, 2021), https://english.ahram.org.eg/NewsContent/1/64/408124/Egypt/Politics-/No-one-can-take-a-drop-of-water-from-Egypt,-Sisi-s.aspx.

Meron Teferi Taye et al., T869 *Climate Change: From Science to Lived Experience. The Lived Experience of Climate Change: Water Case Study on the Nile and Rhine River Basins*, UK. OPEN UNIV (2012).

MESFIN WOLDEMARIAM, AN INTRODUCTION TO GEOGRAPHY OF ETHIOPIA (1972).

Michelle Nichols, *U.N. Security Council Backs AU Bid to Broker Ethiopia Dam Deal*, REUTERS (July 9, 2021), https://www.reuters.com/world/un-security-council-backs-au-bid-broker-ethiopia-dam-deal-2021-07-08/.

Minister Romero to U.S. Secretary of State Richard Olney, 21 Oct. 1895, U.S. Appendix, p. 202.

Mohamed Elmenshawy, *Egypt's War on Terror: ISIS, President Sisi, and the U.S.-led Coalition*, Middle East Inst. (Nov. 6, 2014), https://www.mei.edu/publications/egypts-war-terror-isis-president-sisi-and-us-led-coalition.

Mohamed Helal, *Inheriting International Rivers: State Succession to Territorial Obligations; South Sudan, and the 1959 Nile Waters Agreement*, 27 EMORY INT'L L. REV. (2013).

Mohamed Salman Tayie, *The Grand Ethiopian Renaissance Dam and the Ethiopian Challenge of Hydropolitcal Hegemony on the Nile Basin*, in GRAND ETHIOPIAN RENAISSANCE DAM VERSUS ASWAN HIGH DAM 485, 501 (Abdelazim M. Negm & Sommer Abdel-Fattah eds., 2019).

MOHAMED-HATEM EL-ATAWY, NILOPOLITICS: A HYDROLOGICAL REGIME, 1870–1990 (1996).

Mohammed Abdo, *The Nile Question: The Accords on the Water of the Nile and their Implication on Cooperative Schemes in the Basin*, 9 PERCEPTIONS J. INT'L AFF. 51 (2004).

Mohammed S. Helal, *Sharing Blue Gold: The 1997 UN Convention on the Law of the Non-Navigational Uses of International Watercourses Ten Years On*, 18 COLO. J. INT'L ENVT'L. L. & POL'Y (2007).

Mosaad Shetewy, *Legal Commitments Regulating the Establishment of Water Projects on International Rivers Application Study over the Nile Basin*, 11 (39) AFRICAN PERSPECTIVES 35 (2013).

Mu Xuequan, *Egypt Seeks World Bank as Technical Mediator in Ethiopia's Dam Issue*, XINHUA (Dec. 26, 2017), http://www.xinhuanet.com/english/2017-12/27/c_136853702.htm.

MWANGI KIMENYI & JOHN MBAKU, GOVERNING THE NILE RIVER BASIN: THE SEARCH FOR A NEW LEGAL REGIME (2015).

Nurit Kliot et al, *Institutions for Management of Transboundary Water Resources: Their Nature, Characteristics and Shortcomings*, 3 WATER POL'Y, 229–255 (2001).

Nada Zaki, *60 Million More Egyptians by 2050: UN Report*, AHRAMONLINE (July 3, 2019), https://english.ahram.org.eg/NewsContent/1/64/337249/Egypt/Politics-/-million-more-Egyptians-by--UN-report.aspx.

NASA, *The Mars Exploration Program*, https://mars.nasa.gov/programmissions/overview/.

NBI website https://www.nilebasin.org/.

NBI website, http://entro.nilebasin.org/index.php/our-projects.

NBI website, http://nelsap.nilebasin.org/index.php/en/.

NBI website, http://nilesec.nilebasin.org/index.php/what-we-do/basin-cooperation-program.

NBI website, https://nilebasin.org/index.php/nbi/governance.

NBI website, https://nilebasin.org/index.php/nbi/who-we-are.

NBI website, https://nilebasin.org/index.php/south-sudan.

Nicholas Hildyard, *Neutral? Against What? Bystanders and Human Rights Abuses: The Case of Merowe Dam*, THE SUDAN STUDIES SOCIETY OF THE UNITED KINGDOM, 2 (2008).

Nigel Arnell et al., *Hydrology and Water Resources*, in CLIMATE CHANGE 2001: IMPACTS, ADAPTATION, AND VULNERABILITY (James J. McCarthy et al. eds., Cambridge University Press 2001).

Nigel W. Arnell et al., *Freshwater Resources*, in CLIMATE CHANGE 2014: IMPACTS, ADAPTATION, AND VULNERABILITY. PART A: GLOBAL SECTORAL ASPECTS. CONTRIBUTION OF WORKING GROUP II TO THE FIFTH ASSESSMENT REPORT OF THE INTERGOVERNMENTAL PANEL ON CLIMATE CHANGE (C.B. Field et al. eds., Cambridge University Press 2014).

Nigel W. Arnell, *Climate Change and Global Water Resources: SRES Emissions and Socio-Economic Scenarios*, 14 GLOBAL ENV'T CHANGE (2004).

Nile Basin Initiative, *The NBI Secretariat Strategic Plan 2012–2016*, 3, https://nilesec.nilebasin.org/images/docs/Nile_sec_strategicplan_final.pdf.

NILE BASIN INITIATIVE, THE WATER RESOURCES OF THE NILE BASIN, *in* STATE OF THE RIVER NILE BASIN 27–28 (2012), http://nileis.nilebasin.org/system/files/Nile%20SoB%20Report%20Chpater%202%20-%20Water%20resources.pdf.

Nile Dam Talks: Unlocking a Dangerous Stalemate, INT'L CRISIS GROUP (Mar. 16, 2020).

NILE RIVER BASIN DRAFT ACTION PLAN, TECCONILE, 4 (1994), https://www.ircwash.org/sites/default/files/824-AAF94-14893.pdf.

Noha Donia & Abdelazim Negm, *Impacts of Filling Scenarios of GERD on Egypt's Water Resources and Their Impact on Agriculture Sector*, in CONVENTIONAL WATER RESOURCE AND AGRICULTURE IN EGYPT 391 (Abdelazim Negm ed., 2018).

NURIT KLIOT, WATER RESOURCES AND CONFLICT IN THE MIDDLE EAST (1994).

PATRICIA BIRNIE ET AL., INTERNATIONAL LAW AND THE ENVIRONMENT (3rd ed. 2009).

Patricia Zengerle, *U.S. to Cut $100 Million in Aid to Ethiopia Over Dam Dispute*, REUTERS (Sept. 15, 2020), https://www.reuters.com/article/usa-ethiopia-int/u-s-to-cut-100-million-in-aid-to-ethiopia-over-dam-dispute-idUSKBN25T2ZD.

Patsy Widakuswara, *No Deal from US-Brokered Nile Dam Talks*, VOICE OF AMERICA (Feb. 29, 2020), https://www.voanews.com/africa/no-deal-us-brokered-nile-dam-talks.

PEACE TO PROSPERITY: THE ECONOMIC PLAN: PROGRAMS AND PROJECTS 49 (2020), https://www.whitehouse.gov/wp-content/uploads/2019/06/MEP_programs andprojects.pdf.

Permanent Rep. of Egypt to the U.N., Letter dated 1 May 2020 from the Permanent Rep. of Egypt to the United Nations addressed to the President of the Security Council, U.N. Doc. S/2020/355 (May 1, 2020).

Permanent Rep. of Egypt to the U.N., Letter dated 11 June 2021 from the Permanent Rep. of Egypt to the United Nations addressed to the President of the Security Council, U.N. Doc. S/2021/565, (June 11, 2021).

Permanent Rep. of Egypt to the U.N., Letter dated 15 April 2021 from the Permanent Rep. of Egypt to the United Nations addressed to the President of the Security Council, U.N. Doc. A/75/858 (April 15, 2021).

Permanent Rep. of Egypt to the U.N., Letter dated 19 June 2020 from the Permanent Rep. of Egypt to the United Nations addressed to the President of the Security Council, U.N. Doc. S/2020/566 (June 19, 2020).

Permanent Rep. of Ethiopia to the U.N., Letter dated 16 April 2021 from the Permanent Rep. of Ethiopia to the United Nations addressed to the President of the Security Council, U.N. Doc. S/2021/376 (April 16, 2021).

Permanent Rep. of Ethiopia to the U.N., Letter dated 23 June 2021 from the Permanent Rep. of Ethiopia to the United Nations addressed to the President of the Security Council, U.N. Doc. S/2021/600, (June 23, 2021).

Permanent Rep. of Ethiopia to the U.N., Letter dated 28 June 2021 from the Permanent Rep. of Ethiopia to the United Nations addressed to the President of the Security Council, U.N. Doc. S/2021/613 (June 28, 2021).

PETER GLEICK & GILBERT WHITE, WATER IN CRISIS: A GUIDE TO THE WORLD'S FRESH WATER RESOURCES (1993).

PHILIPPE SANDS, PRINCIPLES OF INTERNATIONAL ENVIRONMENTAL LAW (1995).

Piotr Klimaszyk & Ryszard Gołdyn, *Water Quality of Freshwater Ecosystems in a Temperate Climate*, 12(9) WATER (2020).

Pnina Lahav, *The Suez Crisis of 1956 and Its Aftermath: A Comparative Study of Constitutions, Use of Force, Diplomacy, and International Relations*, 95 B.U. L. REV. (2015).

POPULATION REFERENCE BUREAU, 2020 WORLD POPULATION DATA SHEET (2020), https://www.prb.org/wp-content/uploads/2020/07/letter-booklet-2020-world-population.pdf.

Power Generation Capacity of the GERD Slashed to 5150 MW—Ethiopian Minister, EZEGA NEWS (Oct. 17, 2019) https://www.ezega.com/News/NewsDetails/7331/Power-Generation-Capacity-of-GERD-Slashed-to-5150MW-Ethiopian-Minister.

Press Release, Embassy of Eth., London, Statement of Ethiopia on the Negotiations on the Grand Ethiopian Renaissance Dam (Feb. 29, 2020), https://www.ethioembassy.org.uk/statement-of-ethiopia-on-the-negotiations-on-the-grand-ethiopian-renaissance-dam/.

Press Release, Embassy of Eth., Washington DC, Ethiopia invites Sudan and Egypt to nominate dam operators for data exchange before the filling of GERD in upcoming rainy seasons (April 10, 2021), https://ethiopianembassy.org/ethiopia-invites-sudan-and-egypt-to-nominate-dam-operators-for-data-exchange-before-the-filling-of-gerd-in-upcoming-rainy-seasons-april-10-2021/.

Press Release, Embassy of Eth., Washington DC, Press Release on the Trilateral Negotiations on the GERD, Kinshasa, Democratic Republic of the Congo (April 6, 2021), https://ethiopianembassy.org/press-release-on-the-trilateral-negotiations-on-the-gerd-kinshasa-democratic-republic-of-the-congo-april-6-2021/.

Press Release, Sec'y-Gen., Secretary-General Encouraged by Good Progress in Trilateral Talks to Reach Agreement over Grand Ethiopian Renaissance Dam, U.N. Press Release SG/SM/20088 (May 19, 2020) [Press Release of the Sec'y-Gen]. https://www.un.org/press/en/2020/sgsm20088.doc.htm.

Press Release, Steven T. Mnuchin, U.S. Sec'y of the Treasury, Statement on the Grand Ethiopian Renaissance Dam (Feb. 28, 2020), https://home.treasury.gov/news/secretary-statements-remarks/statement-by-the-secretary-of-the-treasury-on-the-grand-ethiopian-renaissance-dam.

Press Release, U.S. Dep't of the Treasury, Joint Statement of Egypt, Ethiopia, Sudan, the United States, and the World Bank (Nov. 6, 2019), https://home.treasury.gov/.

Press Release, U.S. Dep't of the Treasury, Joint Statement of Egypt, Ethiopia, Sudan, the United States and the World Bank, (Jan. 15, 2020), https://home.treasury.gov/news/press-releases/sm875.

Press Release, U.S. Dep't of the Treasury, Joint Statement of Egypt, Ethiopia, Sudan, the United States, and the World Bank (Feb. 13, 2020), https://home.treasury.gov/news/press-releases/sm907.

Press Release, United Nations Secretary-General, *Secretary-General, in Message to Inaugural Asia-Pacific Water Summit, Warns That Scarcity Threatens Socio-Economic Gains, Could Fuel Conflicts* (December 3, 2007). Available https://www.un.org/press/en/2007/sgsm11311.doc.htm (Accessed on Nov. 2, 2021).

Press Release, United Nations Secretary-General, *World's Water Problems Can Be Catalyst for Cooperation*, (Feb 26, 2002), https://www.un.org/press/en/2002/sgsm8139.doc.htm.

Problems of State Succession in Africa: Statement of the Prime Minister of Tanganyika, 11 INT'L & COMP. L.Q. (1962).

R. K. Batstone, *The Utilisation of the Nile Waters*, 8 INT'L & COMP. L.Q. (1959).

R.A.C. Parker, *Great Britain, France and the Ethiopian Crisis 1935–1936*, 89 ENG. HIST. REV. (1974).

Rawia Tawfik, *Revisiting Hydro-Hegemony from a Benefit-Sharing Perspective: The Case of the Grand Ethiopian Renaissance Dam* (German Dev. Inst. Discussion Paper 5/2015, 2015).

Rawia Tawfik, *The Grand Ethiopian Renaissance Dam: A Benefit-Sharing Project in the Eastern Nile?*, 41 WATER INT'L. (2016).

Reinhard Voss et al., *Enhanced Resolution Modelling Study on Anthropogenic Climate Change: Changes in Extremes of the Hydrological Cycle*, 22 INT'L J. CLIMATOLOGY (2002).

Report of the Commission to the General Assembly on the Work of Its Forty-Sixth Session, [1994] 2 Y.B. INT'L L. COMM'N, 96–97, U.N. Doc. A/CN.4/SER.A/1994/Add.l (Part 2).

Report of the Commission to the General Assembly, 1974 U.N.Y.B. Int'l L. Comm'n 157 (1974).

Report of the Hydrometeorological Survey of the Catchments of Lakes Victoria, Kyoga, and Albert (Burundi, Egypt, Kenya, Rwanda, Sudan, United Republic of Tanzania, and Uganda) 1 METEOROLOGY AND HYDROLOGY OF THE BASIN PART 1, (1974) (UNDP and WMO, RAL 66–025 Tech. Report No. 1).

REPORT OF THE UNITED NATIONS CONFERENCE ON ENVIRONMENT AND DEVELOPMENT, UN Doc. A/CONF.15/26/Rev.1 (Vol. I), (1993).

Richard Kyle Paisley, *Why the 11 Countries That Rely on the Nile Need to Reach a River Deal Soon*, CONVERSATION (Aug. 27, 2017) https://theconversation.com/why-the-11-countries-that-rely-on-the-nile-need-to-reach-a-river-deal-soon-75868.

Richard Pankhurst, *Ethiopia's Alleged Control of the Nile,* in THE NILE: HISTORIES, CULTURES, MYTHS 79, 99 (Haggai Erlich & Israel Gershoni eds., 2000).

RICHARD PANKHURST, THE ETHIOPIANS, A HISTORY (1998).

Riek Machar Teny-Dhurgon, *South Sudan: A History of Political Domination—A Case of Self-Determination,* UNIV. PEN. AF. STUD. C., Nov. 19, 1995, https://www.africa.upenn.edu/Hornet/sd_machar.html.

River Nile Dam: Reservoir Filling Up, Ethiopia Confirms, BBC NEWS (July 15, 2020), https://www.bbc.com/news/world-africa-53416277.

ROBERT COLLINS, THE WATERS OF THE NILE: HYDROPOLITICS AND THE JONGLEI CANAL, 1900–1988 (1990).

Robert Engelman, When It Comes to Water Scarcity, Population Growth Tops Climate Change, WILSON CENTER, (August 1, 2016), https://www.newsecuritybeat.org/2016/08/water-scarcity-population-growth-trumps-climate-change/.

ROBERT G. BERSCHINSKI, AFRICOM'S DILEMMA: THE "GLOBAL WAR ON TERRORISM," "CAPACITY BUILDING," HUMANITARIANISM, AND THE FUTURE OF U.S. SECURITY POLICY IN AFRICA 42 (2007).

ROBERT G. WIRSING ET AL., INTERNATIONAL CONFLICT OVER WATER RESOURCES IN HIMALAYAN ASIA (2013).

Robert O. Collins, *History, Hydropolitics and the Nile: Myth Or Reality?,* in THE NILE: SHARING A SCARCE RESOURCE (Paul P. Howell & J. Antonio Allan eds., 1994).

ROBERT O. COLLINS, THE NILE (2002).

Robert Rangeley et al., *International River Basin Organizations in Sub-Saharan Africa,* 7–8 (World Bank, Technical Paper No. 250, 1994).

Roger Thurow, *Ravaged by Famine: Ethiopia Finally Gets Help From the Nile,* WALL ST. J. (Nov. 26, 2003), https://www.wsj.com/articles/SB106979937643978400.

Sabine Schulze & Susanne Schmeier, *Governing Environmental Change in International River Basins: The Role of River Basin Organizations,* at 7 (Paper presented in Berlin Conference on the Human Dimensions of Global Environmental Change, 2010). https://papers.ssrn.com/sol3/papers.cfm?abstract_id=1690244&download=yes.

Sabine Schulze & Susanne Schmeier, *Governing Environmental Change in International River Basins: The Role of River Basin Organizations,* 10 INT'L J. RIVER BASIN MGMT. 229 (2012).

Salem Solomon & Mohamed Elshinnawi, *Ethiopia Condemns Egyptian Proposal for Nile Water Usage,* VOICE OF AMERICA (Oct. 10, 2019), https://www.voanews.com/africa/ethiopia-condemns-egyptian-proposal-nile-water-usage.

Salman M. A. Salman, *Downstream Riparians Can Also Harm Upstream Riparians: The Concept of Foreclosure of Future Uses,* 35 WATER INT'L (2010).

Salman M. A. Salman, *Equitable and Reasonable Utilization and the Obligation against Causing Significant Harm— Are They Reconcilable?,* 115 AJIL UNBOUND (2021).

Salman M. A. Salman, *Good Offices and Mediation and International Water Disputes*, in RESOLUTION OF INTERNATIONAL WATER DISPUTES 155, (International Bureau of the Permanent Court of Arbitration ed., 2002).

Salman M. A. Salman, *Grand Ethiopian Renaissance Dam: Challenges and Opportunities*, CIP REPORT (Oct. 2011).

Salman M. A. Salman, *South Sudan Road to Independence: Broken Promises and Lost Opportunities*, 26 PAC. MCGEORGE GLOBAL BUS. & DEV. L.J. (2013).

Salman M. A. Salman, *The Declaration of Principles on the Grand Ethiopian Renaissance Dam: An Analytical Overview, in* ETHIOPIAN YEARBOOK OF INTERNATIONAL LAW 203, (Zeray Yihdego et al. eds., 2017).

Salman M. A. Salman, *The GERD and the Revival of the Egyptian-Sudanese Dispute Over the Nile Waters*, in ETHIOPIAN YEARBOOK OF INTERNATIONAL LAW 79, 90 (Zeray Yihdego et al. eds., 2018).

Salman M. A. Salman, *The Grand Ethiopian Renaissance Dam: The Road to the Declaration of Principles and the Khartoum Document*, 42 WATER INT'L (2016).

Salman M. A. Salman, *The New State of South Sudan and the Hydro-Politics of the Nile Basin*, 36 WATER INT'L (2011).

Salman M. A. Salman, *The Nile Basin Cooperative Framework Agreement: A Peacefully Unfolding African Spring?*, 38 WATER INT'L (2012).

Salman M. A. Salman, *The Nile Basin Cooperative Framework Agreement: Disentangling the Gordian Knot*, THE GRAND ETHIOPIAN RENAISSANCE DAM AND THE NILE BASIN: IMPLICATIONS FOR TRANSBOUNDARY WATER COOPERATION (Zeray Yihdego et al. eds. 2018).

Samar Samir, *Egypt Slams Ethiopia for Renaissance Dam Remark*, EGYPT TODAY (Mar. 1, 2020), https://www.egypttoday.com/Article/2/82175/Egypt-slams-Ethiopia-for-Renaissance-dam-remarks.

Samir Ahmed, *Principles and Precedents in International Law Governing the Sharing of Nile Waters*, in THE NILE: SHARING A SCARCE RESOURCE, (Paul P. Howell & J. Antonio Allan eds., 1994).

Second Report on the Law of the Non-Navigational Uses of International Watercourses, Doc. A/CN.4/399, ILC Yearbook 1986, Vol. II (Part 1).

SEIFULAZIZ MILAS, SHARING THE NILE: EGYPT, ETHIOPIA AND THE GEO-POLITICS OF WATER (2013).

SERGEI VINOGRADOV ET AL., TRANSFORMING POTENTIAL CONFLICT INTO COOPERATION POTENTIAL: THE ROLE OF INTERNATIONAL WATER LAW (2003), https://www.semanticscholar.org/paper/Transforming-potential-conflict-into-cooperation-of-VinogradovWouters/e1faef020e5e2da65f0d83b02f8c3ed4e799656f.

SIDNEY PEEL, THE BINDING OF THE NILE AND THE NEW SUDAN (1904), https://archive.org/details/bindingofnilenew00peel/page/134/mode/2up.

ŠIHAB AD-DIN AHMAD BIN ABD AL-QADER BIN SALEM BIN UTMAN, FUTUH AL-HABAŠA: THE CONQUEST OF ABYSSINIA (Paul Lester Stenhouse & Richard Pankhurst, trans., 2003).

SIMON A. MASON, FROM CONFLICT TO COOPERATION IN THE NILE BASIN, (2003).

Sir Humphrey Waldock, *First Report on the Law of Treaties*, [1962] 2 Y.B. INT'L L. COMM'N 27, 32, U.N. Doc. A/CN.4/144.

Stephen C. McCaffrey, *Intertwined General Principles*, in RESEARCH HANDBOOK ON INTERNATIONAL WATER LAW (Stephen C. McCaffrey et al. eds., 2019).

STEPHEN C. MCCAFFREY, THE LAW OF INTERNATIONAL WATERCOURSES (2019).

Stephen C. McCaffrey, *The Need for Flexibility in Freshwater Treaty Regimes*, 27 NAT. RES. F. (2003).

STEPHEN J. WARE, PRINCIPLES OF ALTERNATIVE DISPUTE RESOLUTION 12–13 (2016).

STEPHEN MCCAFFREY ET AL., PUBLIC INTERNATIONAL LAW: CASES, PROBLEMS AND TEXTS (2010).

Stephen McCaffrey, *The Harmon Doctrine One Hundred Years Later: Buried, Not Praised*, 36 NAT. RESOURCES J. (1996).

STEPHEN MCCAFFREY, UNDERSTANDING INTERNATIONAL LAW (2015).

Stephen McCaffrey, *Water, Water Everywhere, But Too Few Drops to Drink: The Coming Fresh Water Crisis and International Environmental Law*, 28 DENV. J. INT'L L. & POL'Y (2000).

Sudan rejects Ethiopian proposal of "partial agreement" on GERD, EGYPT TODAY (May 12, 2020), https://www.egypttoday.com/Article/1/86699/Sudan-rejects-Ethiopian-proposal-of-%E2%80%9Cpartial agreement%E2%80%9D-on-GERD.

Sudan, Egypt, Ethiopia Agree on 90% of Controversial GERD Points, EGYPT INDEPENDENT (June 23, 2020), https://egyptindependent.com/sudan-egypt-ethiopia-agrees-on-90-percent-of-controversial-points-regarding-gerd/.

SUEZ CANAL PROBLEM, JULY 26—SEPTEMBER 22, 1956 (1956).

Susanne Schmeier, *Opening the Black Box of River Basin Organizations*, GLOBAL WATER F., Oct. 16, 2012, http://www.globalwaterforum.org/2012/10/16/opening-the-black-box-of-river-basin-organizations/.

TADDESSE TAMRAT, CHURCH AND STATE IN ETHIOPIA: 1270–1527 (2009).

Tadesse Kassa Woldetsadik, *International Law and Moderations of Physical Geography: The Nile Setting*, in A HISTORY OF WATER SERIES II, VOLUME 3. WATER, GEOPOLITICS AND THE NEW WORLD ORDER (Terje Tvedt et al. eds., 2010).

TADESSE KASSA WOLDETSADIK, INTERNATIONAL WATERCOURSES LAW IN THE NILE RIVER BASIN: THREE STATES AT A CROSSROADS (2013).

Tadesse Woldetsadik, *The Grand Ethiopian Renaissance Dam and Ethiopia's Succession in Hydro-Legal Prominence: A Script in Legal History of Diplomatic Confront (1957–2013)*, 9 MIZAN L. REV. (2015).

Tadesse Woldetsadik, *The Nile Basin Initiative and the Cooperative Framework Agreement: Failing Institutional Enterprises*, 11 MIZAN L. REV. 201 (2017).

Takele Soboka Bulto, *Between Ambivalence and Necessity: Occlusions on the Path Toward a Basin-Wide Treaty in the Nile Basin*, 20 COLO. J. INT'L ENVT'L L. & POL'Y (2009).

Talking Point: Ask Boutros Boutros Ghali, BBC NEWS (June 10, 2002), http://news.bbc.co.uk/1/hi/talking_point/2951028.stm (Accessed on Nov. 2, 2021).

Tamar Meshel, *Swimming against the Current: Revisiting the Principles of International Water Law in the Resolution of Fresh Water Disputes*, 61 HARV. INT'L. L.J. (2020).

Tara Kavaler, *Khartoum Says No to Planned 2nd Filling of Ethiopian Mega-Dam*, THE JERUSALEM POST (June 30, 2021), https://www.jpost.com/international/khartoum-says-no-to-planned-2nd-filling-of-ethiopian-mega-dam-672403.

Taslim O. Elias, *The Doctrine of Intertemporal Law*, 74 AM. J. INT'L L. (1980).

Terje Tvedt, *About the Importance of Studying the Modern History of the Countries of the Nile Basin in a Nile Perspective*, in THE RIVER NILE IN THE POST-COLONIAL AGE: CONFLICT AND COOPERATION AMONG THE NILE BASIN COUNTRIES, (Terje Tvedt ed., 2010).

Terje Tvedt, *Hydrology and Empire: The Nile, Water Imperialism and the Partition of Africa*, 39(2) THE J. OF IMPERIAL AND COMMONWEALTH HIS. (2011).

TERJE TVEDT, THE RIVER NILE IN THE AGE OF THE BRITISH: POLITICAL ECOLOGY AND THE QUEST FOR ECONOMIC POWER (2004).

Tesfaye Tafesse, *Ethiopia's Position on the Nile Water Agreements*, in COOPERATIVE DIPLOMACY, REGIONAL STABILITY AND NATIONAL INTERESTS: THE NILE RIVER AND THE RIPARIAN STATES, 75 (Korwa Adar & Nicasius Check eds. 2011).

TESFAYE TAFESSE, THE NILE QUESTION: HYDROPOLITICS, LEGAL WRANGLING, MODUS VIVENDI AND PERSPECTIVES (2001).

THE ANNUAL REGISTER, THE ANNUAL REGISTER: A REVIEW OF PUBLIC EVENTS AT HOME AND ABROAD FOR THE YEAR 1924, (1925).

THE EGYPTIAN STATE INFORMATION SERVICE, SINAI DEVELOPMENT PROJECTS (2006), http://www.sis.gov.eg/newVR/sinia/html/esinia10.htm.

THE NBI, STATE OF THE RIVER NILE BASIN, CHANGE AND ITS IMPLICATIONS FOR THE NILE REGION, (2012), http://nileis.nilebasin.org/system/files/Nile%20SoB%20Report%20Chapter%208%20%20Climate%20Change.pdf.

THE NILE BASIN INITIATIVE, THE NILE BASIN RESOURCES ATLAS (2016), http://atlas.nilebasin.org/treatise/location-of-the-nile-basin-in-africa/.

THE OAKLAND INSTITUTE, UNDERSTANDING LAND INVESTMENT DEALS IN AFRICA COUNTRY REPORT: ETHIOPIA 4 (2011).

The October Arab-Israeli War of 1973: What Happened?, AL JAZEERA (Oct. 8, 2018), https://www.aljazeera.com/features/2018/10/8/the-october-arab-israeli-war-of-1973-what-happened.

The Role of River Basin Organizations, 10 INT'L J. RIVER BASIN MGMT. 229 (2012).

The White House, Executive Order on Imposing Sanctions on Certain Persons with Respect to the Humanitarian and Human Rights Crisis in Ethiopia (September 17, 2021), https://www.whitehouse.gov/briefing-room/presidential-actions/2021/09/17/executive-order-on-imposing-sanctions-on-certain-persons-with-respect-to-the-humanitarian-and-human-rights-crisis-in-ethiopia/.

THE WHITE HOUSE, PEACE TO PROSPERITY: A NEW VISION FOR THE PALESTINIAN PEOPLE AND THE MIDDLE EAST REGION (2020), https://www.whitehouse.gov/wp-content/uploads/2020/01/Peace-to-Prosperity-0120.pdf.

THE WORLD BANK DEV. RES. GROUP POL'Y RES. WORKING PAPER NO. 4294 (2007).

TRANSBOUNDARY FRESHWATER DISPUTE DATABASE, NEWS EVENT DATA IN THE NILE BASIN (2008), http://gis.nacse.org/tfdd/event.php?BCODE_Input=NILE&.

Trump comment on 'blowing up' Nile Dam angers Ethiopia, BBC NEWS (October 24, 2020), https://www.bbc.com/news/world-africa-54674313.

Tuula Honkonen, *Water Security and Climate Change: The Need for Adaptive Governance*, 20 POTCHEFSTROOM ELEC. L.J. 1, 2 (2017).

U.K. FOREIGN & COMMONWEALTH OFFICE, https://treaties.fco.gov.uk/awweb/pdfopener?md=1&did=74175.

U.S. NATIONAL INTELLIGENCE, GLOBAL WATER SECURITY, INTELLIGENCE COMMUNITY ASSESSMENT (2012).

U.S. to De-link Ethiopian Aid Pause from Dam Policy, REUTERS (Feb. 20. 2021), https://www.reuters.com/article/us-ethiopia-dam-usa/u-s-to-de-link-ethiopian-aid-pause-from-dam-policy-idUSKBN2AK08O.

U.S.B.R, LAND AND WATER RESOURCES OF THE BLUE NILE BASIN, ETHIOPIA (1964).

U.S.B.R, LAND AND WATER RESOURCES OF THE BLUE NILE BASIN, ETHIOPIA (1964a).

U.S.B.R, LAND AND WATER RESOURCES OF THE BLUE NILE BASIN, ETHIOPIA, (1964 b).

Ulf Laessing, *Sudan Launches Major Dam to Boost Agricultural Production Investment*, REUTERS (Jan. 1, 2013), https://www.reuters.com/article/us-sudan-dam/sudan-launches-major-dam-to-boost-agricultural-production-investment-idUSBRE900 0B320130101.

UN Ready to Promote 'Win-win Solution' for Blue Nile Dam Project, UN NEWS (July 8, 2021), https://news.un.org/en/story/2021/07/1095552.

UN. FOOD & AGRIC. FAO IN EMERGENCY, HELPING A WORLD WITHOUT HUNGER—ETHIOPIA (2021), https://www.fao.org/emergencies/countries/detail/en/c/151593/.

UN. FOOD & AGRIC., AQUASTAT COUNTRY PROFILE—EGYPT (2016).

UN. FOOD & AGRIC., AQUASTAT COUNTRY PROFILE—SUDAN (2015).

UNCCD, *Word of the Week: Water Stress* (Oct. 2021), https://knowledge.unccd.int/knowledge-products-and-pillars/unccd-e-library/fact-month-word-week.

UNDP, HUMAN DEVELOPMENT REPORT, ETHIOPIA (2022).

UNEP, CLIMATE CHANGE ADAPTATION CAPACITIES IN THE NILE RIVER BASIN (2015), http://wedocs.unep.org/bitstream/handle/20.500.11822/14068/Nile%20 Climate%20change%20fa.pdf?sequence=1&isAllowed=y.

UNEP, GLOBAL INTERNATIONAL WATERS ASSESSMENT: PATAGONIAN SHELF, GIWA REGIONAL ASSESSMENT (2004).

Ungtae Kim & Jagath J. Kaluarachchi, *Climate Change Impacts on Water Resources in the Upper Blue Nile River Basin, Ethiopia.* J. AM. WATER RSRC. ASS. (2009).

United Nations Conference on Succession of States in Respect of Treaties, (1977–1978), https://digitallibrary.un.org/record/36222?ln=en#record-files-collapse-header.

UNITED NATIONS DEVELOPMENT PROGRAM, HUMAN DEVELOPMENT REPORTS (2020), http://hdr.undp.org/en/indicators/137506#.

UNITED NATIONS ENVIRONMENT PROGRAMME, GLOBAL ENVIRONMENT OUTLOOK 5 (GEO-5): ENVIRONMENT FOR THE FUTURE WE WANT, 125 (2012).

United Nations General Assembly, Official Records Fifty-first Session, 99th plenary meeting (1997).

UNITED NATIONS WORLD WATER ASSESSMENT PROGRAM (WWAP), THE UNITED NATIONS WORLD WATER DEVELOPMENT REPORT 2018: NATURE-BASED SOLUTIONS FOR WATER (2018).

UNITED NATIONS, DEPARTMENT OF ECONOMIC AND SOCIAL AFFAIRS, POPULATION DIVISION, WORLD POPULATION PROSPECTS: THE 2017 REVISION (2017).

United States Bureau of Reclamation (USBR), *Water Facts: Worldwide Water Supply (Nov. 4, 2020)*, https://www.usbr.gov/mp/arwec/water-facts-ww-water-sup.html.

Valerie Knobelsdorf, *The Nile Waters Agreements: Imposition and Impacts of a Transboundary Legal System*, 44 COLUM. J. TRANSNAT'L L. (2006).

Vice President Kamala Harris Warns of Looming "Wars Fought Over Water," CALIFORNIA NEWSTIMES (April 5, 2021), available in https://californianewstimes.com/vice-president-kamala-harris-warns-of-looming-wars-fought-over-water-cbs-san-francisco/255936/.

Vivek K. Arora & George J. Boer, *Effects of Simulated Climate Change on the Hydrology of Major River Basins*, 106 J. GEOPHYSICAL RES. (2001).

Why Ethiopia Rejected the U.S.-Drafted GERD Deal, ETHIOPIAN INSIGHT (Apr. 2, 2020), https://www.ethiopia-insight.com/2020/04/02/why-ethiopia-rejected-the-u-s-drafted-gerd-deal/.

William Claiborne, *Sadat Offers Israel Water from the Nile*, WASH. POST (Sept. 7, 1979), https://www.washingtonpost.com/archive/politics/1979/09/07/sadat-offers-israel-water-from-the-nile/c07ab59e-fde0-489c-88aa-24020196444e/.

WILLIAM GARSTIN, REPORT UPON THE BASIN OF THE UPPER NILE: WITH PROPOSALS FOR THE IMPROVEMENT OF THAT RIVER, 196 (1904), https://archive.org/details/reportuponbasin00dupugoog/page/n280/mode/1up.

WILLIAM KELLY SIMPSON AND WILLIAM W. HALLO, THE ANCIENT NEAR EAST: A HISTORY 261 (1971).

WILLIAM SIMPSON & MARTIN JONES, EUROPE 1783–1914 (2009).

Wondyifraw Qerenso, *Egypt: Better to Unshackle the Nile*, REPORTER (May 12, 2018), https://www.thereporterethiopia.com/article/egypt-better-unshackle-nile.

Work begins to heighten Sudan's 280-MW Roseires Dam, HYDRO REVIEW (Aug. 29, 2008), https://sudantribune.com/spip.php?article26912.

Worku Aberra, *Biden's Blunder on Ethiopia*, E-INTERNATIONAL RELATIONS (November 17, 2021), https://www.e-ir.info/2021/11/17/opinion-bidens-blunder-on-ethiopia/.

World Bank, *OP 7.50—Projects on International Waterways*, http://web.worldbank.org/archive/website01541/WEB/0__C-137.HTM.

WORLD BANK, WORLD BANK GROUP ARCHIVISTS' CHRONOLOGY 1944–2013 (2013).

WORLD COMMISSION ON ENVIRONMENT AND DEVELOPMENT, REPORT OF THE WORLD COMMISSION ON ENVIRONMENT AND DEVELOPMENT: OUR COMMON FUTURE (1987).

WORLD ECONOMIC FORUM, 2016 GLOBAL RISK REPORT (2016), https://www3.weforum.org/docs/GRR/WEF_GRR16.pdf.

World Meteorological Organization (WMO), *Wake Up to the Looming Water Crisis, Report Warns* (Oct. 5, 2021), https://public.wmo.int/en/media/press-release/wake-looming-water-crisis-report-warns.

WORLD WATER ASSESSMENT PROGRAM (WWAP), THE UNITED NATIONS WORLD WATER DEVELOPMENT REPORT 2019: LEAVING NO ONE BEHIND (2019).

WOSSENU ABTEW & SHIELIS BEHAILU DESSU, THE GRAND ETHIOPIAN RENAISSANCE DAM ON THE BLUE NILE (2018).

WWAP, THE UNITED NATIONS WORLD WATER DEVELOPMENT REPORT 2015: WATER FOR A SUSTAINABLE WORLD (2015).

Yaacov Shavit, *Up the River or Down the River? An Afrocentrist Dilemma,* in THE NILE: HISTORIES, CULTURES, MYTHS (Haggai Erlich & Israel Gershoni eds., 2000).

Yacob Arsano & Imeru Tamrat, *Ethiopia and the Eastern Nile Basin,* 67 AQUAT. SCI. (2005).

YACOB ARSANO, ETHIOPIA AND THE NILE DILEMMAS OF NATIONAL AND REGIONAL HYDROPOLITICS (2007).

Yacob Arsano, *Institutional Development and Water Management in the Ethiopian Nile Basin, in* THE RIVER NILE IN THE POST-COLONIAL AGE: CONFLICT AND COOPERATION AMONG THE NILE BASIN COUNTRIES, (Terje Tvedt ed., 2010).

Yehenew Walilegne, *The Nile Basin: From Confrontation to Cooperation,* 27 DALHOUSIE L.J. (2004).

YILMA MAKONNEN, INTERNATIONAL LAW AND THE NEW STATES OF AFRICA (1983).

Yilma Makonnen, *State Succession in Africa: Selected Problems,* 200 RECEUIL DES COURS 93(1987).

Yimer Fisseha, *State Succession and the Legal Status of International Rivers,* in THE LEGAL REGIME OF INTERNATIONAL RIVERS AND LAKES 177 (Ralph Zacklin & Lucius Cafllisch eds., 1981).

Ying Zhang, Solomon Tassew Erkyihum & Paul Block, *Filling the GERD: Evaluating Hydroclimatic Variability and Impoundment Strategies for Blue Nile Riparian Countries,* 41 WATER INT'L (2016).

Zeray Yihdego, *International Law Connotations of US 'Mediated' Nile Dam Negotiations and Outcomes: Why and How the Parties Should Regain Control* 0 (Mar. 18, 2020) (unpublished working paper) https://www.researchgate.net/publication/340341053_International_Law_Connotations_of_USsposored_GERD_'mediation'_WorkingPaper_Zeray_Yihdego_18_March_2020.

ZERAY YIHDEGO, THE FAIRNESS 'DILEMMA' IN SHARING THE NILE WATERS: WHAT LESSONS FROM THE GRAND ETHIOPIAN RENAISSANCE DAM FOR INTERNATIONAL LAW? (2017).

Zeray Yihdego, *Trilateral Negotiations Over a Dam on the Blue Nile: US Meddling and the 'Role' of the UN Security Council, in* ETHIOPIAN YEARBOOK OF INTERNATIONAL LAW 239, 250 (Zeray Yihdego et al. eds., 2019).

Index

Printed in the United States
by Baker & Taylor Publisher Services